Shojo Beat

Yukarism

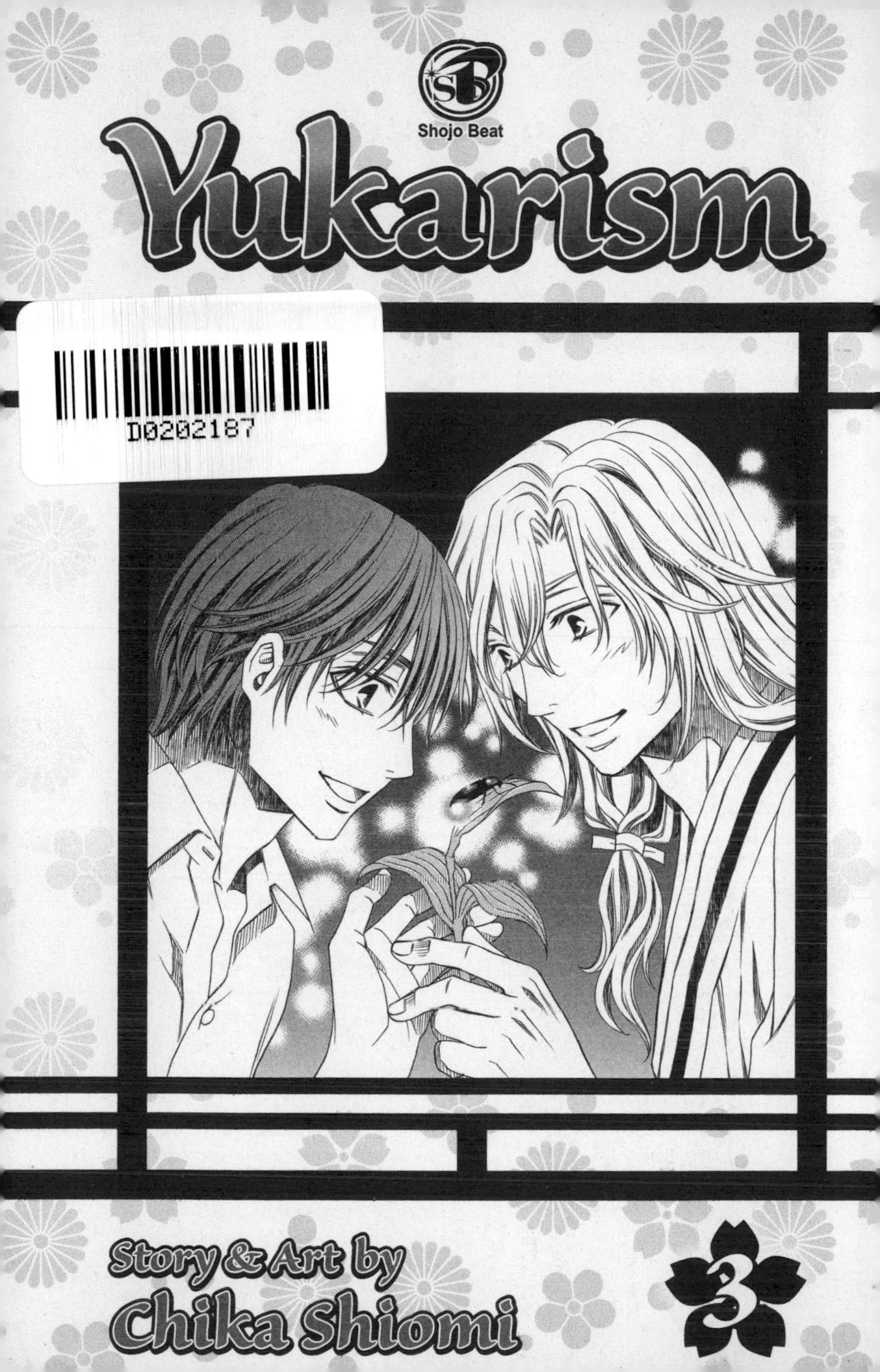

Story & Art by

Chika Shiomi

3

【Cast of Characters】

Yukari Kobayakawa

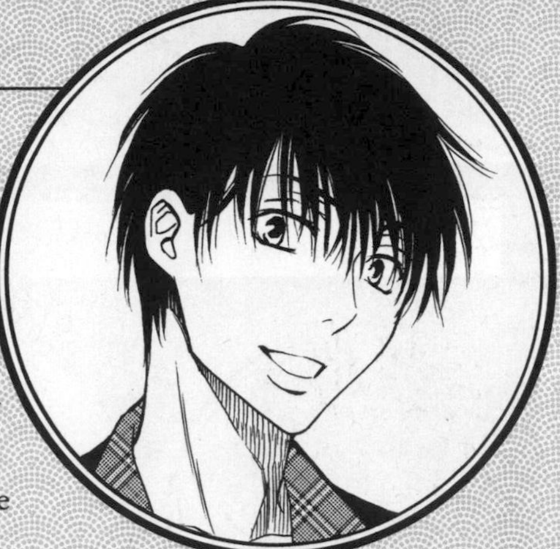

A 17-year-old high school student and author of historical novels. Most of his stories are set in the Edo period. One day, he meets a girl named Mahoro at school. It's their first time meeting, but he feels as if he knows her and suddenly becomes dizzy. Later, his spirit enters the body of Yumurasaki, who he was in a past life.

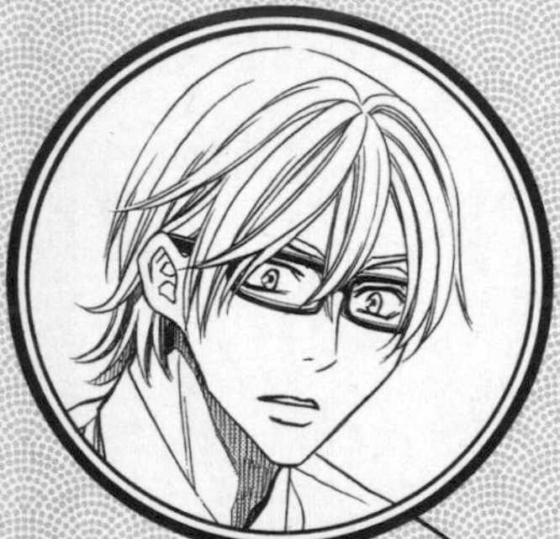

Katsuhiko Satomi

The new housekeeper at Yukari's house. He and Mahoro have been at each other's throats ever since they met. Once when Mahoro came to Yukari's house, she called him "Kazuma"...?!

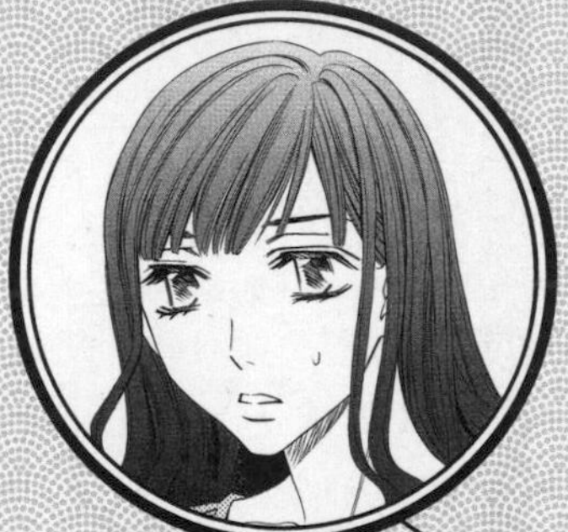

Mahoro Tachibana

Yukari's classmate and a big fan of his novels. She worries about Yukari's tendency to skip school due to illness, so she begins visiting him at his home. Until she was 4, she had a habit of talking like a boy and of writing strange symbols like curses, causing her family to worry.

The Present

The Past

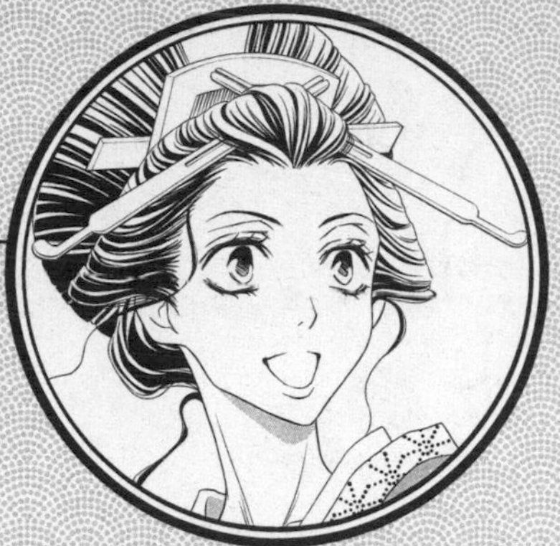

Yumurasaki

The *oiran* of an establishment called Tatsutaya in the Yoshiwara pleasure district of Edo (present-day Tokyo, Japan). Due to his memories of her as his previous incarnation, Yukari knows that someone murdered her...

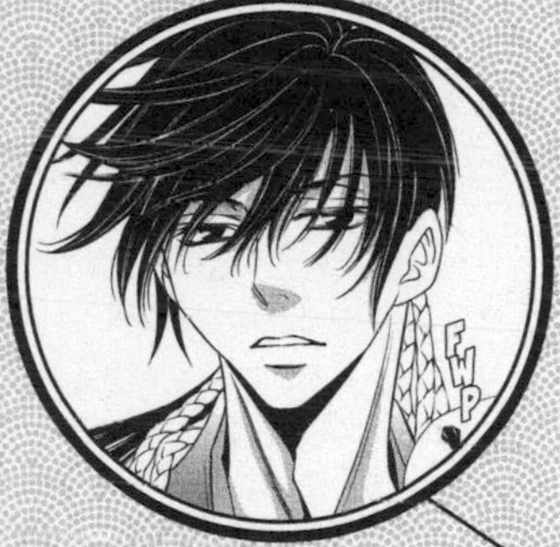
FWP

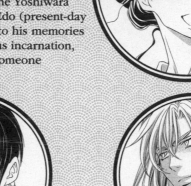

Shizuka Takamura

A frequent customer of Yumurasaki's. He is a powerful witch doctor feared by people because he will cast curses to kill for the right sum.

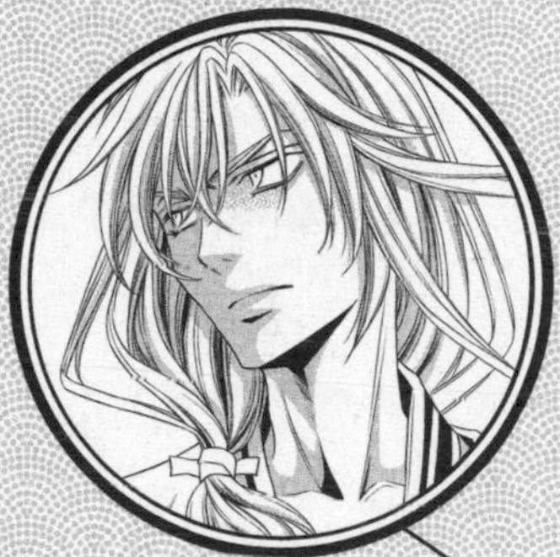

Kazuma

A bodyguard at Tatsutaya where Yumurasaki works. He gently cares for Yumurasaki but mercilessly disposes of her would-be assassins.

The Story

At the young age of 17, high school student Yukari Kobayakawa is a genius author of historical novels set in the Edo period. One day, he meets a girl named Mahoro Tachibana at school. Despite meeting her for the first time, he feels like he knows her... Afterward, he suffers dizzy spells and enters the body of Yumurasaki, an oiran in an Edo period pleasure district. Yukari instinctively realizes she is himself in a past life, and he begins going back and forth between the past and present. Yumurasaki's regular customer Takamura teaches Yukari about reincarnation, but he still doesn't know who has been reborn as who, so he decides to learn more about his acquaintances. He visits Mahoro at her home, but as they return to his house, a change comes over her...

Yukarism

[Volume 3 Contents]

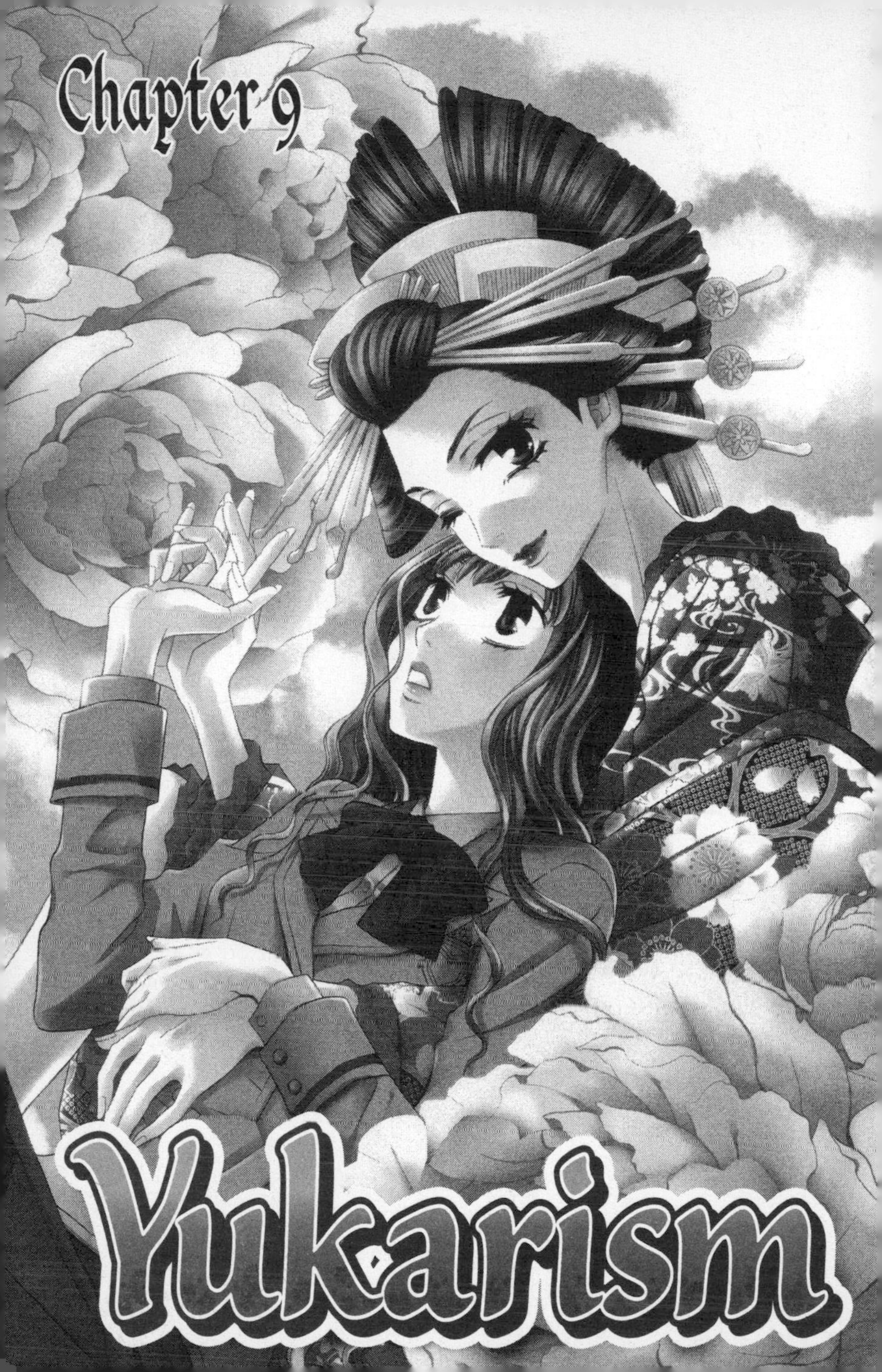
Chapter 9
Yukarism

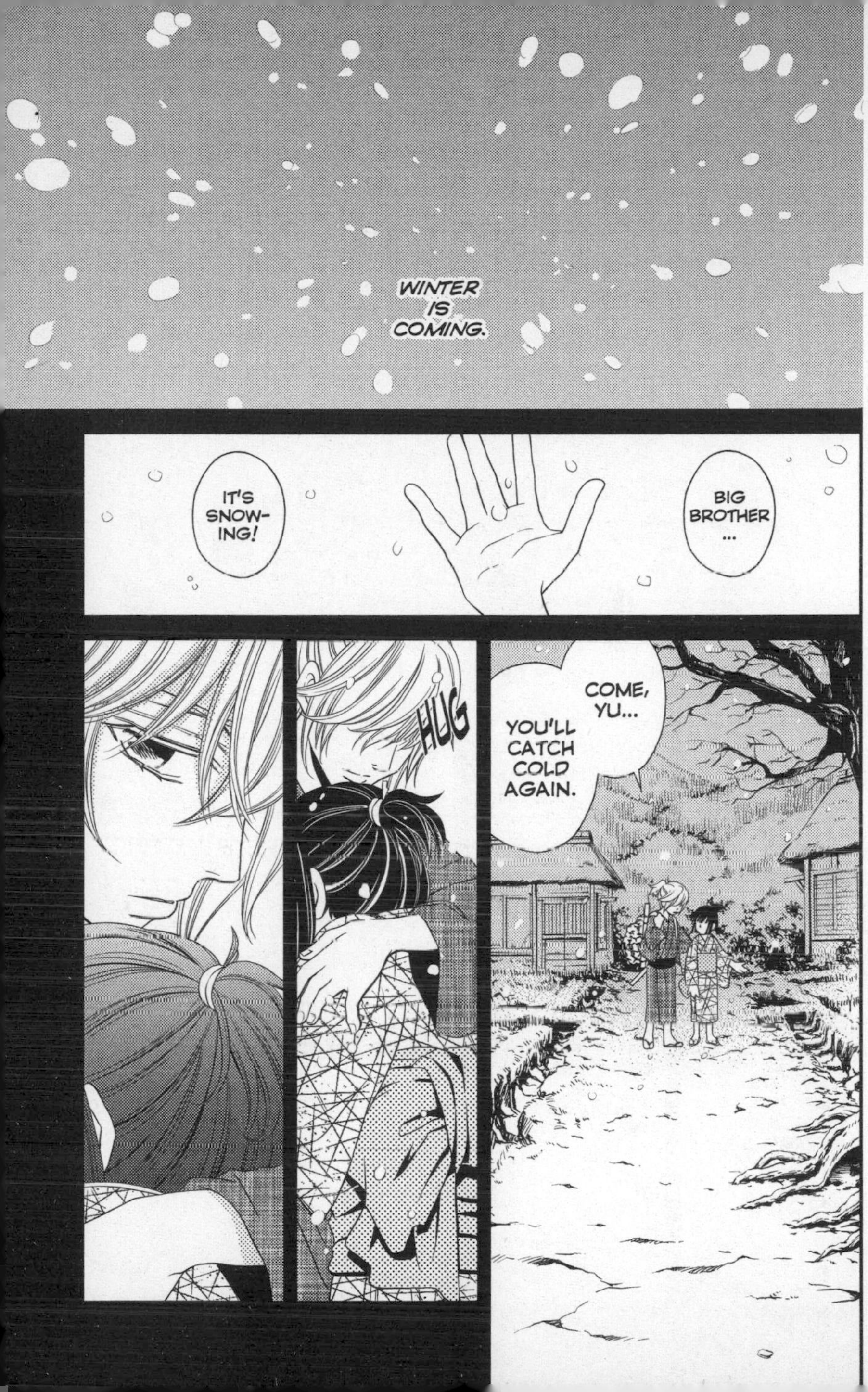
WINTER IS COMING.
BIG BROTHER ...
IT'S SNOWING!
COME, YU... YOU'LL CATCH COLD AGAIN.
HUG

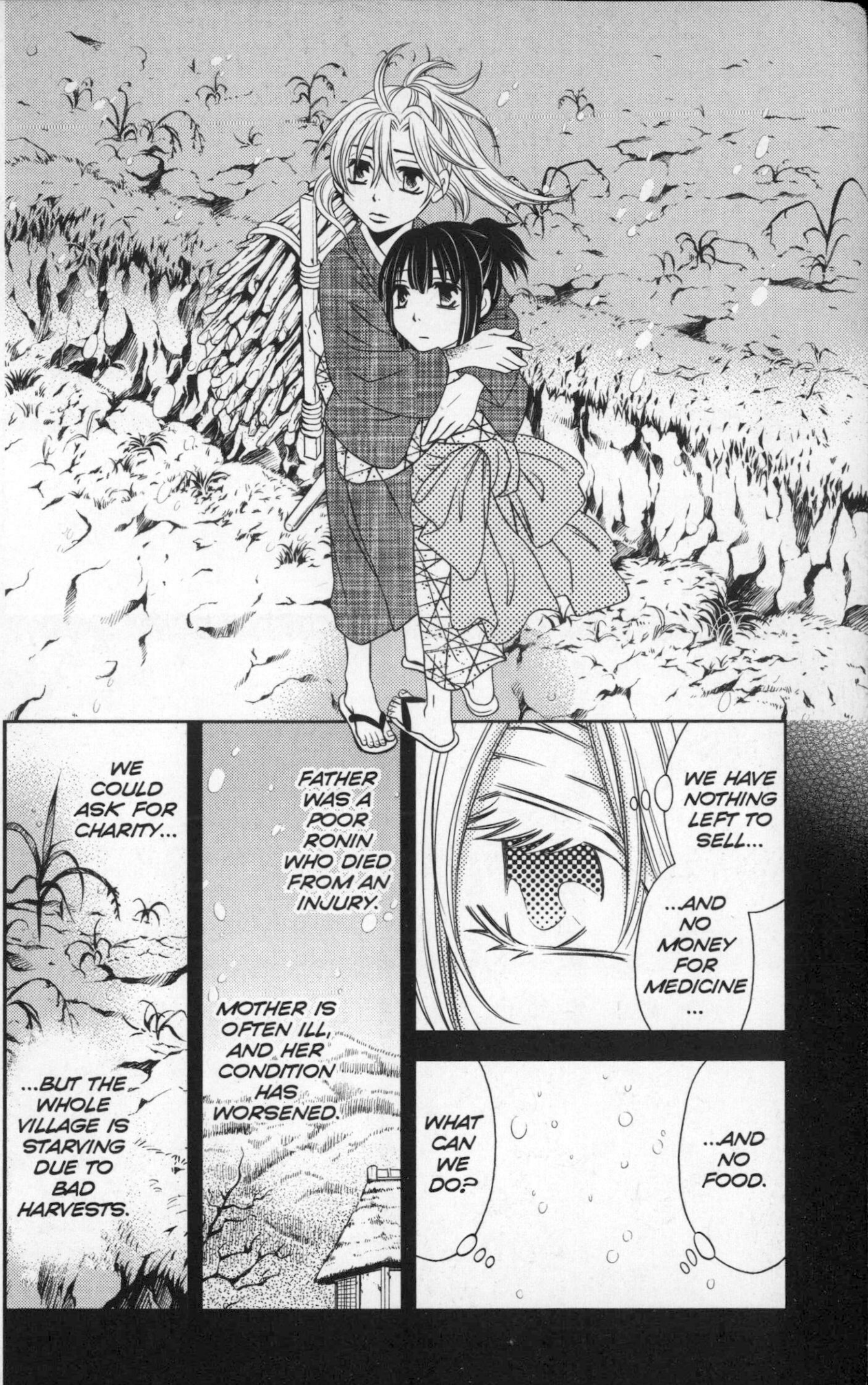
WE HAVE NOTHING LEFT TO SELL...
...AND NO MONEY FOR MEDICINE...
...AND NO FOOD.
WHAT CAN WE DO?
FATHER WAS A POOR RONIN WHO DIED FROM AN INJURY.
MOTHER IS OFTEN ILL, AND HER CONDITION HAS WORSENED.
WE COULD ASK FOR CHARITY...
...BUT THE WHOLE VILLAGE IS STARVING DUE TO BAD HARVESTS.

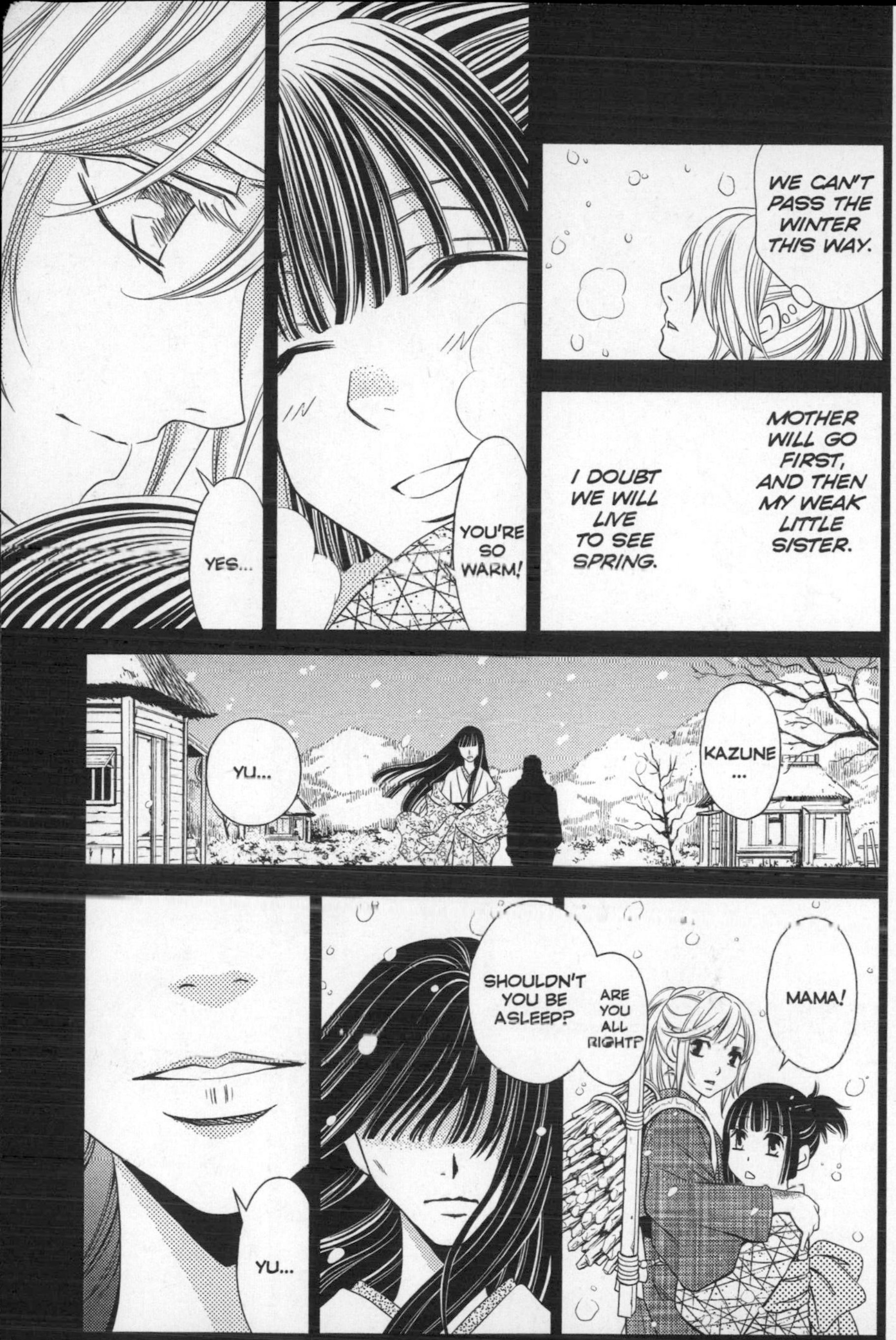
WE CAN'T PASS THE WINTER THIS WAY.
MOTHER WILL GO FIRST, AND THEN MY WEAK LITTLE SISTER.
I DOUBT WE WILL LIVE TO SEE SPRING.
YOU'RE SO WARM!
YES...
KAZUNE ...
YU...
MAMA!
ARE YOU ALL RIGHT?
SHOULDN'T YOU BE ASLEEP?
YU...

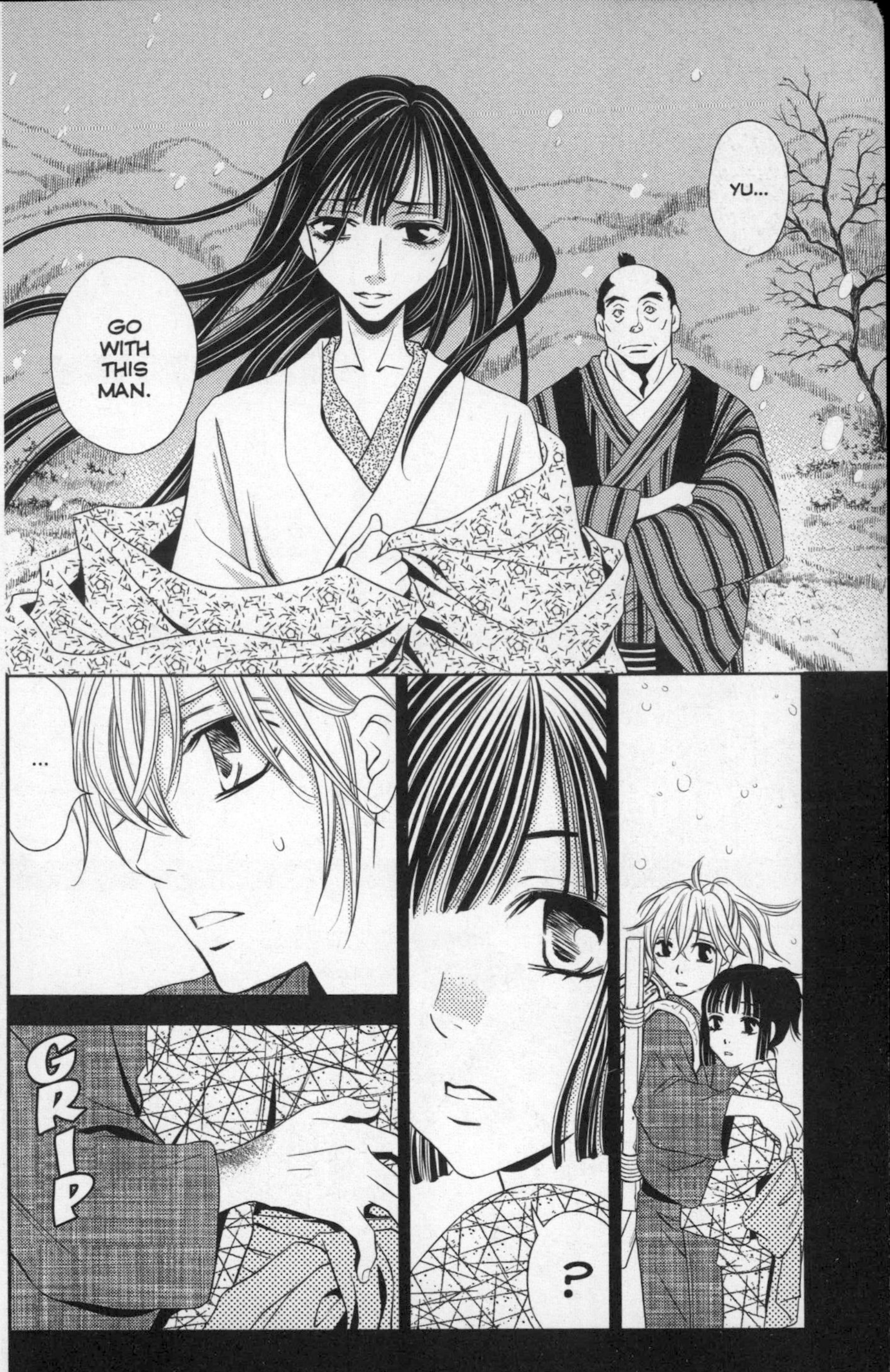
YU...
GO WITH THIS MAN.
?
...
GRIP

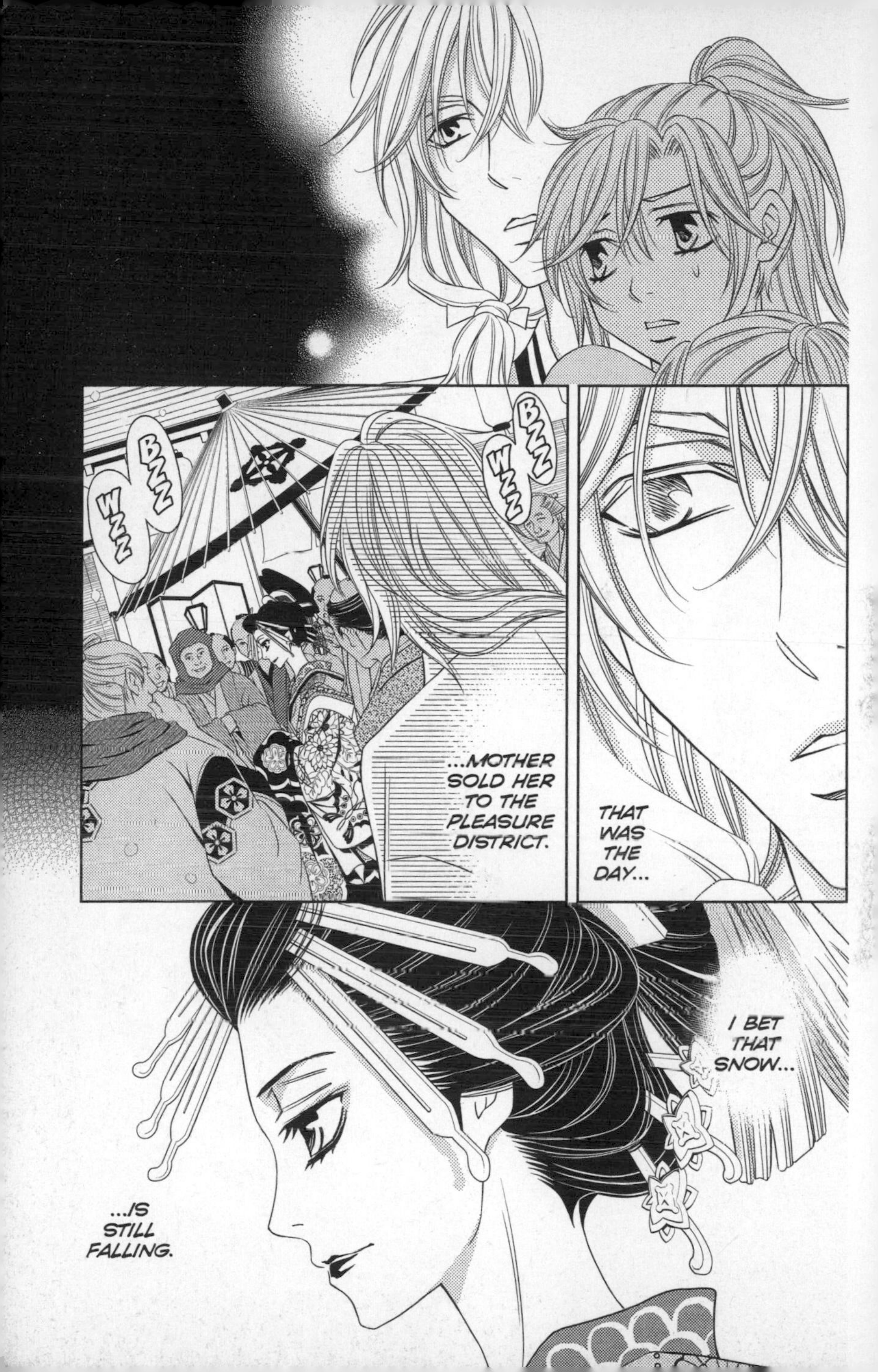
THAT WAS THE DAY...
BZZ WZZ
BZZ WZZ
...MOTHER SOLD HER TO THE PLEASURE DISTRICT.
I BET THAT SNOW...
...IS STILL FALLING.

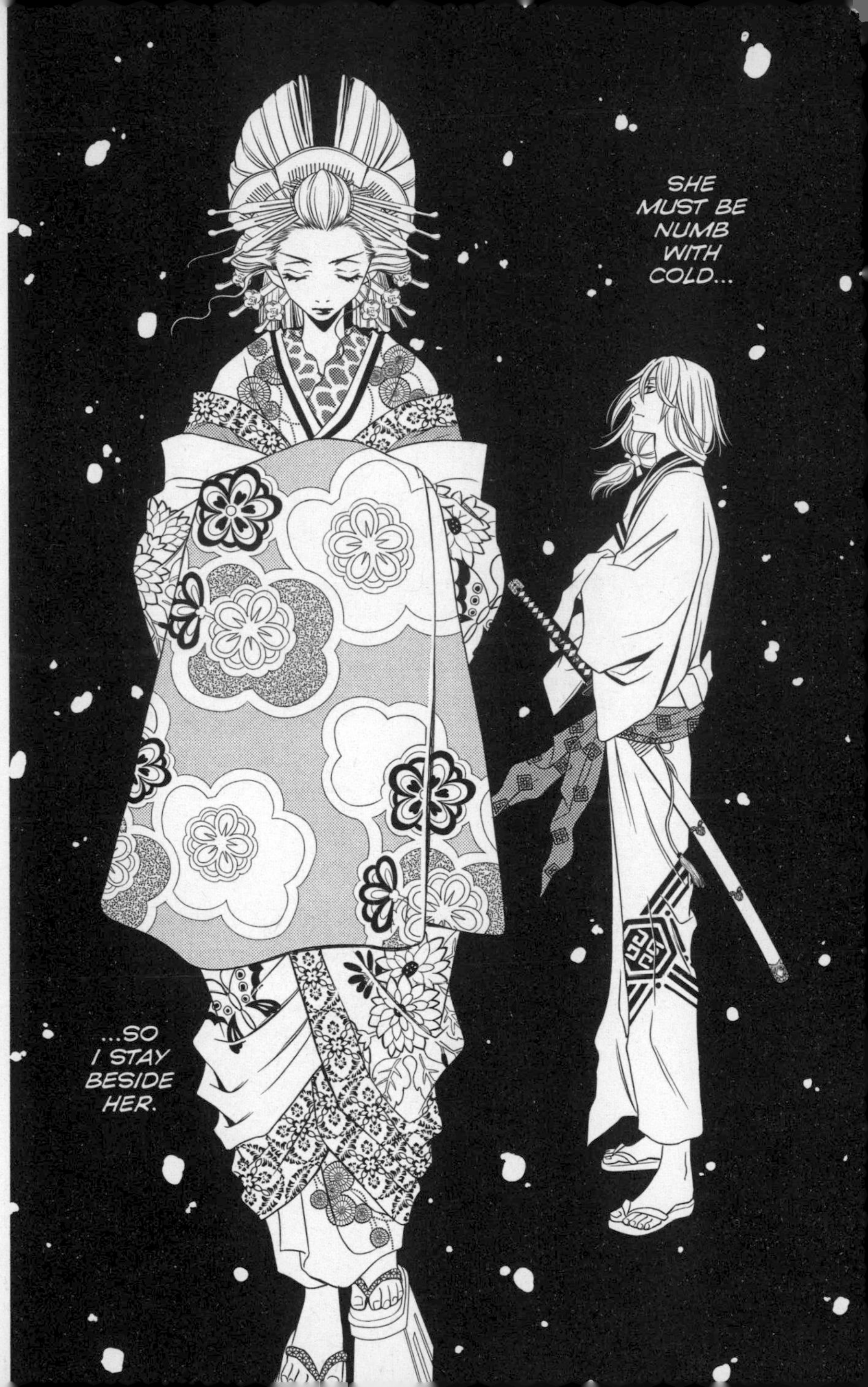
SHE MUST BE NUMB WITH COLD...
...SO I STAY BESIDE HER.

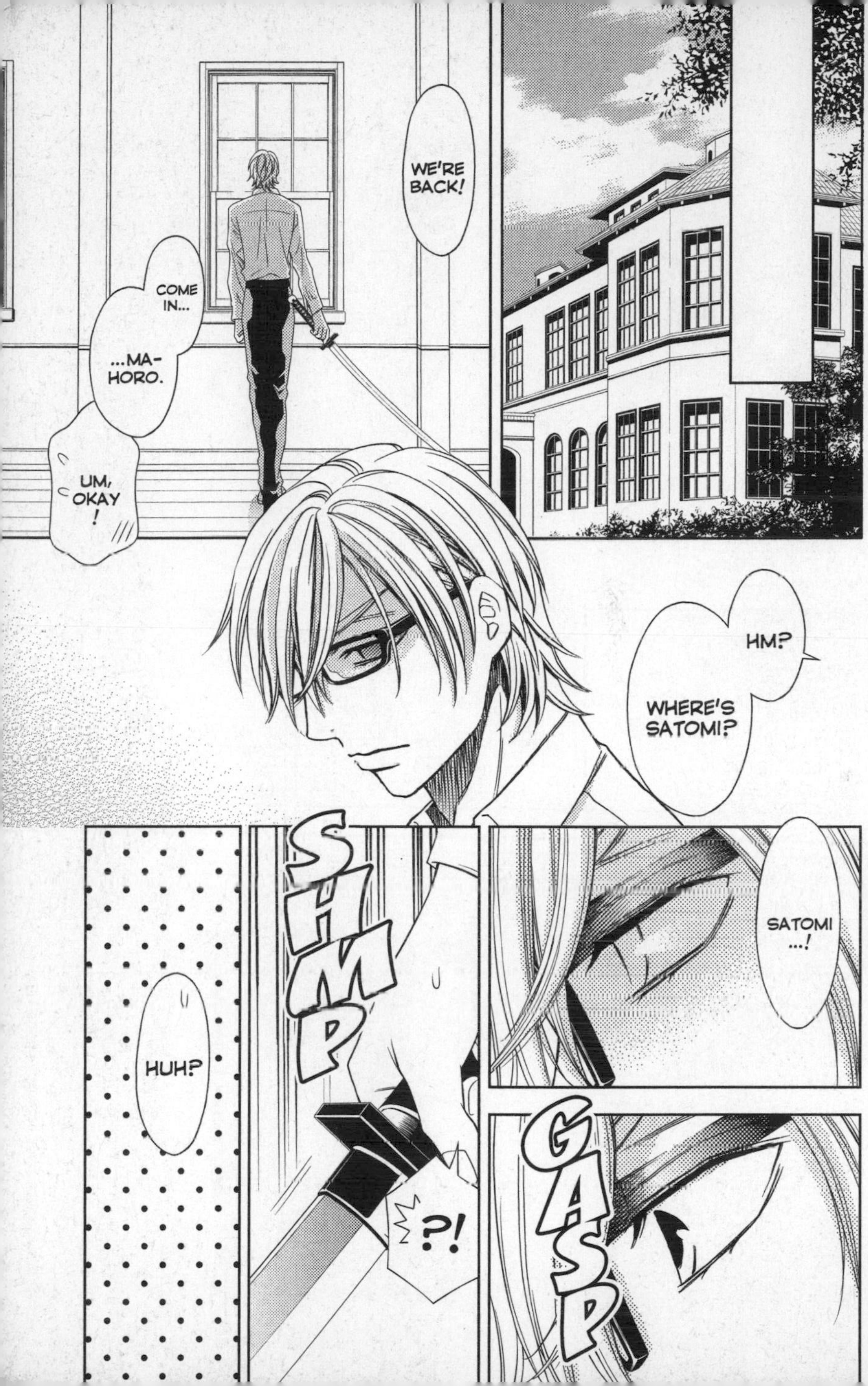
WE'RE BACK!
COME IN...
...MA-HORO.
UM, OKAY!
HM?
WHERE'S SATOMI?
SATOMI ...!
GASP
SHMP
?!
HUH?

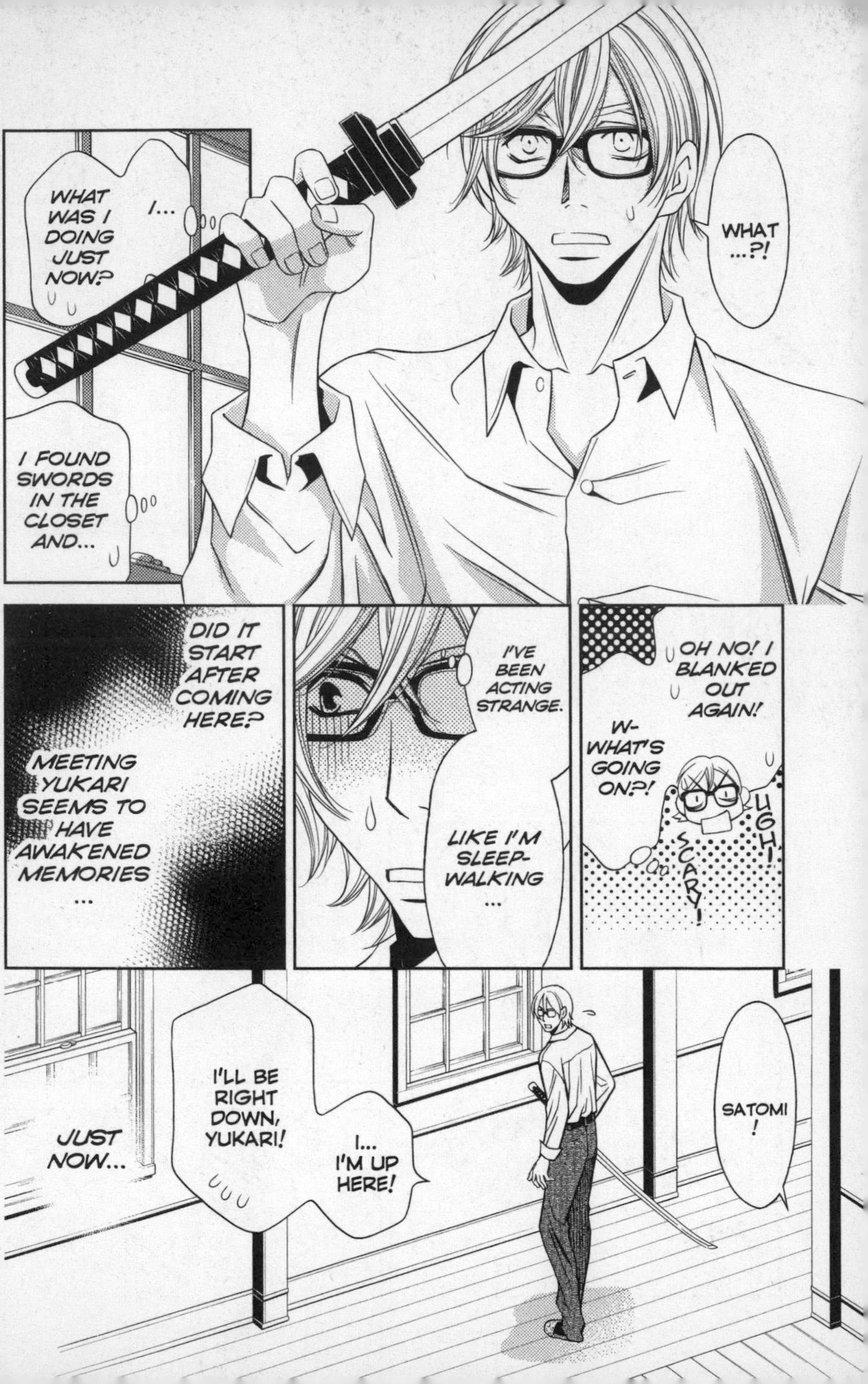
WHAT ...?!
I...
WHAT WAS I DOING JUST NOW?
I FOUND SWORDS IN THE CLOSET AND...
OH NO! I BLANKED OUT AGAIN!
W-WHAT'S GOING ON?!
UGH!
SCARY!
I'VE BEEN ACTING STRANGE.
LIKE I'M SLEEP-WALKING...
DID IT START AFTER COMING HERE?
MEETING YUKARI SEEMS TO HAVE AWAKENED MEMORIES...
SATOMI!
I... I'M UP HERE!
I'LL BE RIGHT DOWN, YUKARI!
JUST NOW...

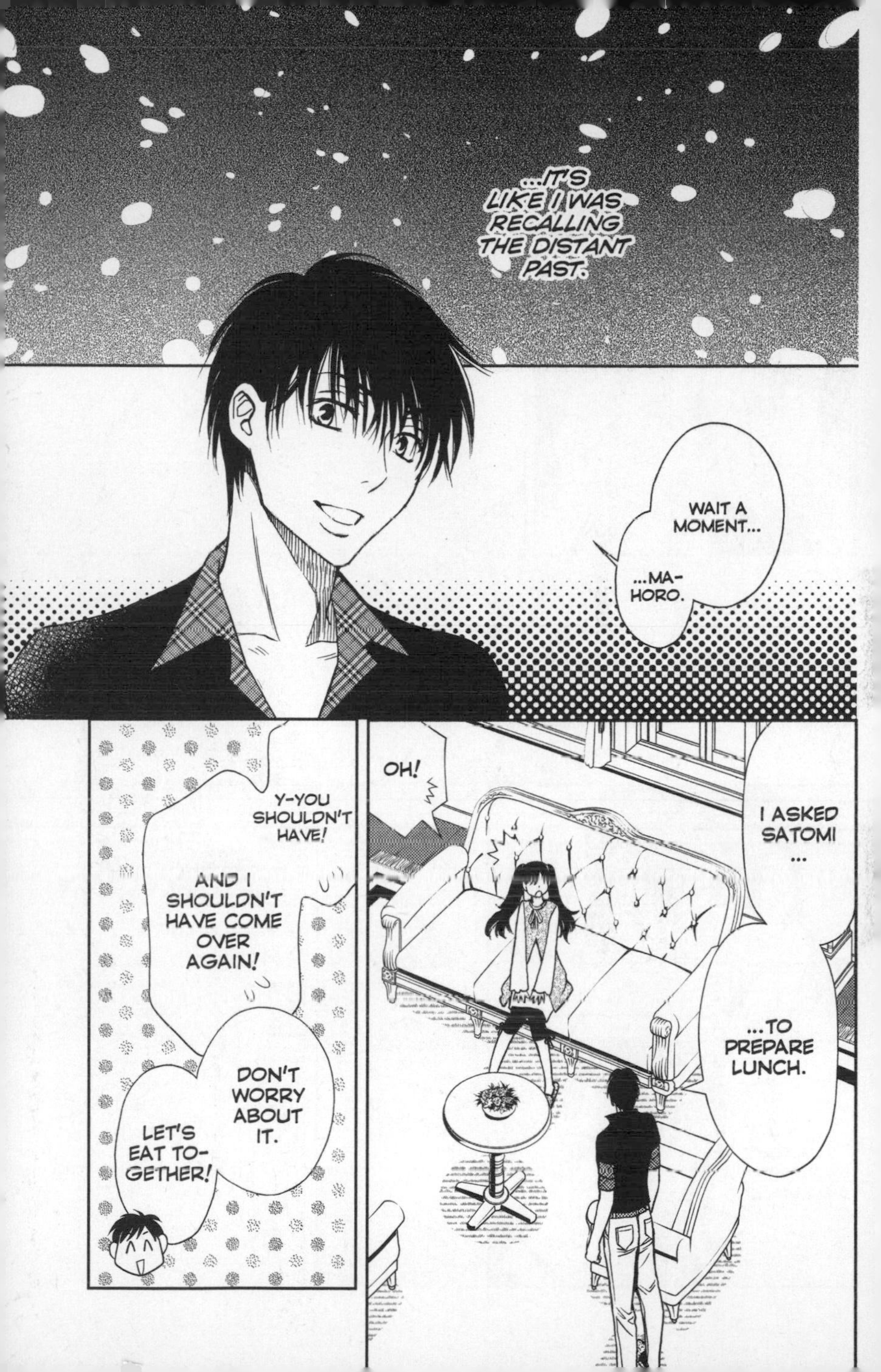
...IT'S LIKE I WAS RECALLING THE DISTANT PAST.
WAIT A MOMENT...
...MA-HORO.
I ASKED SATOMI ...
...TO PREPARE LUNCH.
OH!
Y-YOU SHOULDN'T HAVE!
AND I SHOULDN'T HAVE COME OVER AGAIN!
DON'T WORRY ABOUT IT.
LET'S EAT TO-GETHER!

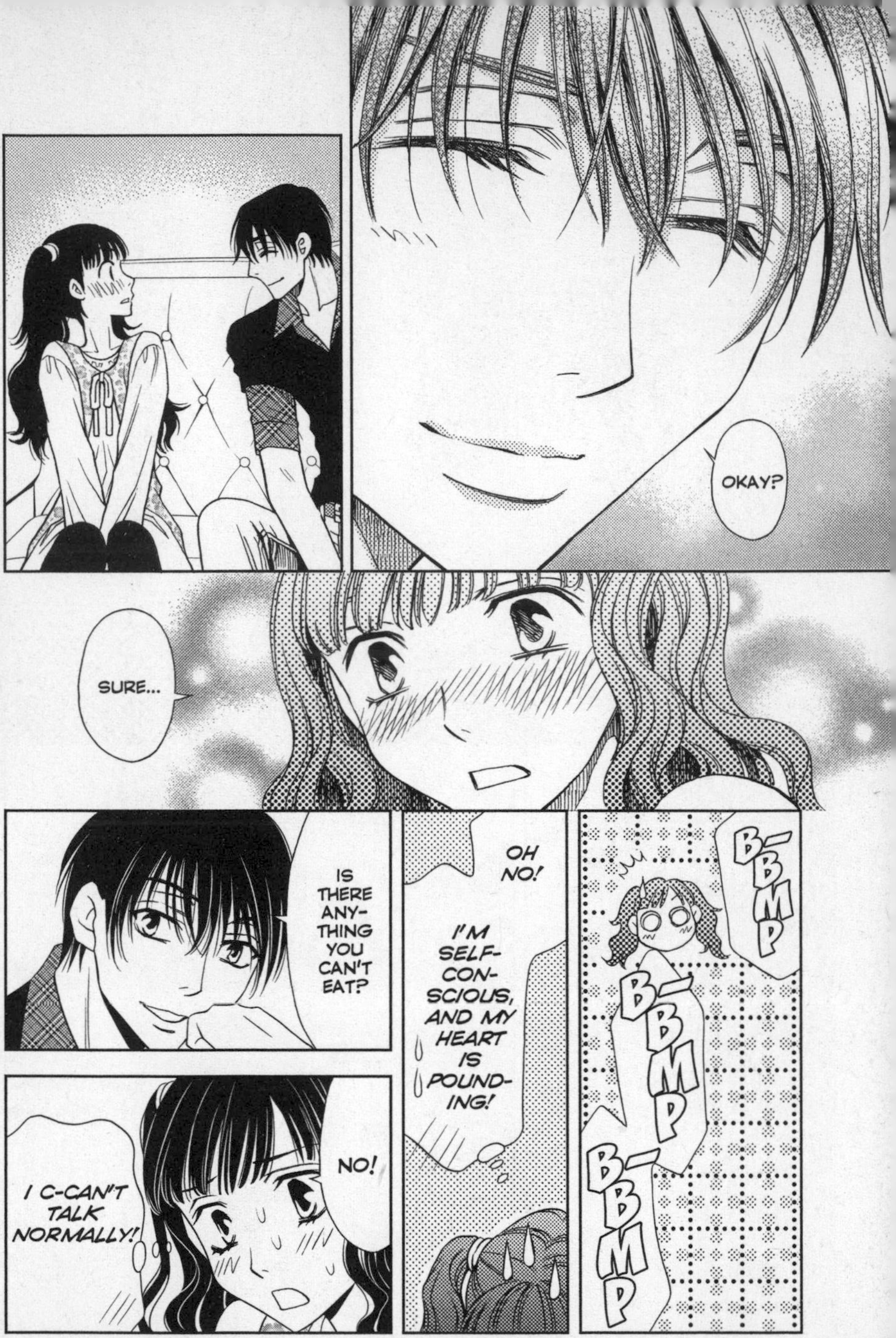
OKAY?
SURE...
B-BMP
B-BMP
B-BMP
OH NO!
I'M SELF-CONSCIOUS, AND MY HEART IS POUNDING!
IS THERE ANYTHING YOU CAN'T EAT?
NO!
I C-CAN'T TALK NORMALLY!

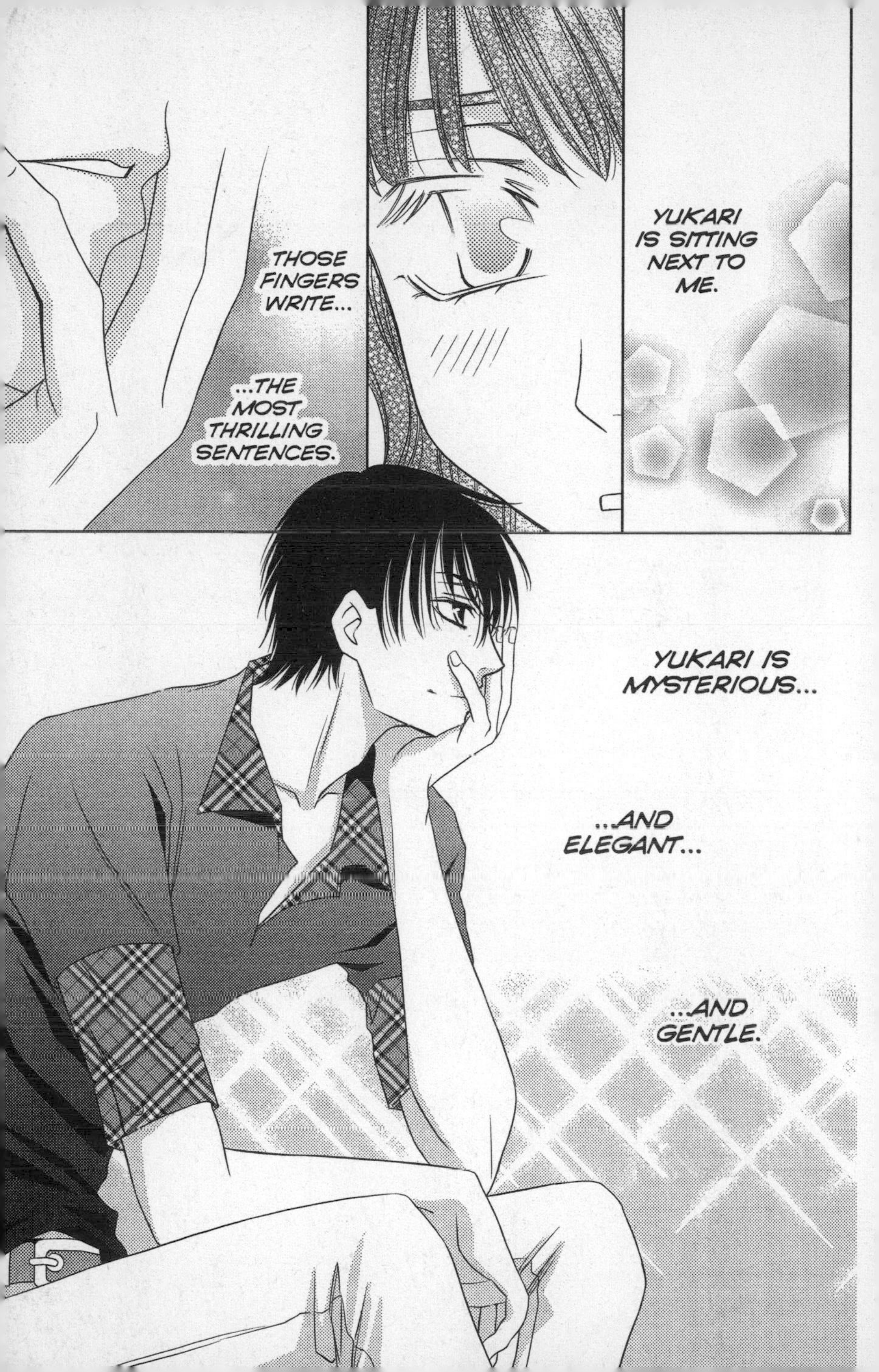
YUKARI IS SITTING NEXT TO ME.
THOSE FINGERS WRITE...
...THE MOST THRILLING SENTENCES.
YUKARI IS MYSTERIOUS...
...AND ELEGANT...
...AND GENTLE.

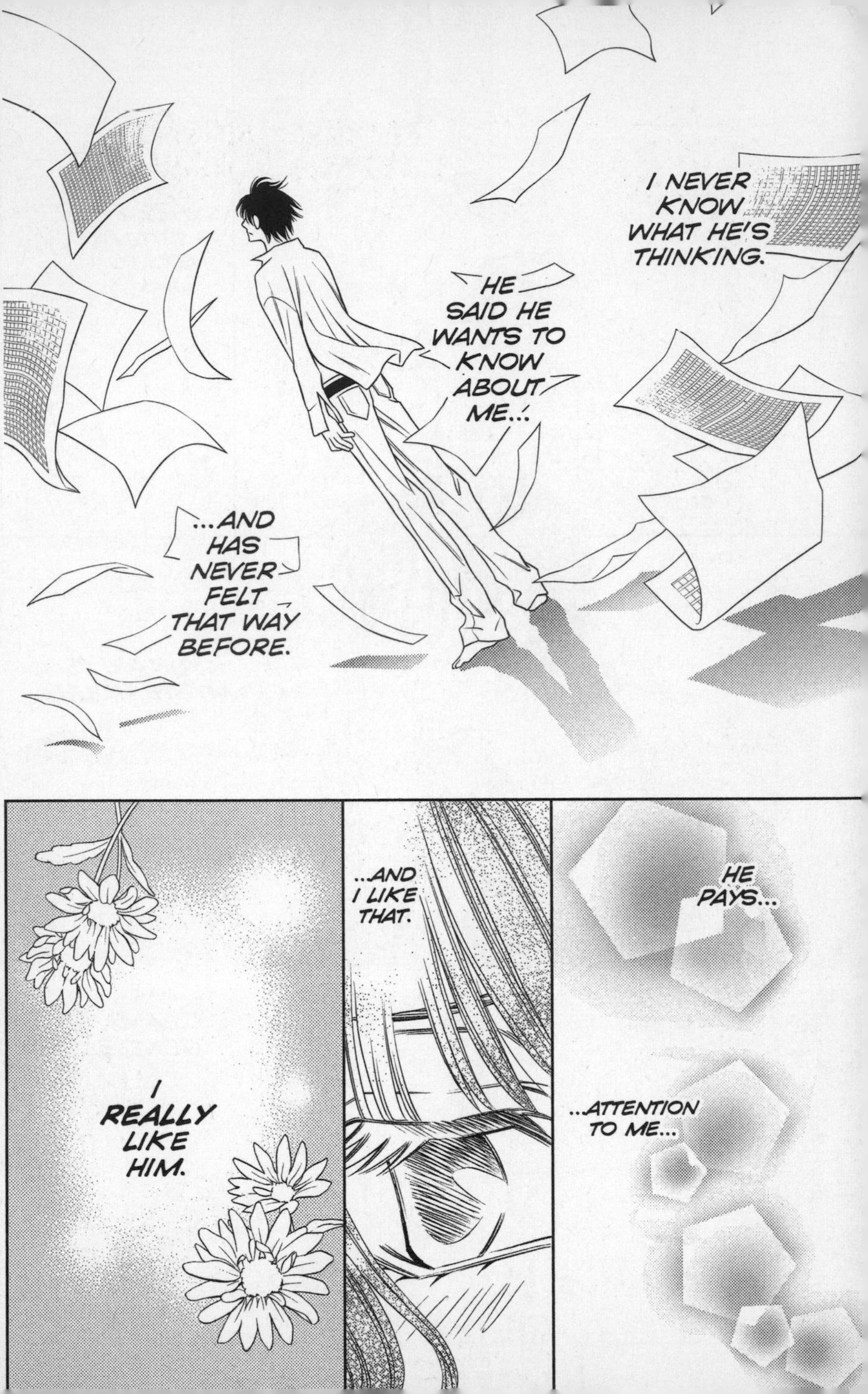
I NEVER KNOW WHAT HE'S THINKING.
HE SAID HE WANTS TO KNOW ABOUT ME...
...AND HAS NEVER FELT THAT WAY BEFORE.
HE PAYS...
...ATTENTION TO ME...
...AND I LIKE THAT.
I REALLY LIKE HIM.

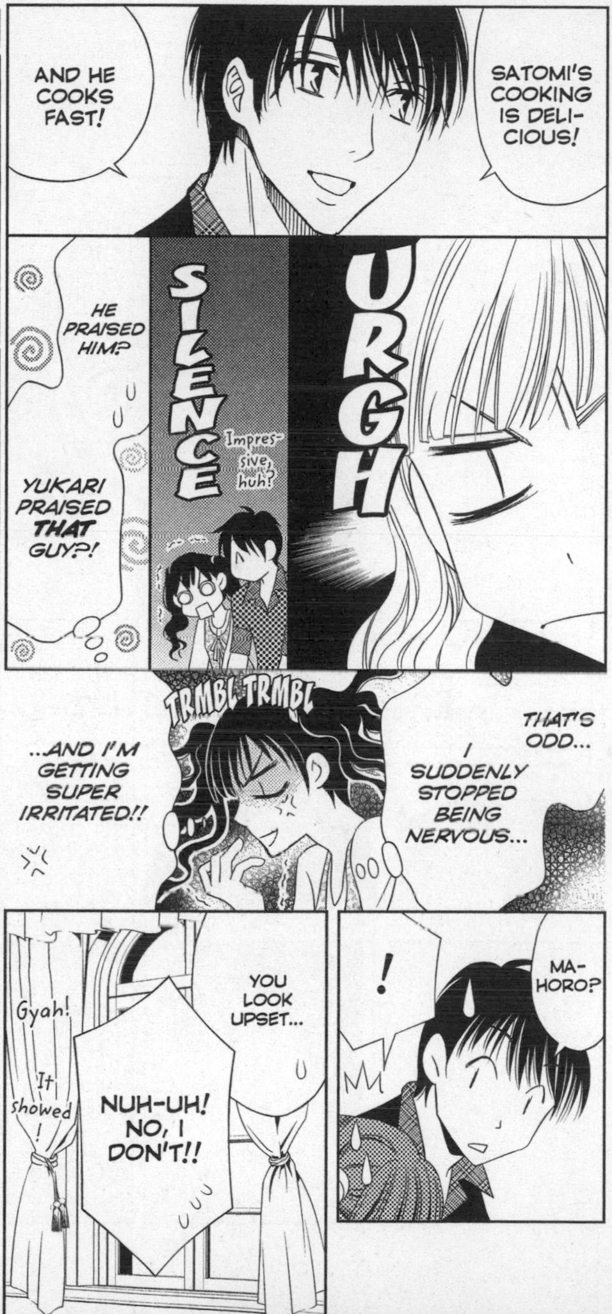
SATOMI'S COOKING IS DELICIOUS!
AND HE COOKS FAST!
URGH
SILENCE
Impressive, huh?
HE PRAISED HIM?
YUKARI PRAISED THAT GUY?!
THAT'S ODD...
I SUDDENLY STOPPED BEING NERVOUS...
TRMBL TRMBL
...AND I'M GETTING SUPER IRRITATED!!
MA-HORO?
!
YOU LOOK UPSET...
NUH-UH! NO, I DON'T!!
Gyah!
It showed!

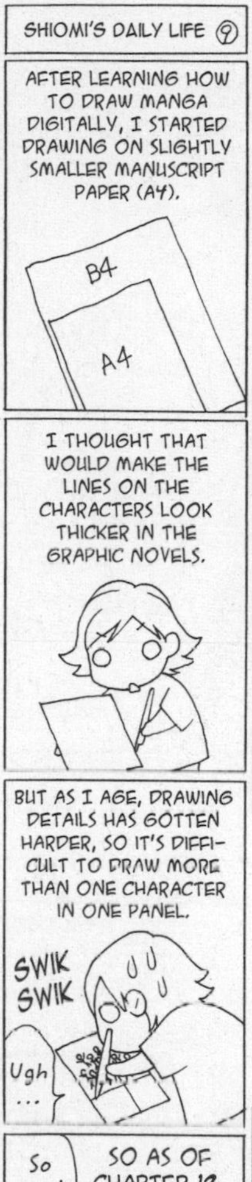
SHIOMI'S DAILY LIFE ⑨
AFTER LEARNING HOW TO DRAW MANGA DIGITALLY, I STARTED DRAWING ON SLIGHTLY SMALLER MANUSCRIPT PAPER (A4).
B4
A4
I THOUGHT THAT WOULD MAKE THE LINES ON THE CHARACTERS LOOK THICKER IN THE GRAPHIC NOVELS.
BUT AS I AGE, DRAWING DETAILS HAS GOTTEN HARDER, SO IT'S DIFFICULT TO DRAW MORE THAN ONE CHARACTER IN ONE PANEL.
SWIK SWIK
Ugh...
SO AS OF CHAPTER 12, I'VE STARTED USING THE B4 SIZE AGAIN.
So much space...
This is easy!

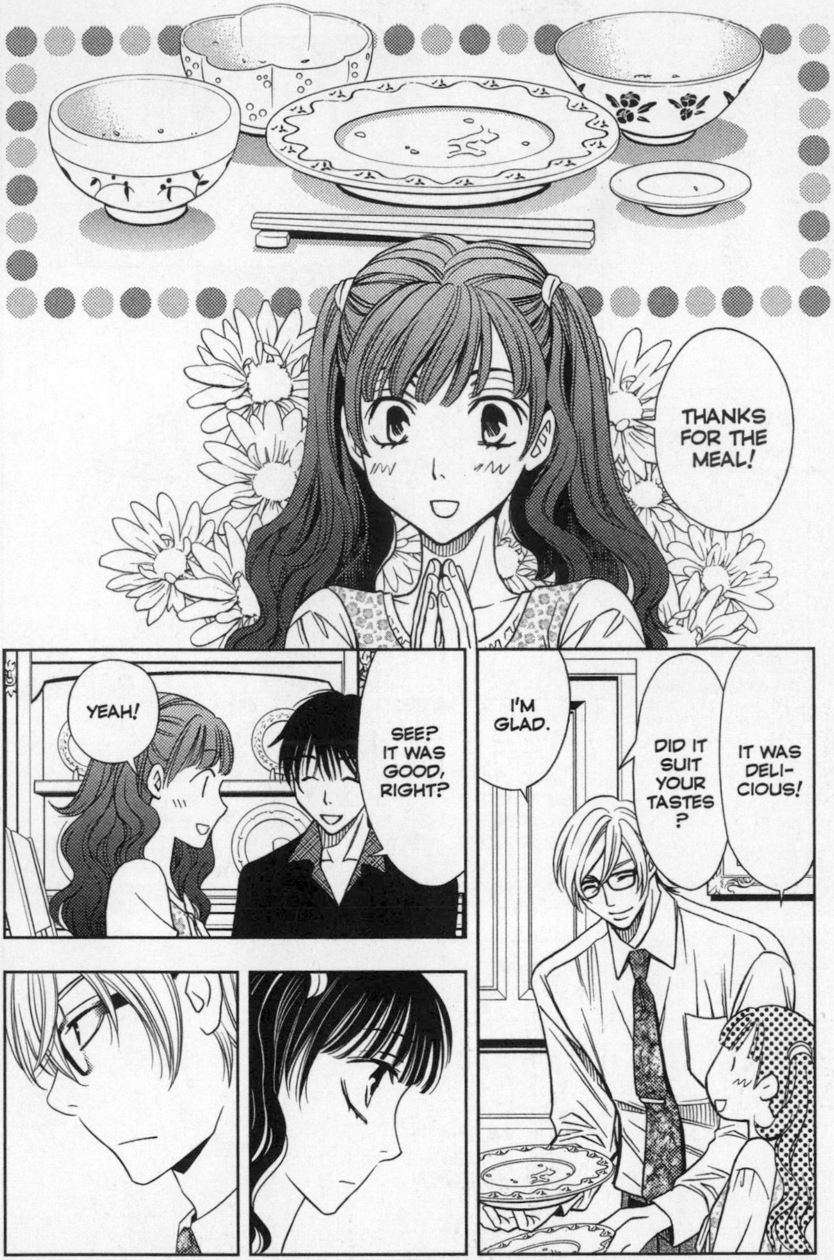
THANKS FOR THE MEAL!
IT WAS DELICIOUS!
DID IT SUIT YOUR TASTES?
I'M GLAD.
SEE? IT WAS GOOD, RIGHT?
YEAH!

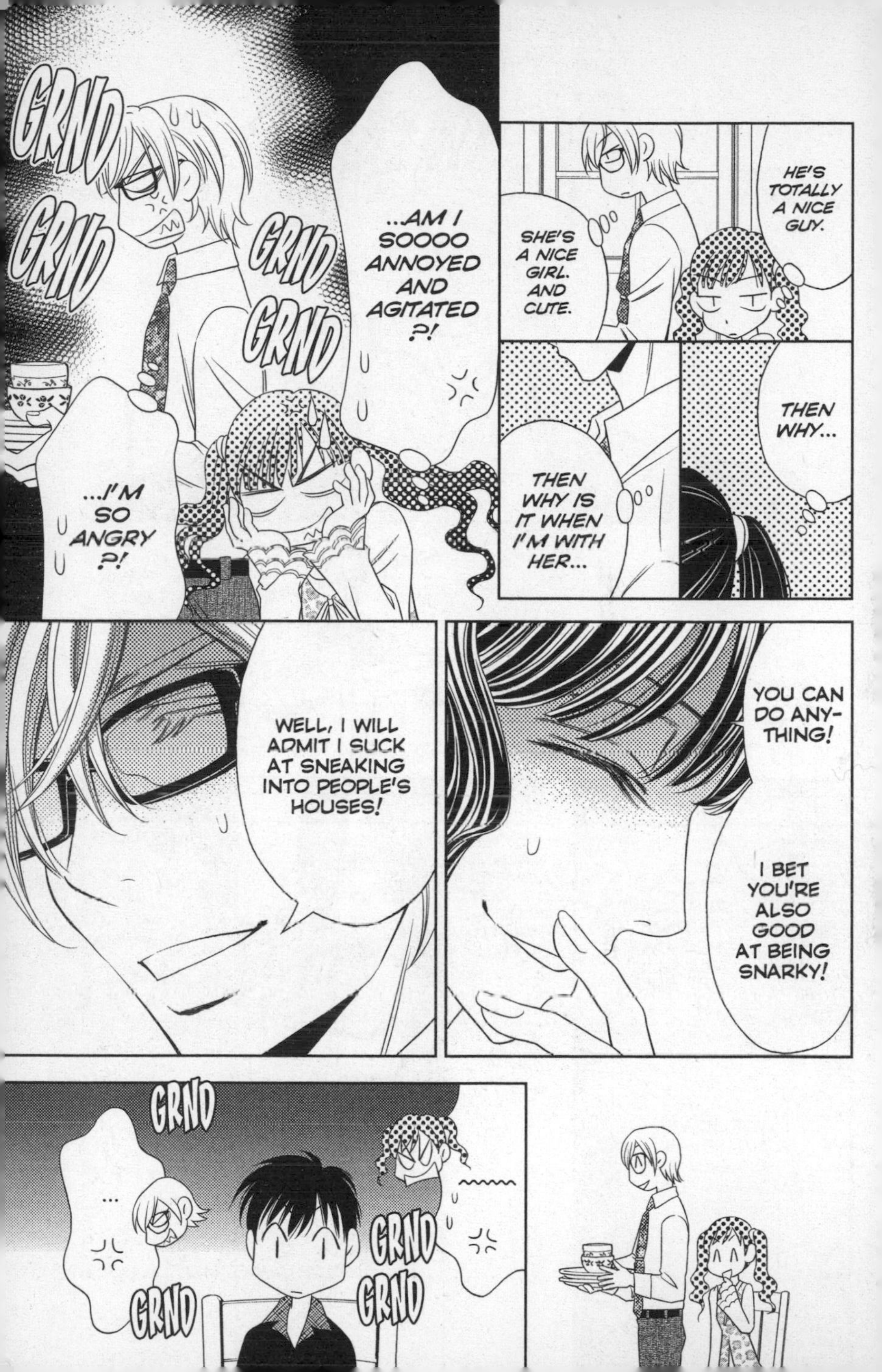
HE'S TOTALLY A NICE GUY.
SHE'S A NICE GIRL. AND CUTE.
THEN WHY...
THEN WHY IS IT WHEN I'M WITH HER...
...AM I SOOOO ANNOYED AND AGITATED ?!
GRND GRND
GRND GRND
...I'M SO ANGRY ?!
YOU CAN DO ANY-THING!
I BET YOU'RE ALSO GOOD AT BEING SNARKY!
WELL, I WILL ADMIT I SUCK AT SNEAKING INTO PEOPLE'S HOUSES!
GRND
~~~~~
GRND GRND
...
GRND
~~~~~

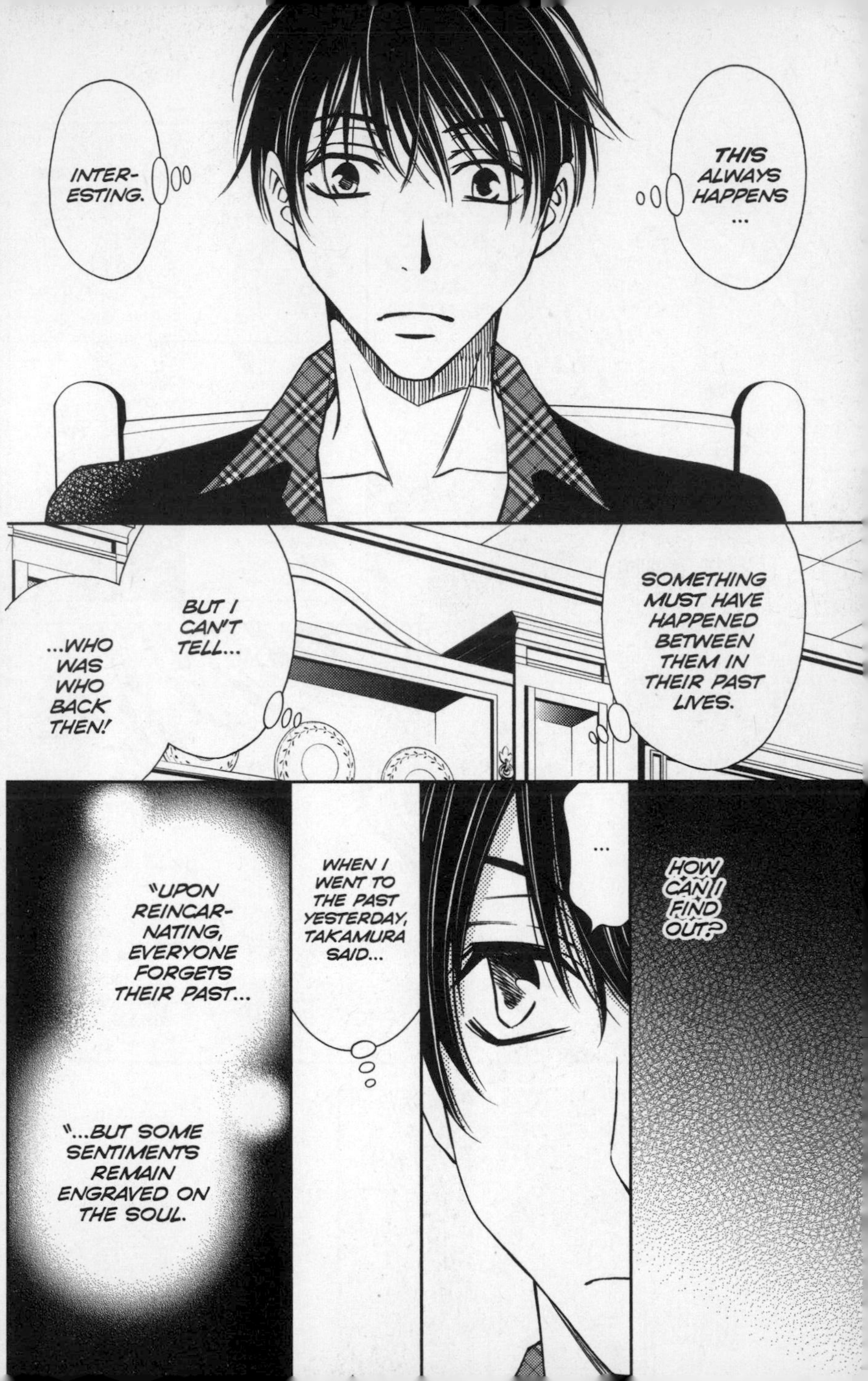
THIS ALWAYS HAPPENS ...
INTER-ESTING.
SOMETHING MUST HAVE HAPPENED BETWEEN THEM IN THEIR PAST LIVES.
BUT I CAN'T TELL...
...WHO WAS WHO BACK THEN!
HOW CAN I FIND OUT?
...
WHEN I WENT TO THE PAST YESTERDAY, TAKAMURA SAID...
"UPON REINCAR-NATING, EVERYONE FORGETS THEIR PAST...
"...BUT SOME SENTIMENTS REMAIN ENGRAVED ON THE SOUL.

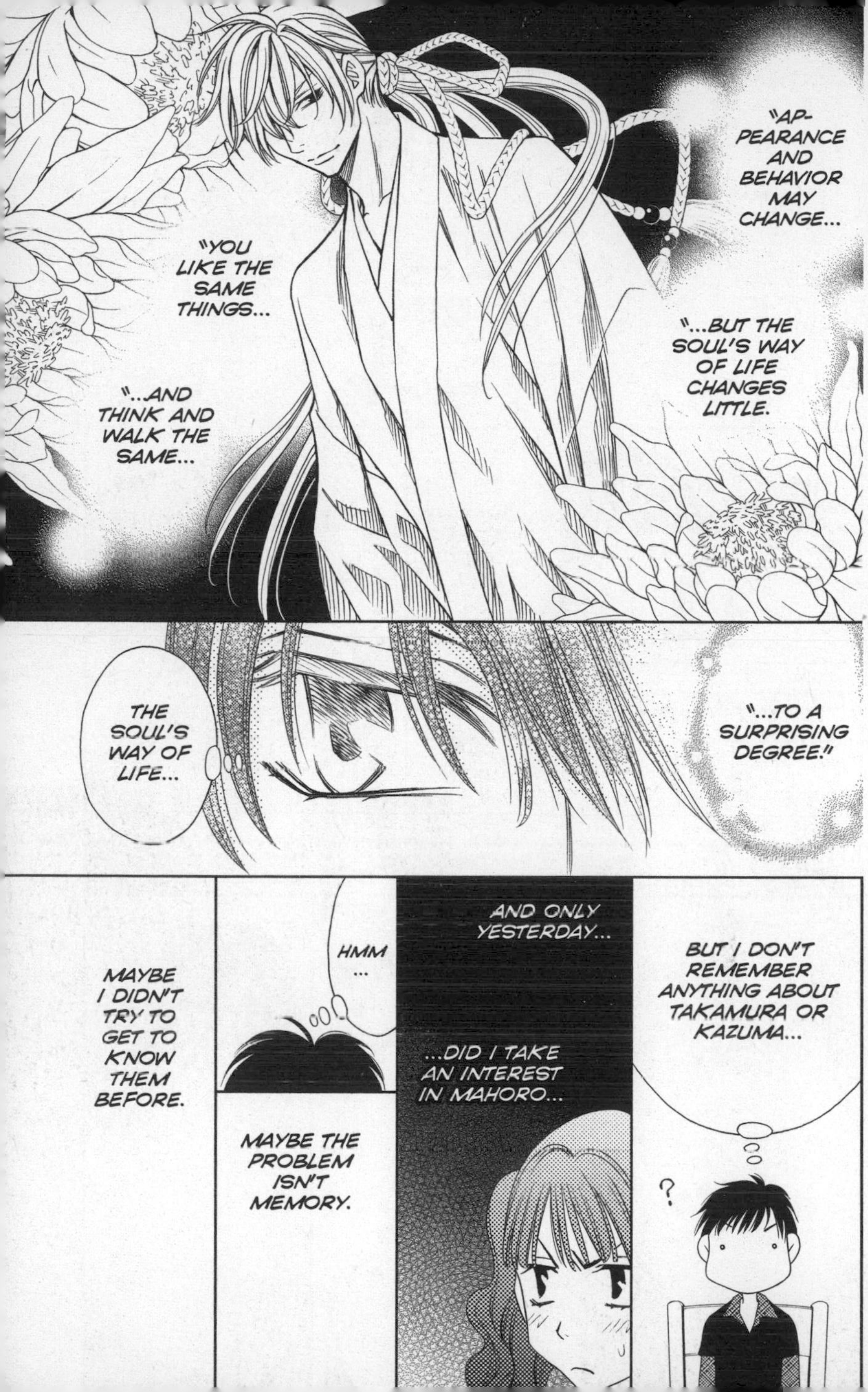
"AP-PEARANCE AND BEHAVIOR MAY CHANGE...
"...BUT THE SOUL'S WAY OF LIFE CHANGES LITTLE.
"YOU LIKE THE SAME THINGS...
"...AND THINK AND WALK THE SAME...
"...TO A SURPRISING DEGREE."
THE SOUL'S WAY OF LIFE...
BUT I DON'T REMEMBER ANYTHING ABOUT TAKAMURA OR KAZUMA...
?
AND ONLY YESTERDAY...
...DID I TAKE AN INTEREST IN MAHORO...
HMM ...
MAYBE THE PROBLEM ISN'T MEMORY.
MAYBE I DIDN'T TRY TO GET TO KNOW THEM BEFORE.

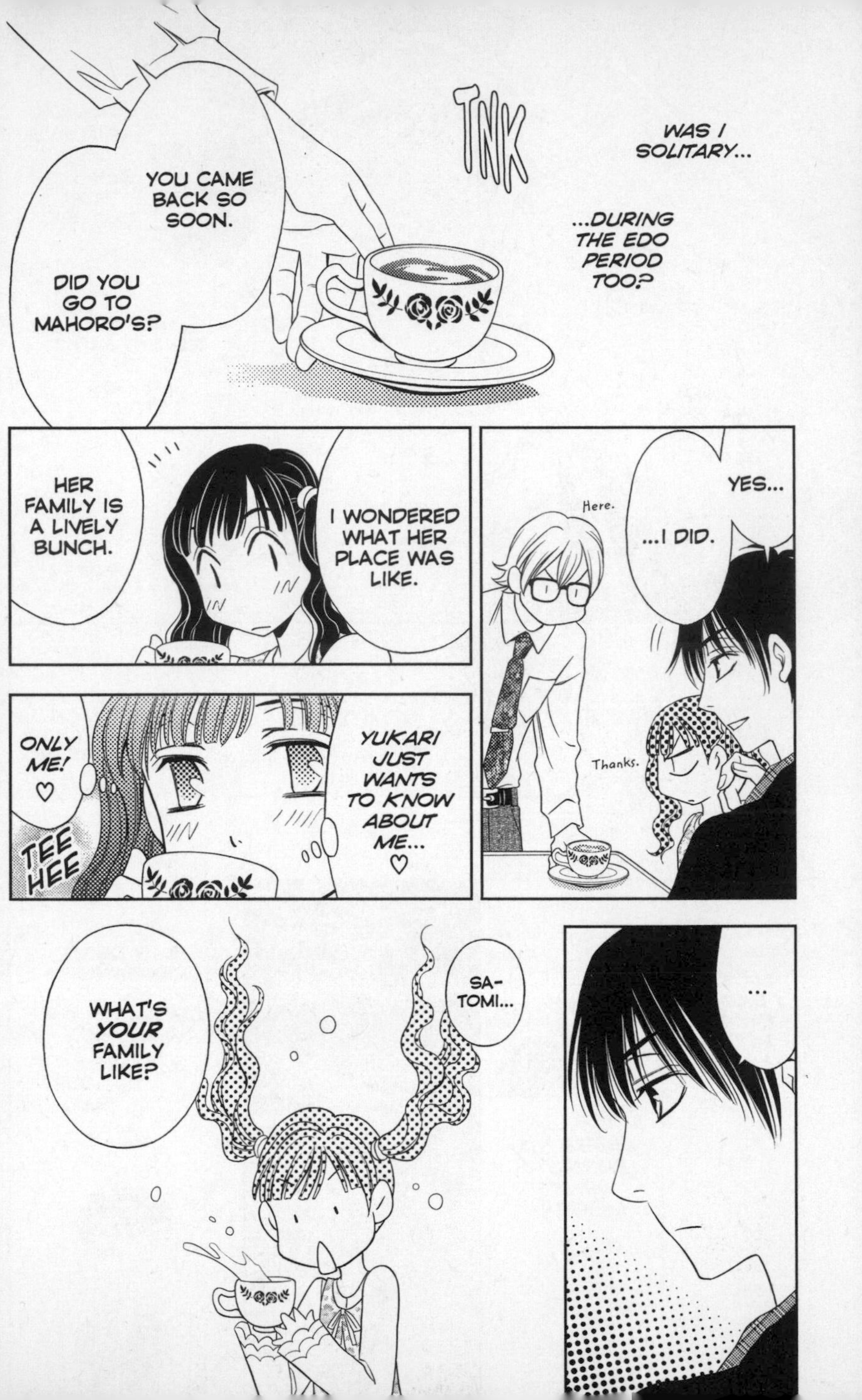
WAS I SOLITARY...
...DURING THE EDO PERIOD TOO?
TNK
YOU CAME BACK SO SOON.
DID YOU GO TO MAHORO'S?
YES...
...I DID.
Here.
Thanks.
I WONDERED WHAT HER PLACE WAS LIKE.
HER FAMILY IS A LIVELY BUNCH.
YUKARI JUST WANTS TO KNOW ABOUT ME... ♡
ONLY ME! ♡
TEE HEE
...
SA-TOMI...
WHAT'S *YOUR* FAMILY LIKE?

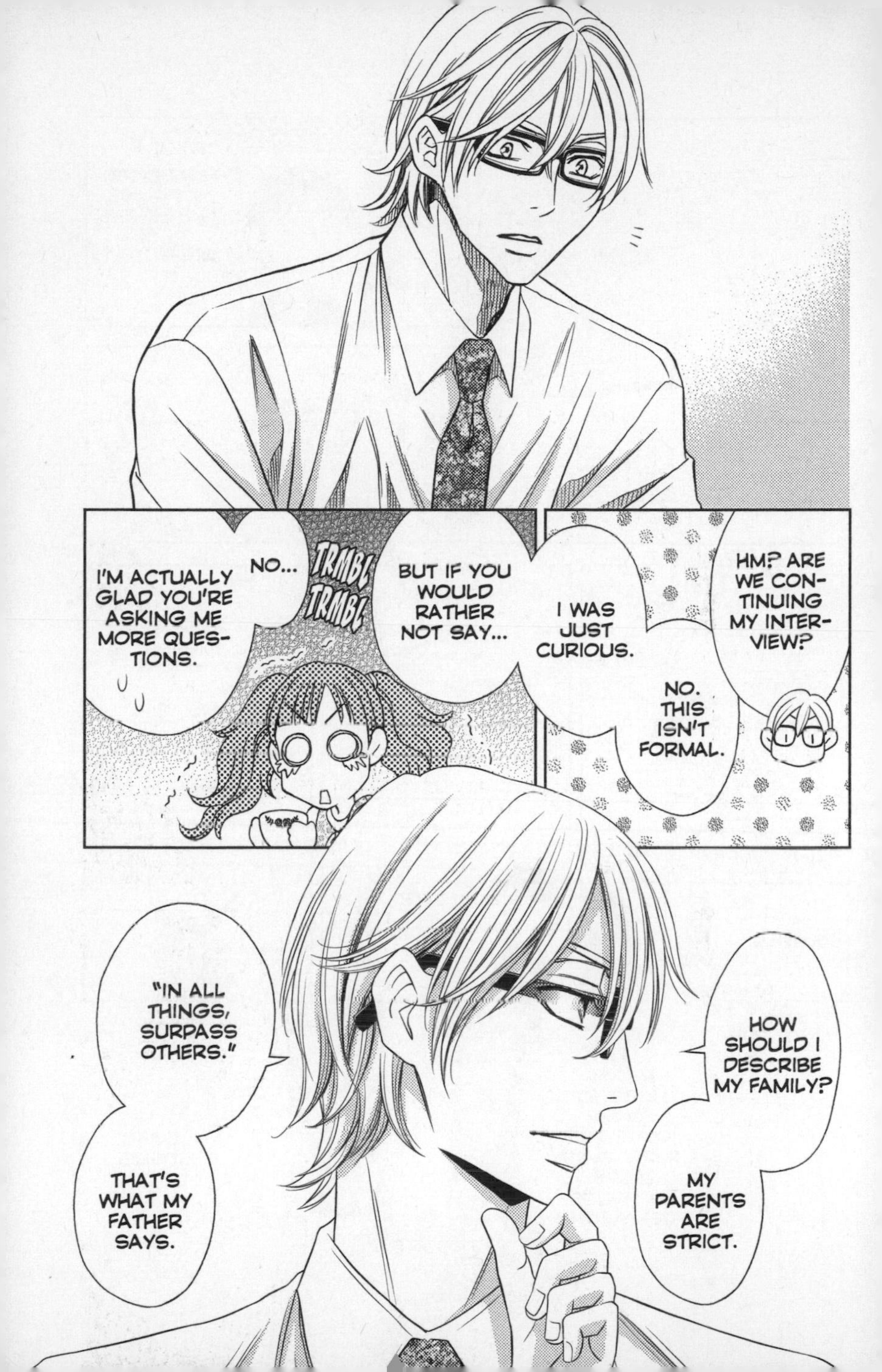
HM? ARE WE CONTINUING MY INTERVIEW?
NO. THIS ISN'T FORMAL.
I WAS JUST CURIOUS.
BUT IF YOU WOULD RATHER NOT SAY...
TRMBL TRMBL
NO...
I'M ACTUALLY GLAD YOU'RE ASKING ME MORE QUESTIONS.
HOW SHOULD I DESCRIBE MY FAMILY?
MY PARENTS ARE STRICT.
"IN ALL THINGS, SURPASS OTHERS."
THAT'S WHAT MY FATHER SAYS.

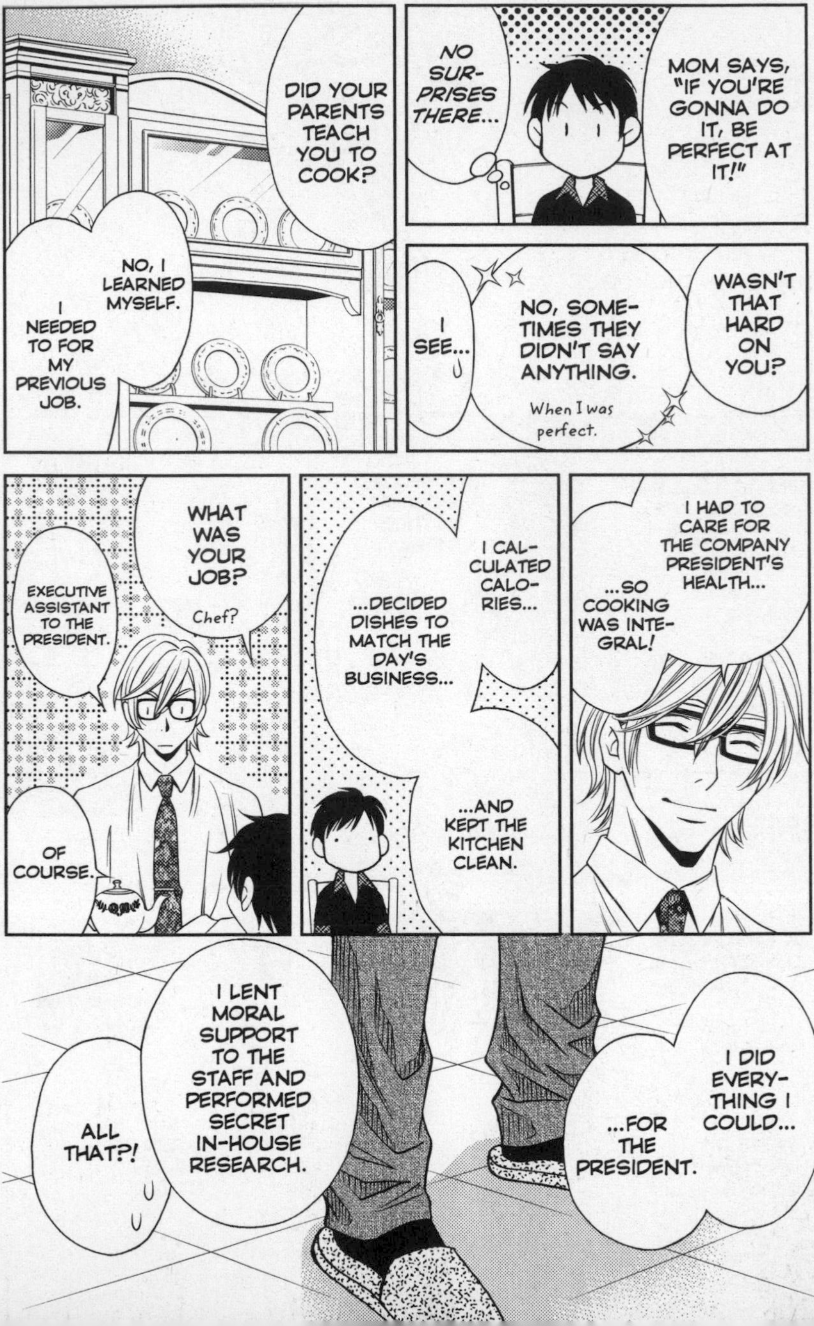
MOM SAYS, "IF YOU'RE GONNA DO IT, BE PERFECT AT IT!"
NO SURPRISES THERE...
WASN'T THAT HARD ON YOU?
NO, SOMETIMES THEY DIDN'T SAY ANYTHING.
When I was perfect.
I SEE...
DID YOUR PARENTS TEACH YOU TO COOK?
NO, I LEARNED MYSELF.
I NEEDED TO FOR MY PREVIOUS JOB.
I HAD TO CARE FOR THE COMPANY PRESIDENT'S HEALTH...
...SO COOKING WAS INTEGRAL!
I CALCULATED CALORIES...
...DECIDED DISHES TO MATCH THE DAY'S BUSINESS...
...AND KEPT THE KITCHEN CLEAN.
WHAT WAS YOUR JOB?
Chef?
EXECUTIVE ASSISTANT TO THE PRESIDENT.
OF COURSE.
I DID EVERYTHING I COULD...
...FOR THE PRESIDENT.
I LENT MORAL SUPPORT TO THE STAFF AND PERFORMED SECRET IN-HOUSE RESEARCH.
ALL THAT?!

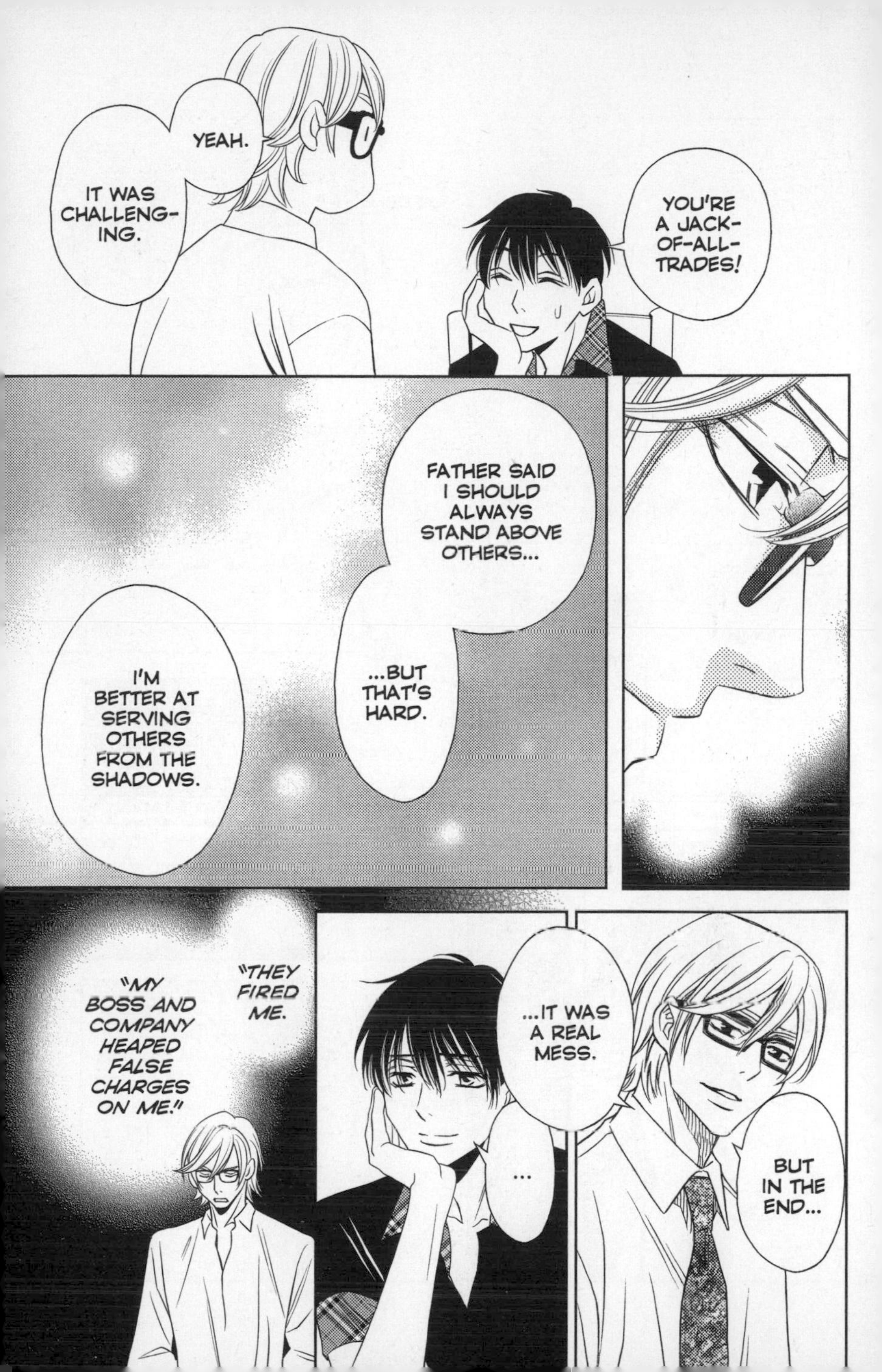
YOU'RE A JACK-OF-ALL-TRADES!
YEAH.
IT WAS CHALLENG-ING.
FATHER SAID I SHOULD ALWAYS STAND ABOVE OTHERS...
...BUT THAT'S HARD.
I'M BETTER AT SERVING OTHERS FROM THE SHADOWS.
...IT WAS A REAL MESS.
BUT IN THE END...
...
"THEY FIRED ME.
"MY BOSS AND COMPANY HEAPED FALSE CHARGES ON ME."

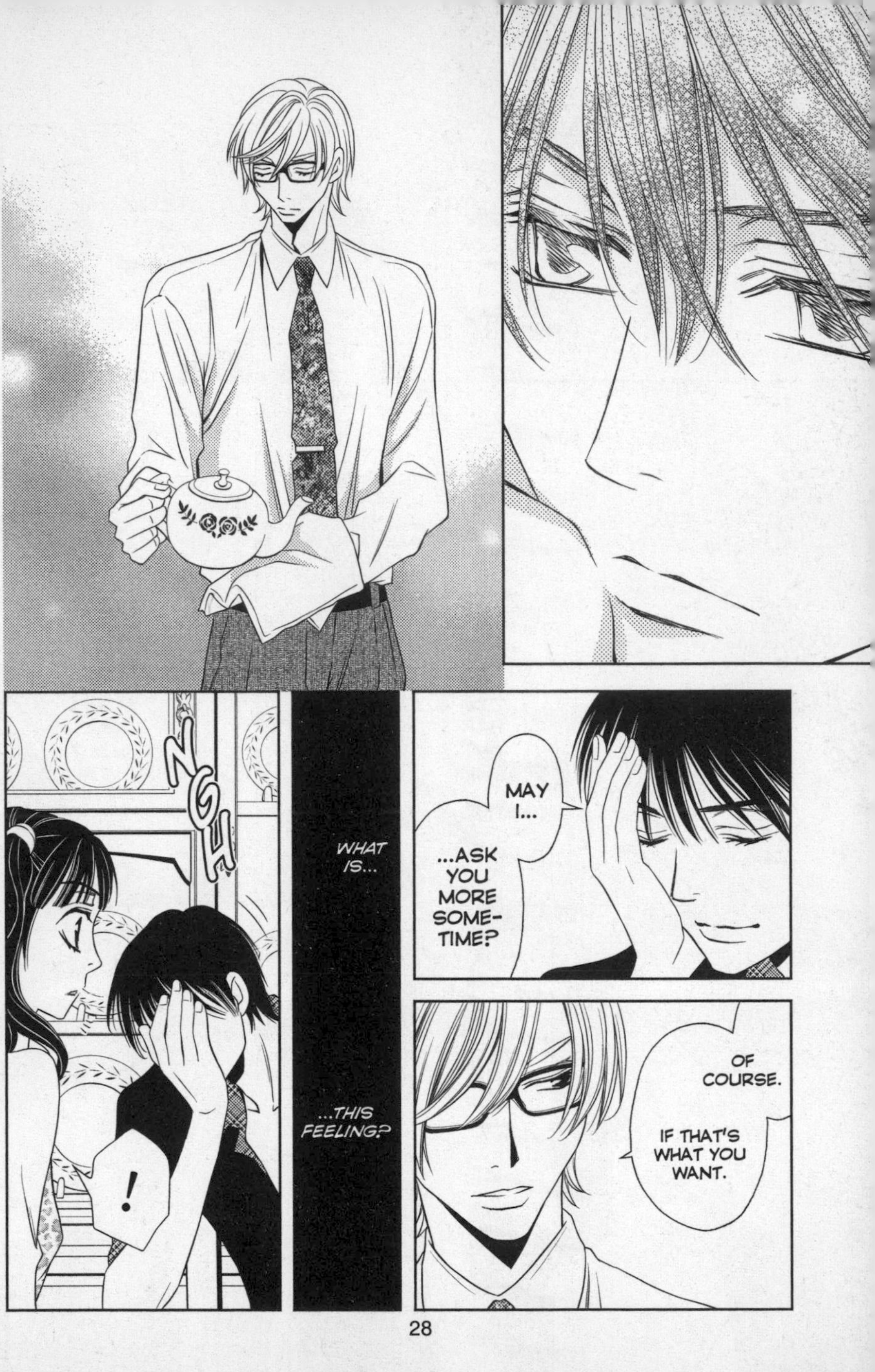
MAY I...
...ASK YOU MORE SOME-TIME?
OF COURSE.
IF THAT'S WHAT YOU WANT.
WHAT IS...
...THIS FEELING?
NGH
!

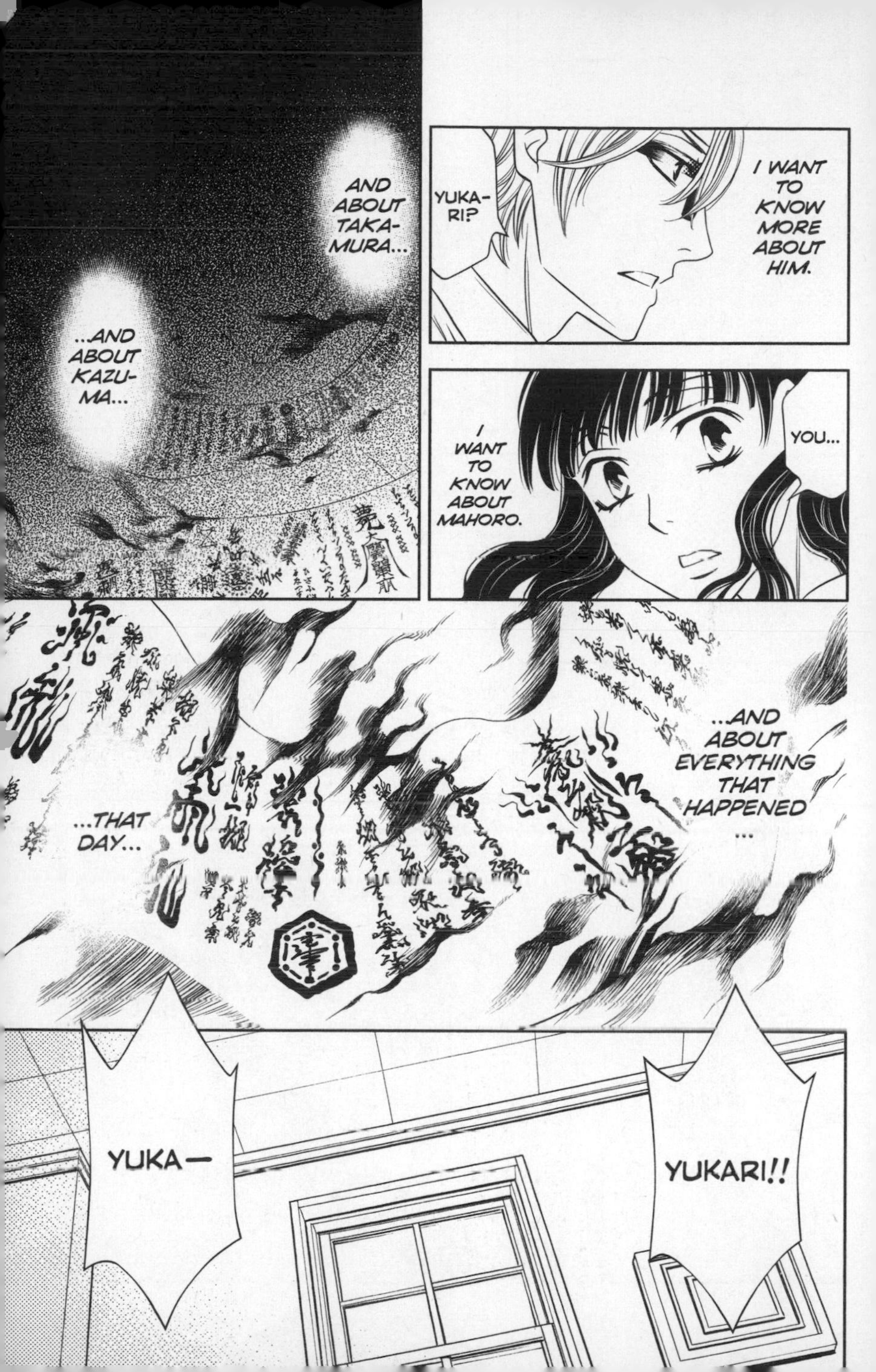
I WANT TO KNOW MORE ABOUT HIM.
YUKA-RI?
YOU...
I WANT TO KNOW ABOUT MAHORO.
AND ABOUT TAKA-MURA...
...AND ABOUT KAZU-MA...
...AND ABOUT EVERYTHING THAT HAPPENED ...
...THAT DAY...
YUKARI!!
YUKA—

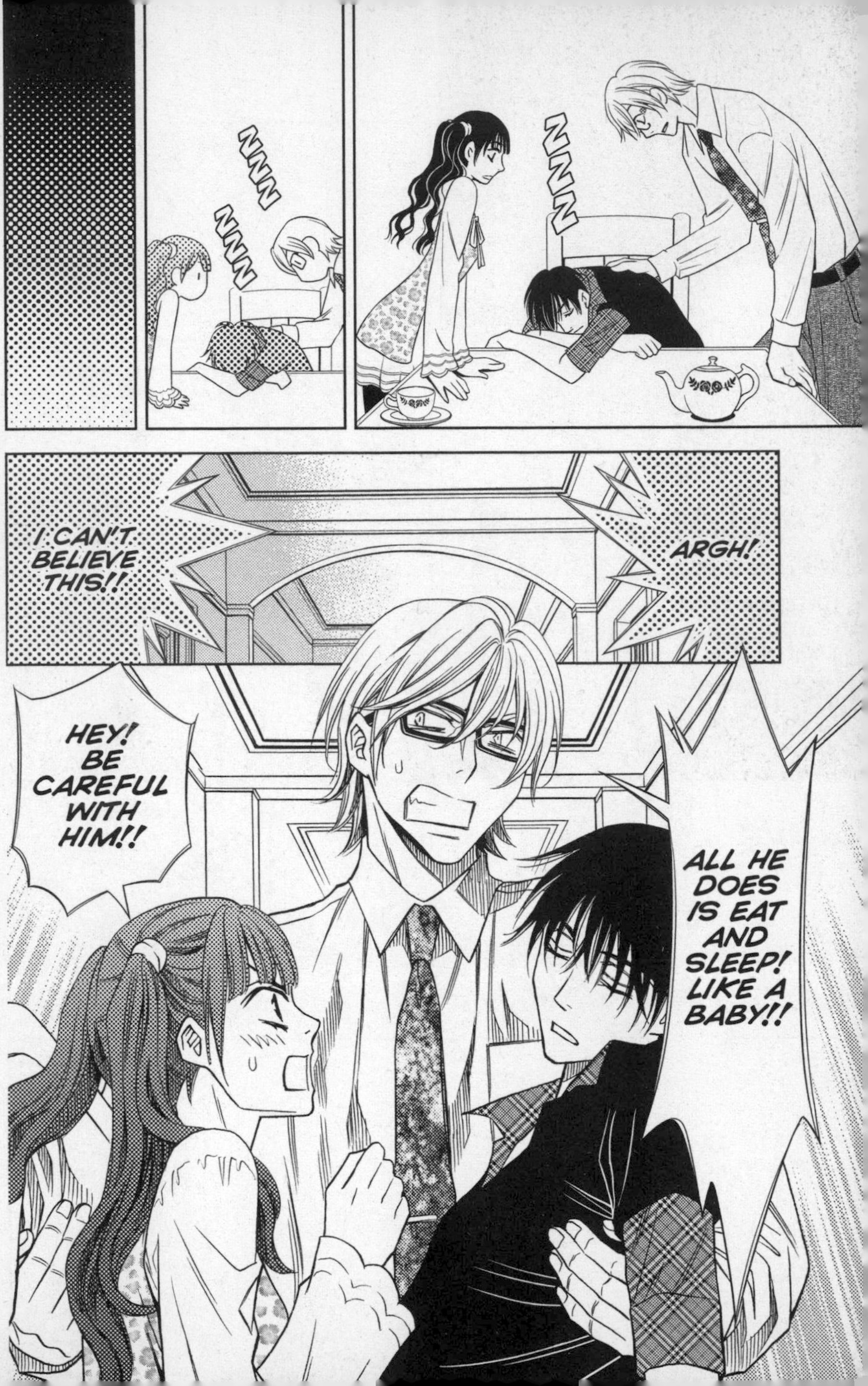
NNN
NNN
NNN
ARGH!
I CAN'T BELIEVE THIS!!
HEY! BE CAREFUL WITH HIM!!
ALL HE DOES IS EAT AND SLEEP! LIKE A BABY!!

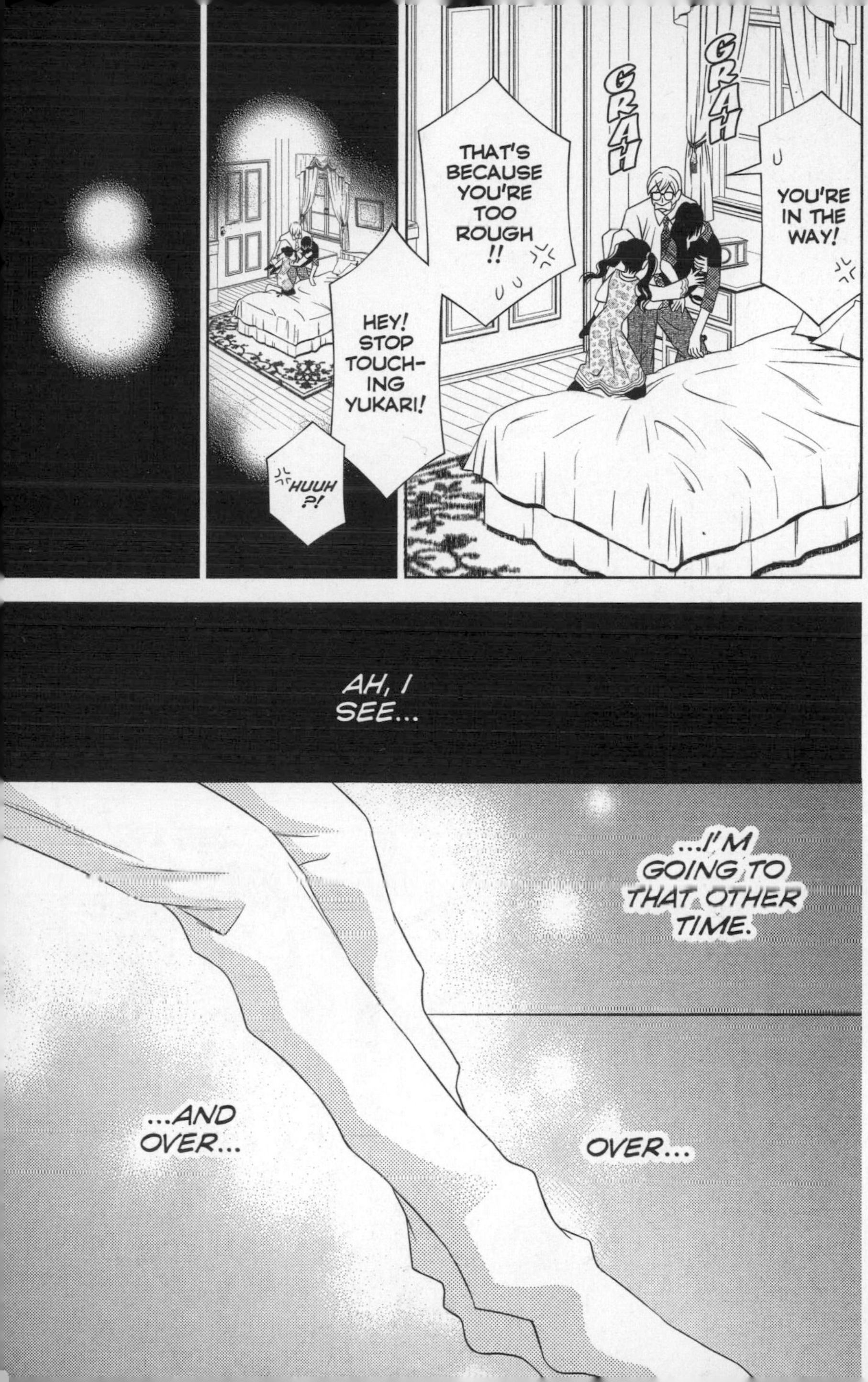

YOU'RE IN THE WAY!
GRAH
GRAH
THAT'S BECAUSE YOU'RE TOO ROUGH!!
HEY! STOP TOUCHING YUKARI!
HUUH?!
AH, I SEE...
...I'M GOING TO THAT OTHER TIME.
OVER...
...AND OVER...

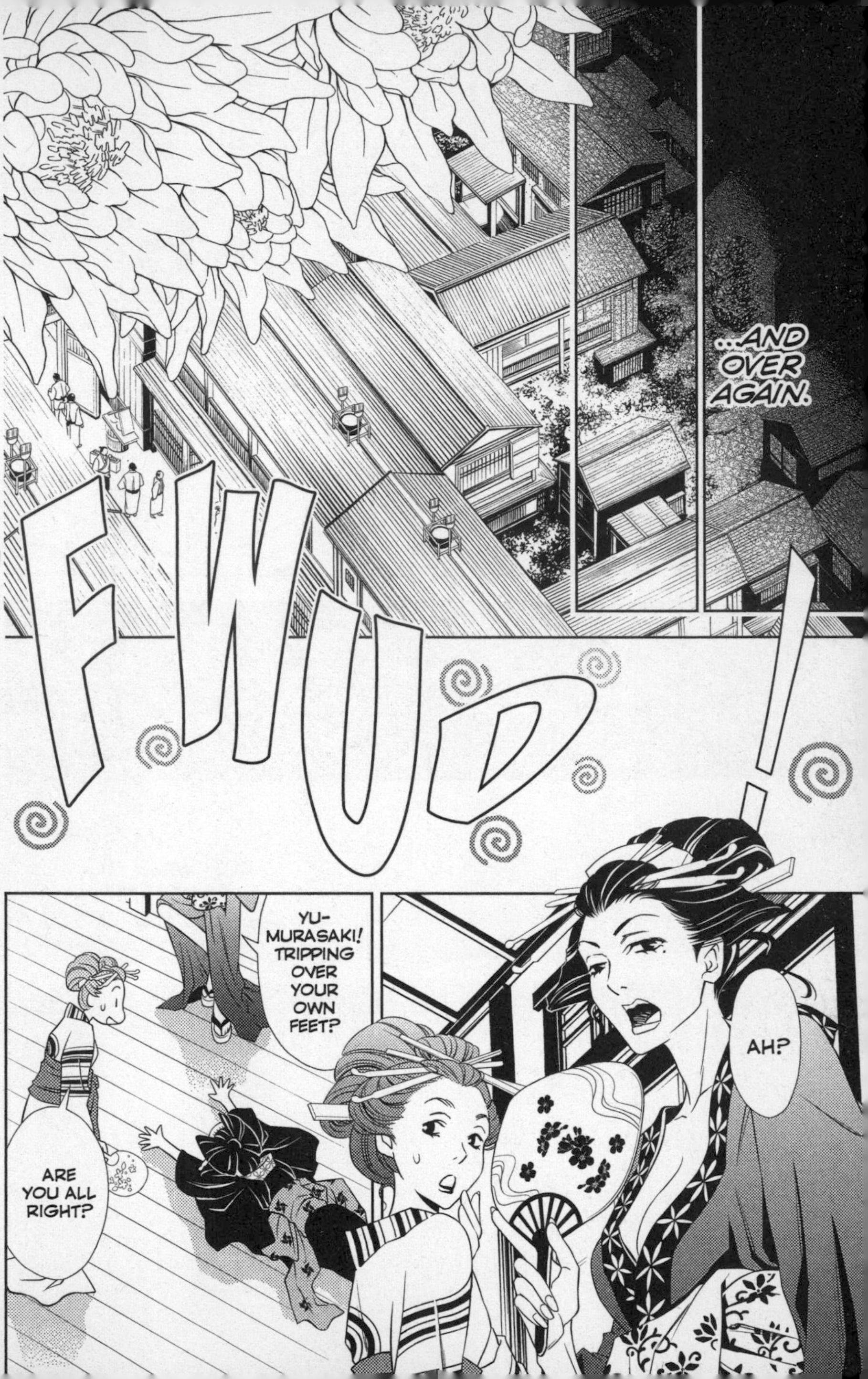
...AND OVER AGAIN.
FWUD!
AH?
YU-MURASAKI! TRIPPING OVER YOUR OWN FEET?
ARE YOU ALL RIGHT?

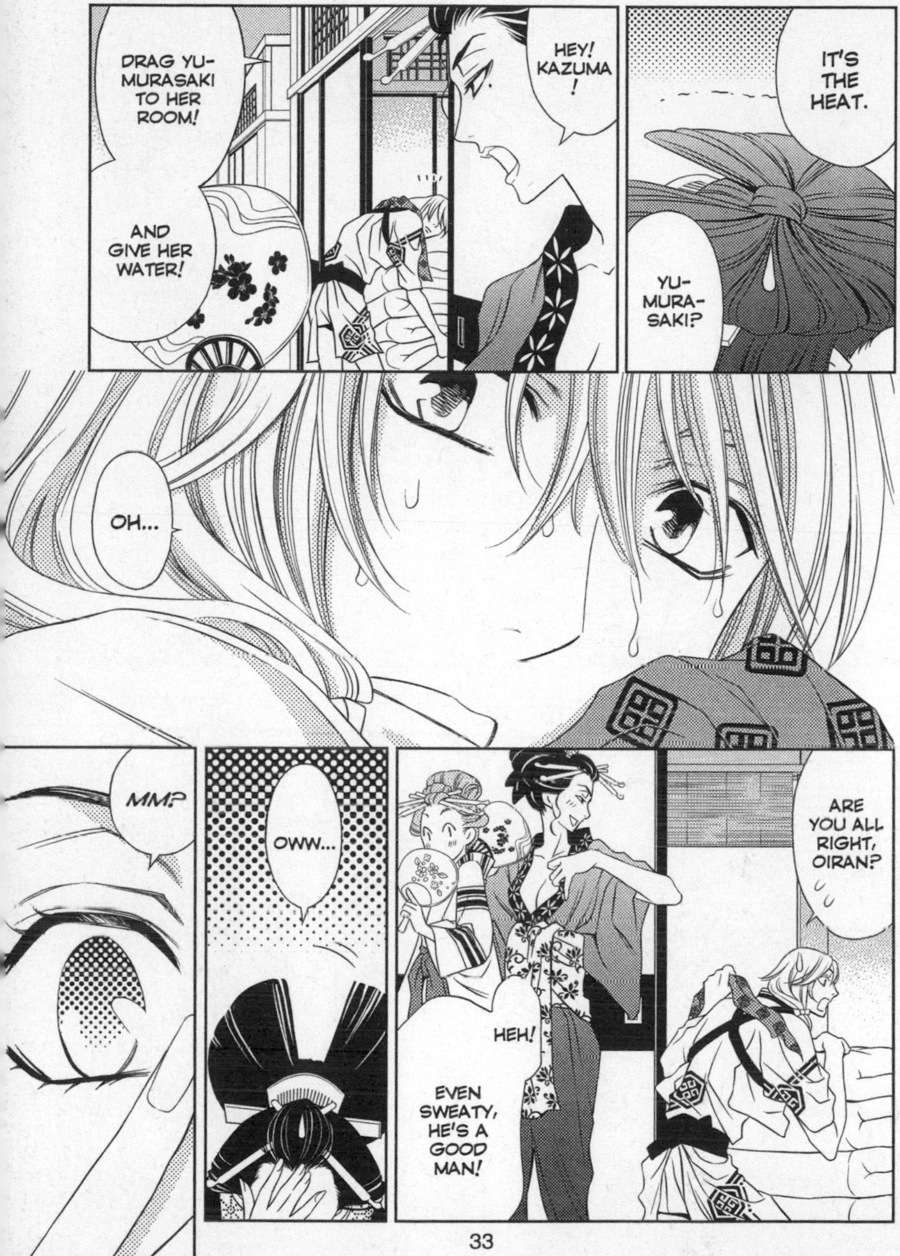
IT'S THE HEAT.
YU-MURA-SAKI?
HEY! KAZUMA!
DRAG YU-MURASAKI TO HER ROOM!
AND GIVE HER WATER!
OH...
ARE YOU ALL RIGHT, OIRAN?
HEH!
EVEN SWEATY, HE'S A GOOD MAN!
OWW...
MM?

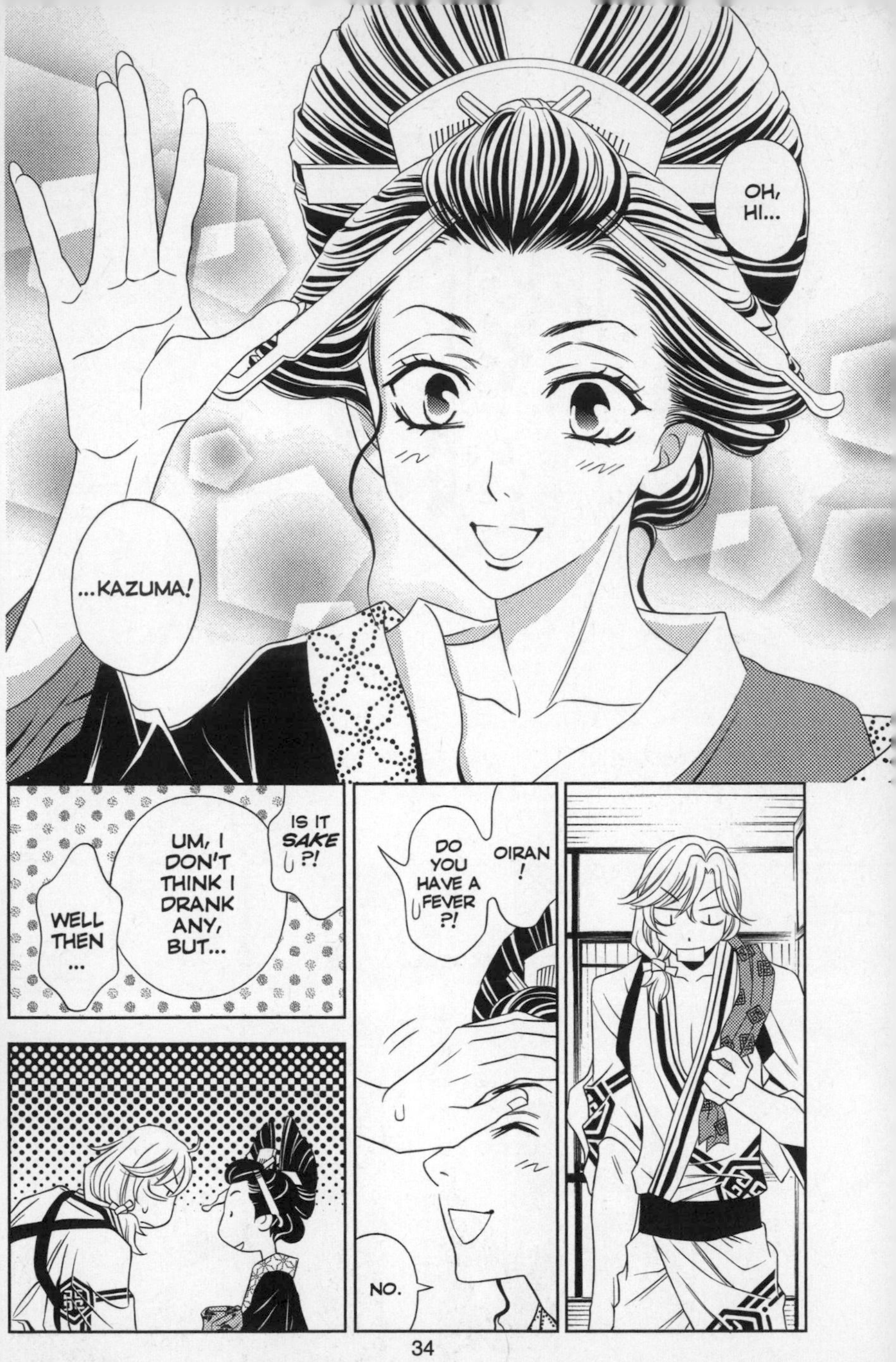
OH, HI...
...KAZUMA!
OIRAN!
DO YOU HAVE A FEVER?!
NO.
IS IT *SAKE*?!
UM, I DON'T THINK I DRANK ANY, BUT...
WELL THEN ...

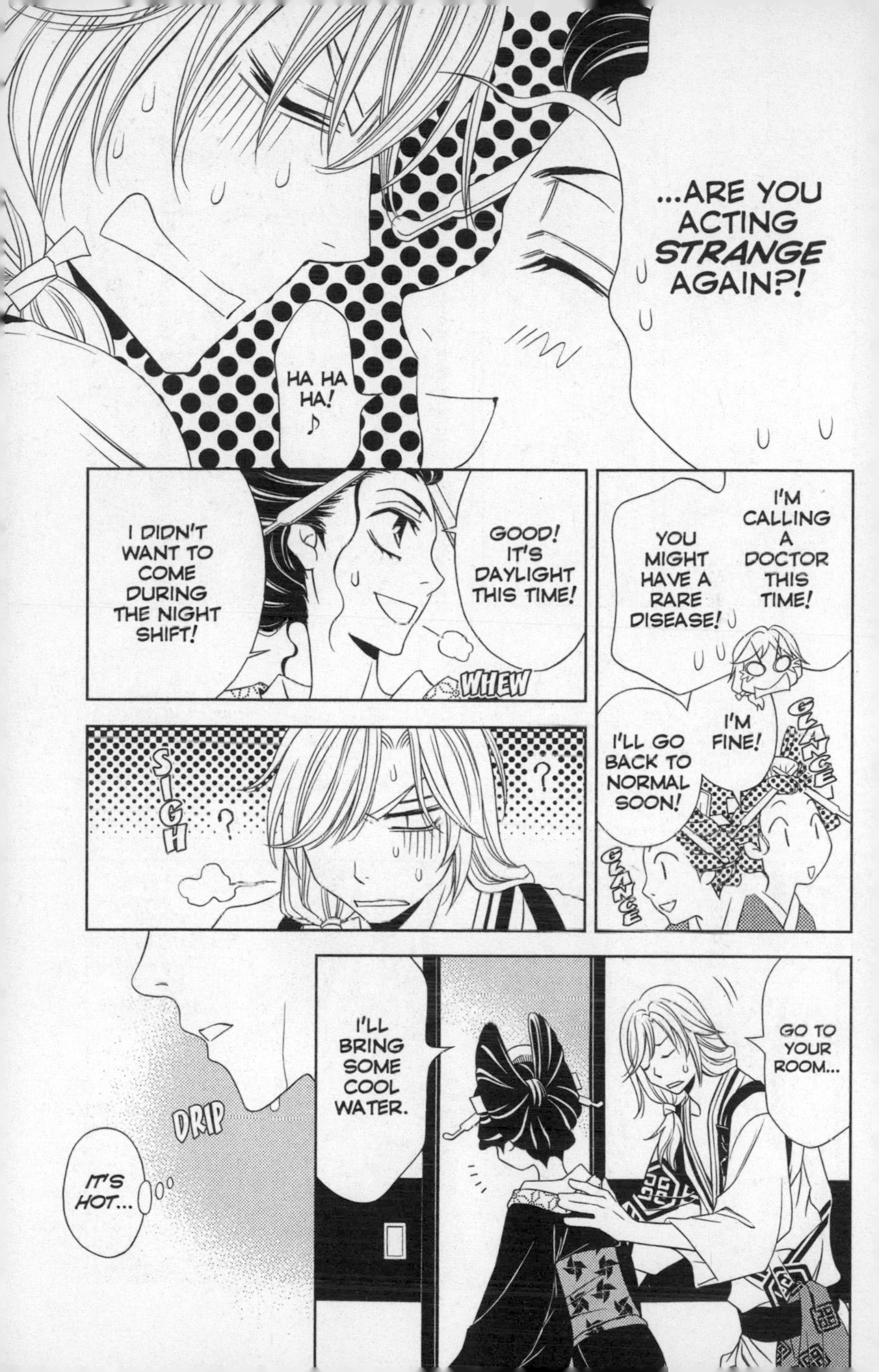
...ARE YOU ACTING STRANGE AGAIN?!
HA HA HA! ♪
I'M CALLING A DOCTOR THIS TIME!
YOU MIGHT HAVE A RARE DISEASE!
GLANCE
I'M FINE!
I'LL GO BACK TO NORMAL SOON!
GLANCE
GOOD! IT'S DAYLIGHT THIS TIME!
WHEW
I DIDN'T WANT TO COME DURING THE NIGHT SHIFT!
SIGH
GO TO YOUR ROOM...
I'LL BRING SOME COOL WATER.
DRIP
IT'S HOT...

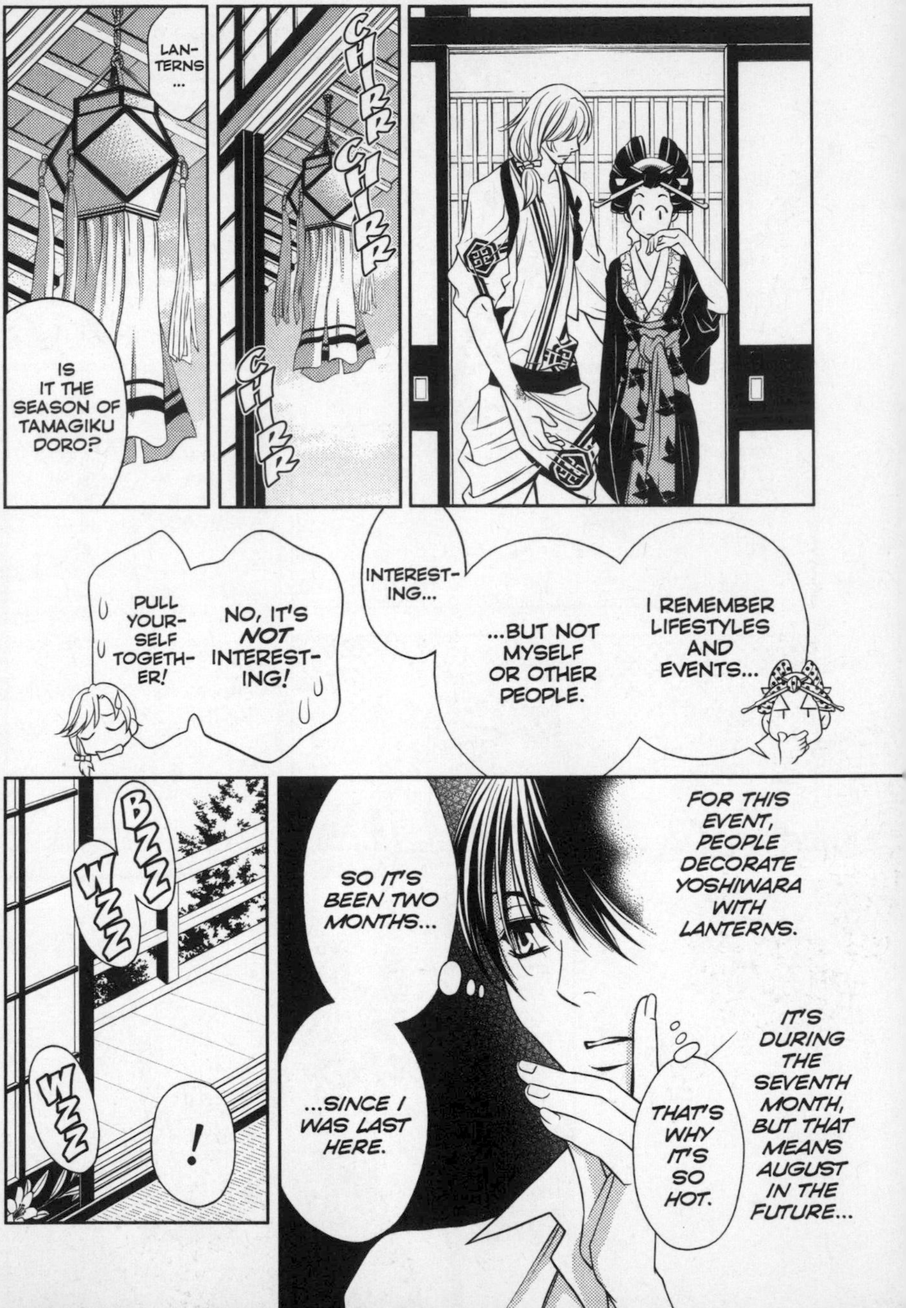
CHIRR CHIRR CHIRR
CHIRR
LAN-TERNS...
IS IT THE SEASON OF TAMAGIKU DORO?
I REMEMBER LIFESTYLES AND EVENTS...
...BUT NOT MYSELF OR OTHER PEOPLE.
INTEREST-ING...
NO, IT'S *NOT* INTEREST-ING!
PULL YOUR-SELF TOGETH-ER!
FOR THIS EVENT, PEOPLE DECORATE YOSHIWARA WITH LANTERNS.
IT'S DURING THE SEVENTH MONTH, BUT THAT MEANS AUGUST IN THE FUTURE...
THAT'S WHY IT'S SO HOT.
SO IT'S BEEN TWO MONTHS...
...SINCE I WAS LAST HERE.
BZZ
WZZ
WZZ
!

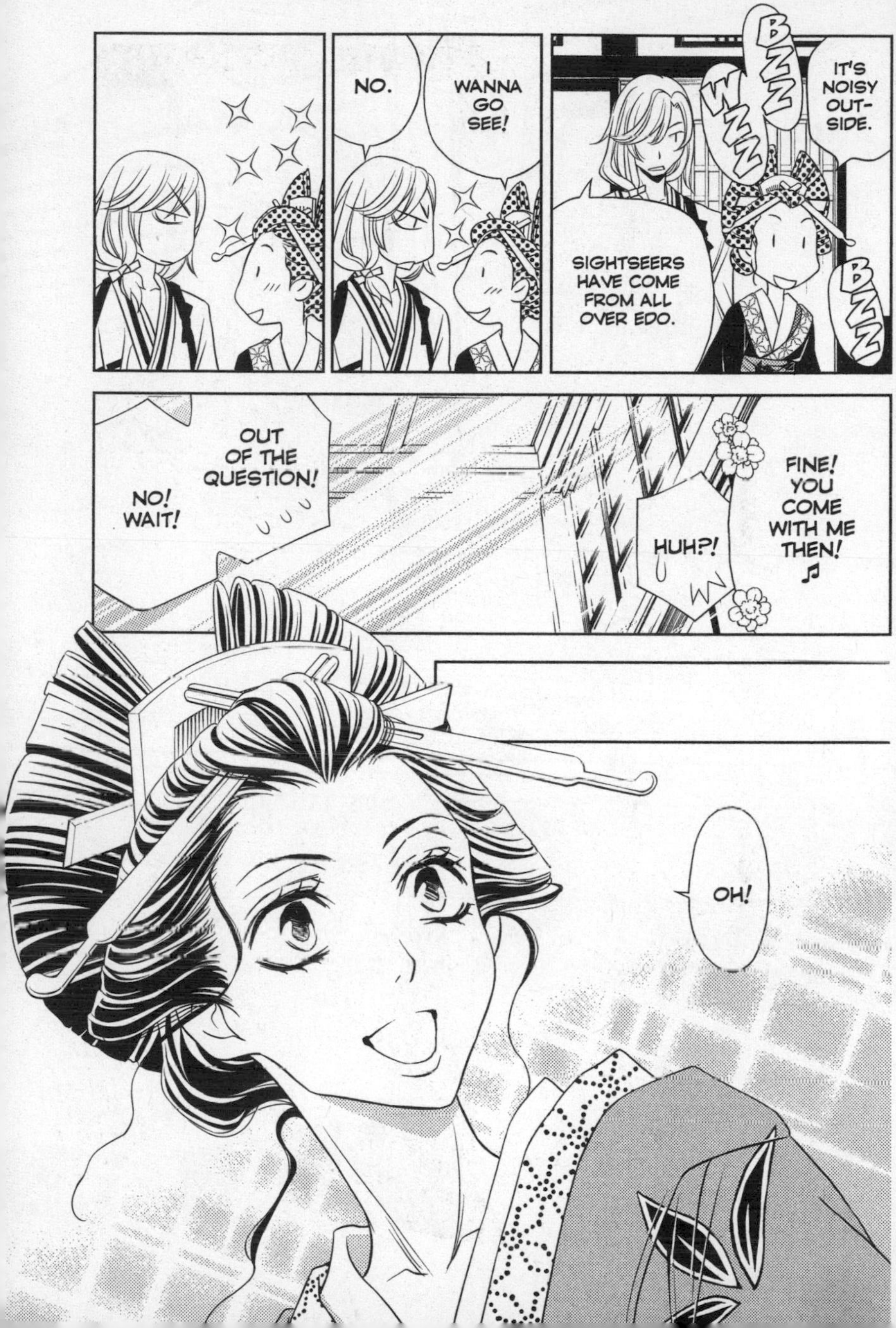
IT'S NOISY OUT-SIDE.
BZZ
WZZ
SIGHTSEERS HAVE COME FROM ALL OVER EDO.
BZZ
I WANNA GO SEE!
NO.
FINE! YOU COME WITH ME THEN! ♫
HUH?!
OUT OF THE QUESTION!
NO! WAIT!
OH!

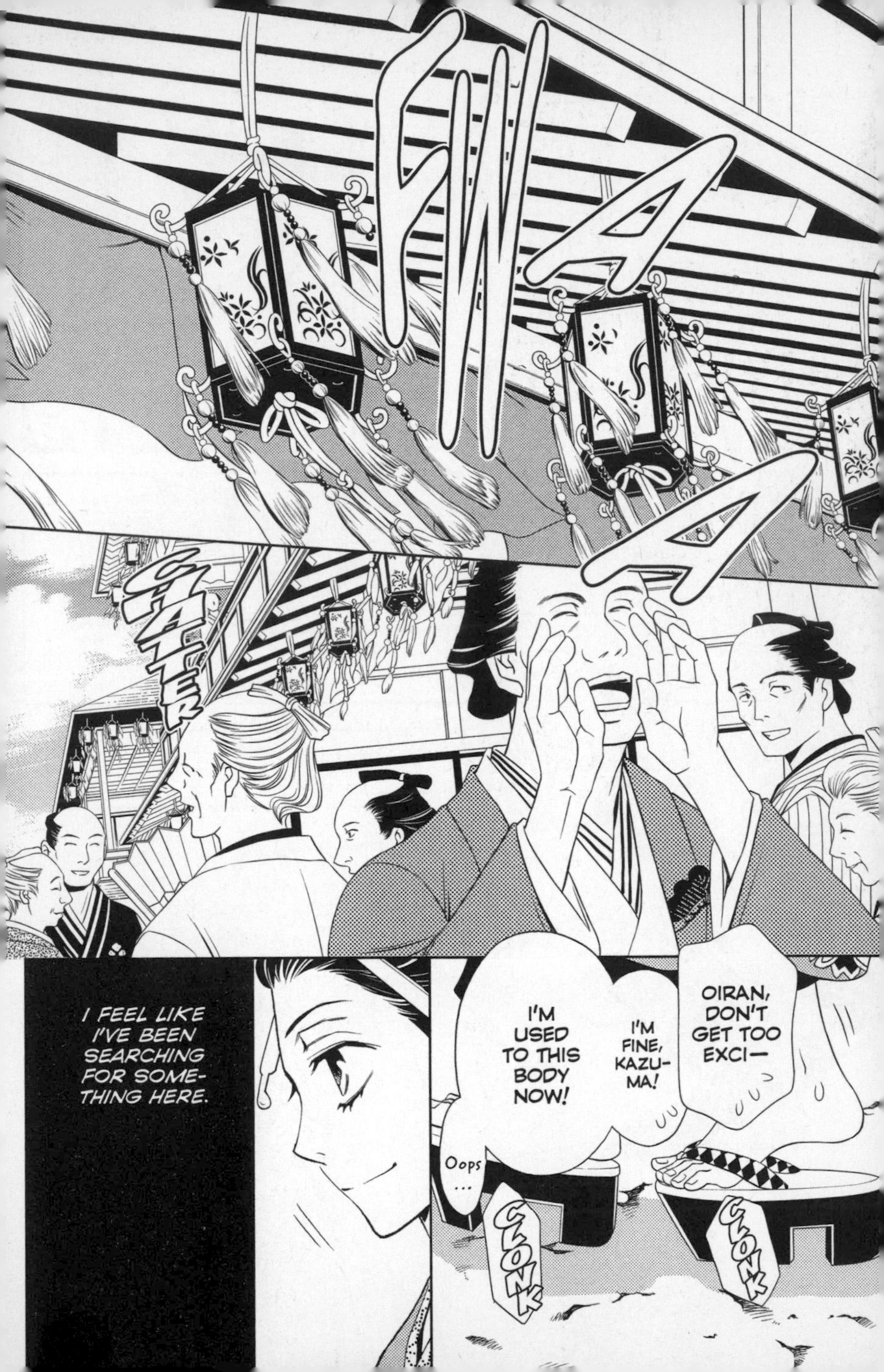
FWAA
CHATTER
OIRAN, DON'T GET TOO EXCI—
I'M FINE, KAZUMA!
I'M USED TO THIS BODY NOW!
Oops...
CLONK
CLONK
I FEEL LIKE I'VE BEEN SEARCHING FOR SOMETHING HERE.

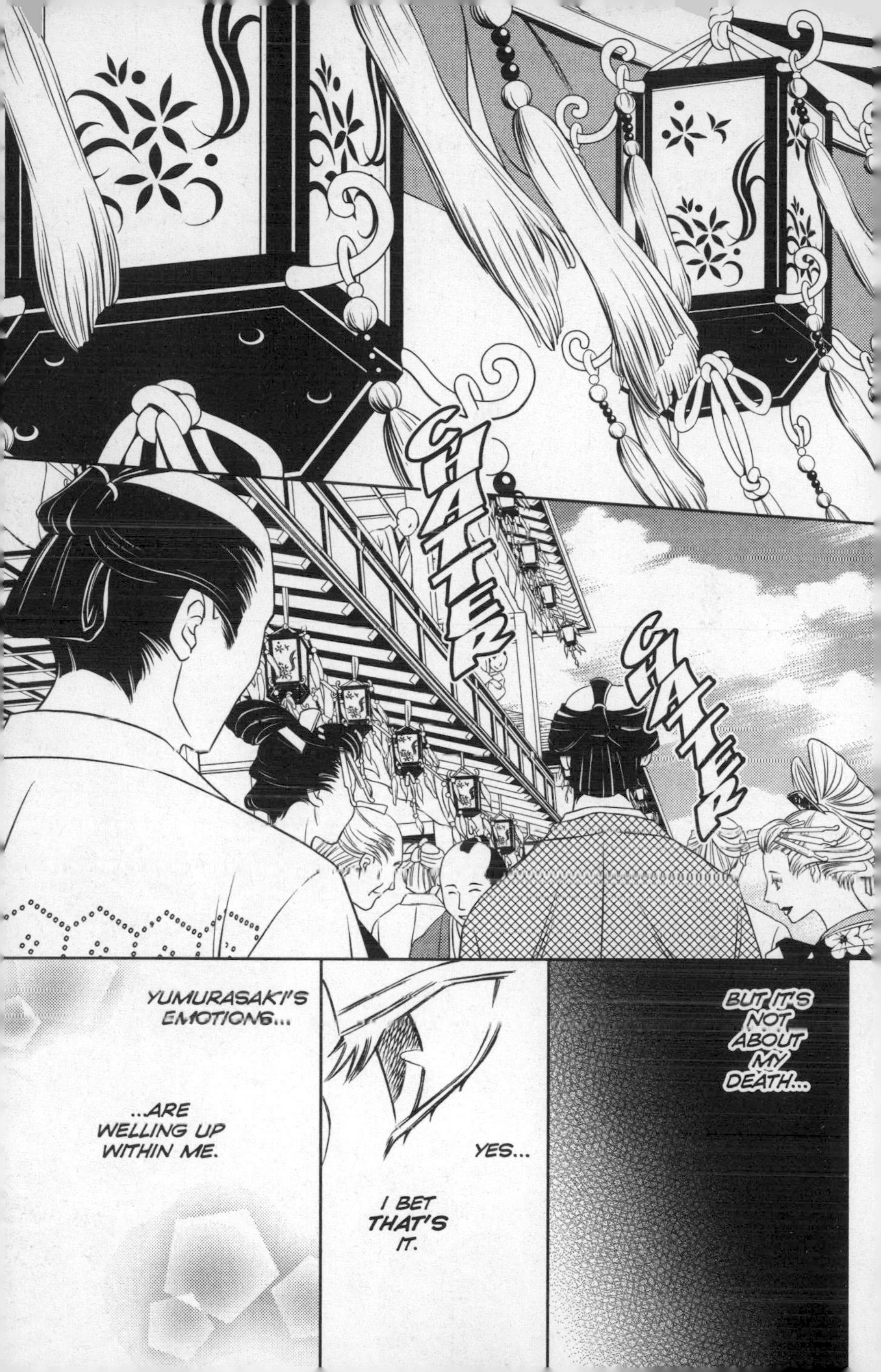
CHATTER
CHATTER
BUT IT'S NOT ABOUT MY DEATH...
YES...
I BET THAT'S IT.
YUMURASAKI'S EMOTIONS...
...ARE WELLING UP WITHIN ME.

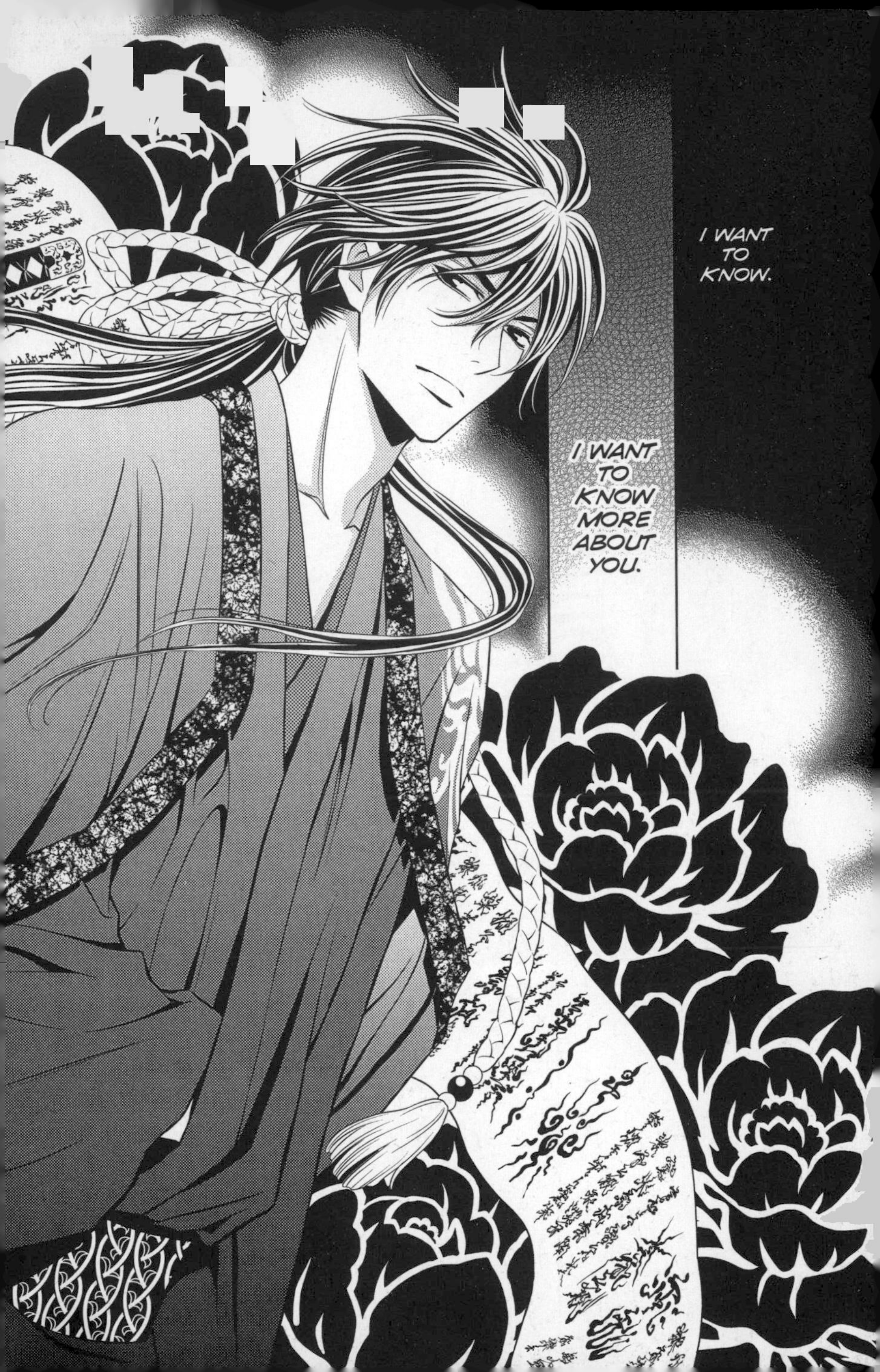
I WANT TO KNOW.
I WANT TO KNOW MORE ABOUT YOU.

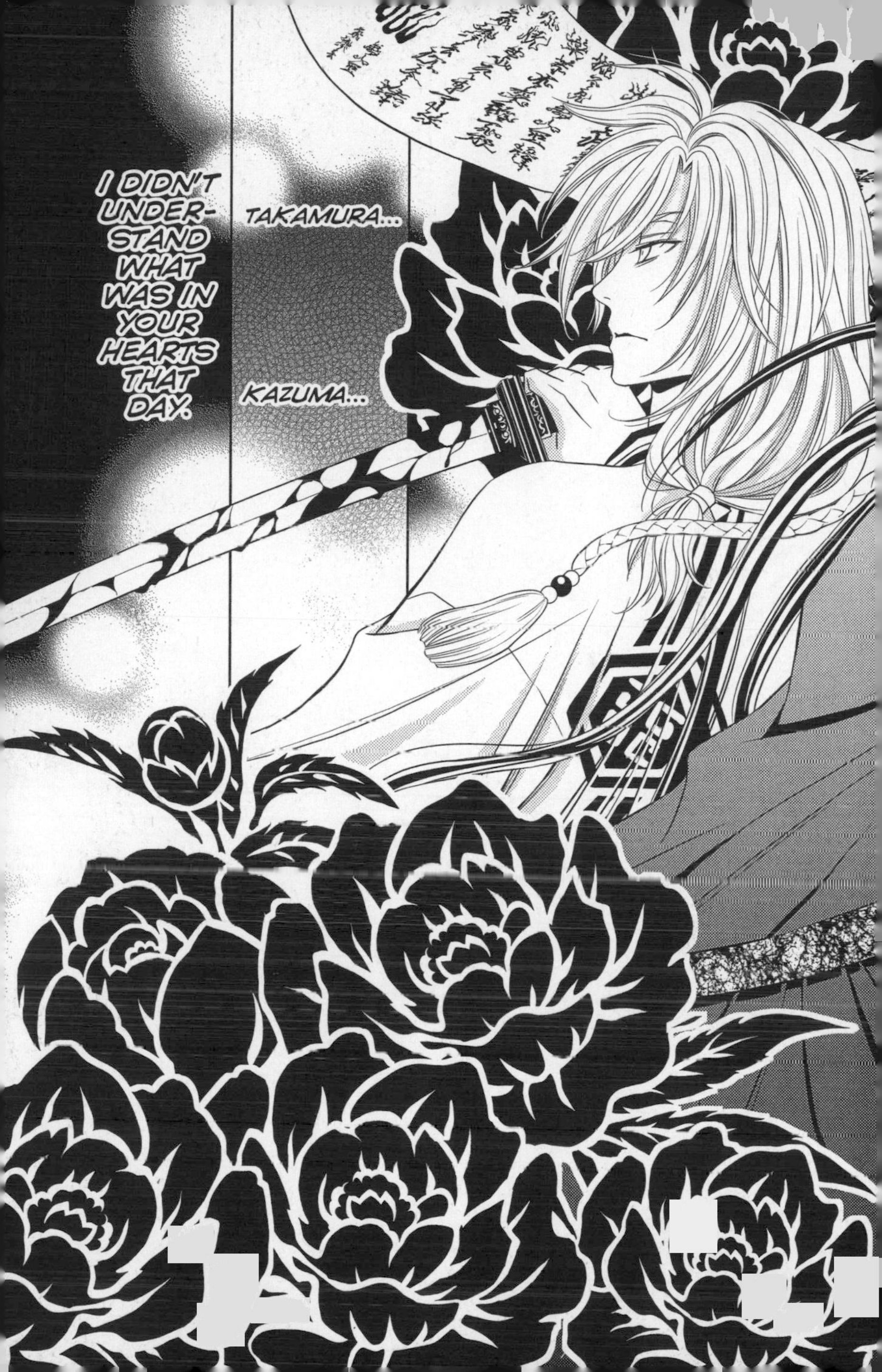
TAKAMURA...
KAZUMA...
I DIDN'T UNDERSTAND WHAT WAS IN YOUR HEARTS THAT DAY.

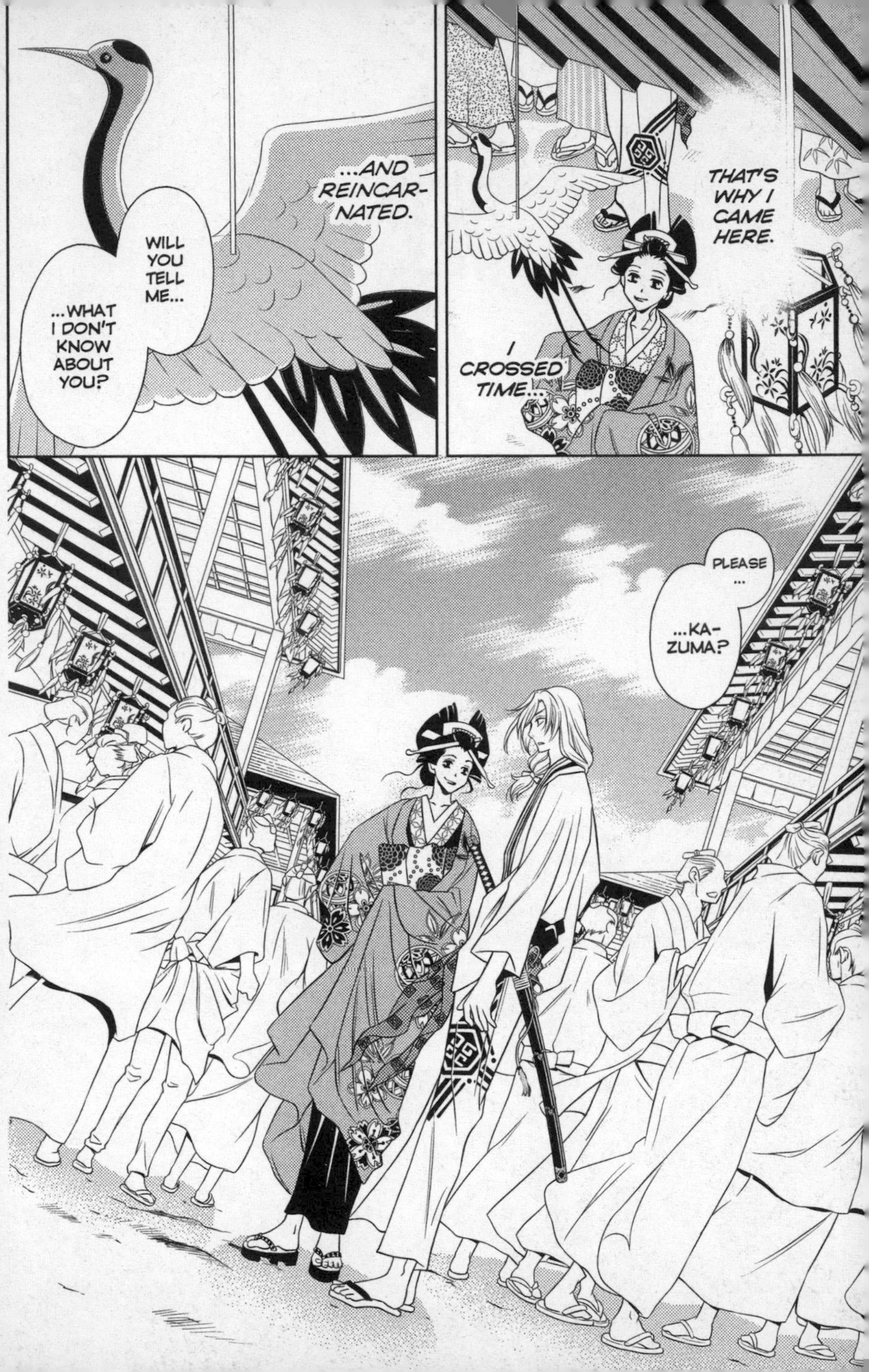
THAT'S WHY I CAME HERE.
I CROSSED TIME...
...AND REINCARNATED.
WILL YOU TELL ME...
...WHAT I DON'T KNOW ABOUT YOU?
PLEASE...
...KAZUMA?

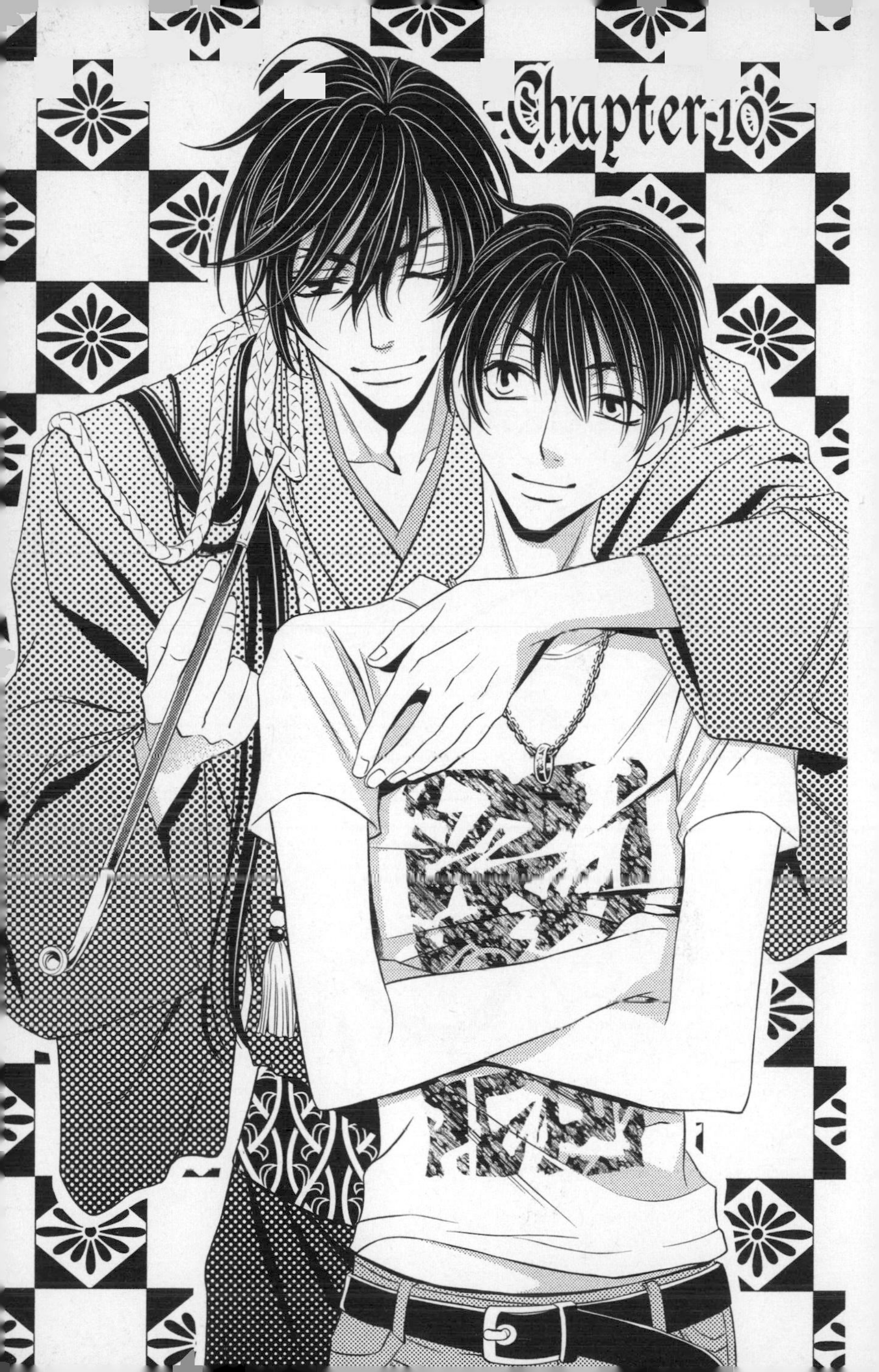
Chapter 10

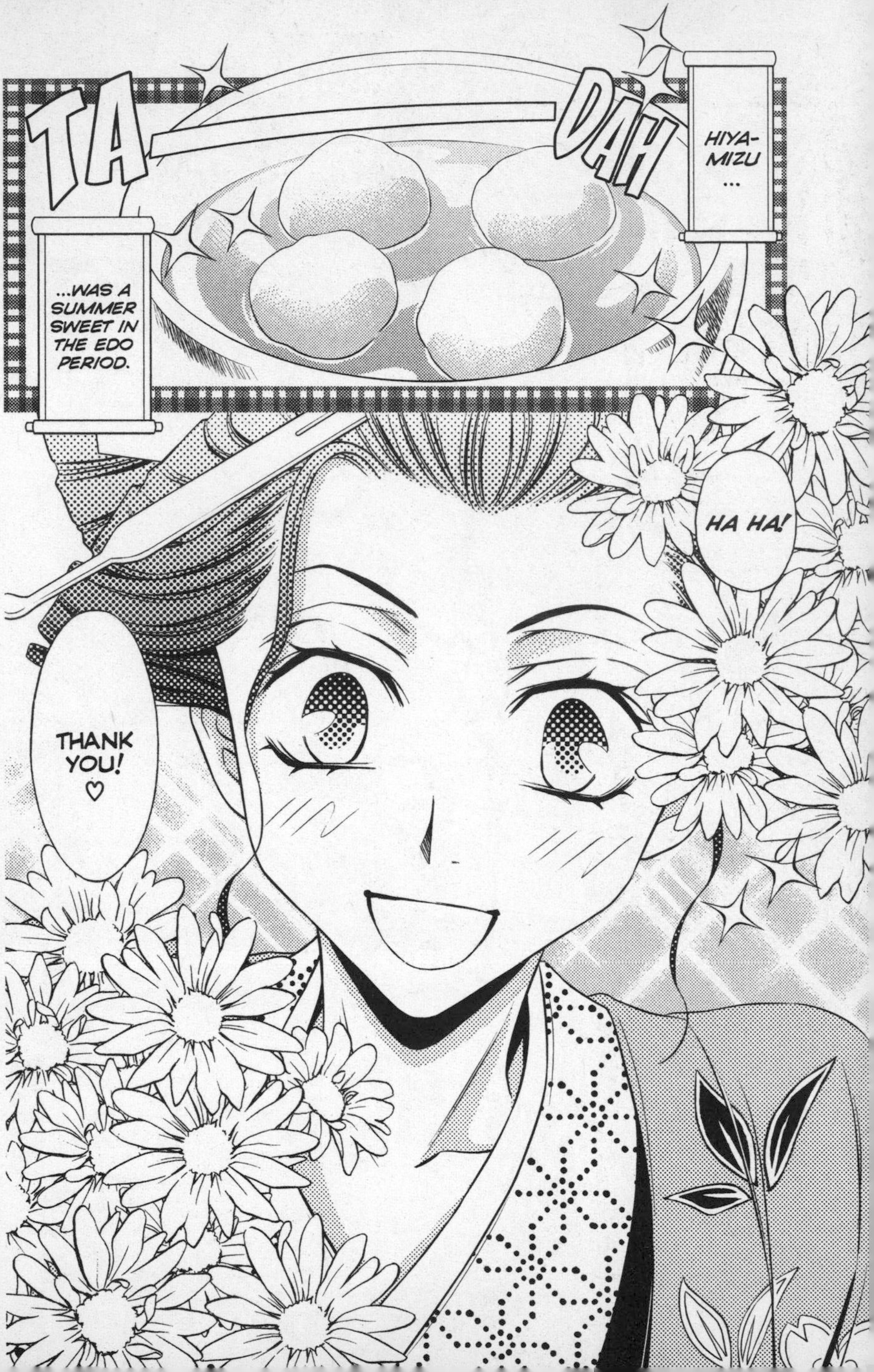
TA-DAH
HIYA-MIZU...
...WAS A SUMMER SWEET IN THE EDO PERIOD.
HA HA!
THANK YOU! ♡

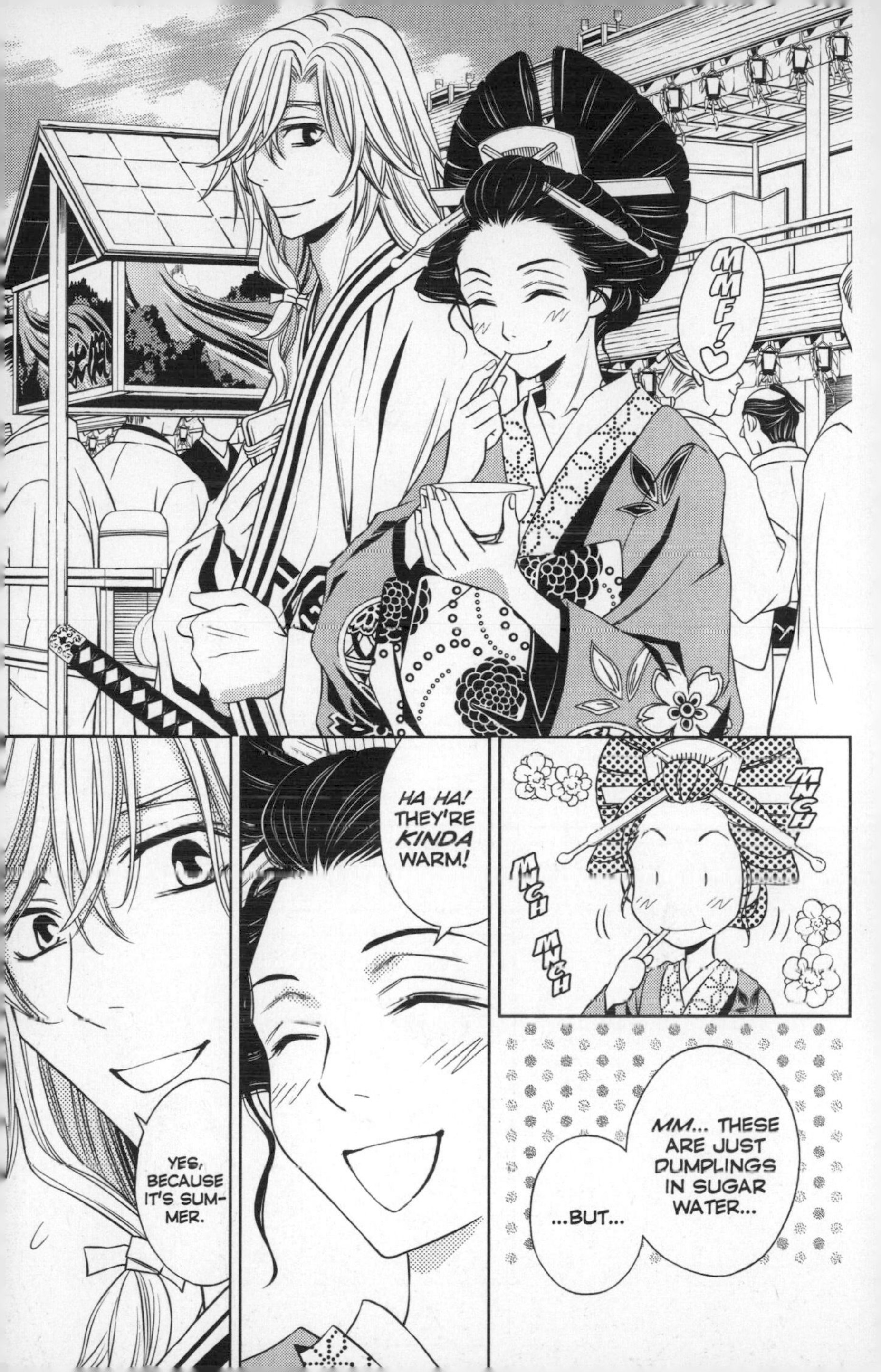
MMF! ♥
MNCH
MNCH
MNCH
MM... THESE ARE JUST DUMPLINGS IN SUGAR WATER...
...BUT...
HA HA! THEY'RE KINDA WARM!
YES, BECAUSE IT'S SUMMER.

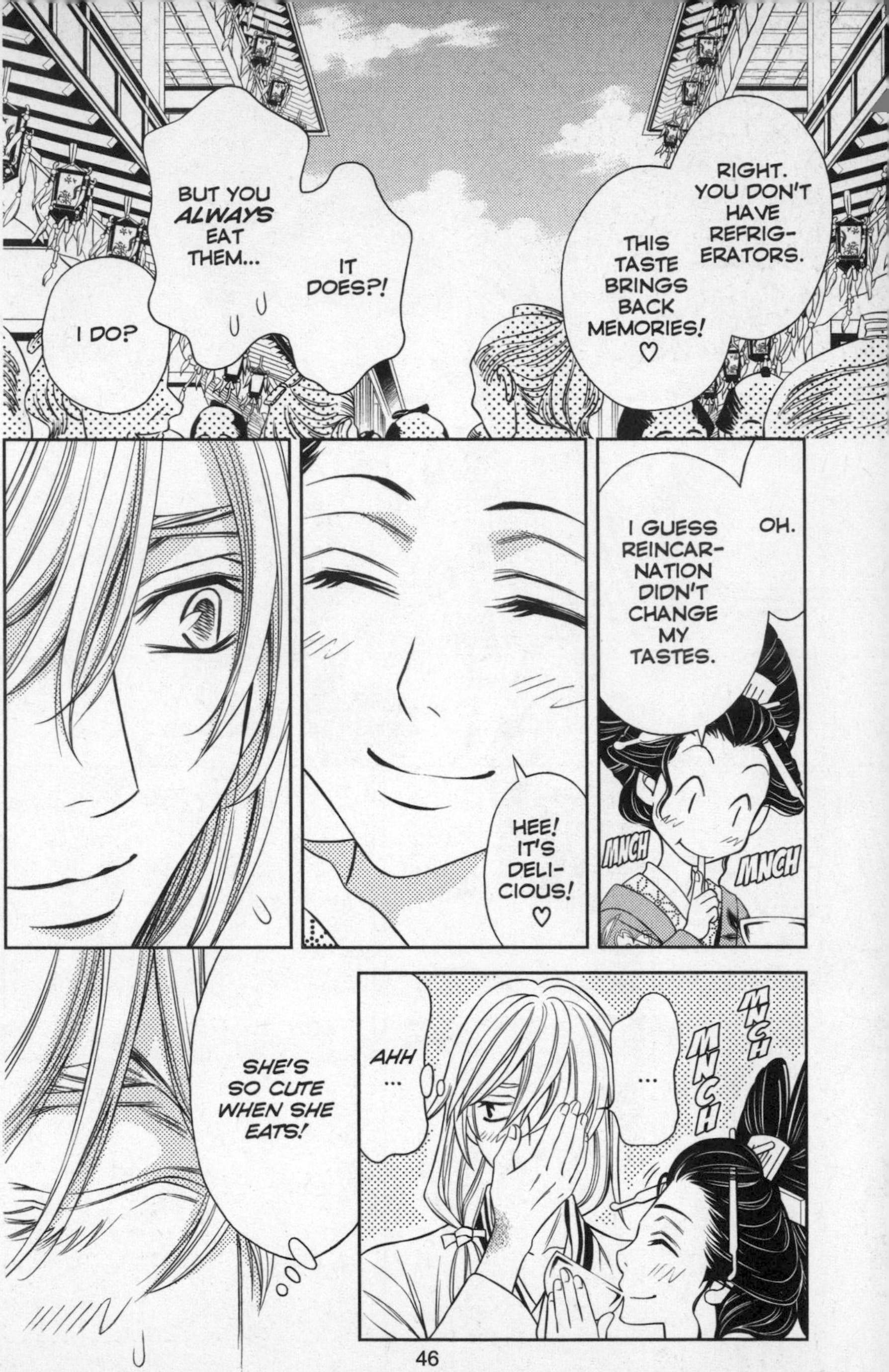
RIGHT. YOU DON'T HAVE REFRIG-ERATORS.
THIS TASTE BRINGS BACK MEMORIES! ♡
IT DOES?!
BUT YOU *ALWAYS* EAT THEM...
I DO?
OH.
I GUESS REINCAR-NATION DIDN'T CHANGE MY TASTES.
MNCH
MNCH
HEE! IT'S DELI-CIOUS! ♡
MNCH
MNCH
...
AHH ...
SHE'S SO CUTE WHEN SHE EATS!

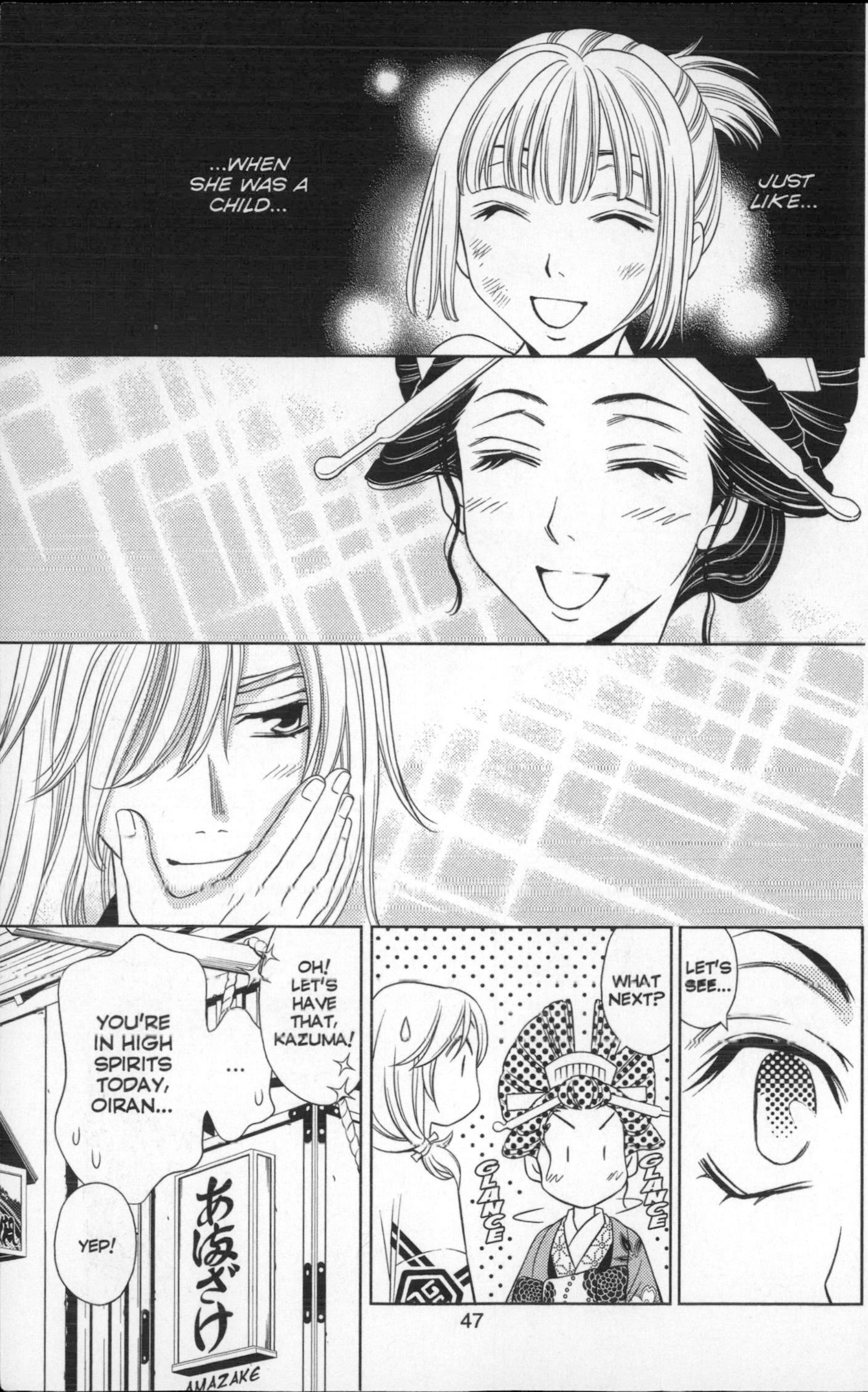
JUST LIKE...
...WHEN SHE WAS A CHILD...
LET'S SEE...
WHAT NEXT?
GLANCE
GLANCE
OH! LET'S HAVE THAT, KAZUMA!
YOU'RE IN HIGH SPIRITS TODAY, OIRAN...
...
YEP!
AMAZAKE

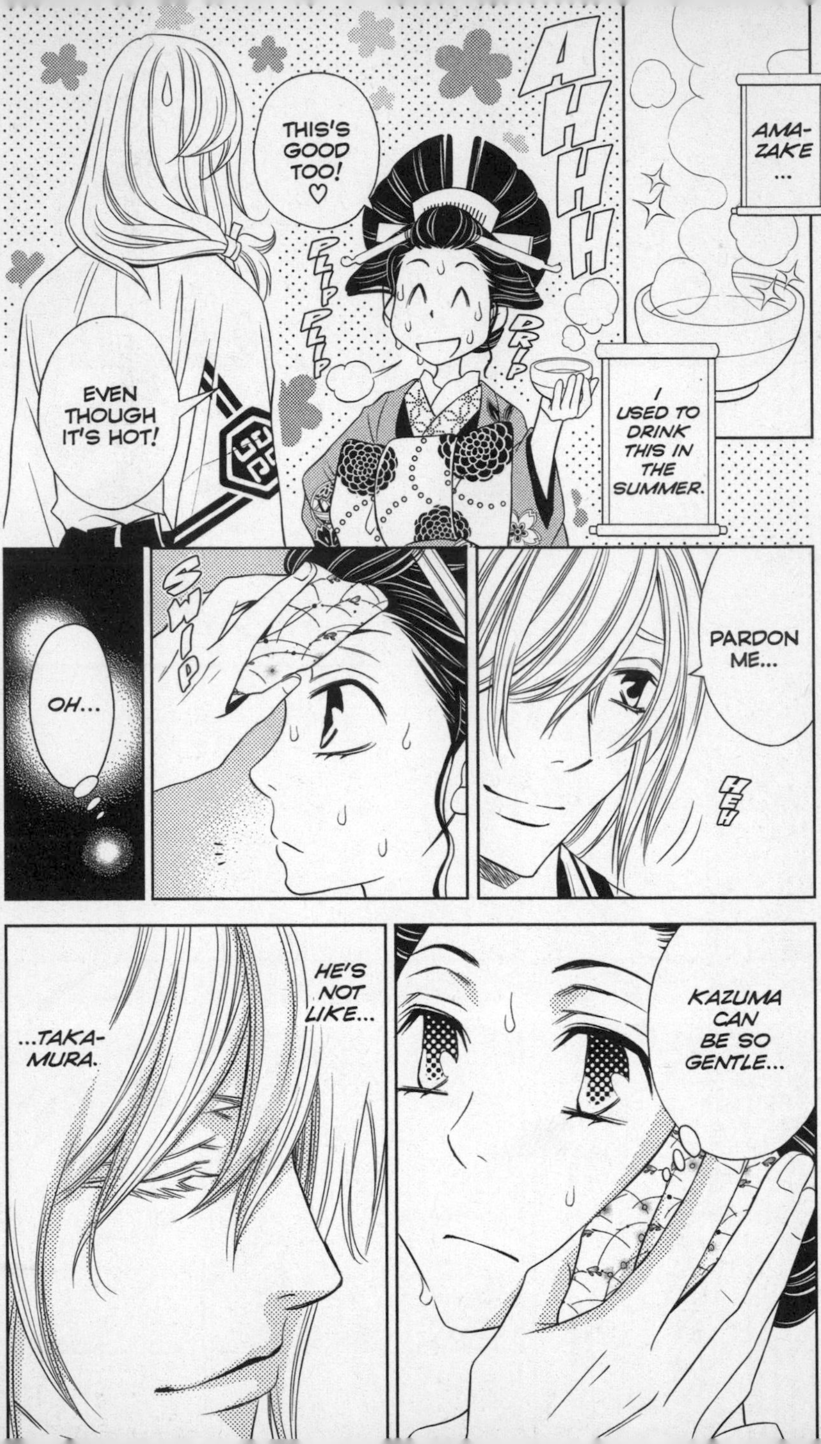
AMA-ZAKE...
AHHHH
THIS'S GOOD TOO! ♡
I USED TO DRINK THIS IN THE SUMMER.
DRIP
PLIP PLIP
EVEN THOUGH IT'S HOT!
PARDON ME...
HEH
SWIP
OH...
KAZUMA CAN BE SO GENTLE...
HE'S NOT LIKE...
...TAKA-MURA.

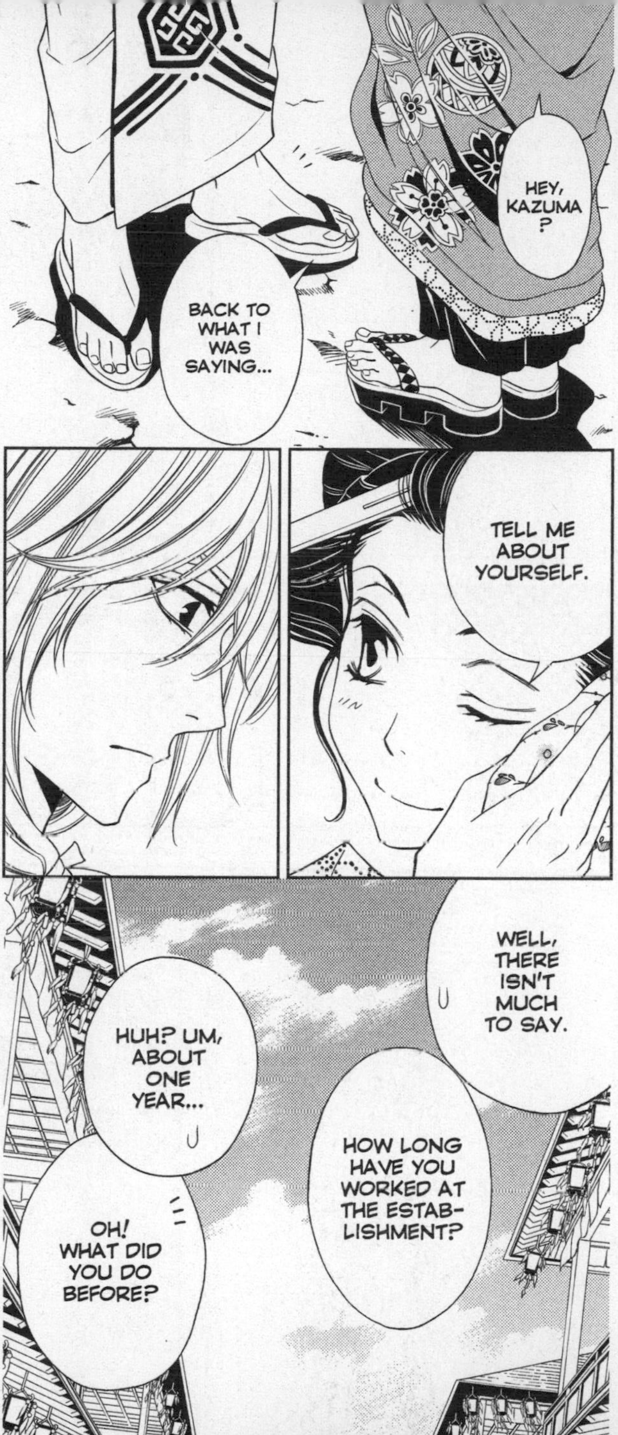
HEY, KAZUMA?
BACK TO WHAT I WAS SAYING...
TELL ME ABOUT YOURSELF.
WELL, THERE ISN'T MUCH TO SAY.
HOW LONG HAVE YOU WORKED AT THE ESTABLISHMENT?
HUH? UM, ABOUT ONE YEAR...
OH! WHAT DID YOU DO BEFORE?

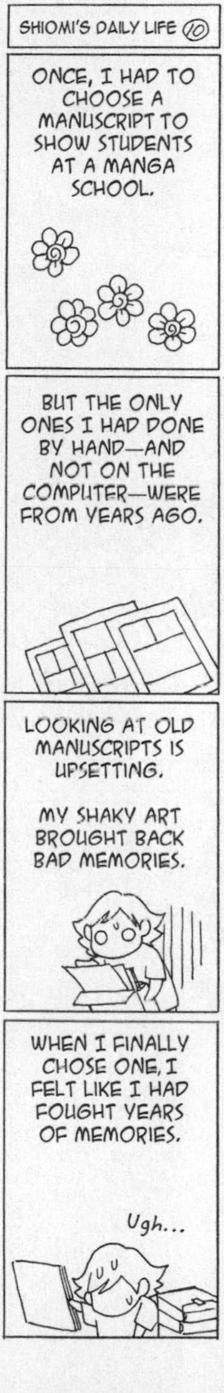
SHIOMI'S DAILY LIFE ⑩
ONCE, I HAD TO CHOOSE A MANUSCRIPT TO SHOW STUDENTS AT A MANGA SCHOOL.
BUT THE ONLY ONES I HAD DONE BY HAND—AND NOT ON THE COMPUTER—WERE FROM YEARS AGO.
LOOKING AT OLD MANUSCRIPTS IS UPSETTING.
MY SHAKY ART BROUGHT BACK BAD MEMORIES.
WHEN I FINALLY CHOSE ONE, I FELT LIKE I HAD FOUGHT YEARS OF MEMORIES.
Ugh...

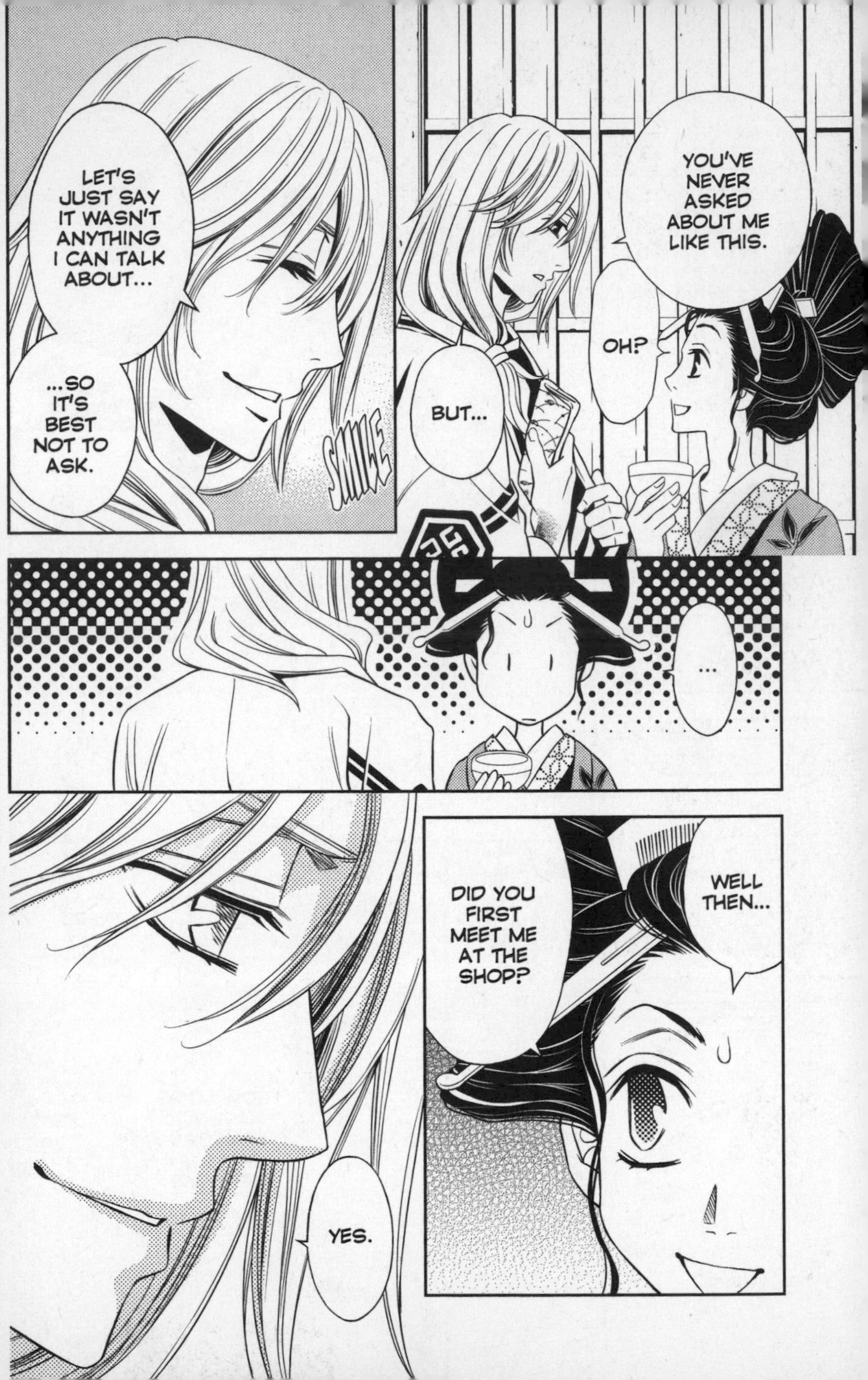
YOU'VE NEVER ASKED ABOUT ME LIKE THIS.
OH?
BUT...
LET'S JUST SAY IT WASN'T ANYTHING I CAN TALK ABOUT...
...SO IT'S BEST NOT TO ASK.
SMILE
...
WELL THEN...
DID YOU FIRST MEET ME AT THE SHOP?
YES.

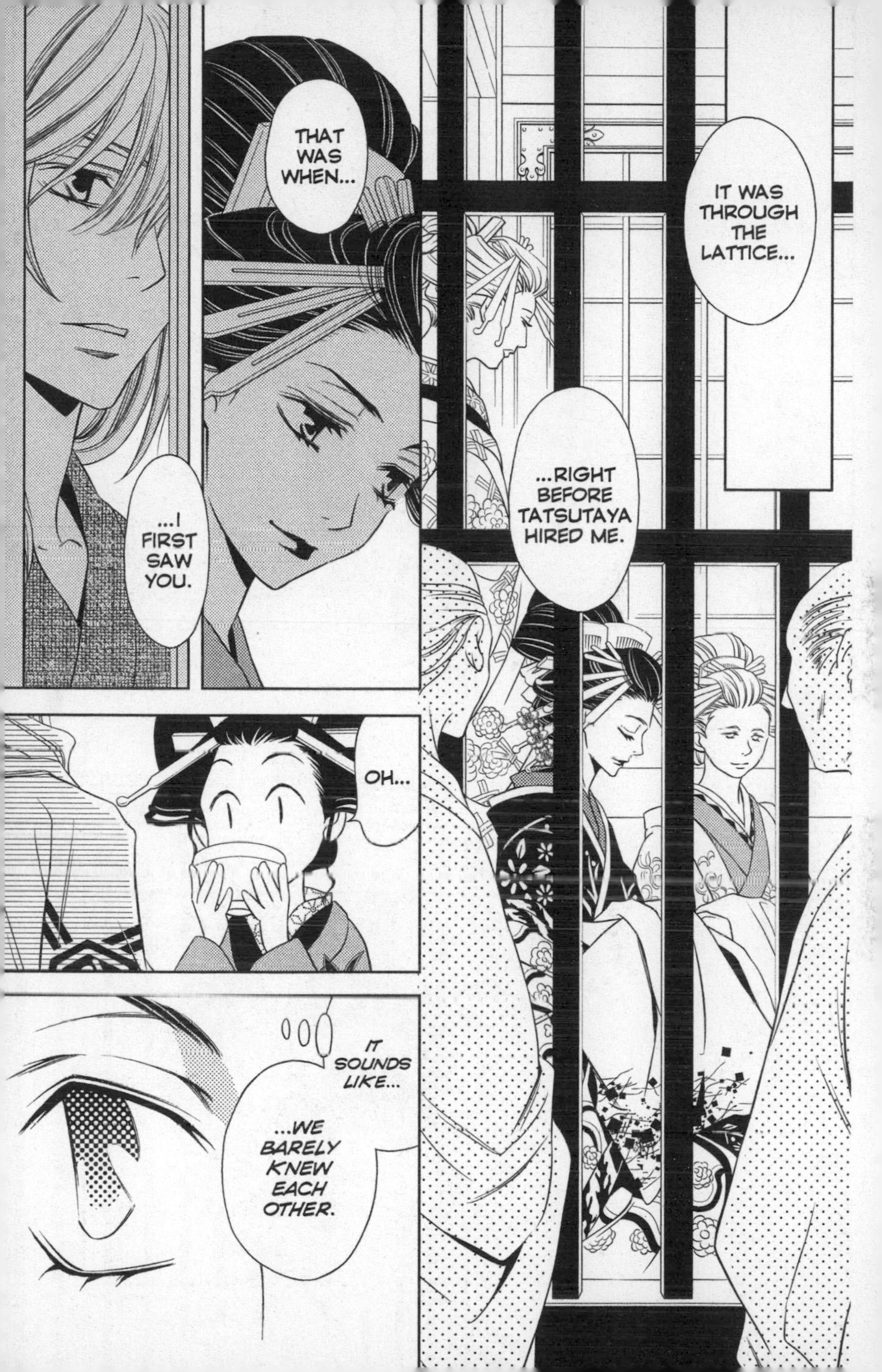
IT WAS THROUGH THE LATTICE...
...RIGHT BEFORE TATSUTAYA HIRED ME.
THAT WAS WHEN...
...I FIRST SAW YOU.
OH...
IT SOUNDS LIKE...
...WE BARELY KNEW EACH OTHER.

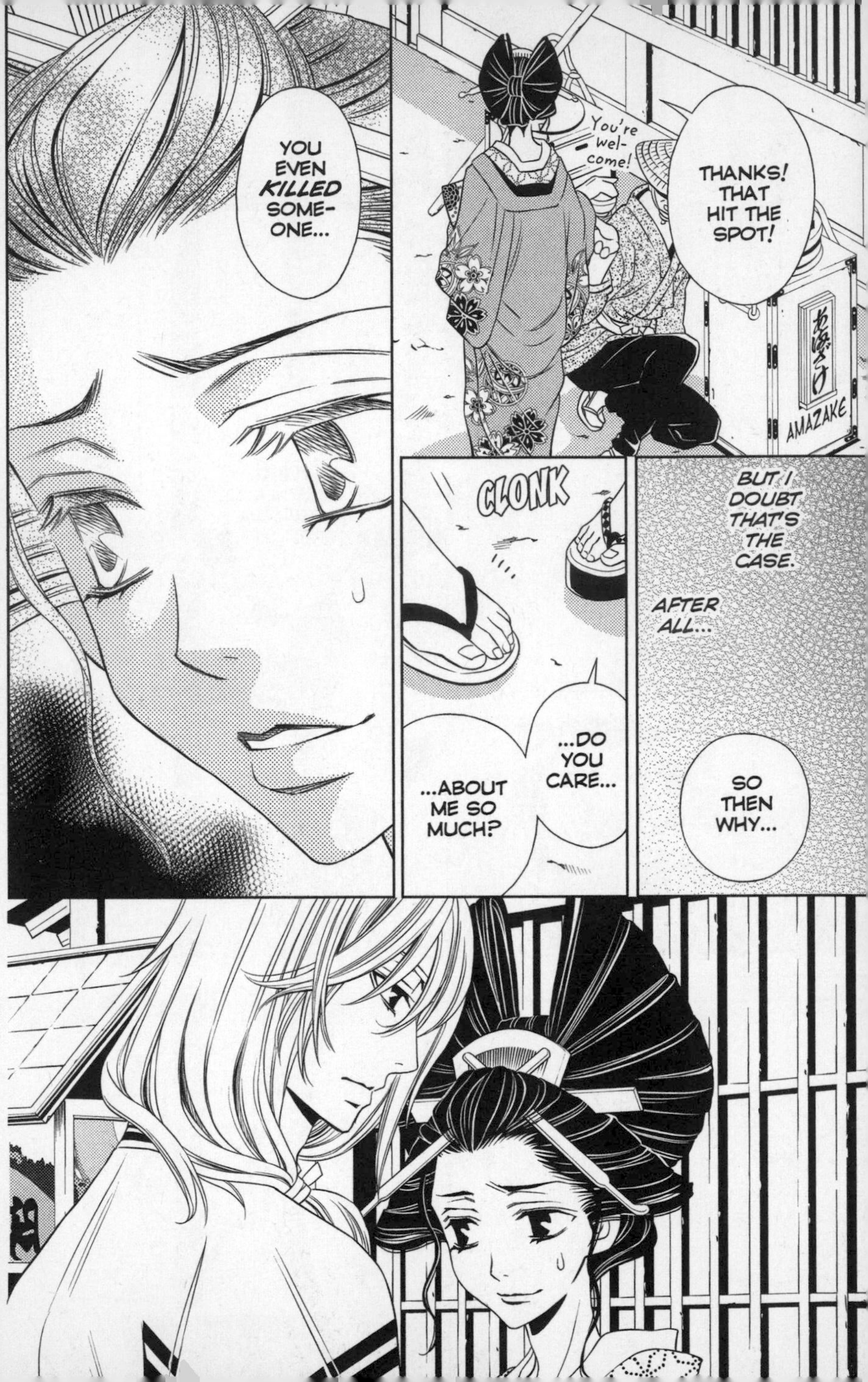
THANKS! THAT HIT THE SPOT!
You're wel-come!
AMAZAKE
BUT I DOUBT THAT'S THE CASE.
AFTER ALL...
SO THEN WHY...
CLONK
...DO YOU CARE...
...ABOUT ME SO MUCH?
YOU EVEN *KILLED* SOME-ONE...

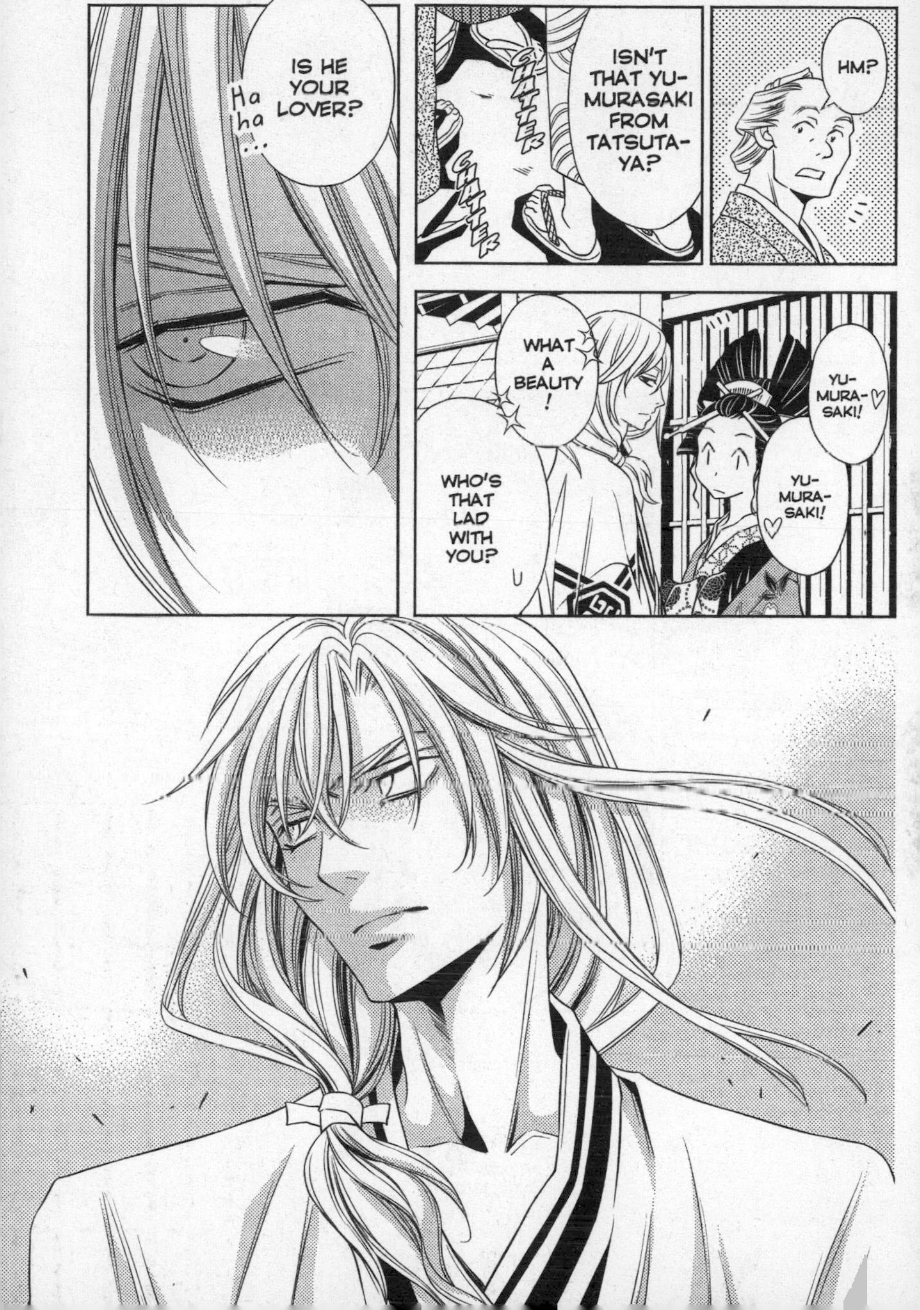
HM?
ISN'T THAT YU-MURASAKI FROM TATSUTA-YA?
CHATTER CHATTER
YU-MURA-SAKI! ♡
YU-MURA-SAKI! ♡
WHAT A BEAUTY!
WHO'S THAT LAD WITH YOU?
IS HE YOUR LOVER?
Ha ha...

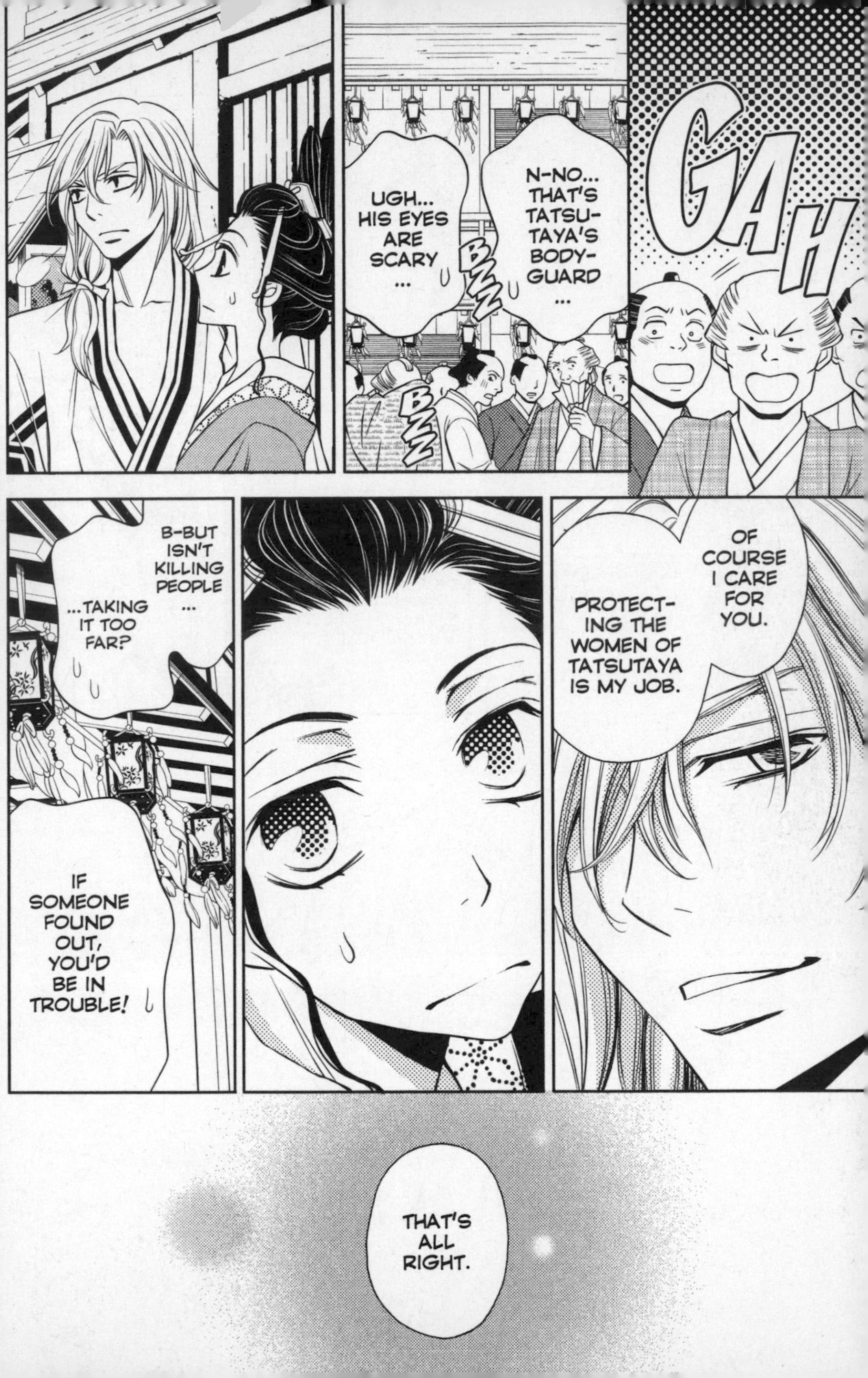
GAH
N-NO... THAT'S TATSU-TAYA'S BODY-GUARD ...
UGH... HIS EYES ARE SCARY ...
BZZ
BZZ
OF COURSE I CARE FOR YOU.
PROTECT-ING THE WOMEN OF TATSUTAYA IS MY JOB.
B-BUT ISN'T KILLING PEOPLE ...
...TAKING IT TOO FAR?
IF SOMEONE FOUND OUT, YOU'D BE IN TROUBLE!
THAT'S ALL RIGHT.

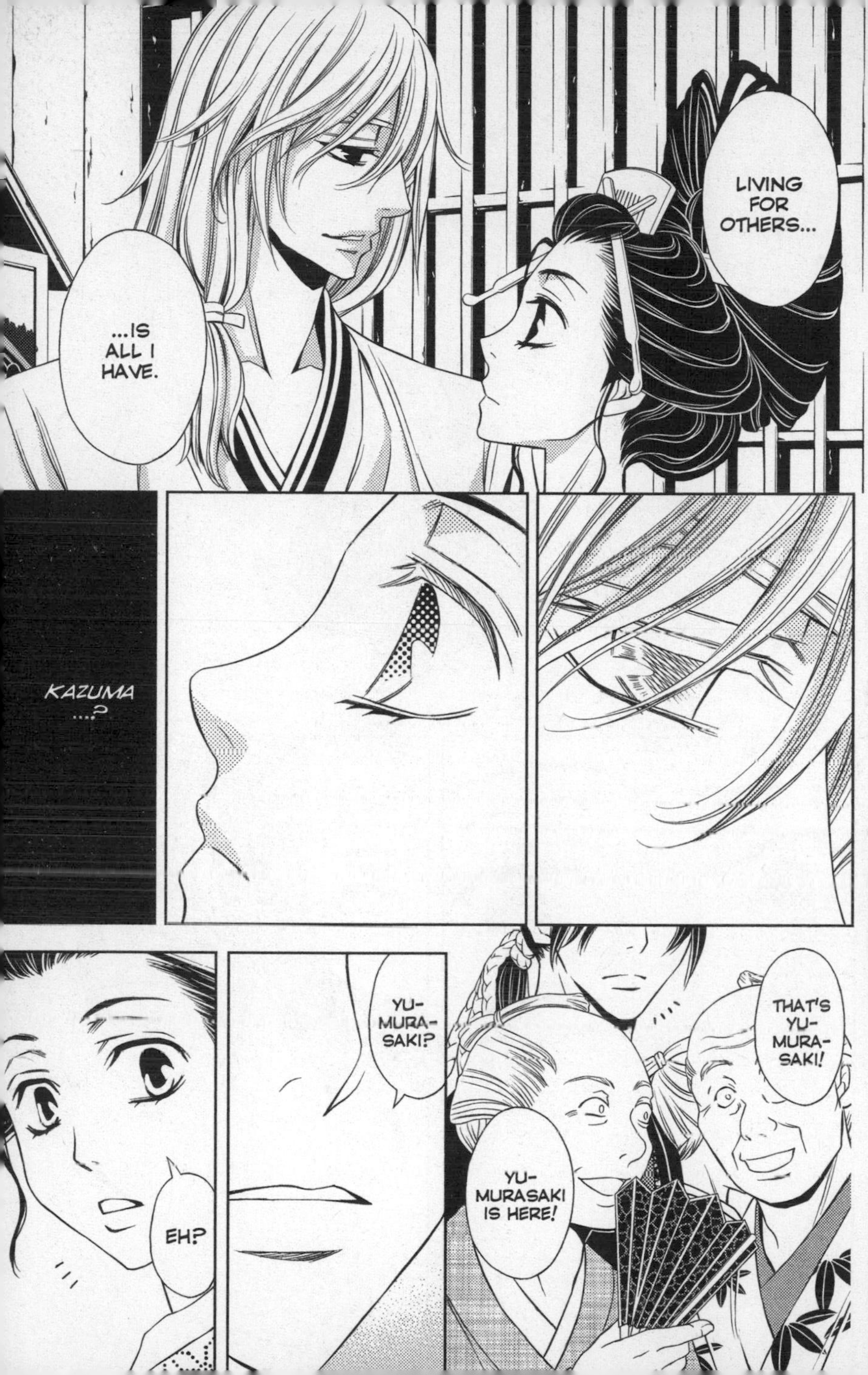
LIVING FOR OTHERS...
...IS ALL I HAVE.
KAZUMA ...?
THAT'S YU-MURA-SAKI!
YU-MURASAKI IS HERE!
YU-MURA-SAKI?
EH?

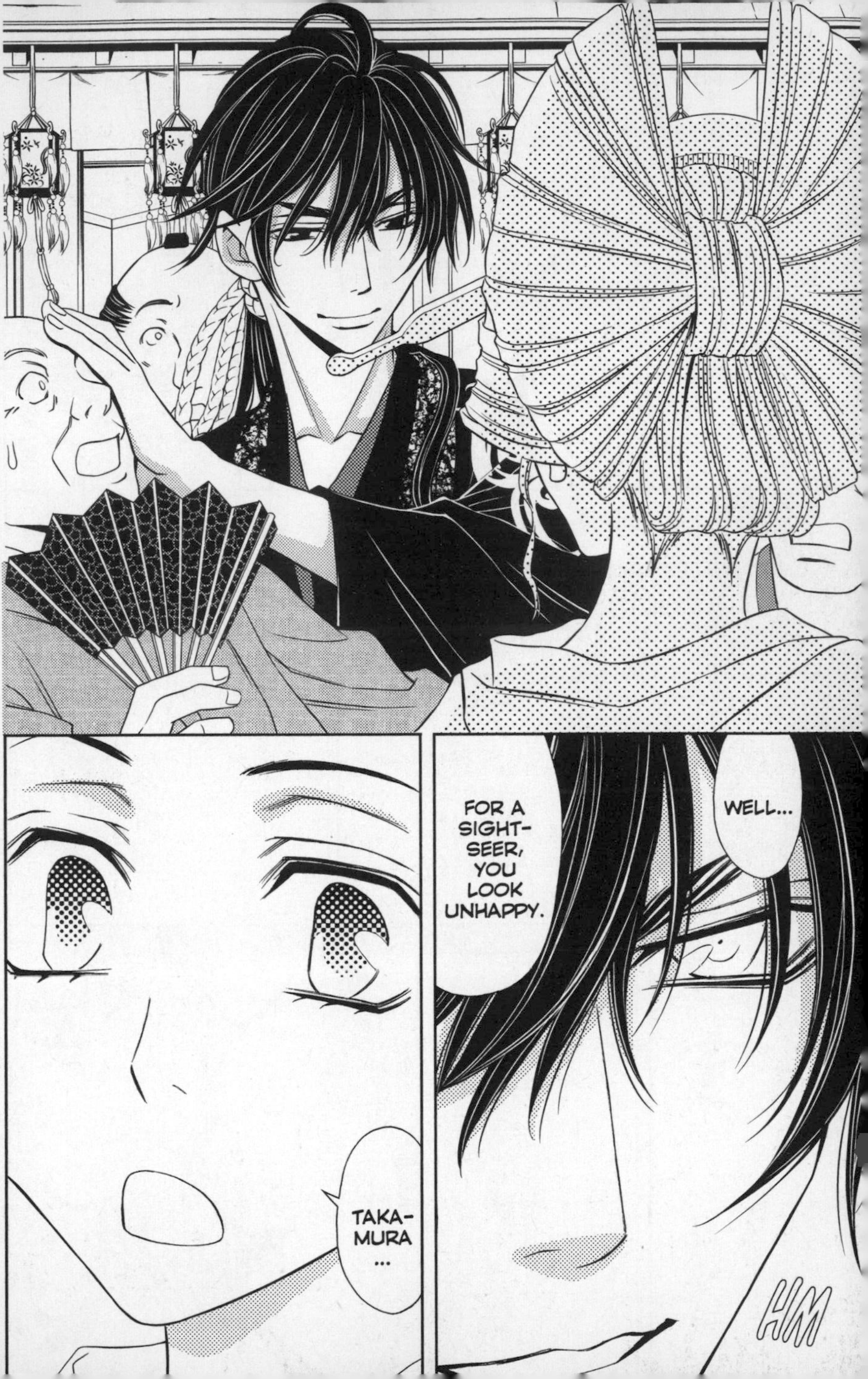
WELL...
FOR A SIGHT-SEER, YOU LOOK UNHAPPY.
HM
TAKA-MURA...

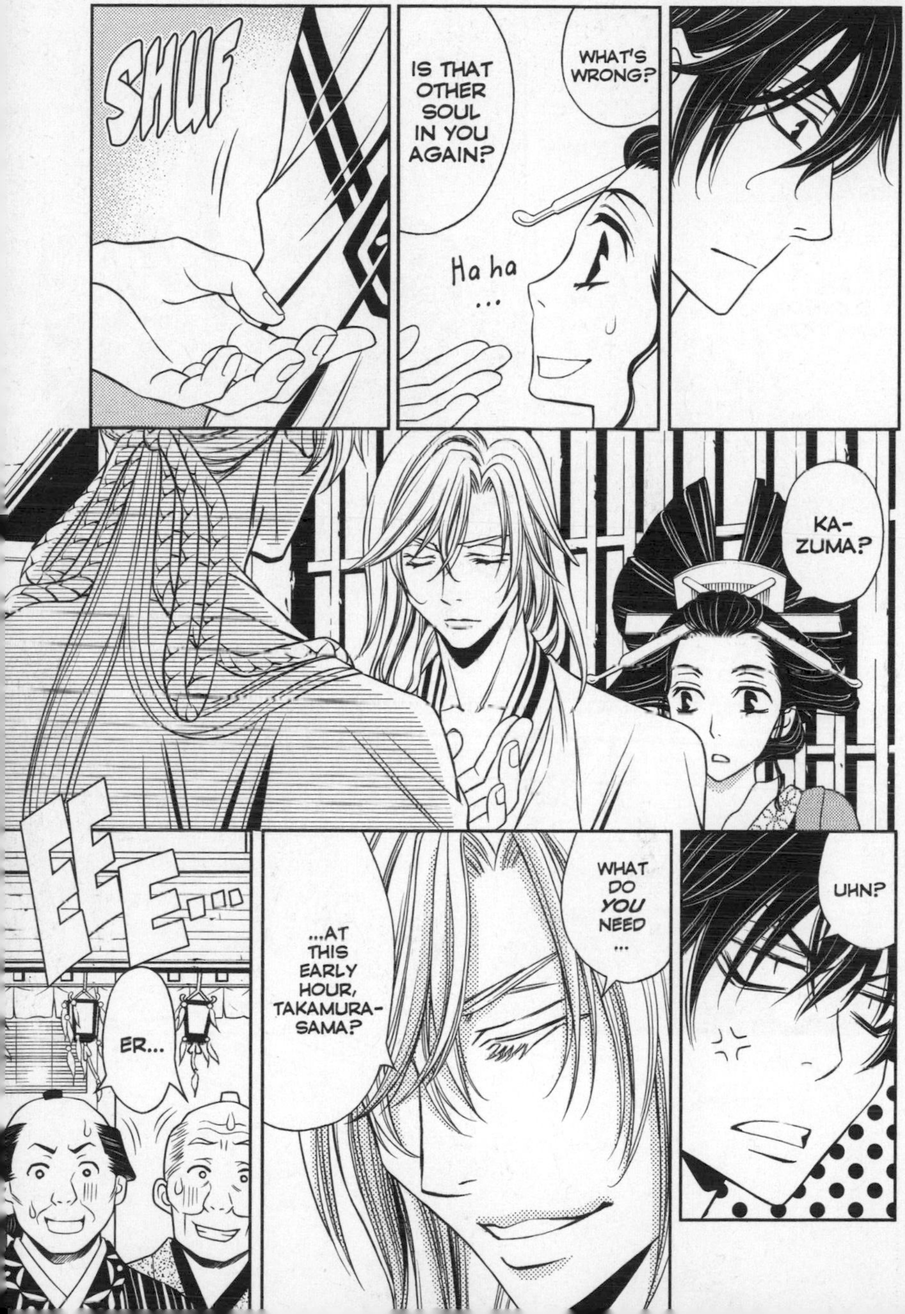
WHAT'S WRONG?
IS THAT OTHER SOUL IN YOU AGAIN?
Ha ha ...
SHUF
KA-ZUMA?
UHN?
WHAT DO *YOU* NEED ...
...AT THIS EARLY HOUR, TAKAMURA-SAMA?
EE...
ER...

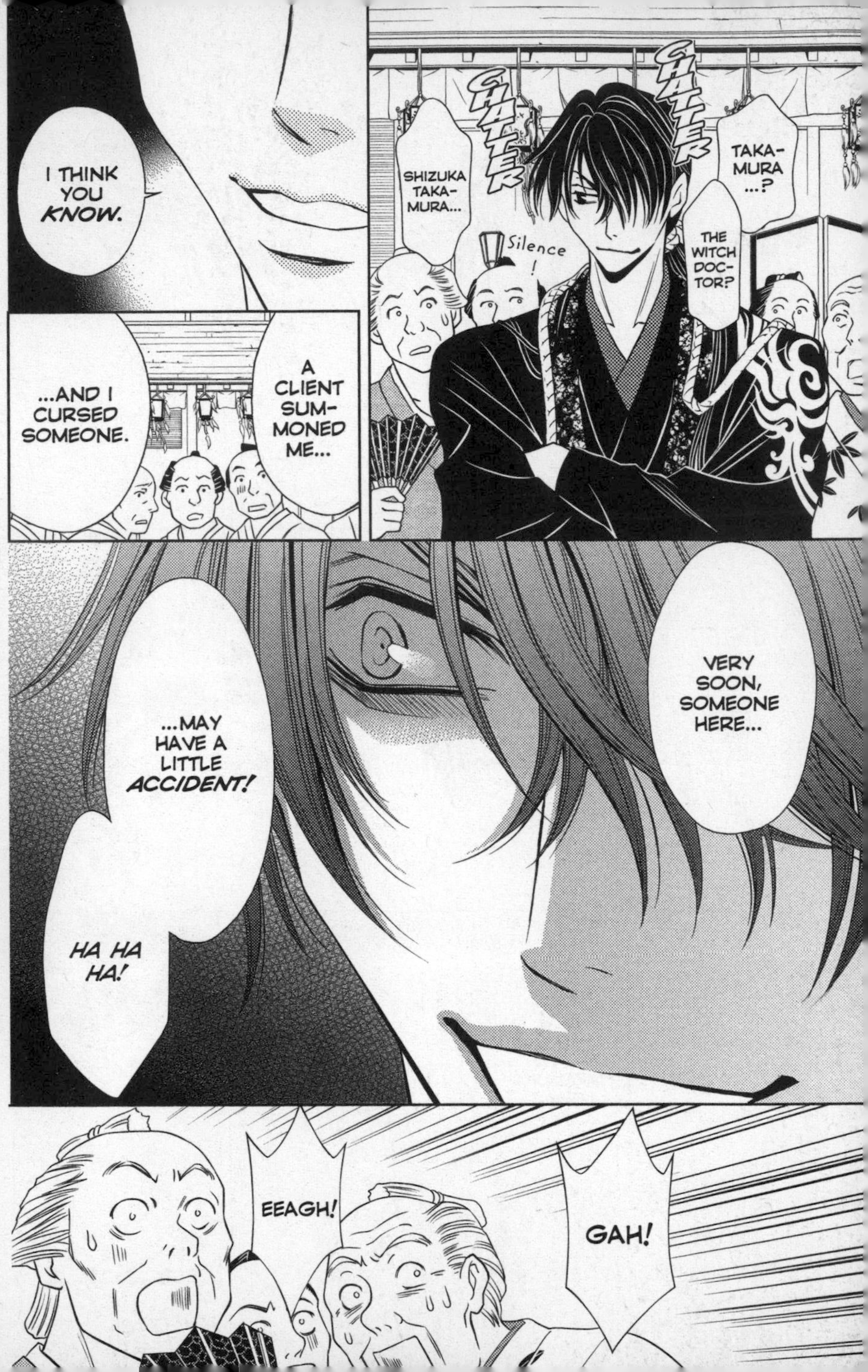
CHATTER
TAKAMURA...?
CHATTER
SHIZUKA TAKAMURA...
THE WITCH DOCTOR?
Silence!
I THINK YOU *KNOW*.
A CLIENT SUMMONED ME...
...AND I CURSED SOMEONE.
VERY SOON, SOMEONE HERE...
...MAY HAVE A LITTLE *ACCIDENT!*
HA HA HA!
GAH!
EEAGH!

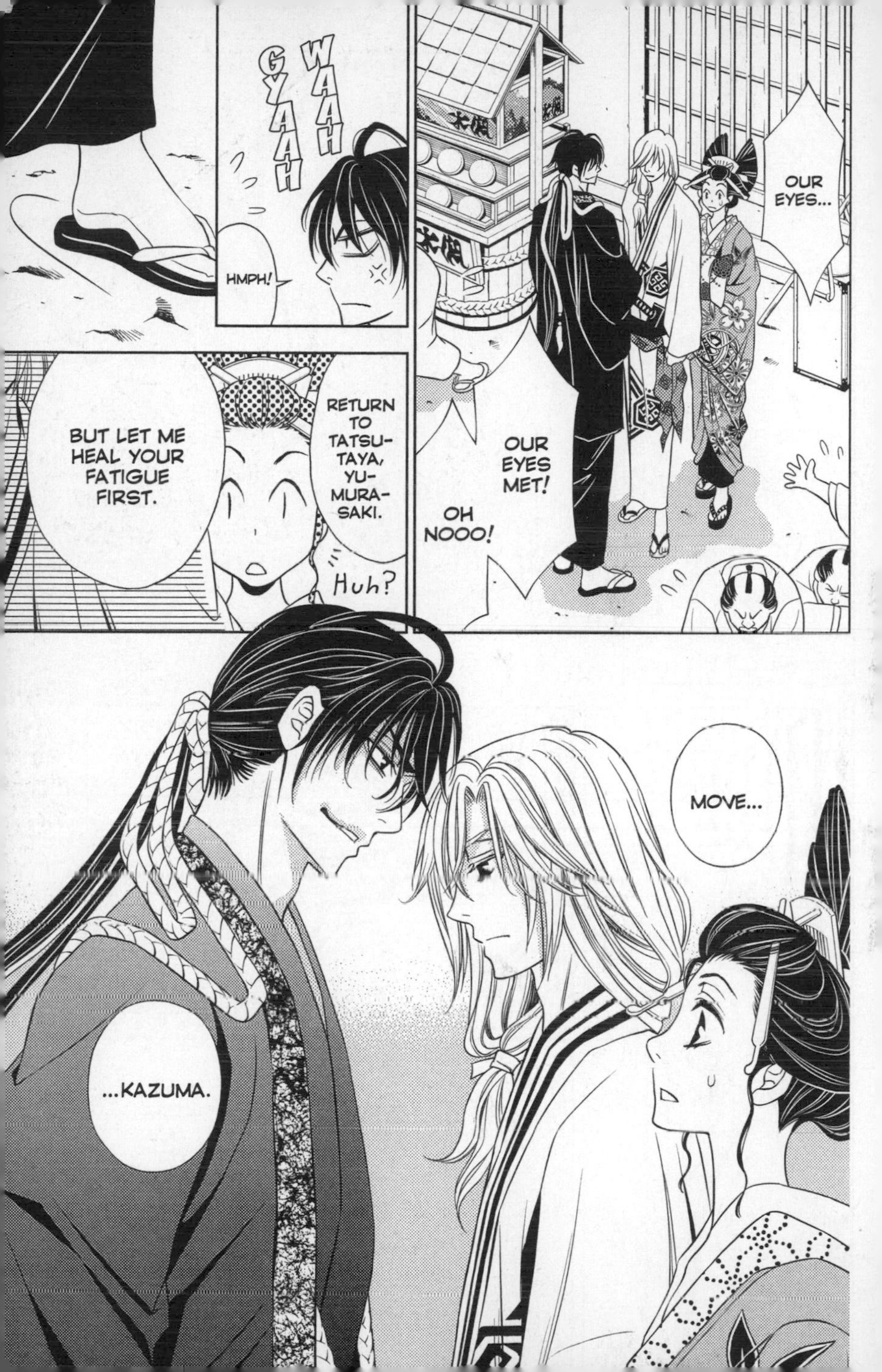
OUR EYES...
OUR EYES MET!
OH NOOO!
WAAH
GYAAH
HMPH!
RETURN TO TATSU-TAYA, YU-MURA-SAKI.
Huh?
BUT LET ME HEAL YOUR FATIGUE FIRST.
MOVE...
...KAZUMA.

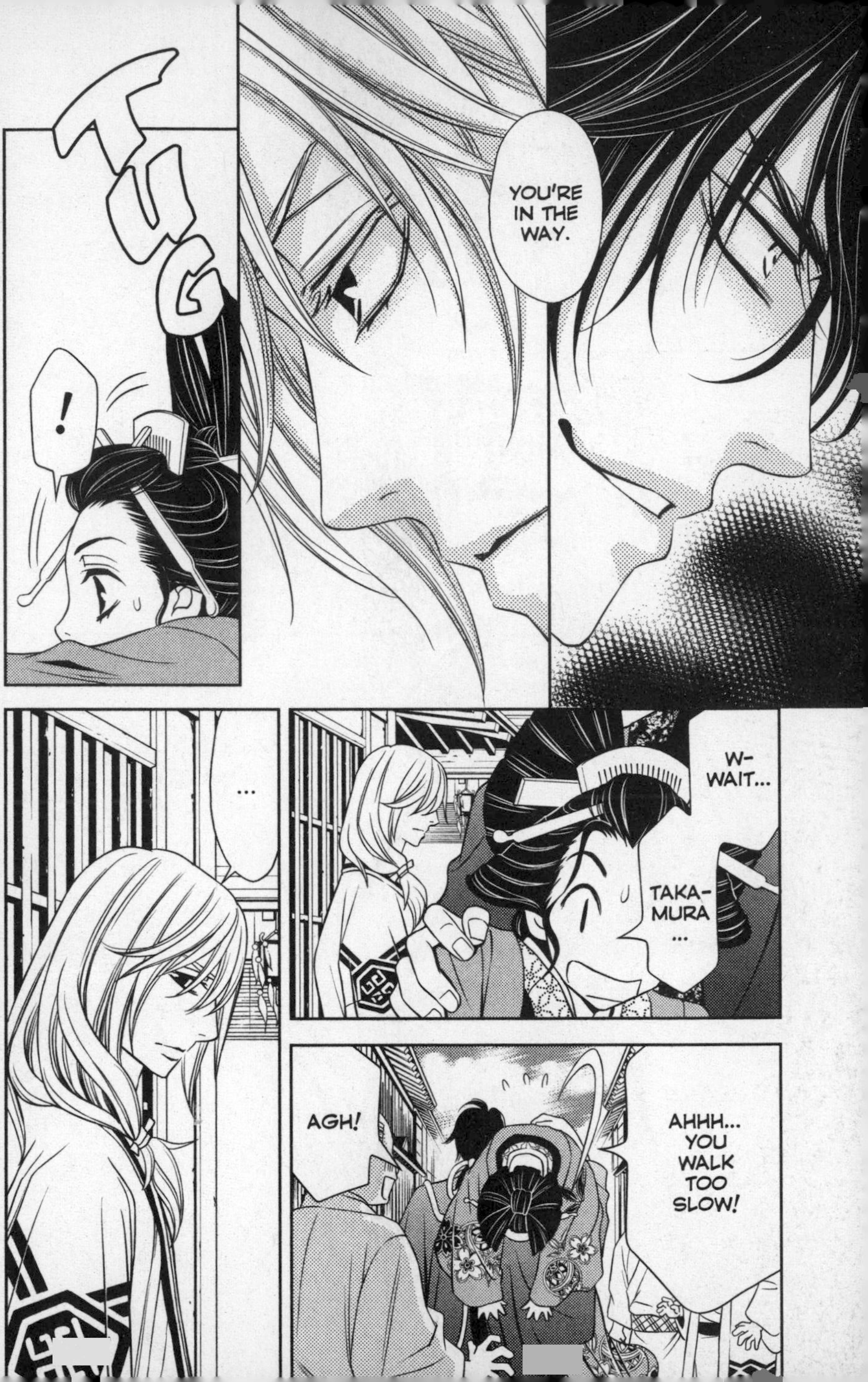
YOU'RE IN THE WAY.
TUG
!
W- WAIT...
TAKAMURA ...
AHHH... YOU WALK TOO SLOW!
AGH!
...

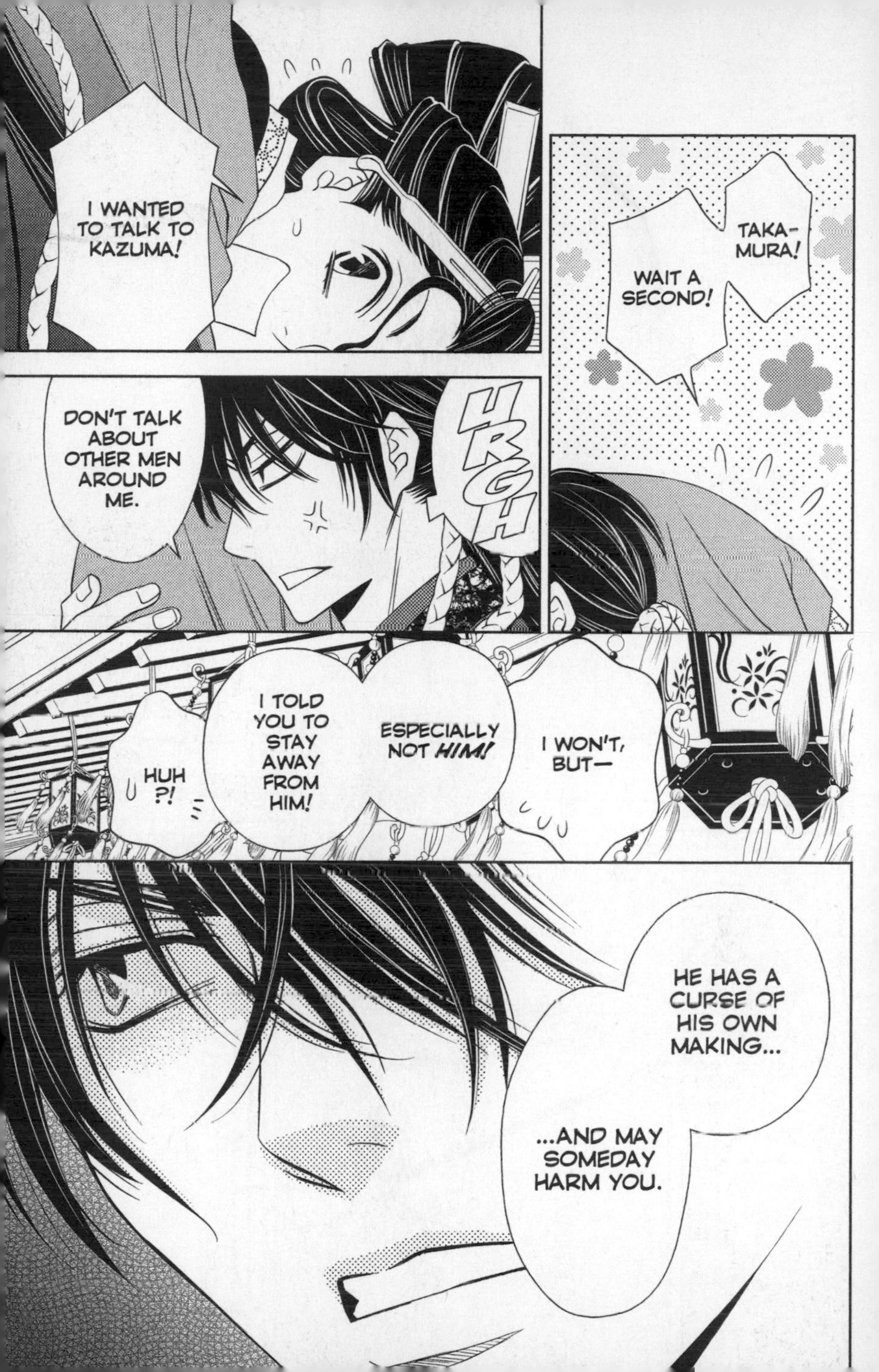
TAKA-MURA!
WAIT A SECOND!
I WANTED TO TALK TO KAZUMA!
DON'T TALK ABOUT OTHER MEN AROUND ME.
URGH
I WON'T, BUT—
ESPECIALLY NOT *HIM!*
I TOLD YOU TO STAY AWAY FROM HIM!
HUH?!
HE HAS A CURSE OF HIS OWN MAKING...
...AND MAY SOMEDAY HARM YOU.

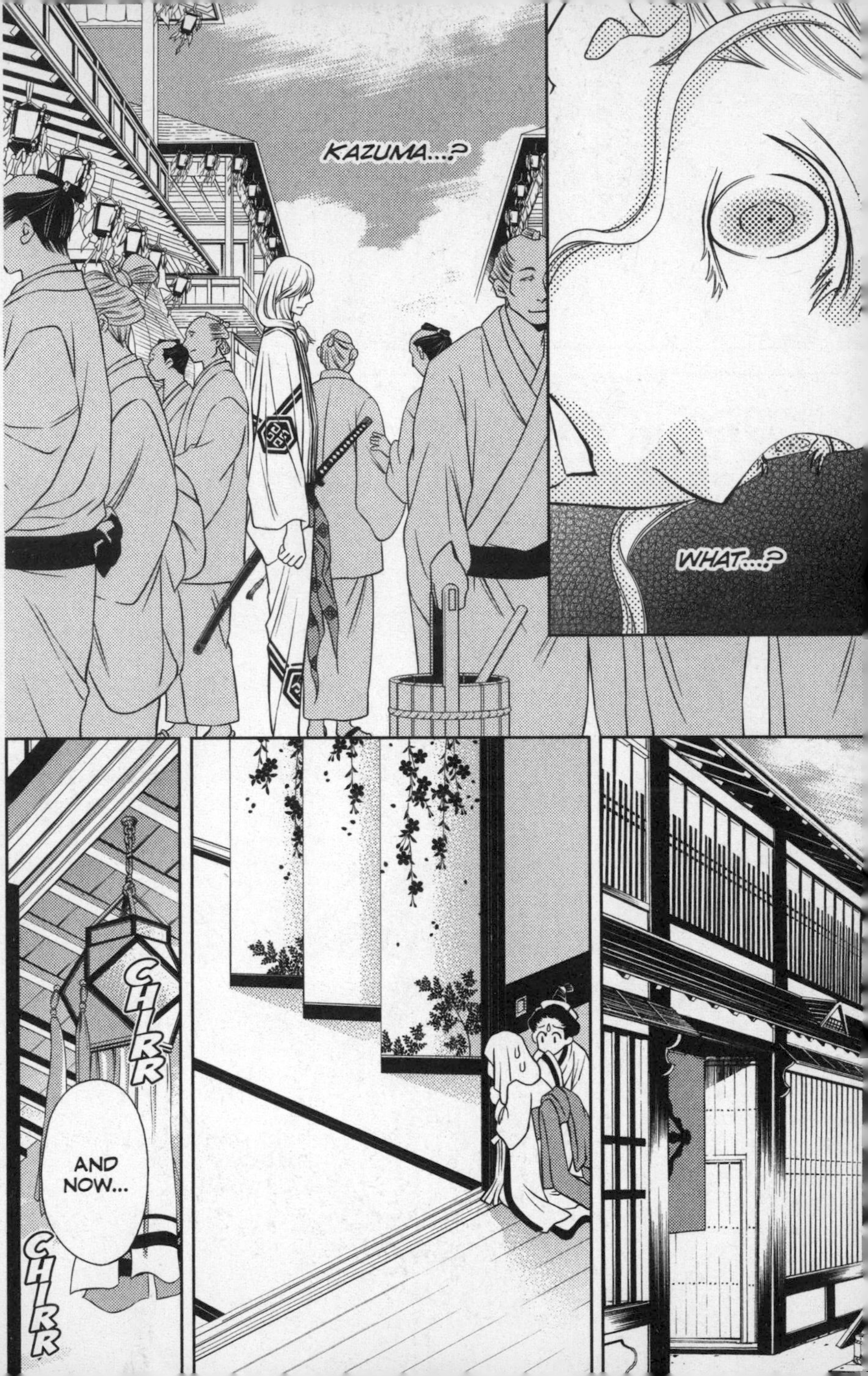
WHAT...?
KAZUMA...?
CHIRR
AND NOW...
CHIRR

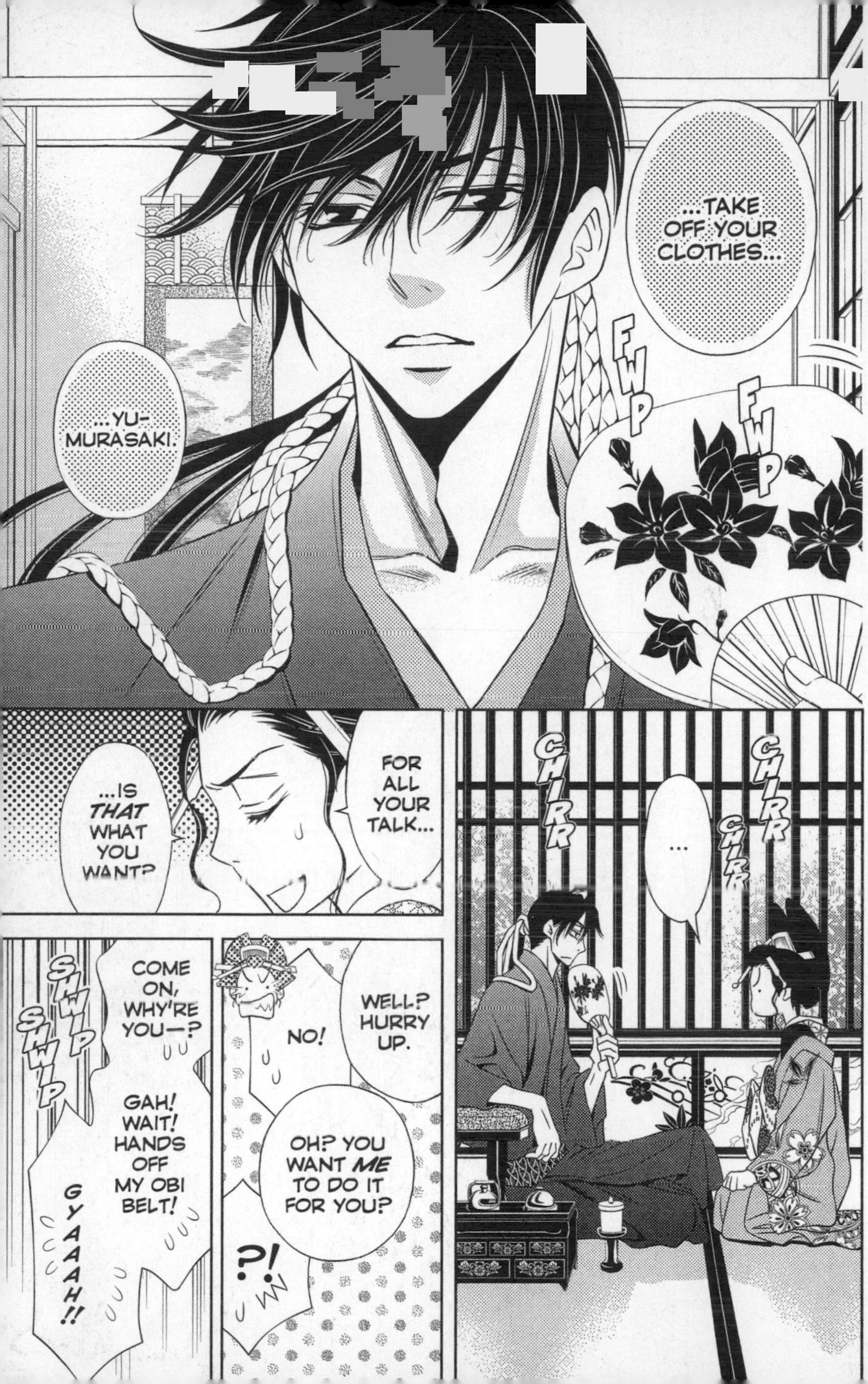
...TAKE OFF YOUR CLOTHES...
FWP
FWP
...YU-MURASAKI.
CHIRR
CHIRR
CHIRR
...
FOR ALL YOUR TALK...
...IS *THAT* WHAT YOU WANT?
WELL? HURRY UP.
NO!
OH? YOU WANT *ME* TO DO IT FOR YOU?
?!
COME ON, WHY'RE YOU—?
SHWIP
SHWIP
GAH! WAIT! HANDS OFF MY OBI BELT!
GYAAAAH!!

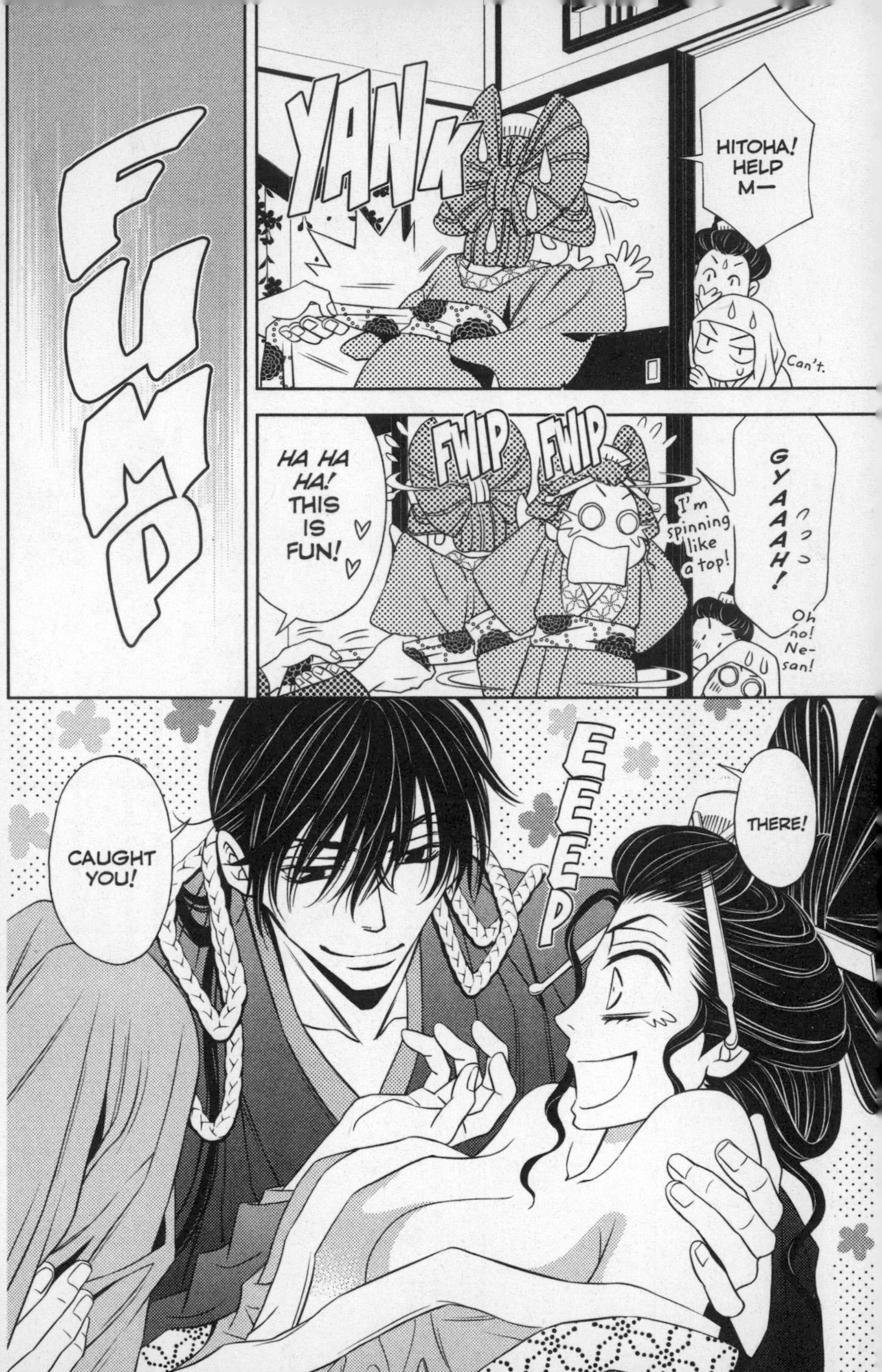
HITOHA! HELP M—
YANK
Can't.
GYAAAH!
I'm spinning like a top!
FWIP FWIP
HA HA HA! THIS IS FUN!
Oh no! Ne-san!
FUMP
THERE!
EEEEP
CAUGHT YOU!

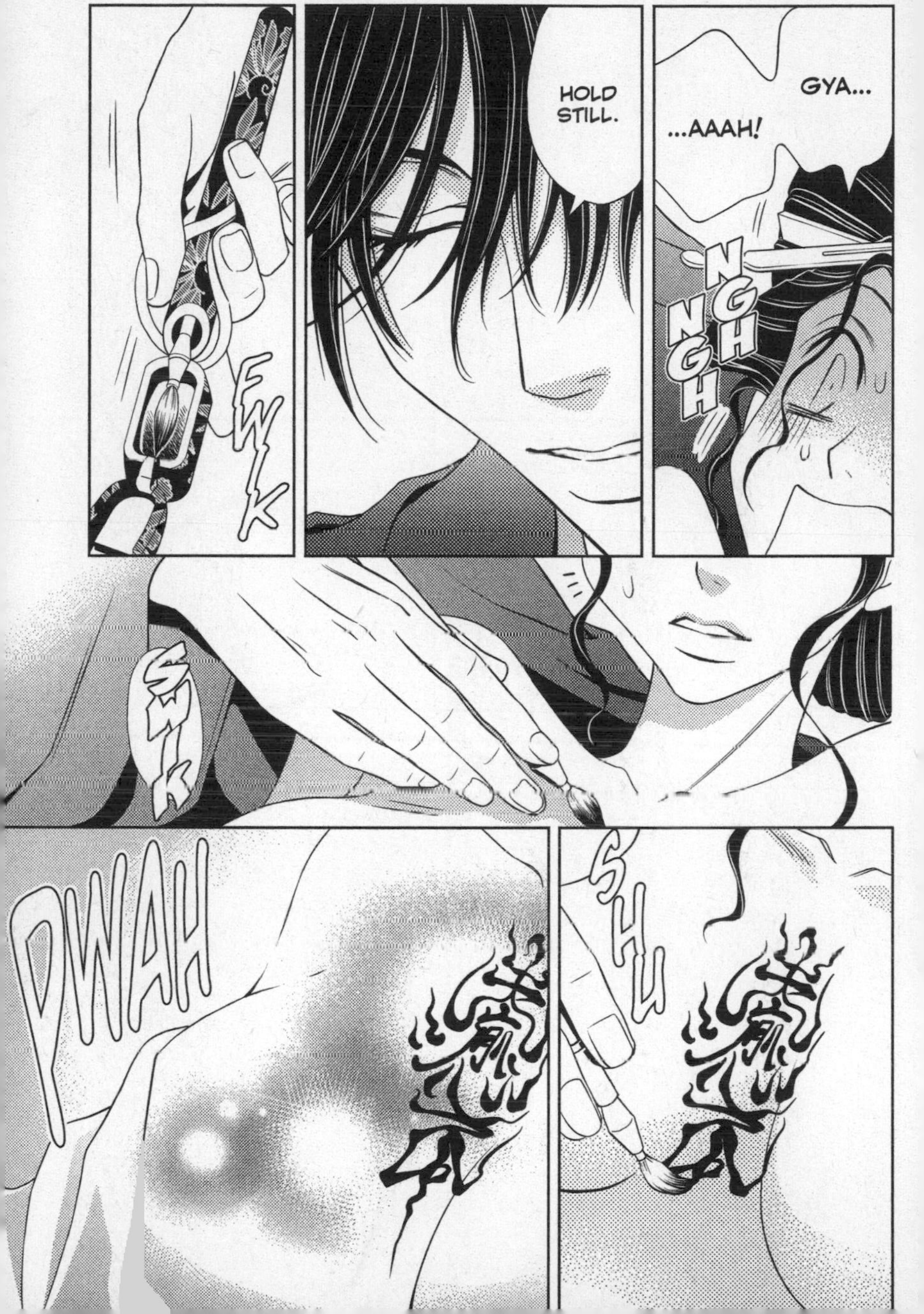
GYA...
...AAAH!
NGH NGH
HOLD STILL.
FWIK
SWIK
SHU
PWAH

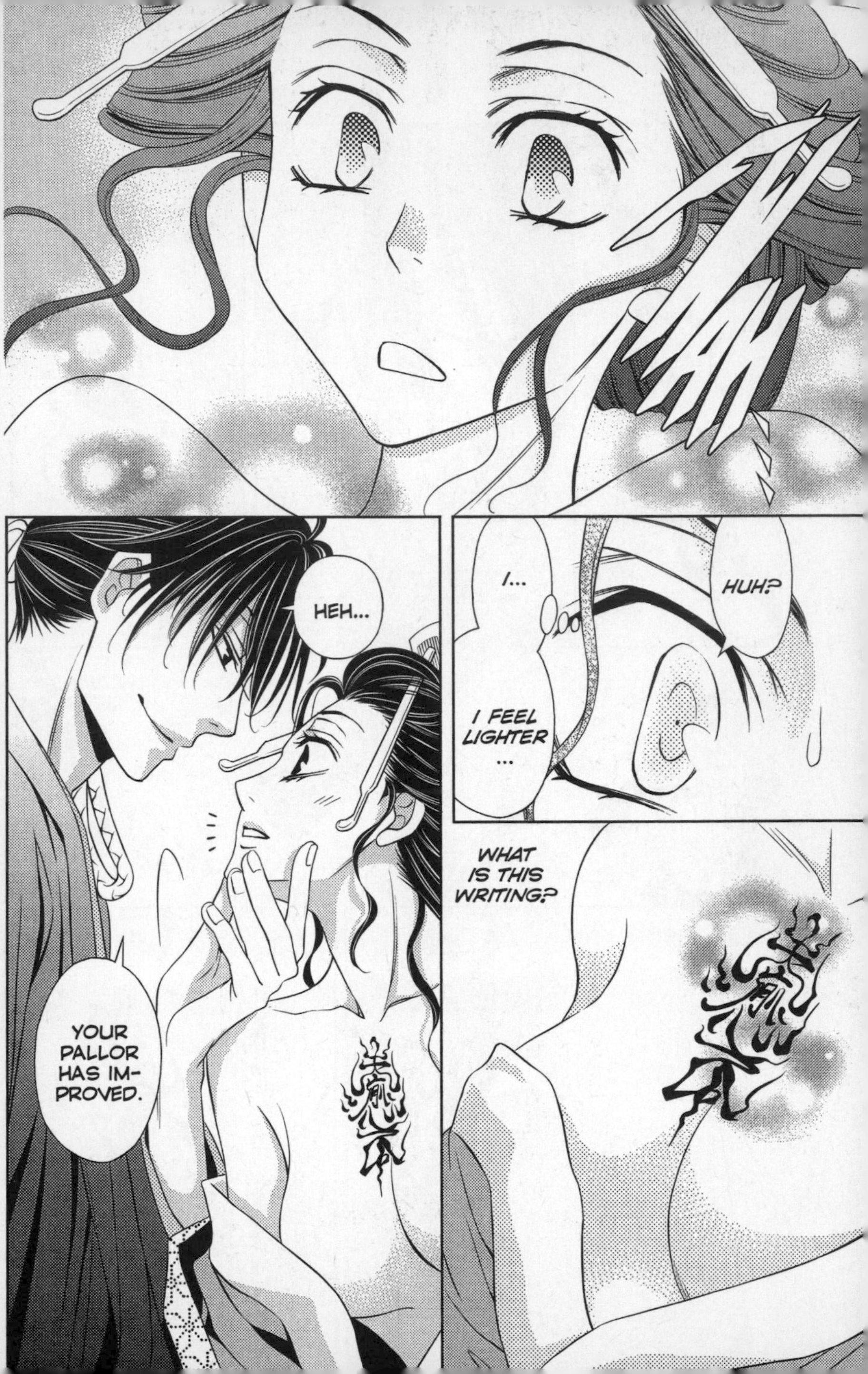
WAH
HUH?
I...
I FEEL LIGHTER ...
WHAT IS THIS WRITING?
HEH...
YOUR PALLOR HAS IM- PROVED.

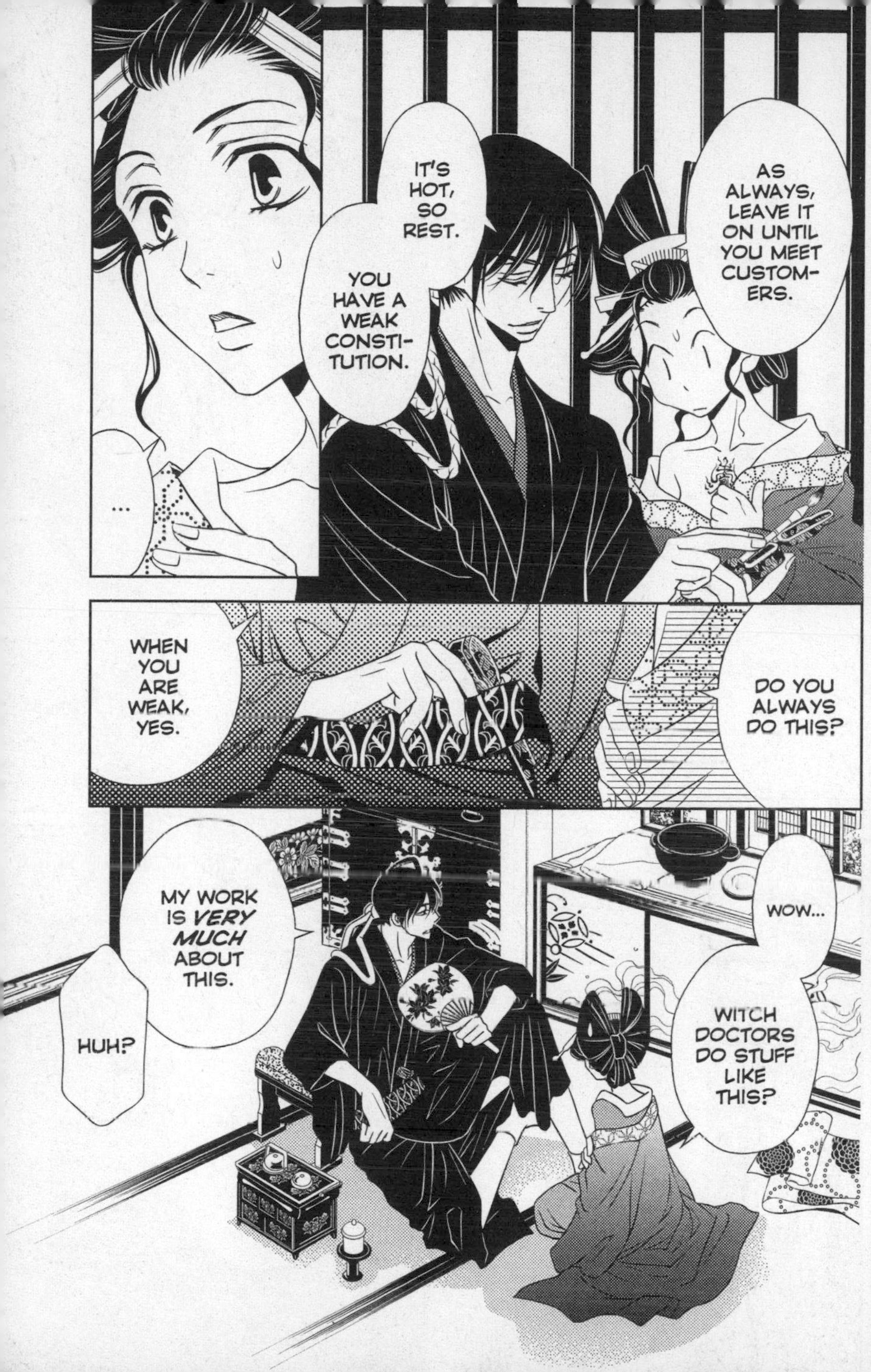
AS ALWAYS, LEAVE IT ON UNTIL YOU MEET CUSTOM-ERS.
IT'S HOT, SO REST.
YOU HAVE A WEAK CONSTI-TUTION.
...
DO YOU ALWAYS DO THIS?
WHEN YOU ARE WEAK, YES.
WOW...
WITCH DOCTORS DO STUFF LIKE THIS?
MY WORK IS *VERY MUCH* ABOUT THIS.
HUH?

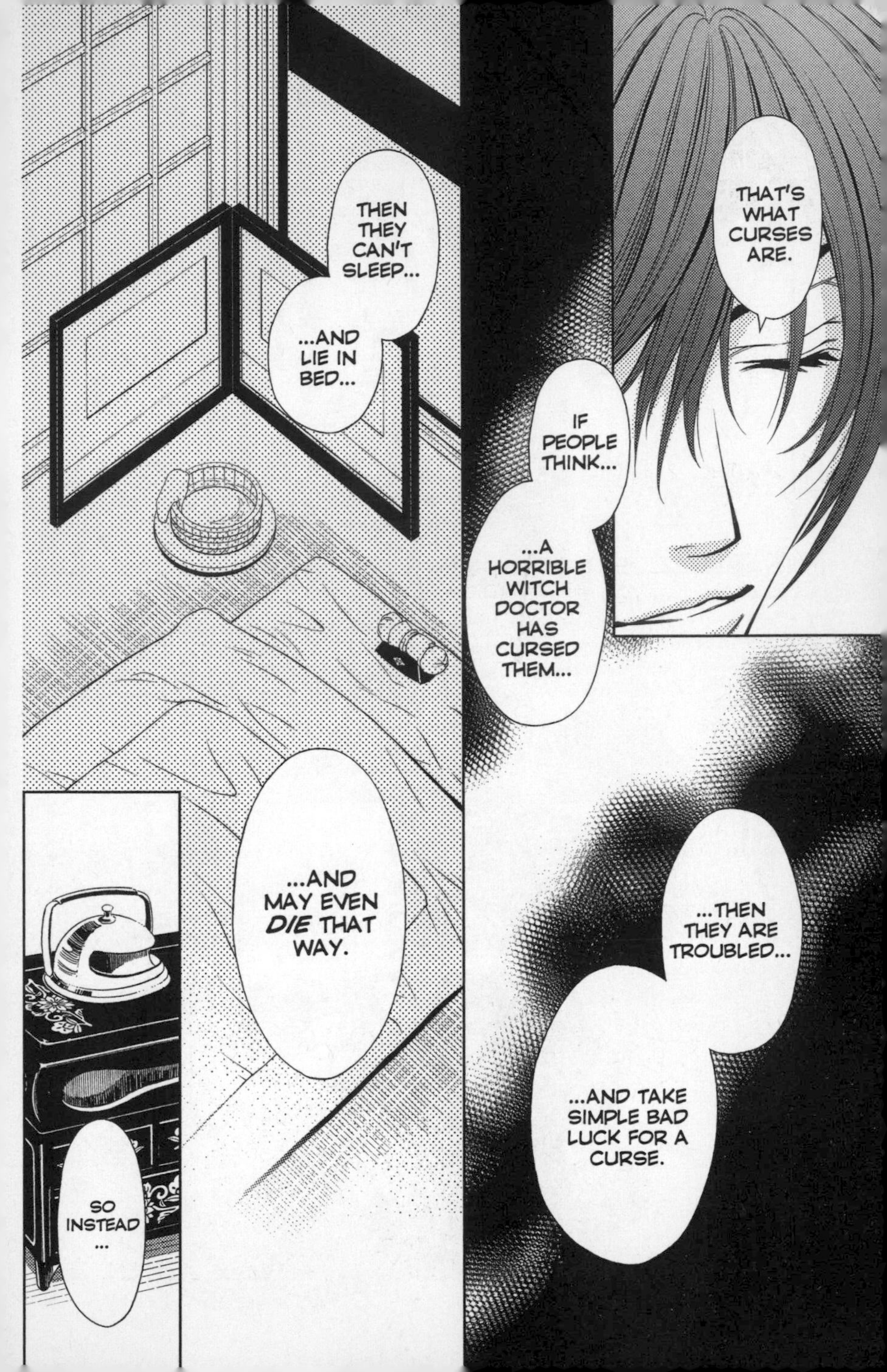
THAT'S WHAT CURSES ARE.
IF PEOPLE THINK...
...A HORRIBLE WITCH DOCTOR HAS CURSED THEM...
...THEN THEY ARE TROUBLED...
...AND TAKE SIMPLE BAD LUCK FOR A CURSE.
THEN THEY CAN'T SLEEP...
...AND LIE IN BED...
...AND MAY EVEN *DIE* THAT WAY.
SO INSTEAD ...

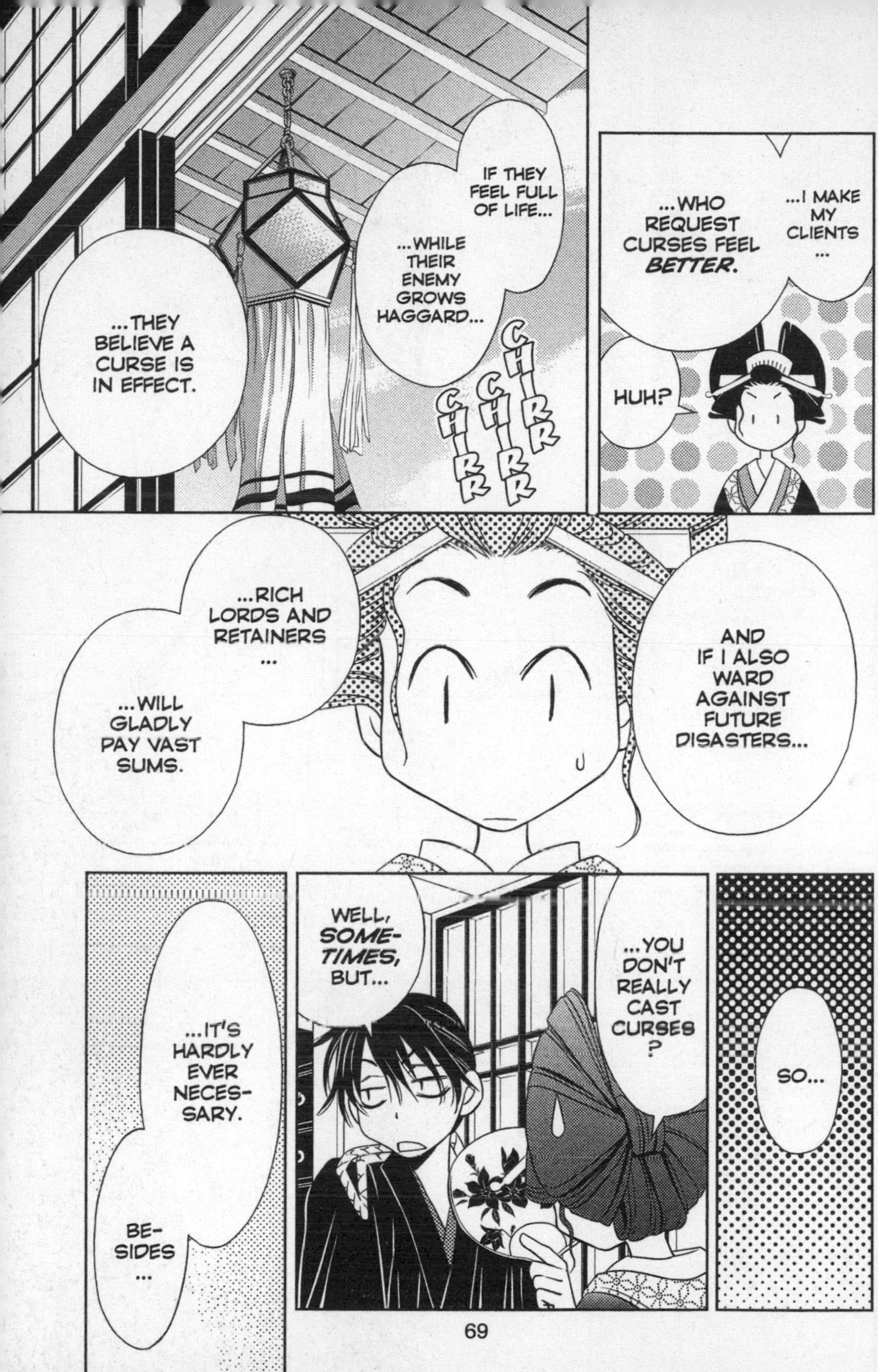
...I MAKE MY CLIENTS ...
...WHO REQUEST CURSES FEEL *BETTER*.
HUH?
IF THEY FEEL FULL OF LIFE...
...WHILE THEIR ENEMY GROWS HAGGARD...
CHIRR CHIRR
...THEY BELIEVE A CURSE IS IN EFFECT.
AND IF I ALSO WARD AGAINST FUTURE DISASTERS...
...RICH LORDS AND RETAINERS ...
...WILL GLADLY PAY VAST SUMS.
SO...
...YOU DON'T REALLY CAST CURSES ?
WELL, *SOMETIMES*, BUT...
...IT'S HARDLY EVER NECESSARY.
BESIDES ...

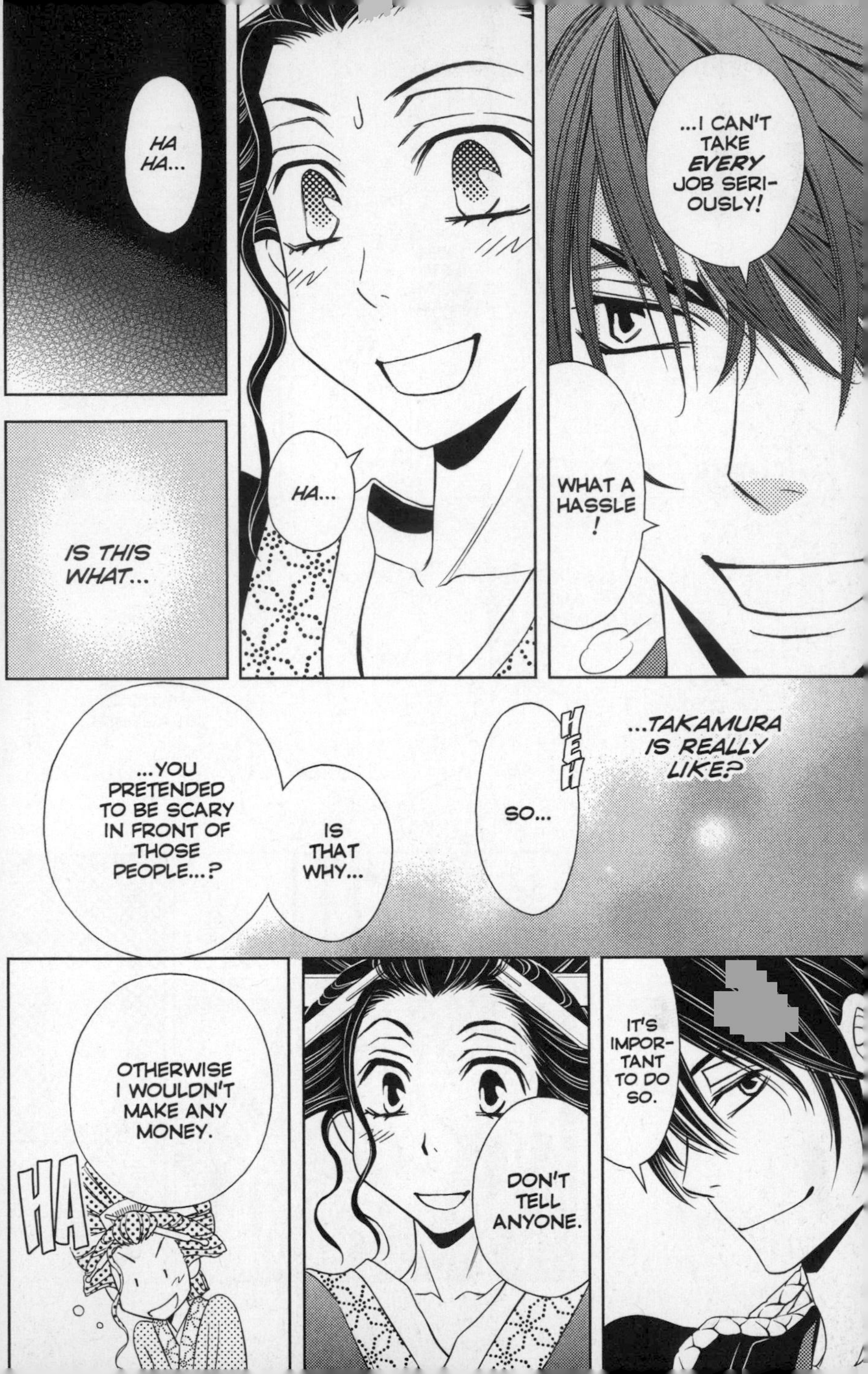
...I CAN'T TAKE *EVERY* JOB SERIOUSLY!
WHAT A HASSLE!
HA...
HA HA...
IS THIS WHAT...
...TAKAMURA IS REALLY LIKE?
HEH
SO...
IS THAT WHY...
...YOU PRETENDED TO BE SCARY IN FRONT OF THOSE PEOPLE...?
IT'S IMPORTANT TO DO SO.
DON'T TELL ANYONE.
OTHERWISE I WOULDN'T MAKE ANY MONEY.
HA

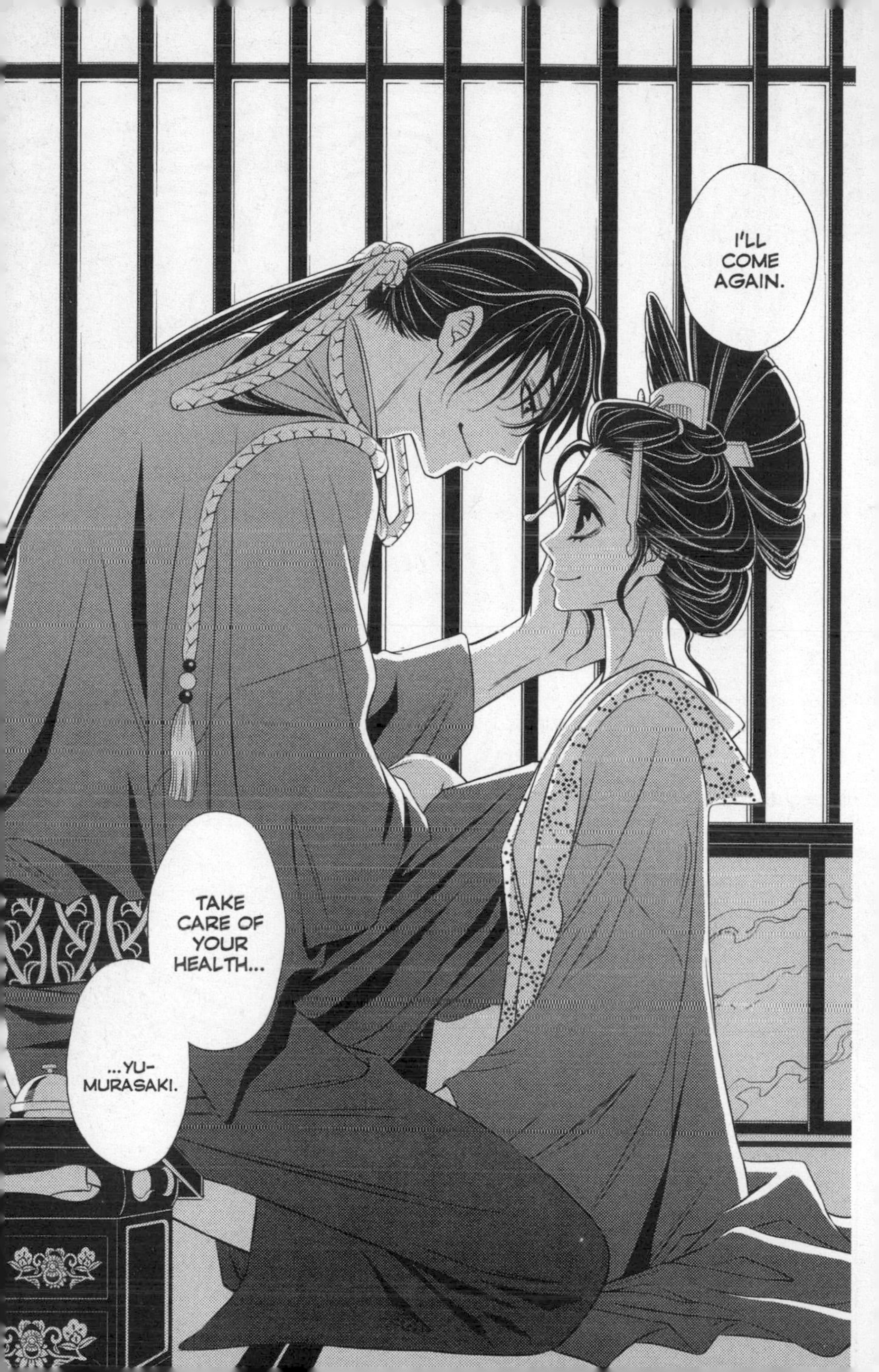
I'LL COME AGAIN.
TAKE CARE OF YOUR HEALTH...
...YU-MURASAKI.

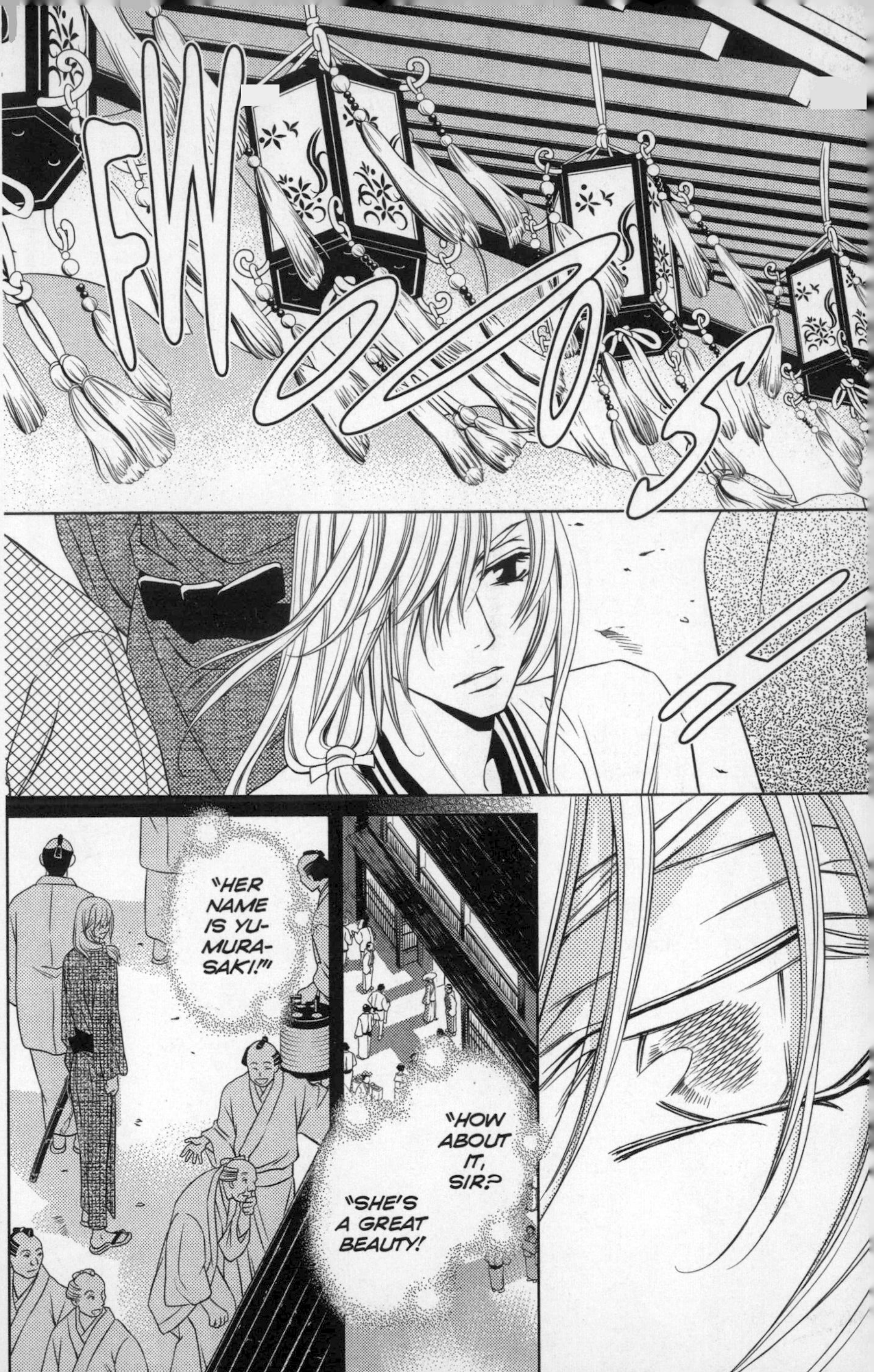
FWOOSH
"HOW ABOUT IT, SIR?
"SHE'S A GREAT BEAUTY!
"HER NAME IS YUMURASAKI!"

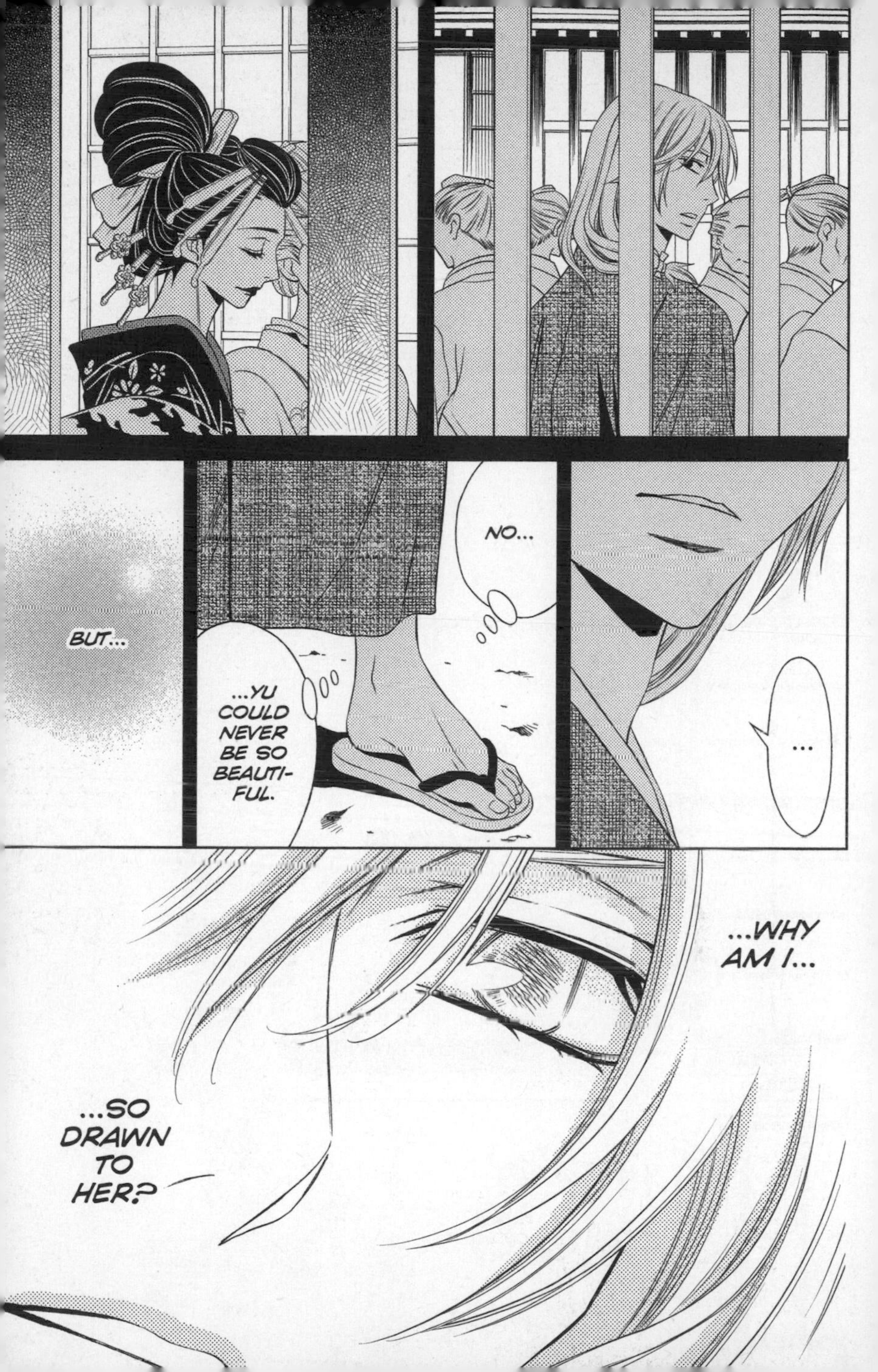
...
NO...
...YU COULD NEVER BE SO BEAUTIFUL.
BUT...
...WHY AM I...
...SO DRAWN TO HER?

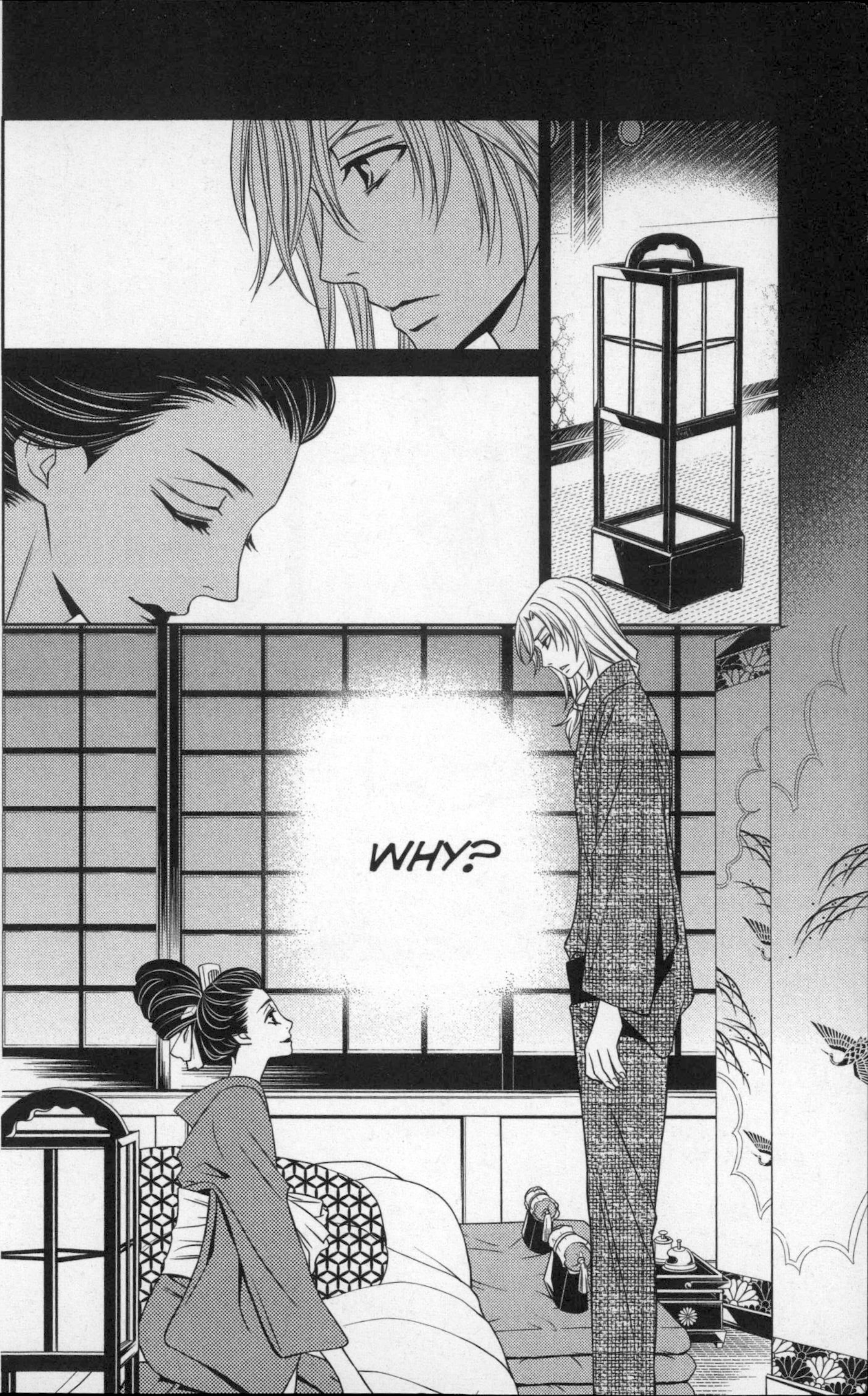
WHY?

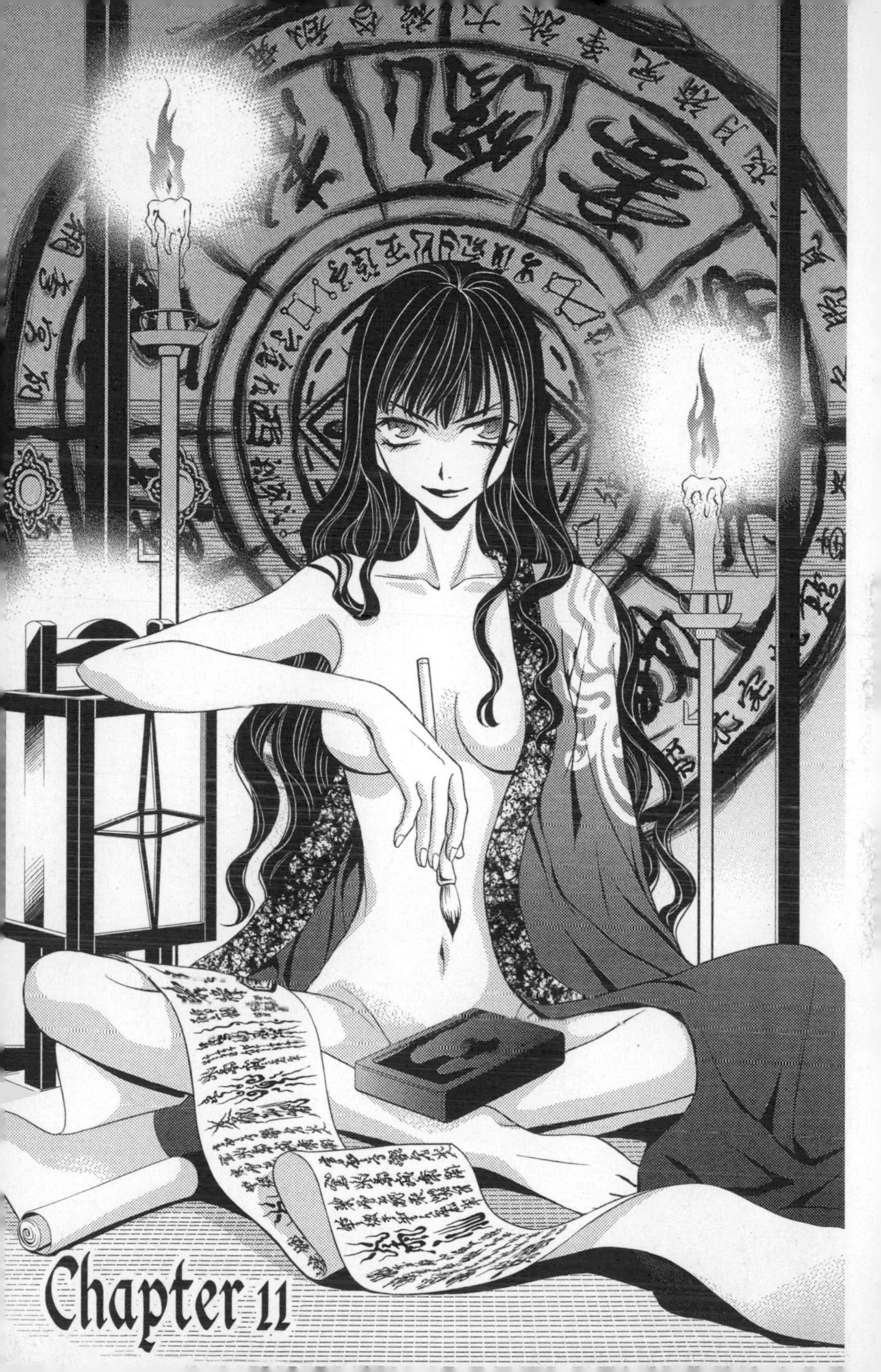
Chapter 11

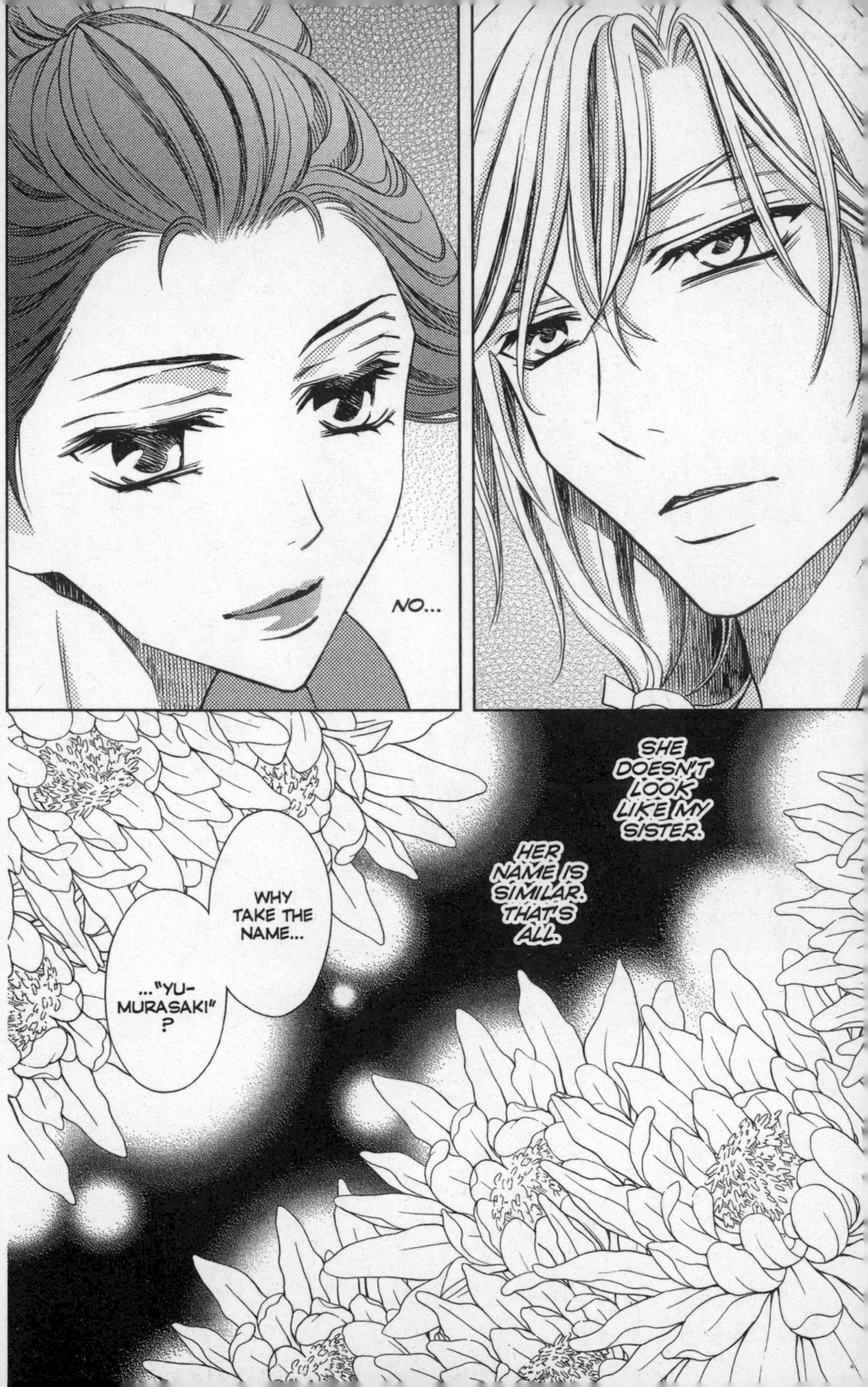
NO...
SHE DOESN'T LOOK LIKE MY SISTER.
HER NAME IS SIMILAR. THAT'S ALL.
WHY TAKE THE NAME...
..."YU-MURASAKI"?

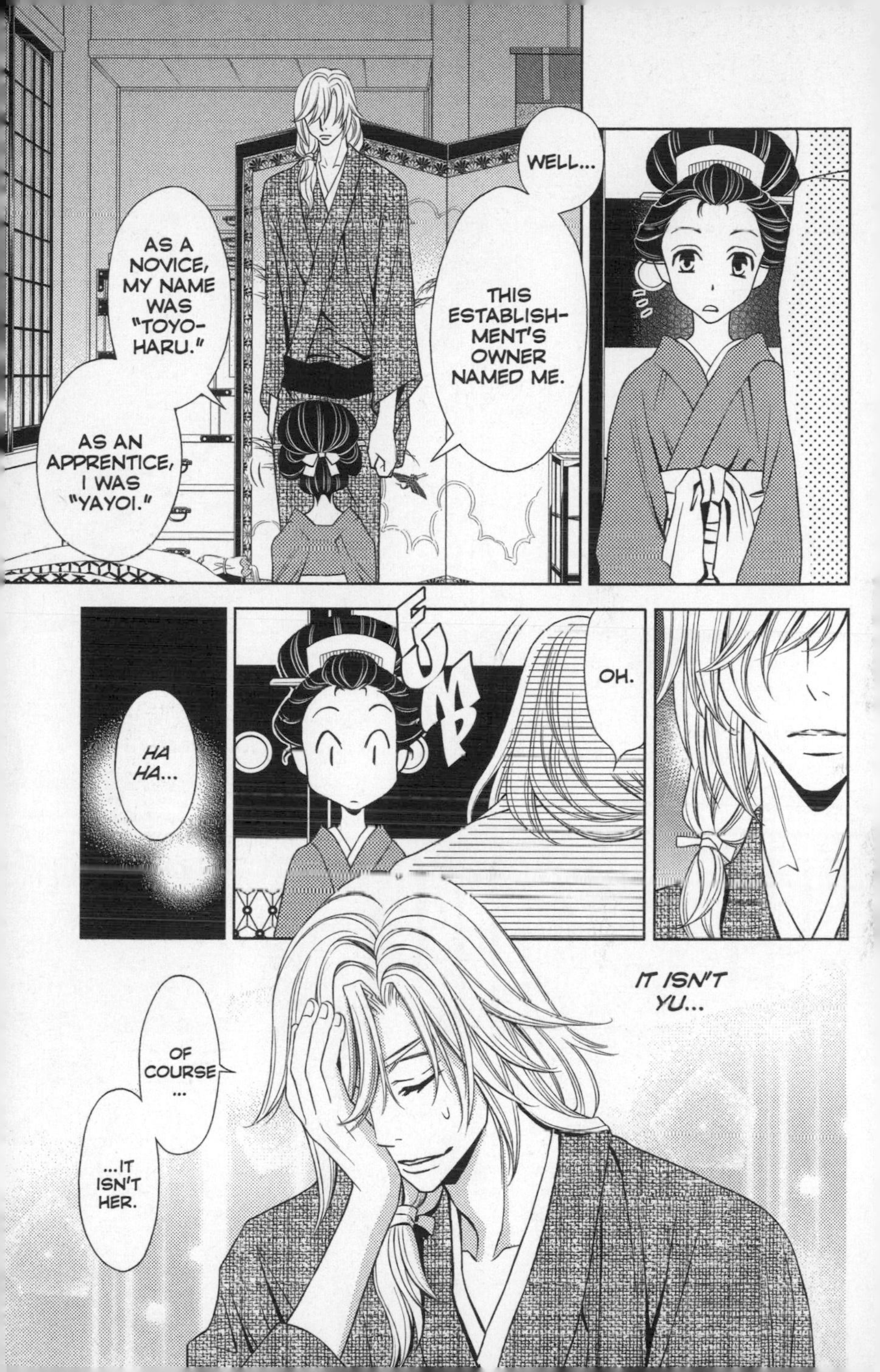
WELL...
THIS ESTABLISHMENT'S OWNER NAMED ME.
AS A NOVICE, MY NAME WAS "TOYOHARU."
AS AN APPRENTICE, I WAS "YAYOI."
OH.
FUMP
HA HA...
IT ISN'T YU...
OF COURSE...
...IT ISN'T HER.

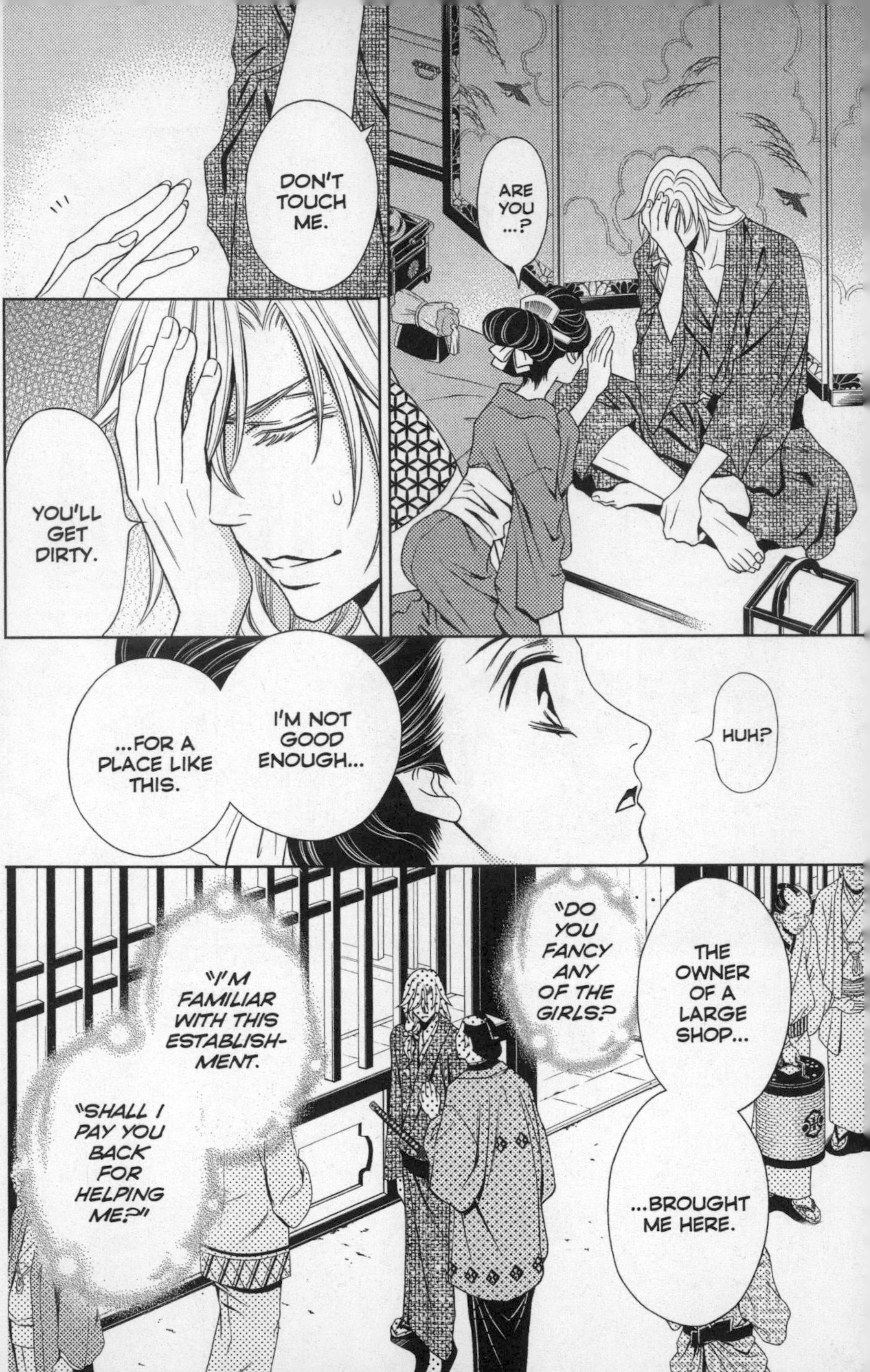
ARE YOU ...?
DON'T TOUCH ME.
YOU'LL GET DIRTY.
HUH?
I'M NOT GOOD ENOUGH...
...FOR A PLACE LIKE THIS.
THE OWNER OF A LARGE SHOP...
...BROUGHT ME HERE.
"DO YOU FANCY ANY OF THE GIRLS?"
"I'M FAMILIAR WITH THIS ESTABLISHMENT.
"SHALL I PAY YOU BACK FOR HELPING ME?"

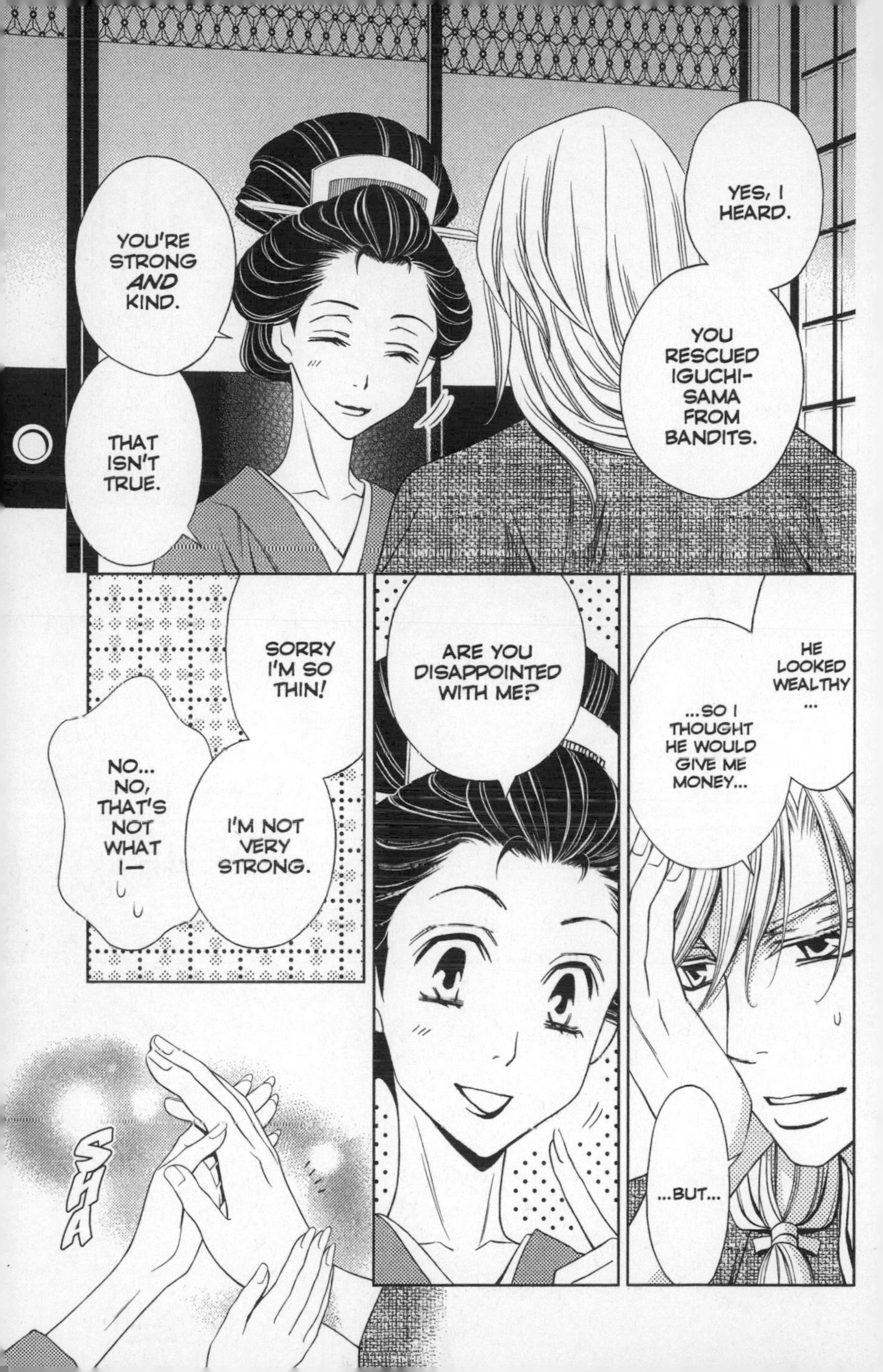
YES, I HEARD.
YOU RESCUED IGUCHI-SAMA FROM BANDITS.
YOU'RE STRONG *AND* KIND.
THAT ISN'T TRUE.
HE LOOKED WEALTHY...
...SO I THOUGHT HE WOULD GIVE ME MONEY...
...BUT...
ARE YOU DISAPPOINTED WITH ME?
SORRY I'M SO THIN!
I'M NOT VERY STRONG.
NO... NO, THAT'S NOT WHAT I—
SHA

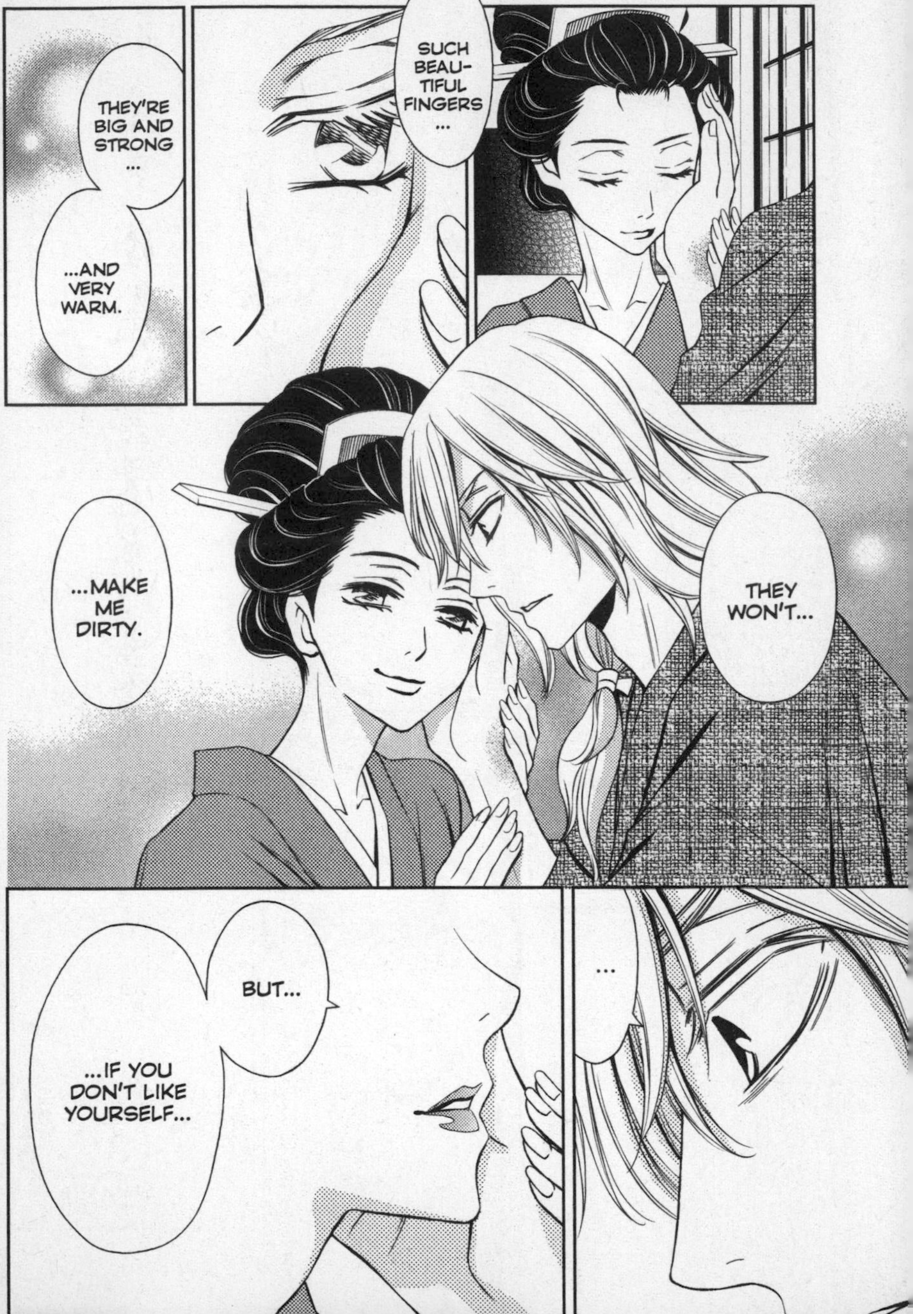
SUCH BEAU-TIFUL FINGERS ...
THEY'RE BIG AND STRONG ...
...AND VERY WARM.
THEY WON'T...
...MAKE ME DIRTY.
...
BUT...
...IF YOU DON'T LIKE YOURSELF...

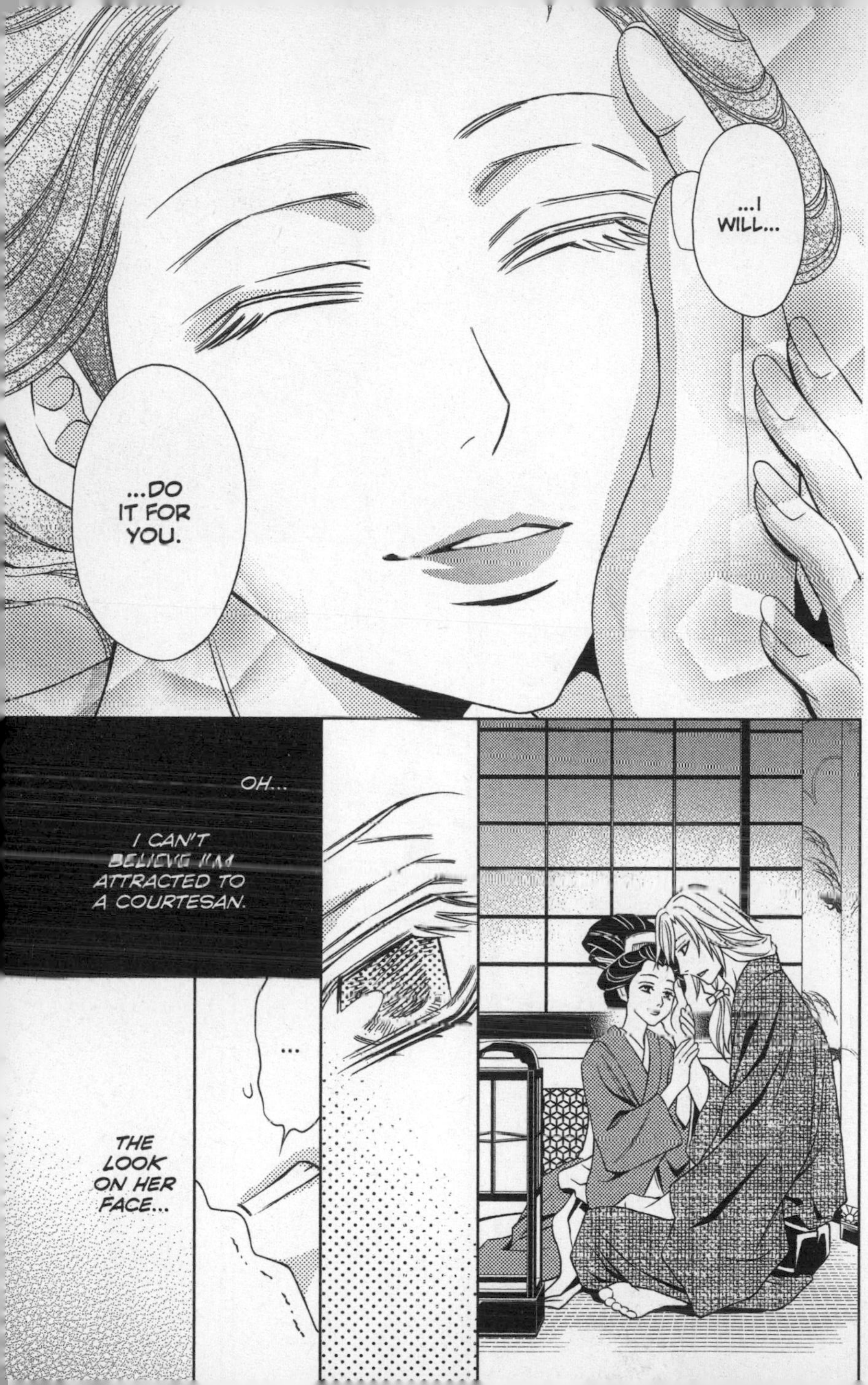
...I WILL...
...DO IT FOR YOU.
OH...
I CAN'T BELIEVE I'M ATTRACTED TO A COURTESAN.
...
THE LOOK ON HER FACE...

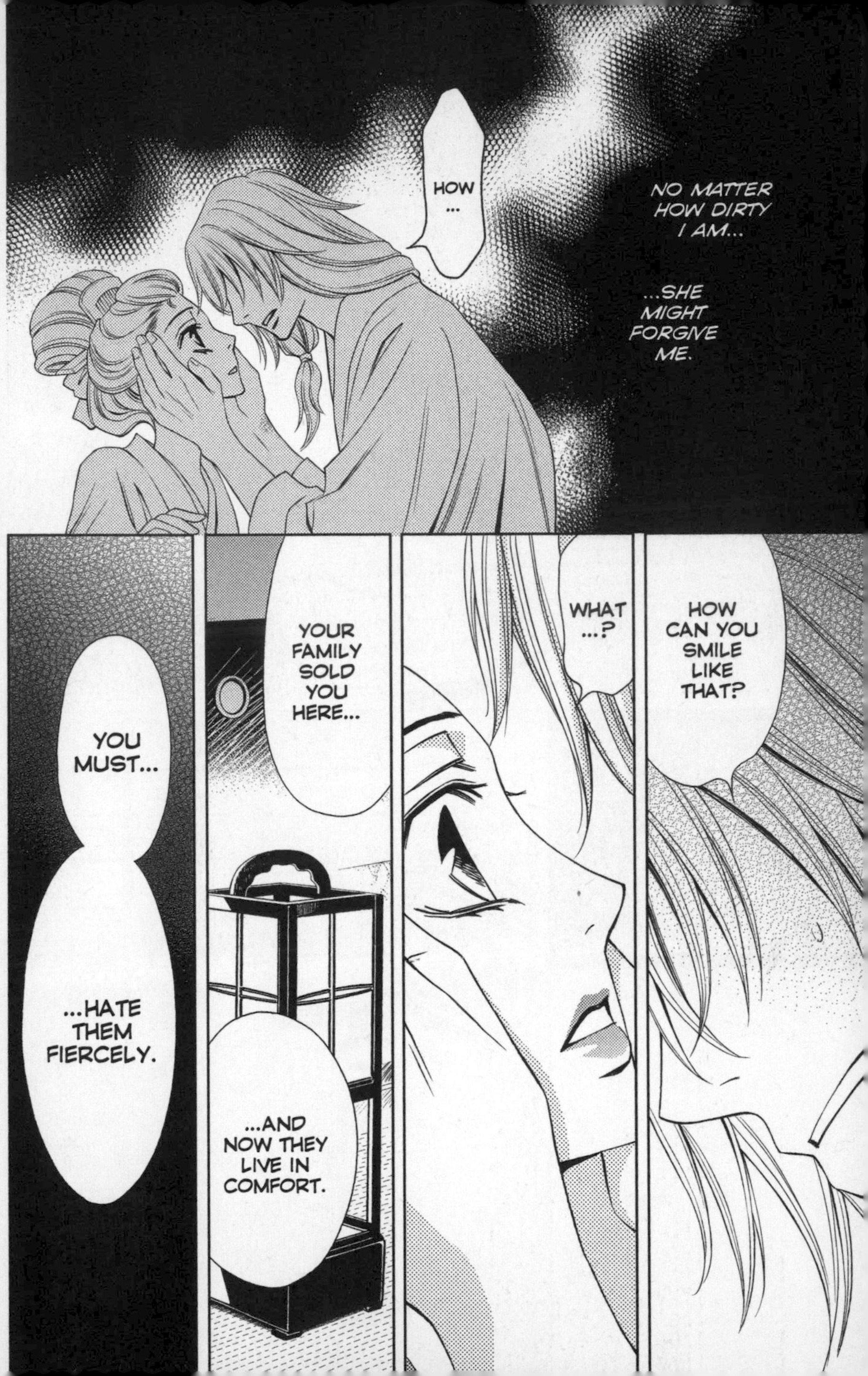
NO MATTER HOW DIRTY I AM...
...SHE MIGHT FORGIVE ME.
HOW ...
HOW CAN YOU SMILE LIKE THAT?
WHAT ...?
YOUR FAMILY SOLD YOU HERE...
...AND NOW THEY LIVE IN COMFORT.
YOU MUST...
...HATE THEM FIERCELY.

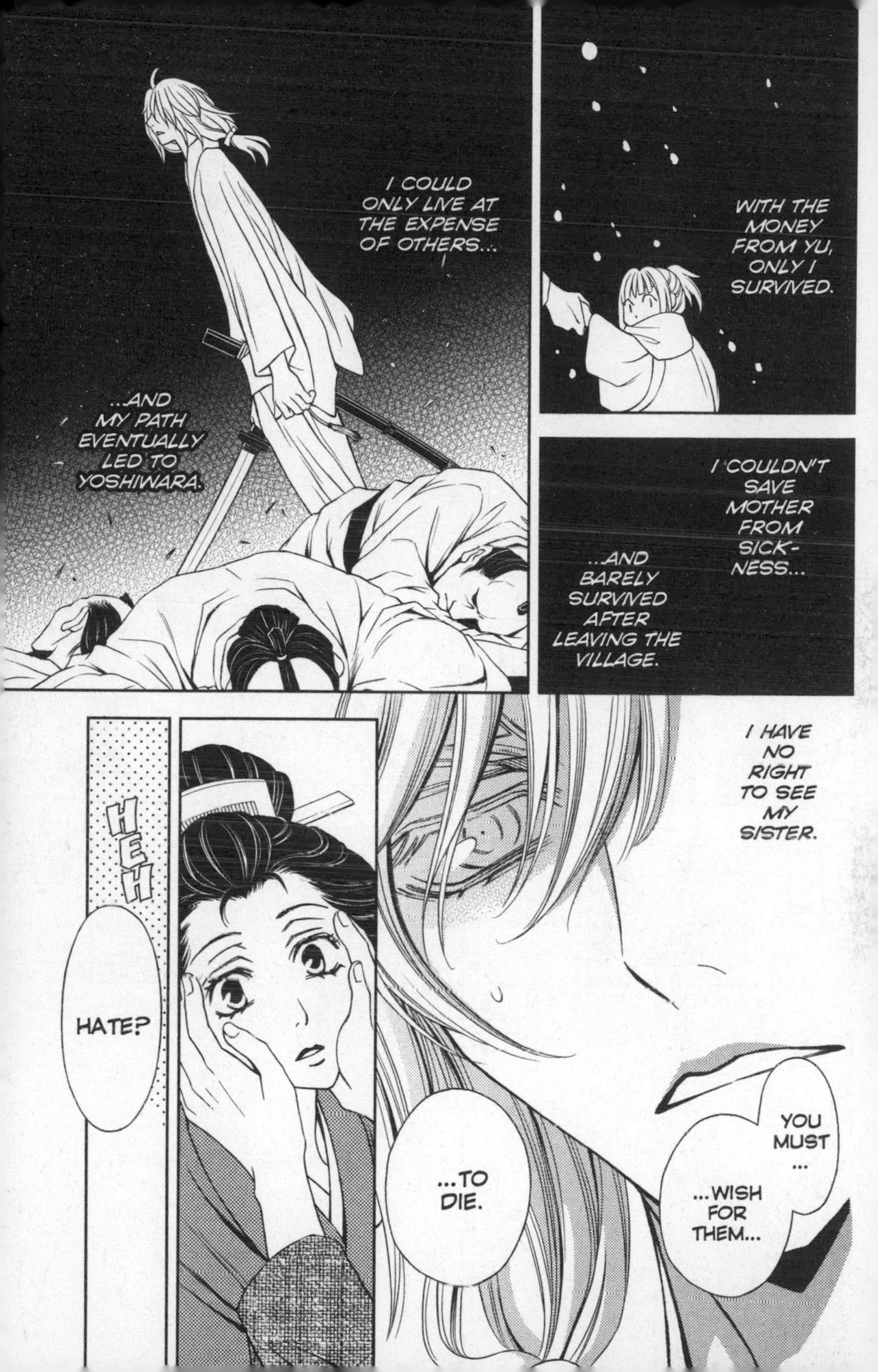
WITH THE MONEY FROM YU, ONLY I SURVIVED.
I COULDN'T SAVE MOTHER FROM SICK-NESS...
...AND BARELY SURVIVED AFTER LEAVING THE VILLAGE.
I COULD ONLY LIVE AT THE EXPENSE OF OTHERS...
...AND MY PATH EVENTUALLY LED TO YOSHIWARA.
I HAVE NO RIGHT TO SEE MY SISTER.
YOU MUST...
...WISH FOR THEM...
...TO DIE.
HATE?
HEH

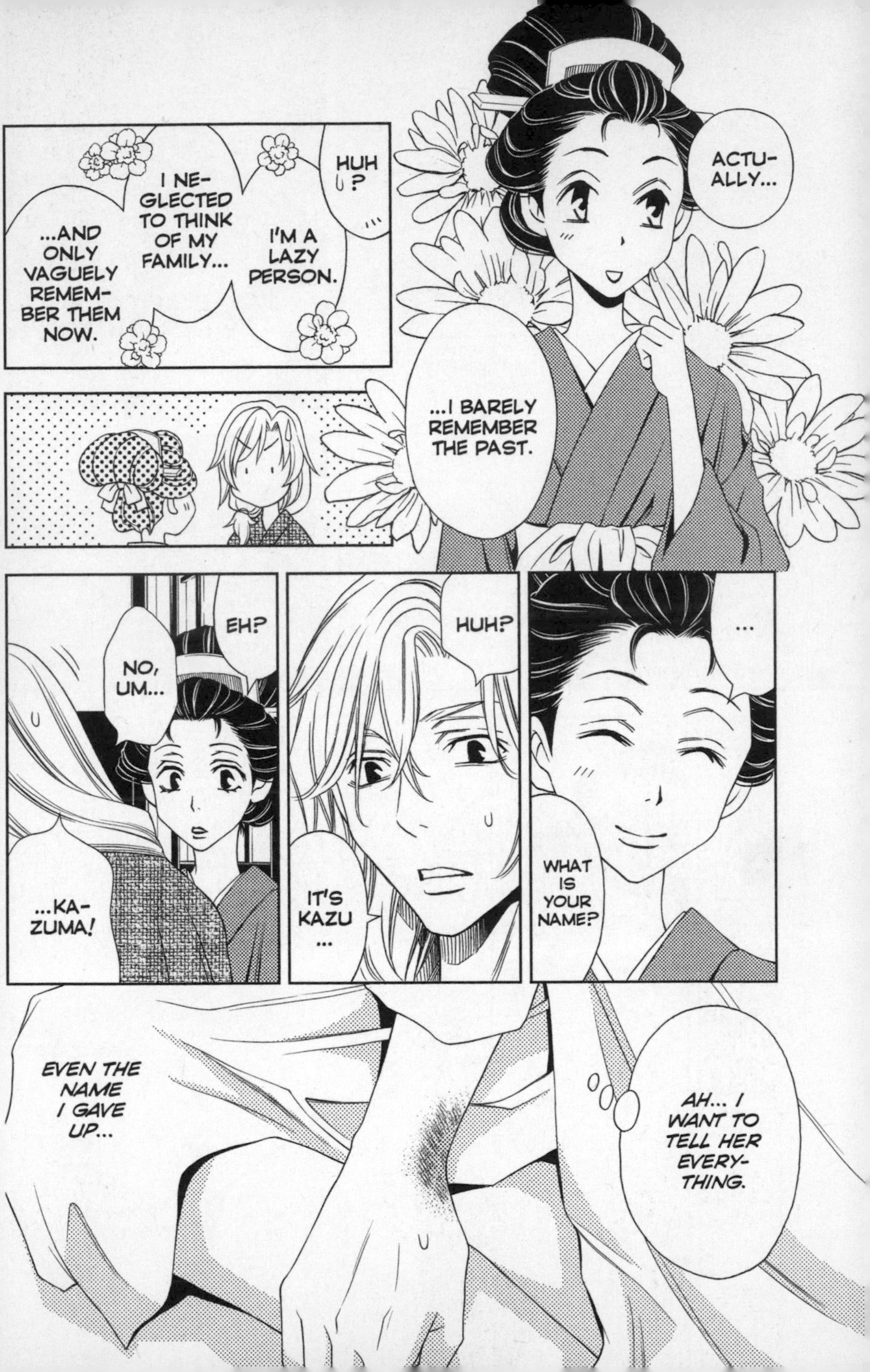
ACTUALLY...
...I BARELY REMEMBER THE PAST.
HUH?
I'M A LAZY PERSON.
I NEGLECTED TO THINK OF MY FAMILY...
...AND ONLY VAGUELY REMEMBER THEM NOW.
...
WHAT IS YOUR NAME?
HUH?
IT'S KAZU...
EH?
NO, UM...
...KAZUMA!
AH... I WANT TO TELL HER EVERYTHING.
EVEN THE NAME I GAVE UP...

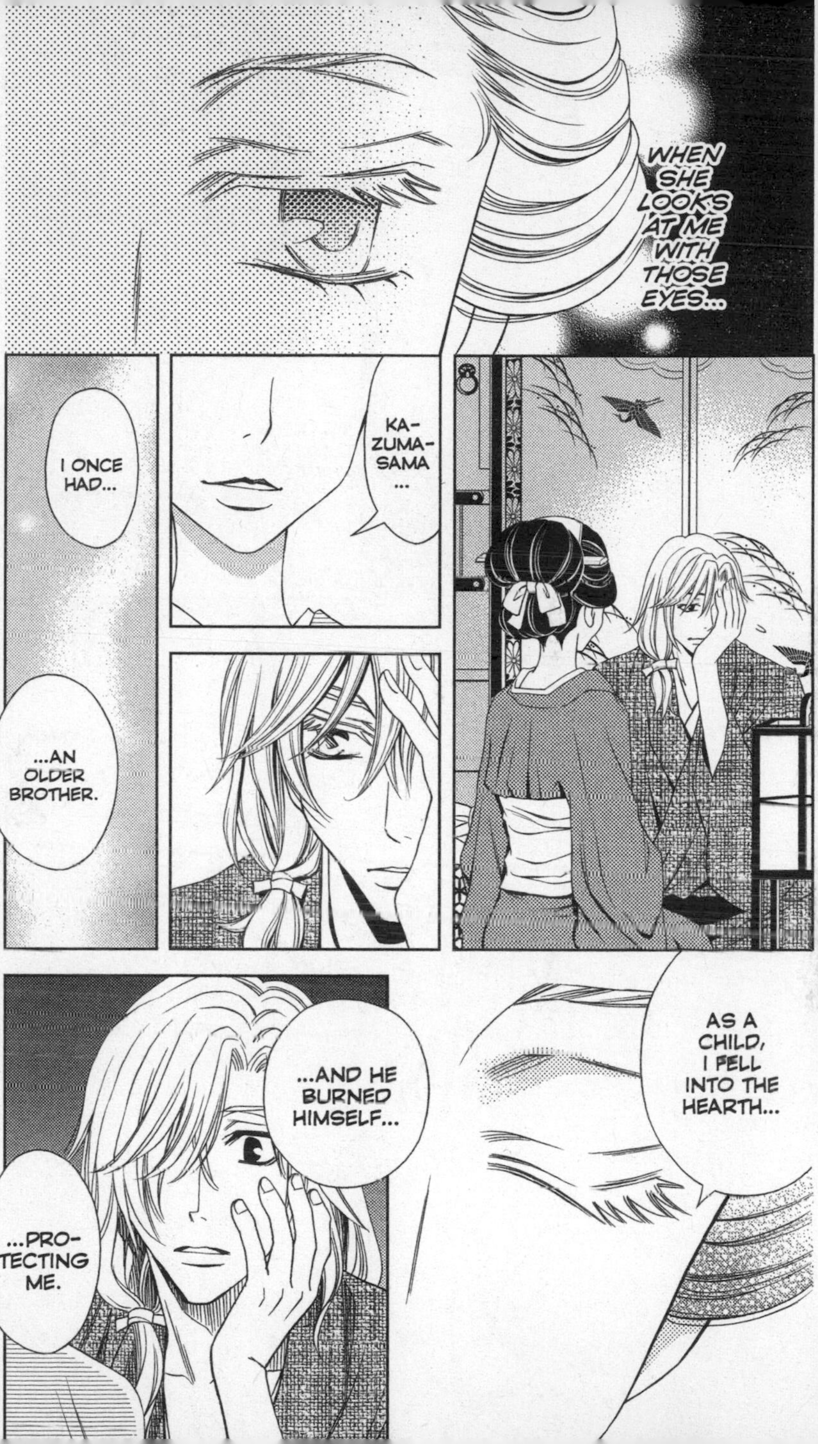
WHEN SHE LOOKS AT ME WITH THOSE EYES...
KA-ZUMA-SAMA ...
I ONCE HAD...
...AN OLDER BROTHER.
AS A CHILD, I FELL INTO THE HEARTH...
...AND HE BURNED HIMSELF...
...PRO-TECTING ME.

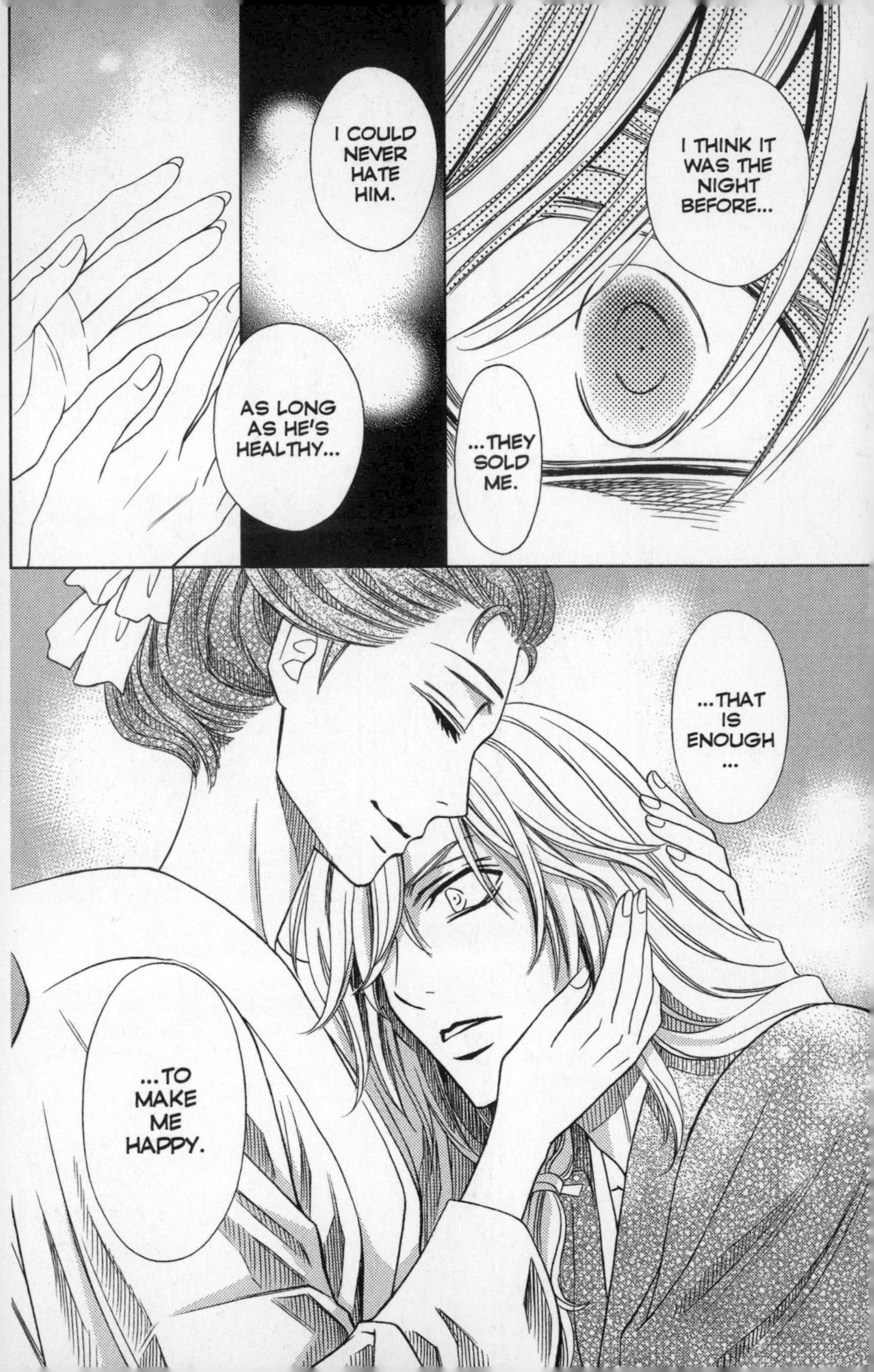
I THINK IT WAS THE NIGHT BEFORE...
...THEY SOLD ME.
I COULD NEVER HATE HIM.
AS LONG AS HE'S HEALTHY...
...THAT IS ENOUGH...
...TO MAKE ME HAPPY.

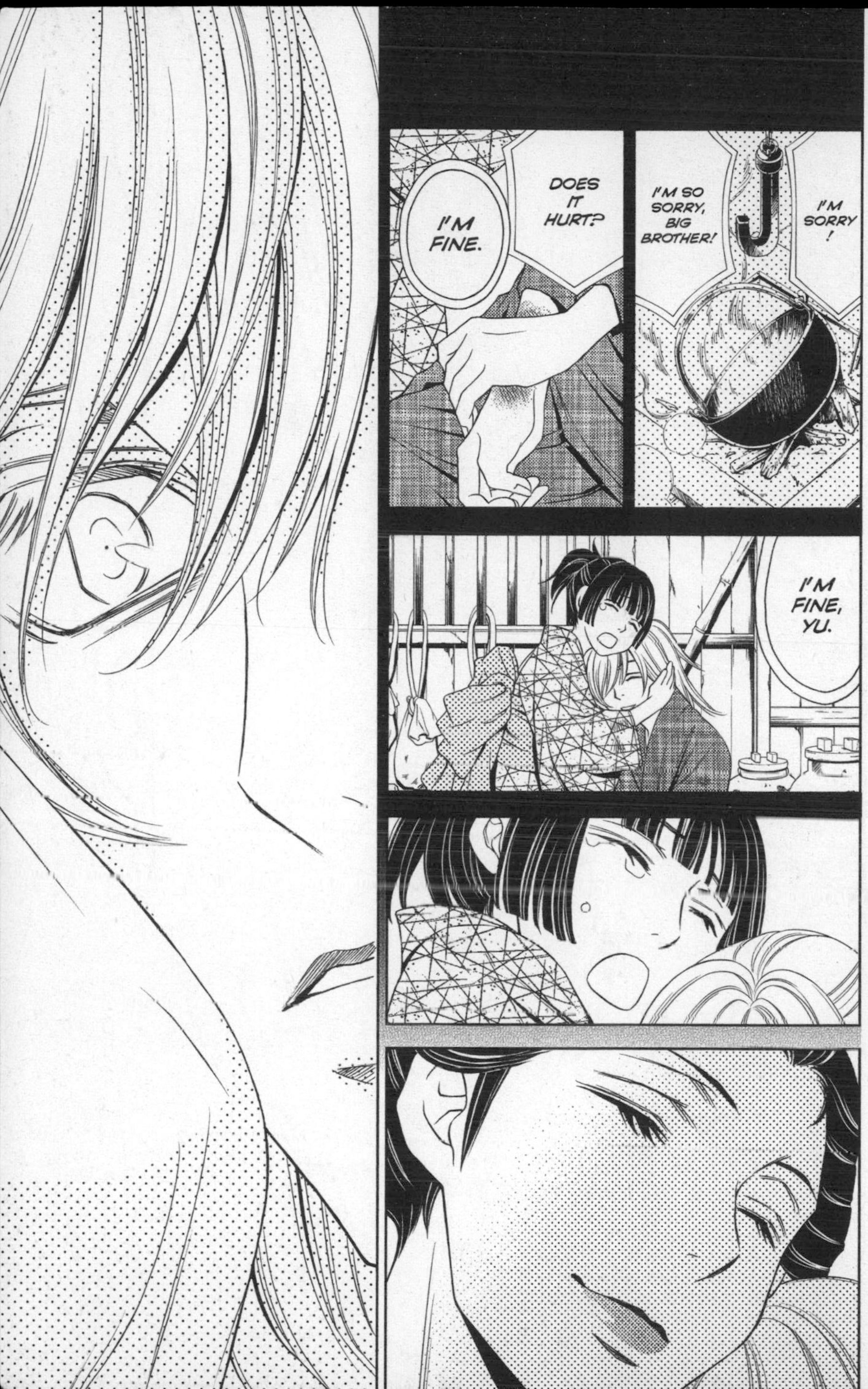
I'M SORRY!
I'M SO SORRY, BIG BROTHER!
DOES IT HURT?
I'M FINE.
I'M FINE, YU.

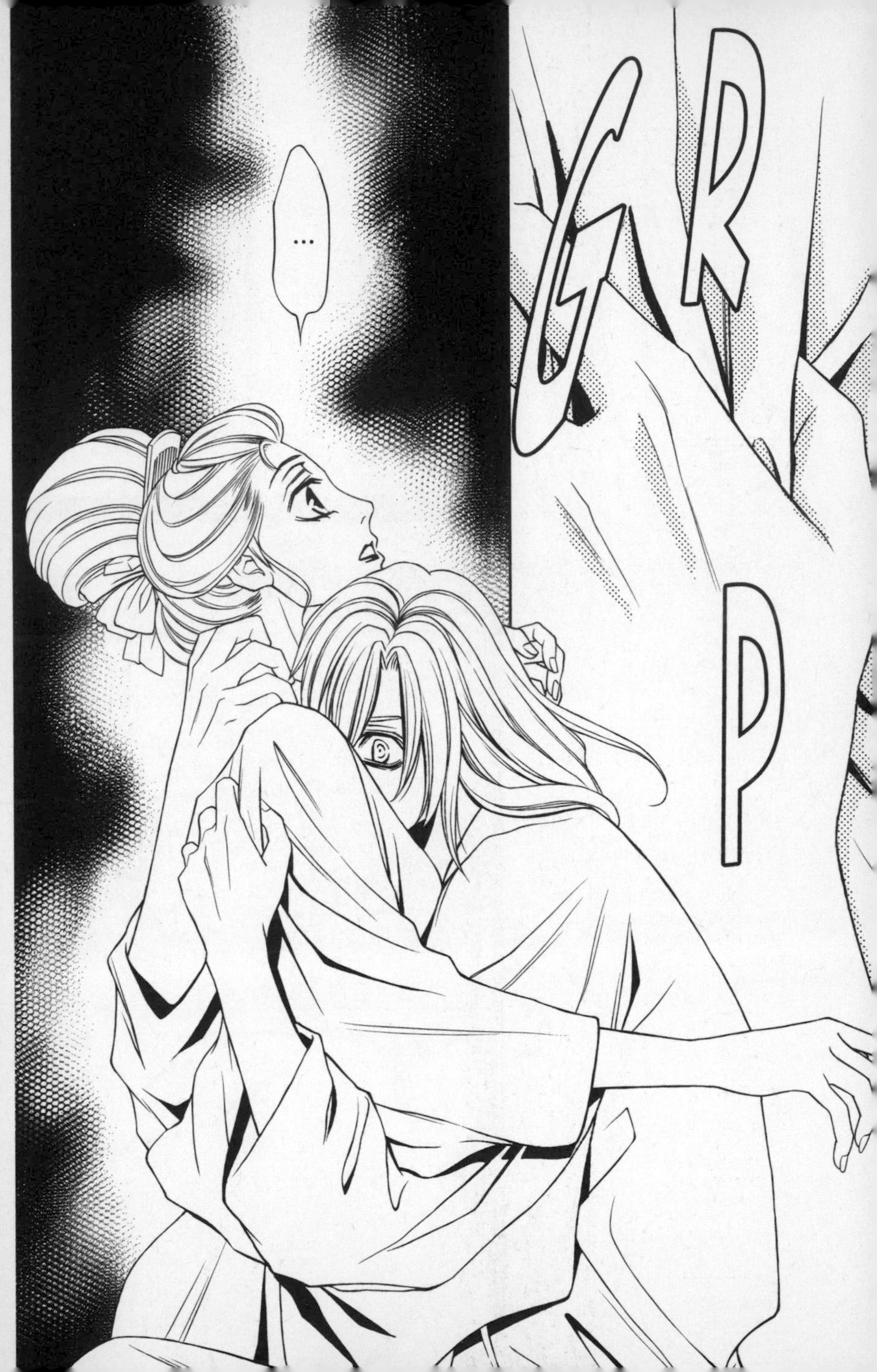
GRP
...

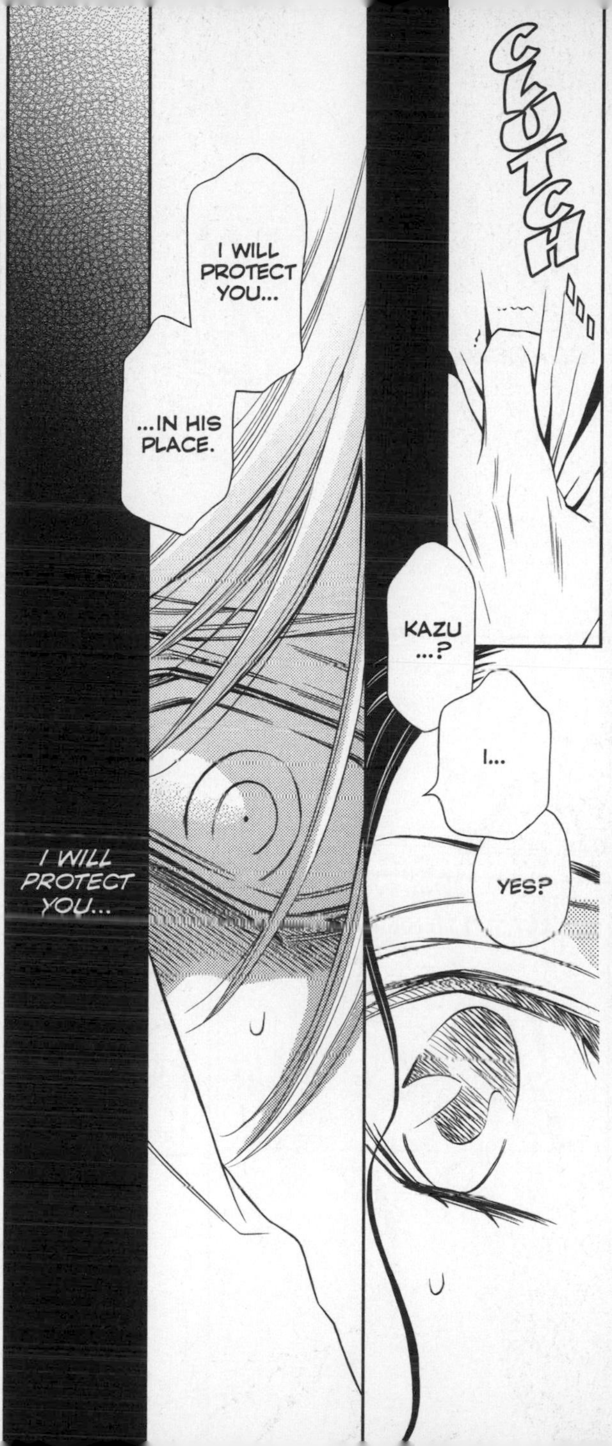
CLUTCH...
KAZU ...?
I...
YES?
I WILL PROTECT YOU...
...IN HIS PLACE.
I WILL PROTECT YOU...

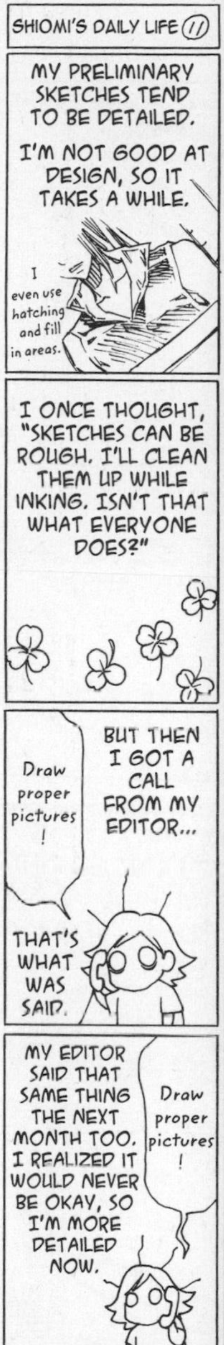
SHIOMI'S DAILY LIFE (11)
MY PRELIMINARY SKETCHES TEND TO BE DETAILED.
I'M NOT GOOD AT DESIGN, SO IT TAKES A WHILE.
I even use hatching and fill in areas.
I ONCE THOUGHT, "SKETCHES CAN BE ROUGH. I'LL CLEAN THEM UP WHILE INKING. ISN'T THAT WHAT EVERYONE DOES?"
BUT THEN I GOT A CALL FROM MY EDITOR...
Draw proper pictures!
THAT'S WHAT WAS SAID.
Draw proper pictures!
MY EDITOR SAID THAT SAME THING THE NEXT MONTH TOO. I REALIZED IT WOULD NEVER BE OKAY, SO I'M MORE DETAILED NOW.

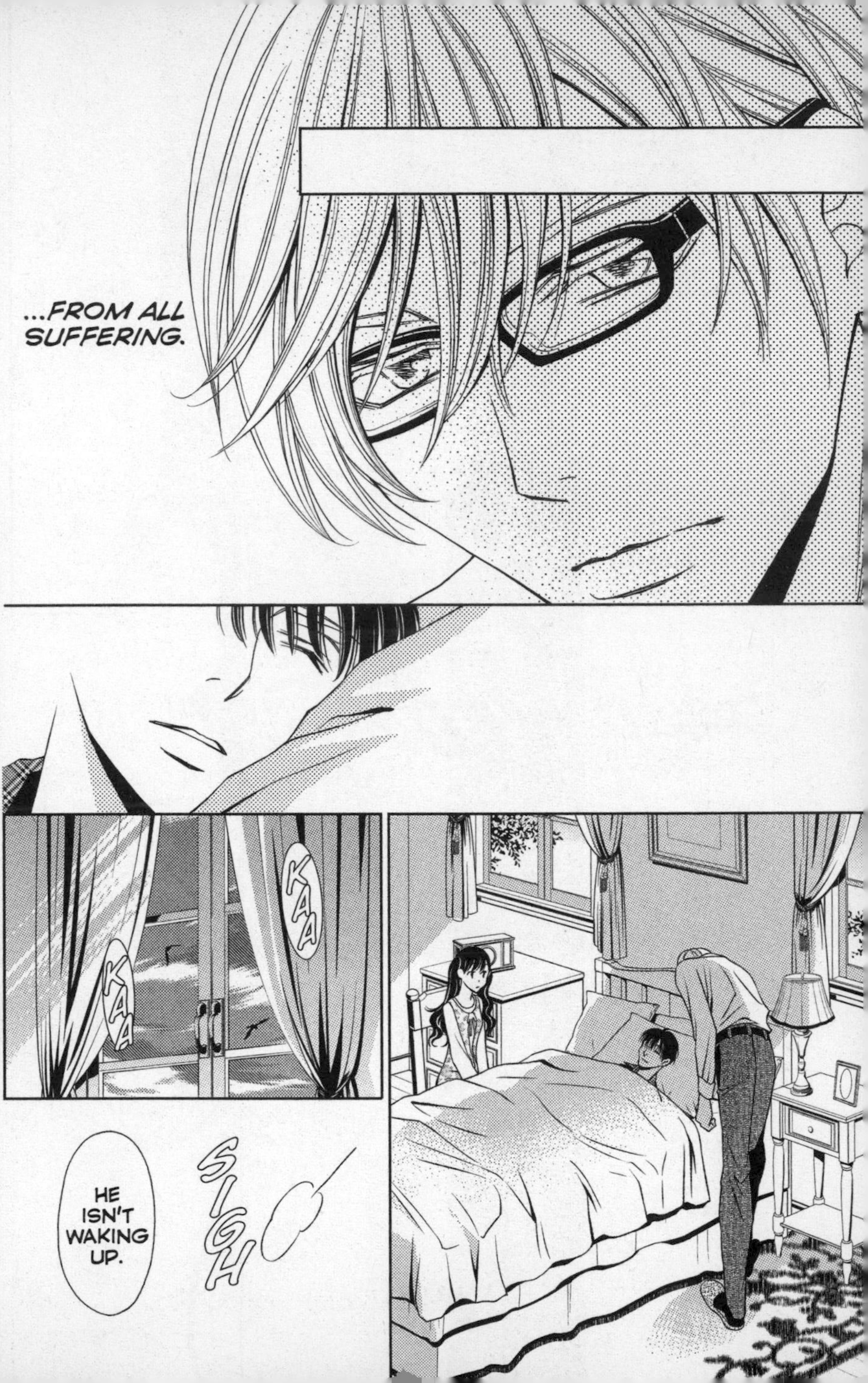
...FROM ALL SUFFERING.
SIGH
HE ISN'T WAKING UP.
KAA
KAA

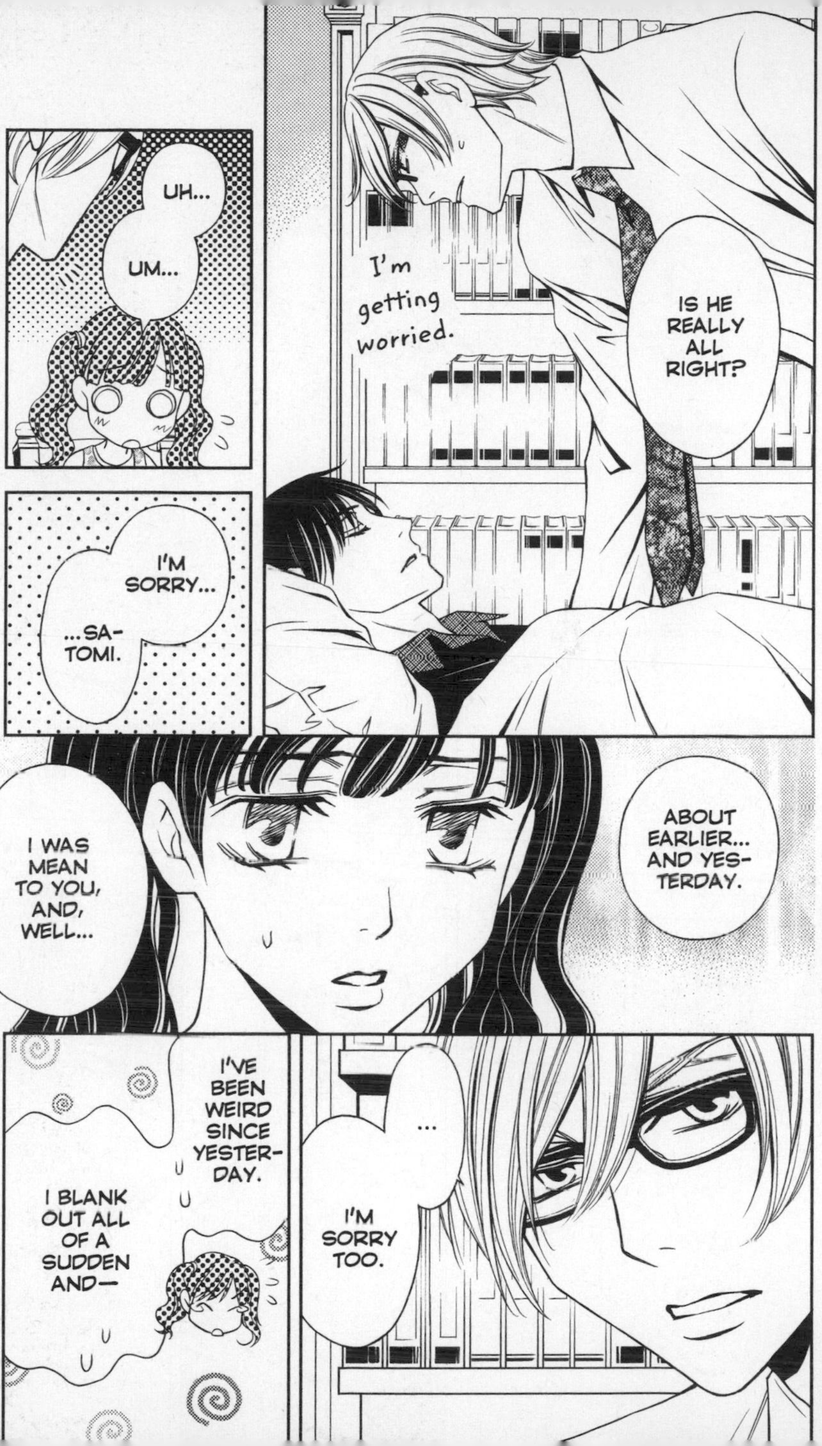
IS HE REALLY ALL RIGHT?
I'm getting worried.
UH...
UM...
I'M SORRY...
...SA-TOMI.
ABOUT EARLIER... AND YES-TERDAY.
I WAS MEAN TO YOU, AND, WELL...
...
I'M SORRY TOO.
I'VE BEEN WEIRD SINCE YESTER-DAY.
I BLANK OUT ALL OF A SUDDEN AND—

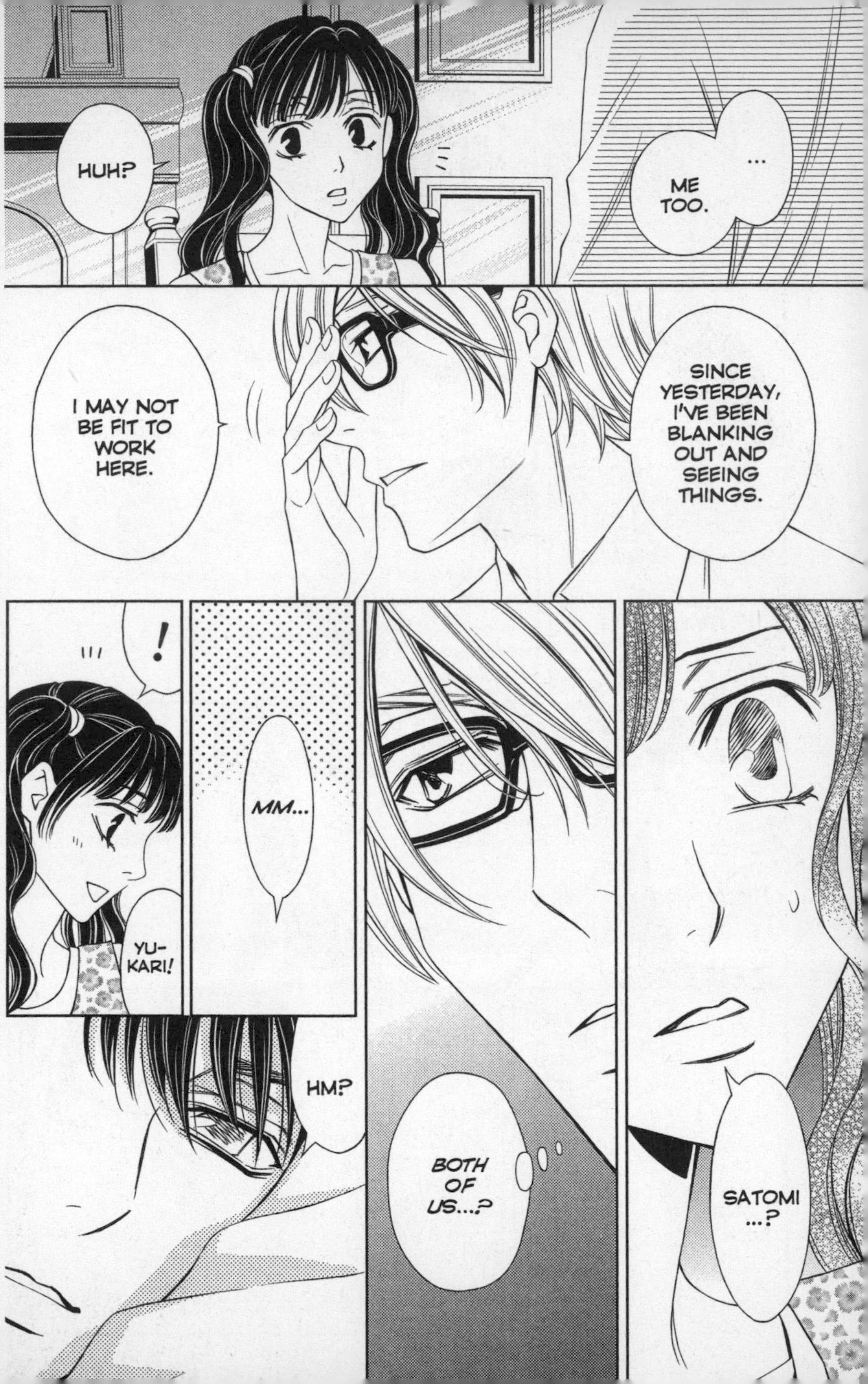
... ME TOO.
HUH?
SINCE YESTERDAY, I'VE BEEN BLANKING OUT AND SEEING THINGS.
I MAY NOT BE FIT TO WORK HERE.
SATOMI ...?
BOTH OF US...?
MM...
!
YU-KARI!
HM?

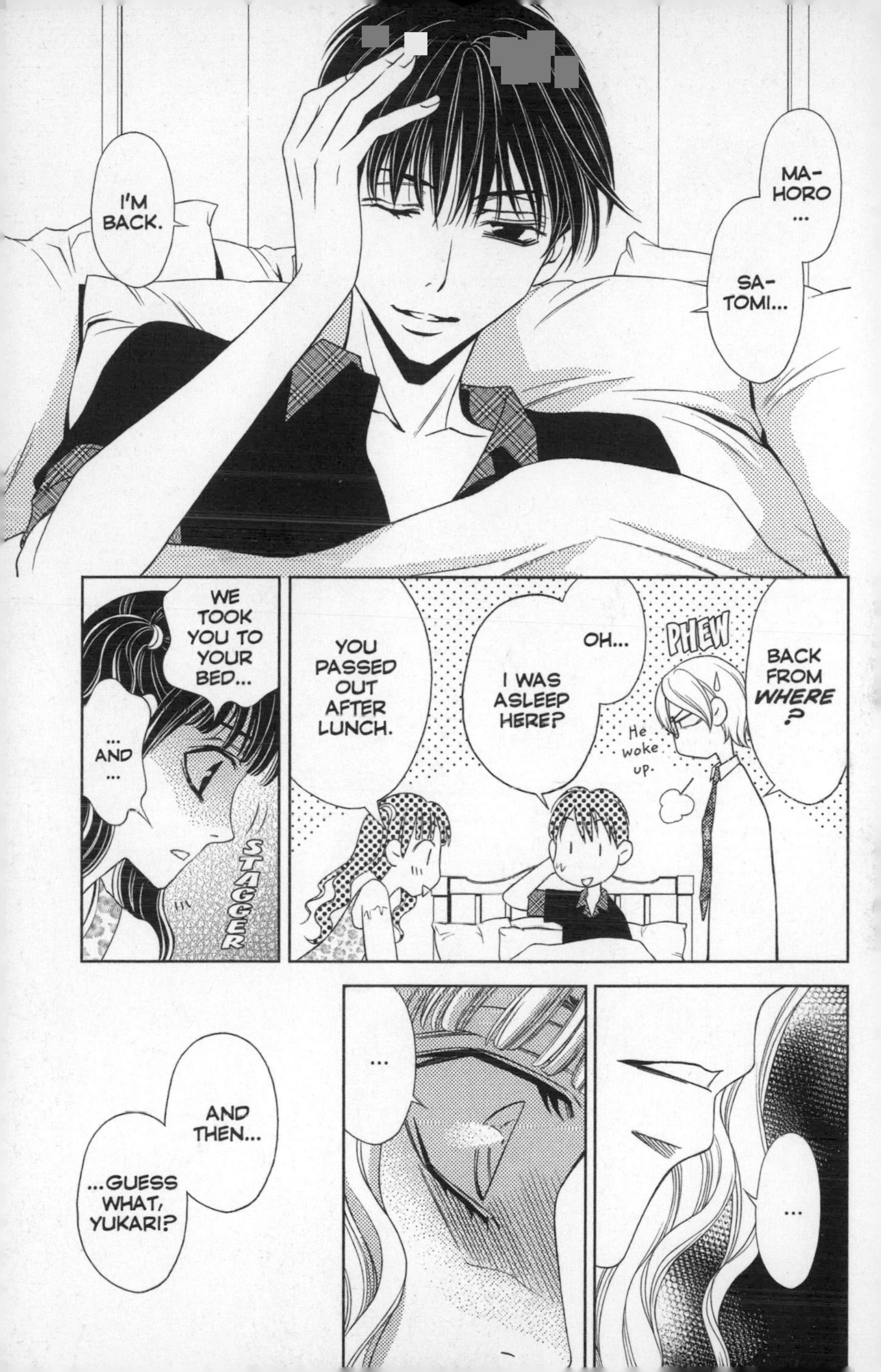
MA-HORO...
SA-TOMI...
I'M BACK.
BACK FROM *WHERE*?
PHEW
He woke up.
OH...
I WAS ASLEEP HERE?
YOU PASSED OUT AFTER LUNCH.
WE TOOK YOU TO YOUR BED...
...AND...
STAGGER
...
...
AND THEN...
...GUESS WHAT, YUKARI?

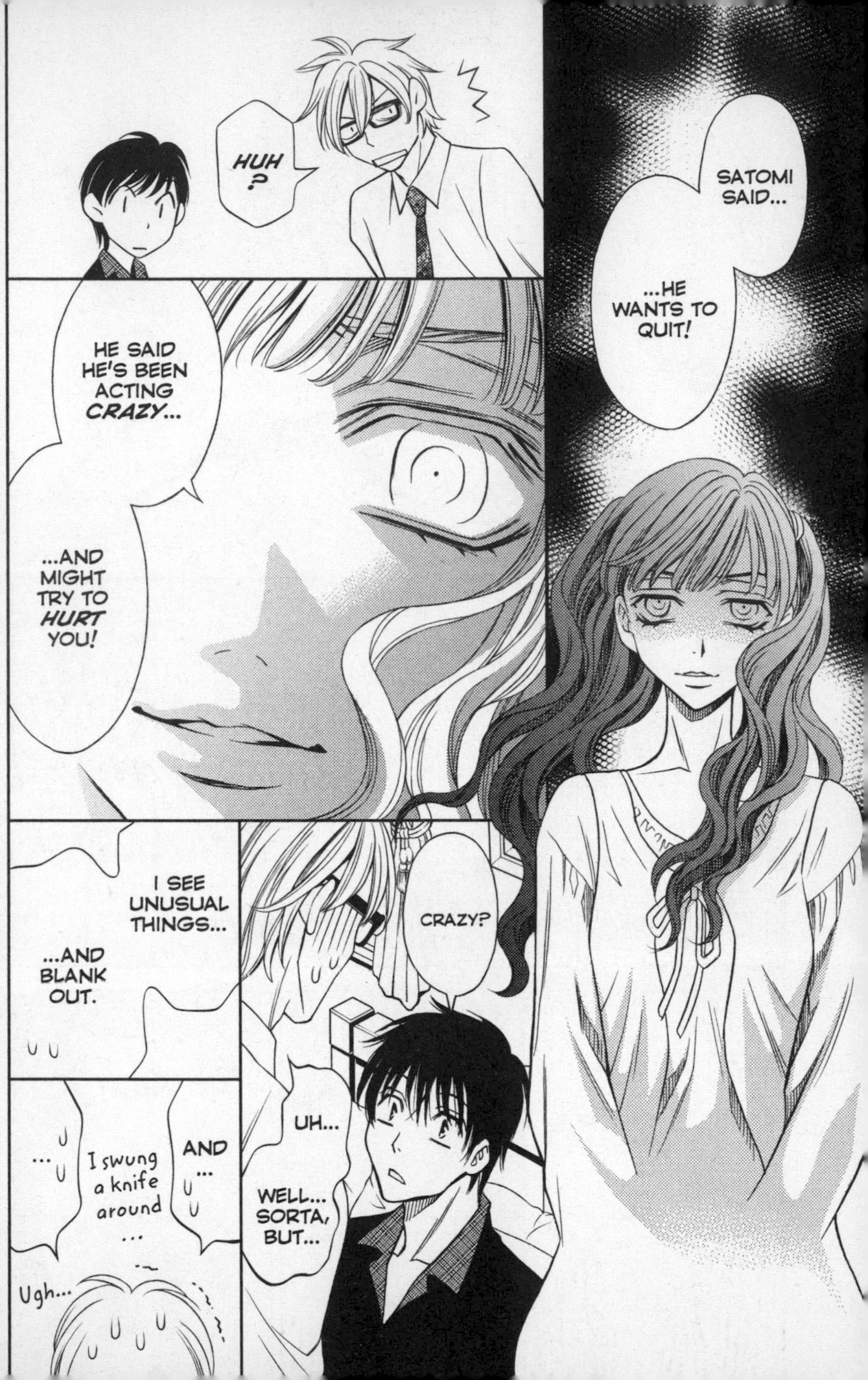
SATOMI SAID...
...HE WANTS TO QUIT!
HUH?
HE SAID HE'S BEEN ACTING CRAZY...
...AND MIGHT TRY TO HURT YOU!
CRAZY?
UH...
WELL... SORTA, BUT...
I SEE UNUSUAL THINGS...
...AND BLANK OUT.
AND ...
I swung a knife around ...
...
Ugh...

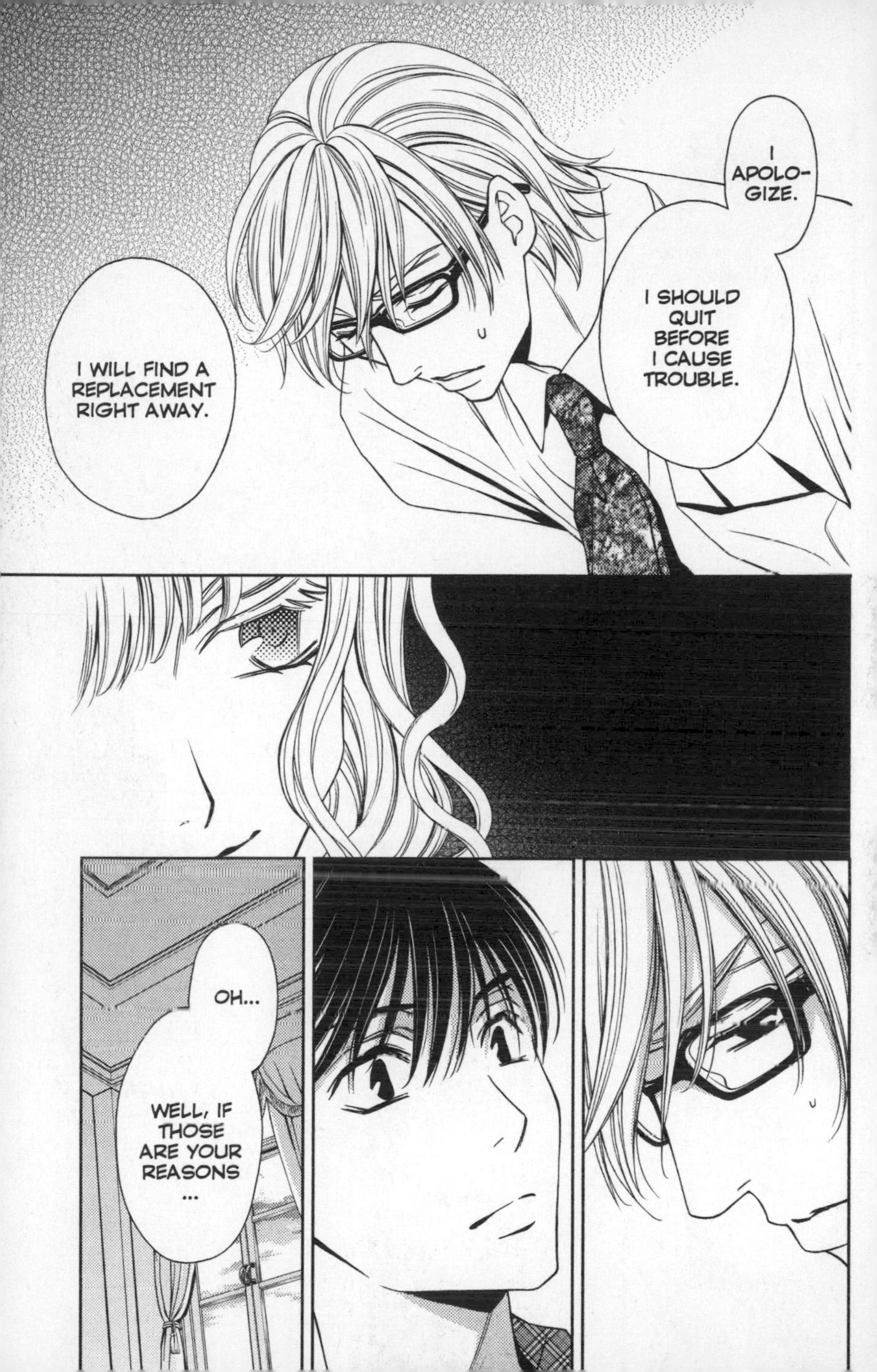
I APOLO-GIZE.
I SHOULD QUIT BEFORE I CAUSE TROUBLE.
I WILL FIND A REPLACEMENT RIGHT AWAY.
OH...
WELL, IF THOSE ARE YOUR REASONS...

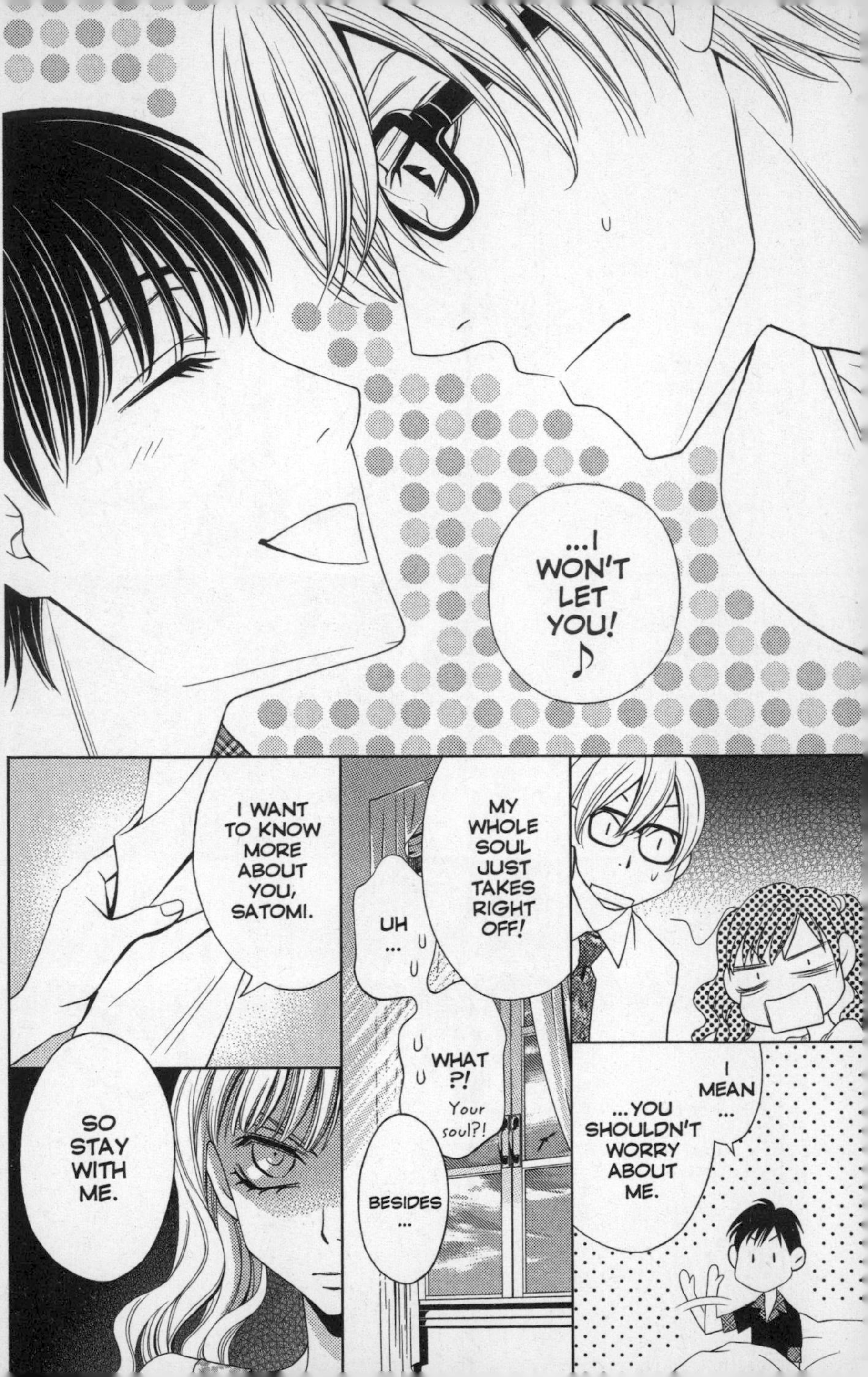
...I WON'T LET YOU! ♪
MY WHOLE SOUL JUST TAKES RIGHT OFF!
I MEAN ...
...YOU SHOULDN'T WORRY ABOUT ME.
UH ...
WHAT ?!
Your soul?!
BESIDES ...
I WANT TO KNOW MORE ABOUT YOU, SATOMI.
SO STAY WITH ME.

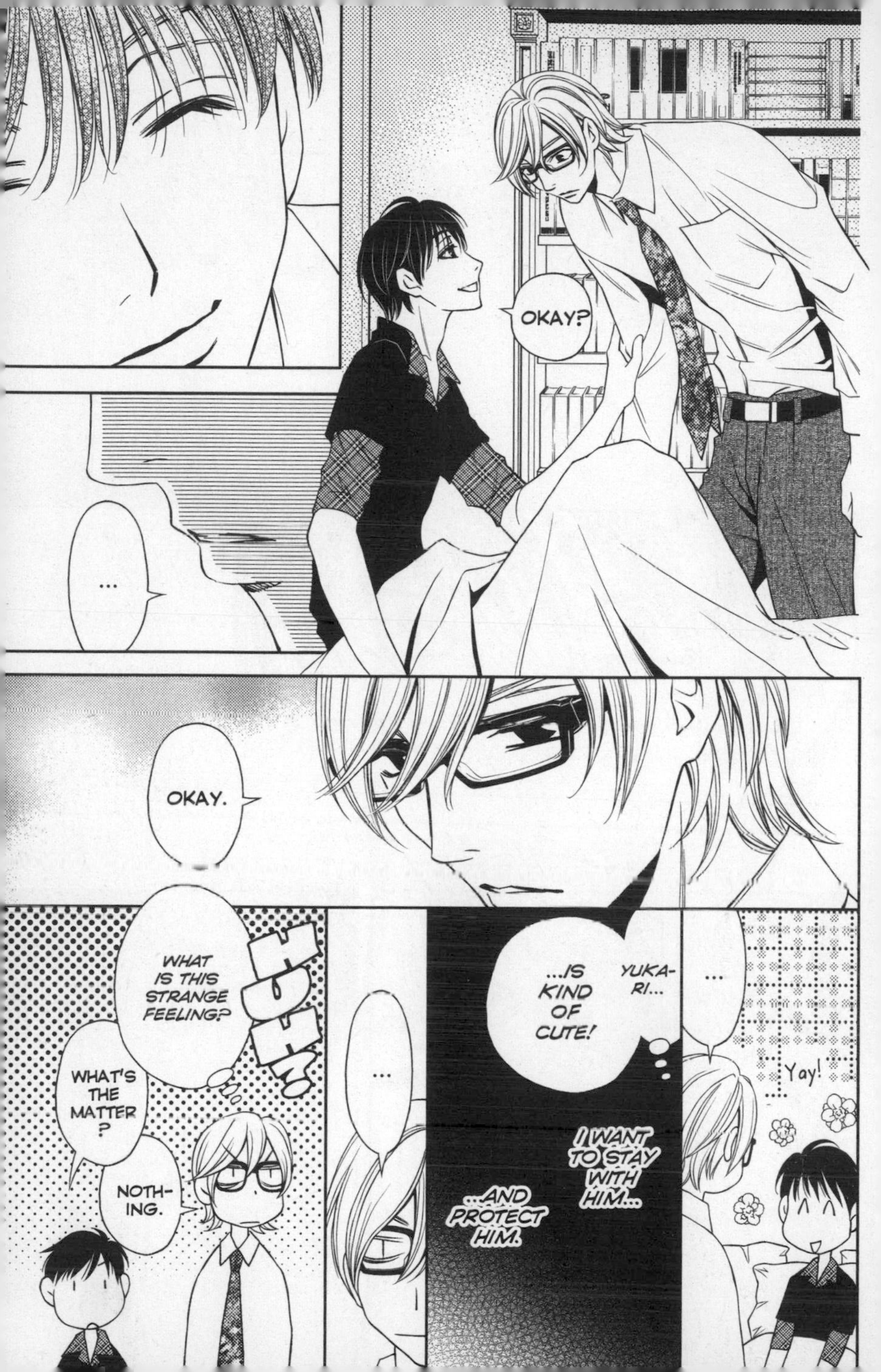
OKAY?
...
OKAY.
...
Yay!
YUKA-RI...
...IS KIND OF CUTE!
I WANT TO STAY WITH HIM...
...AND PROTECT HIM.
...
WHAT IS THIS STRANGE FEELING?
WHAT'S THE MATTER?
NOTH-ING.

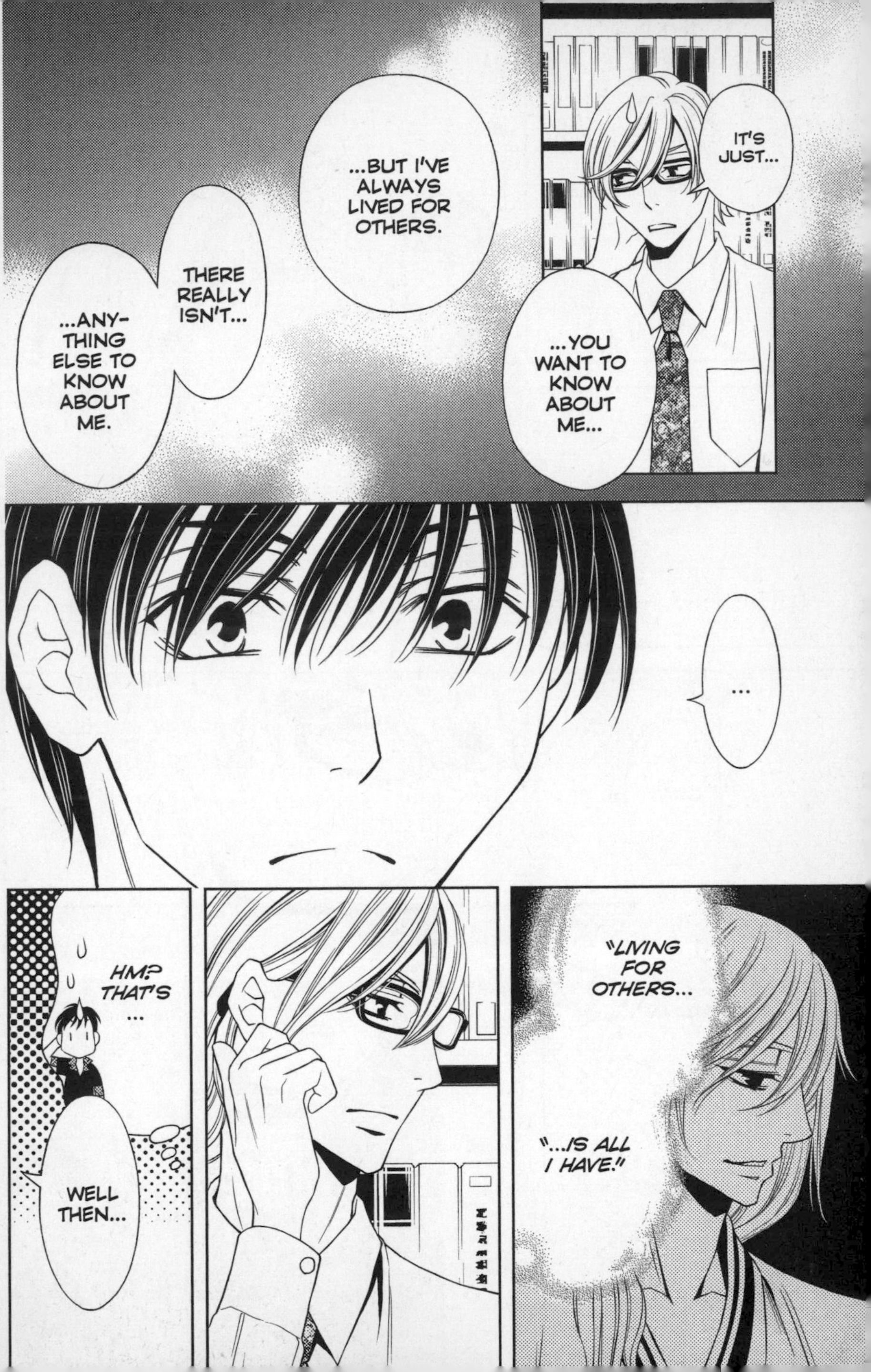
IT'S JUST...
...YOU WANT TO KNOW ABOUT ME...
...BUT I'VE ALWAYS LIVED FOR OTHERS.
THERE REALLY ISN'T...
...ANY-THING ELSE TO KNOW ABOUT ME.
...
"LIVING FOR OTHERS...
"...IS ALL I HAVE."
HM? THAT'S ...
WELL THEN...

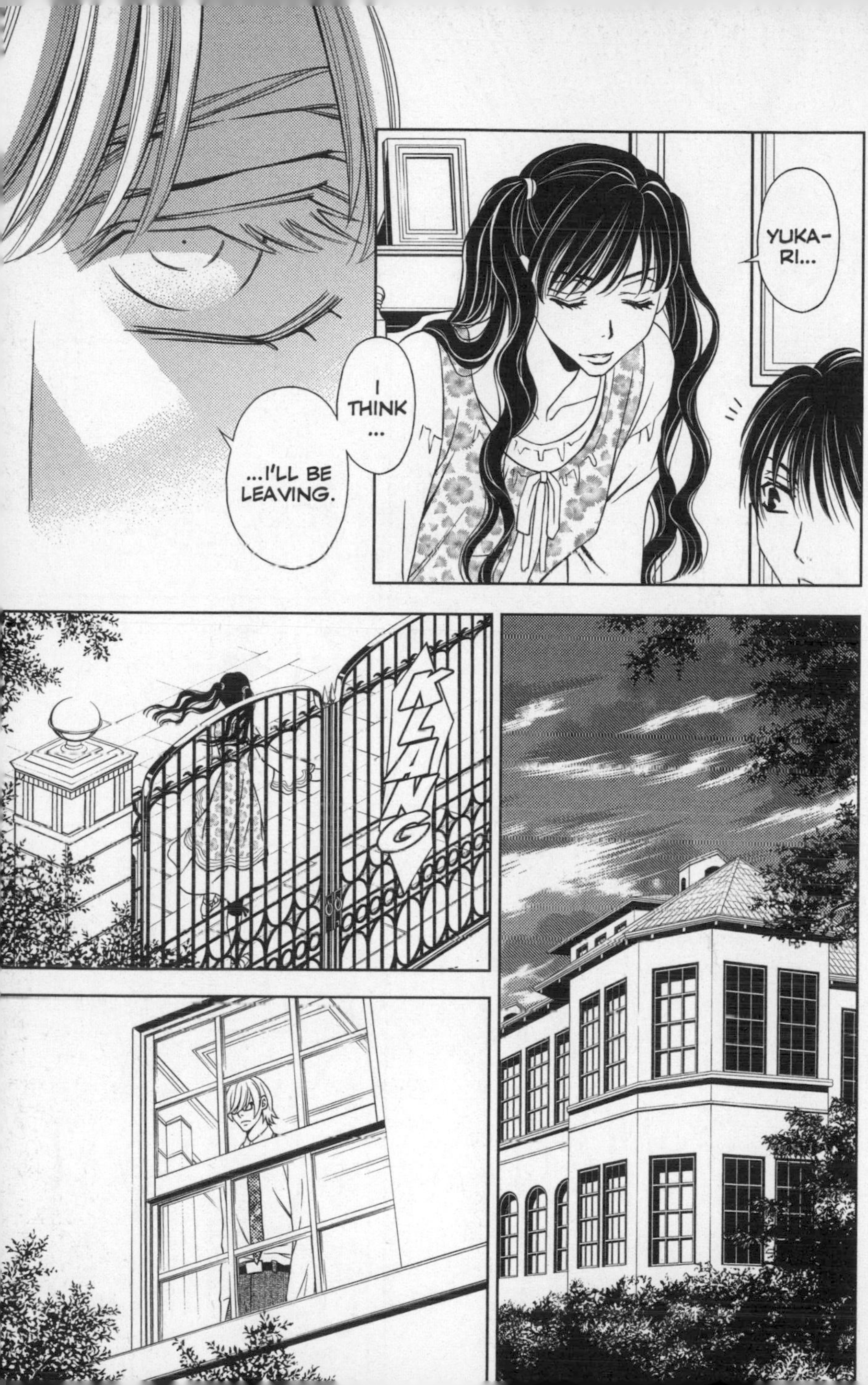
YUKA-RI...
I THINK...
...I'LL BE LEAVING.
KLANG

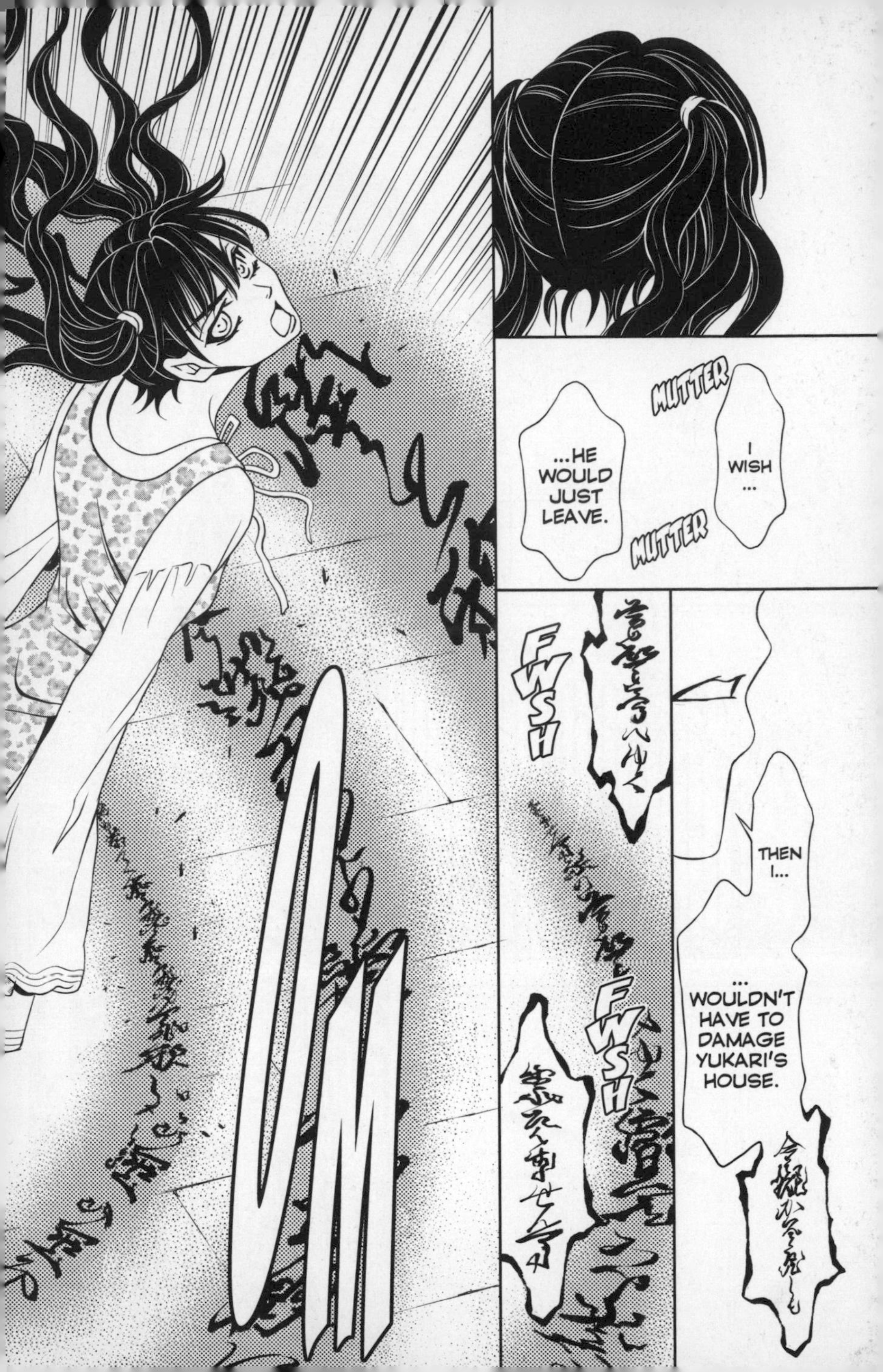
MUTTER
I WISH...
...HE WOULD JUST LEAVE.
MUTTER
FWSH
THEN I...
...WOULDN'T HAVE TO DAMAGE YUKARI'S HOUSE.
FWSH

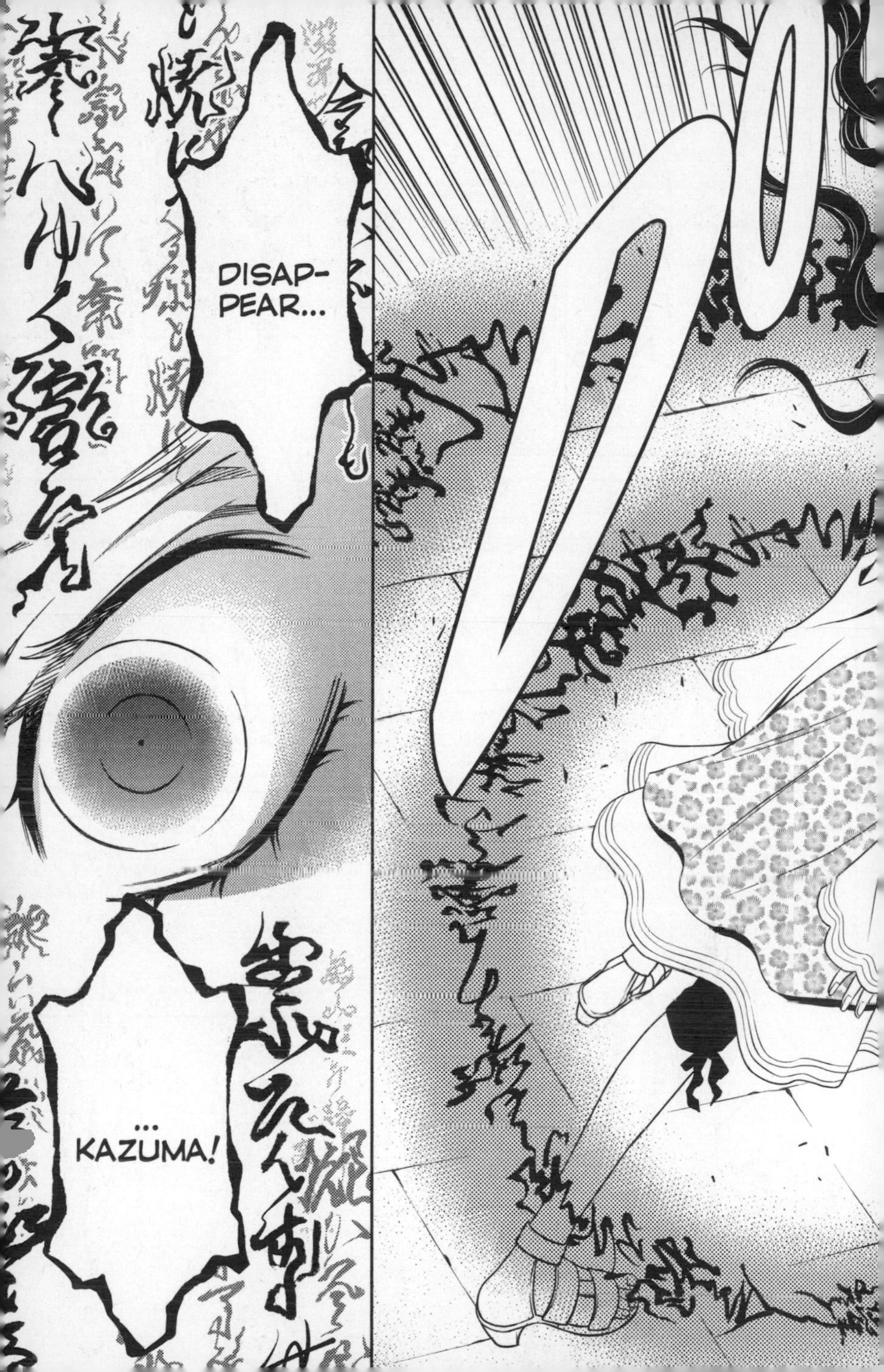
DISAP-PEAR...
...KAZUMA!

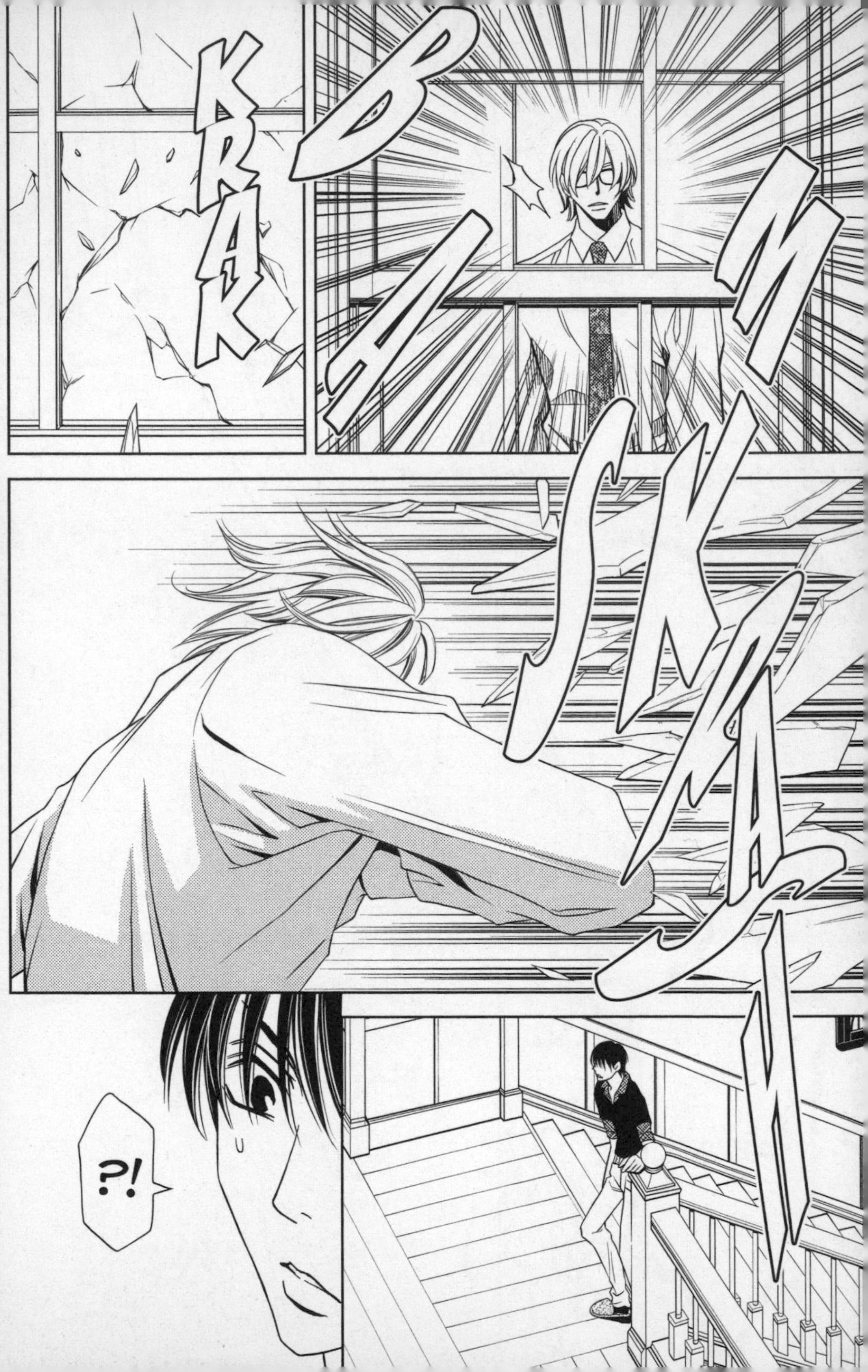
BAM
KRAK
SMASH
?!

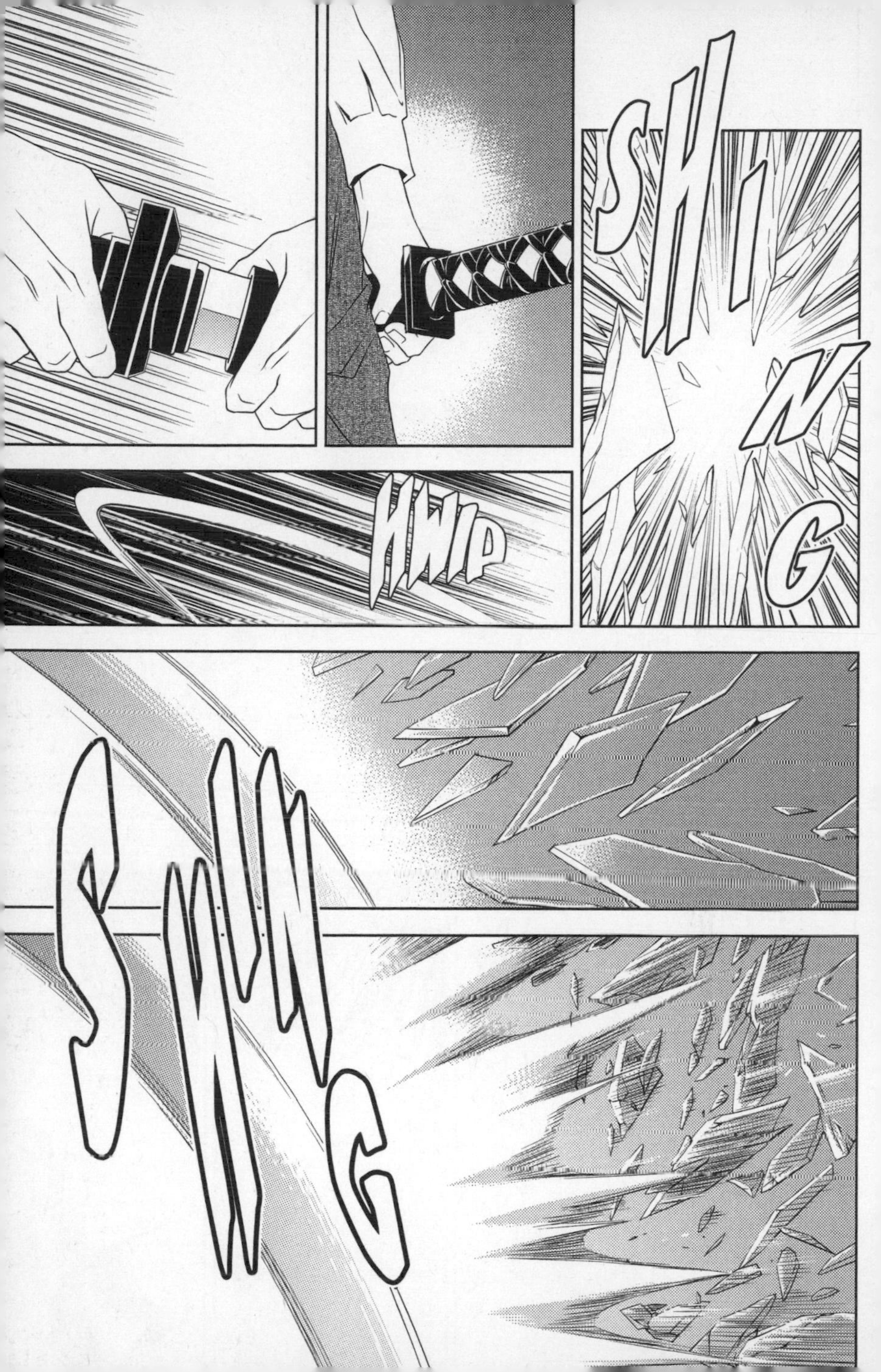
SHING
WHIP
SHING

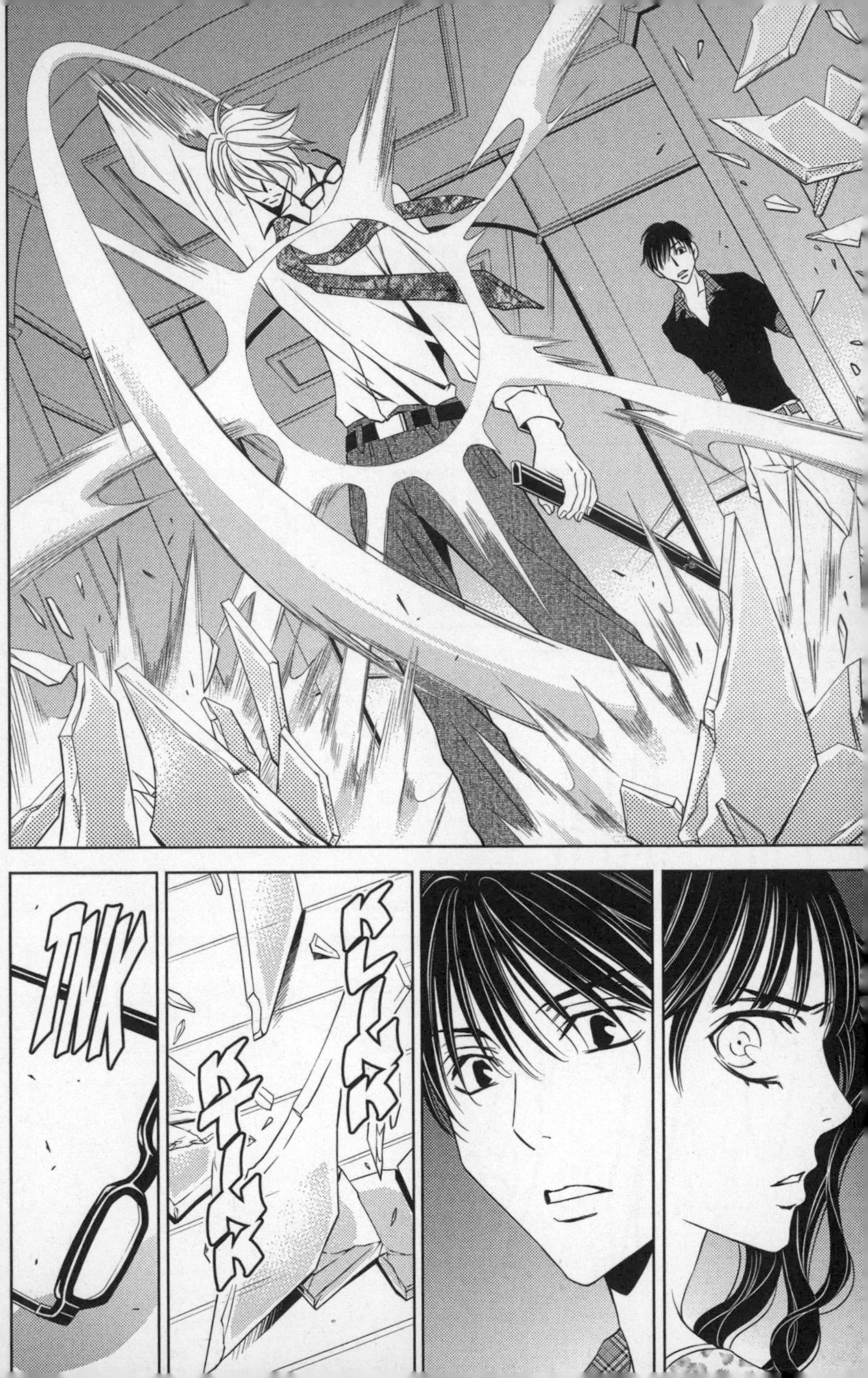
KLINK
KLINK
TINK

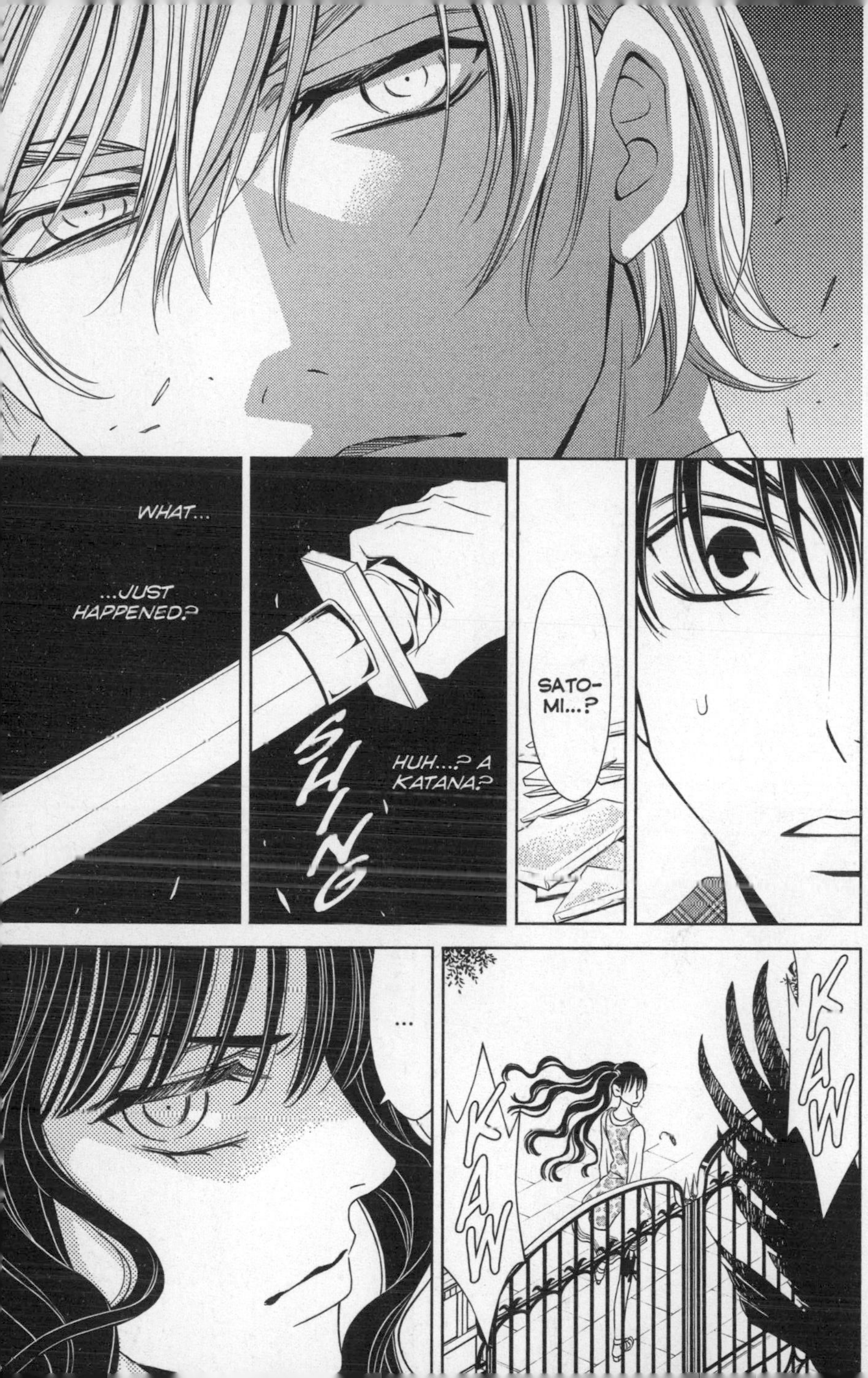
SATO-MI...?
HUH...? A KATANA?
SHING
WHAT...
...JUST HAPPENED?
KAW
KAW
...

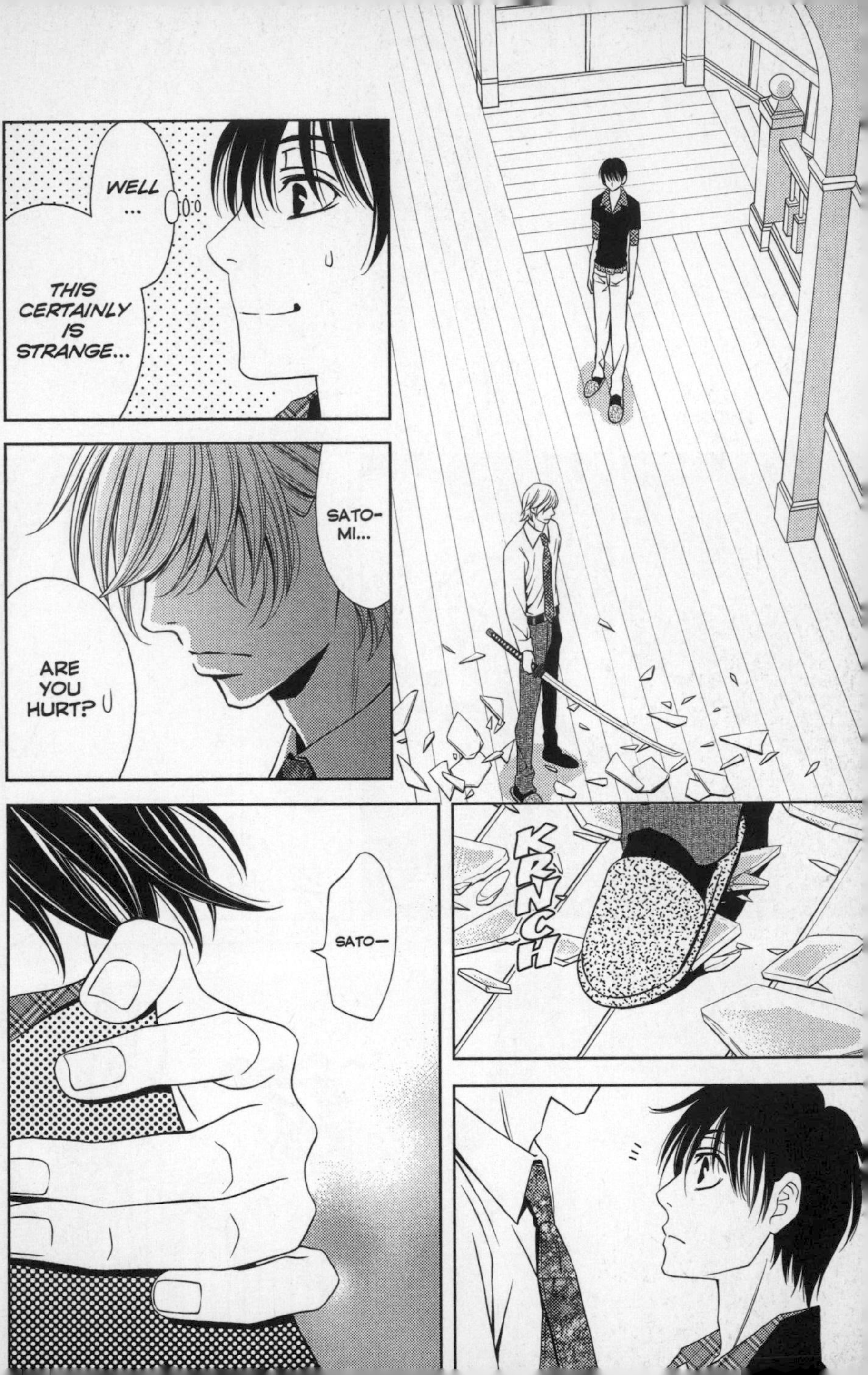
WELL ...
THIS CERTAINLY IS STRANGE...
SATO-MI...
ARE YOU HURT?
KRNCH
SATO—

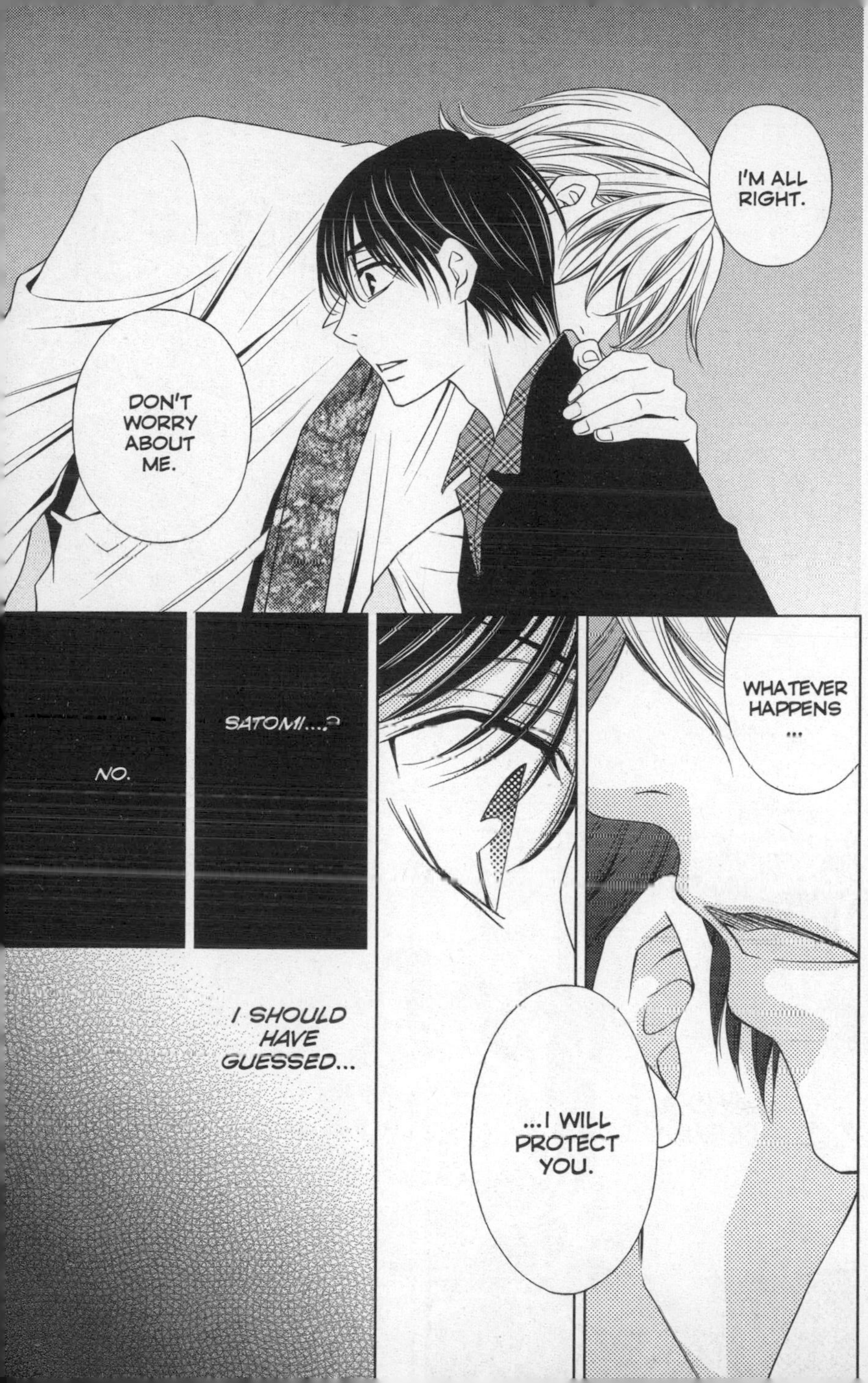
I'M ALL RIGHT.
DON'T WORRY ABOUT ME.
WHATEVER HAPPENS ...
...I WILL PROTECT YOU.
SATOMI...?
NO.
I SHOULD HAVE GUESSED...

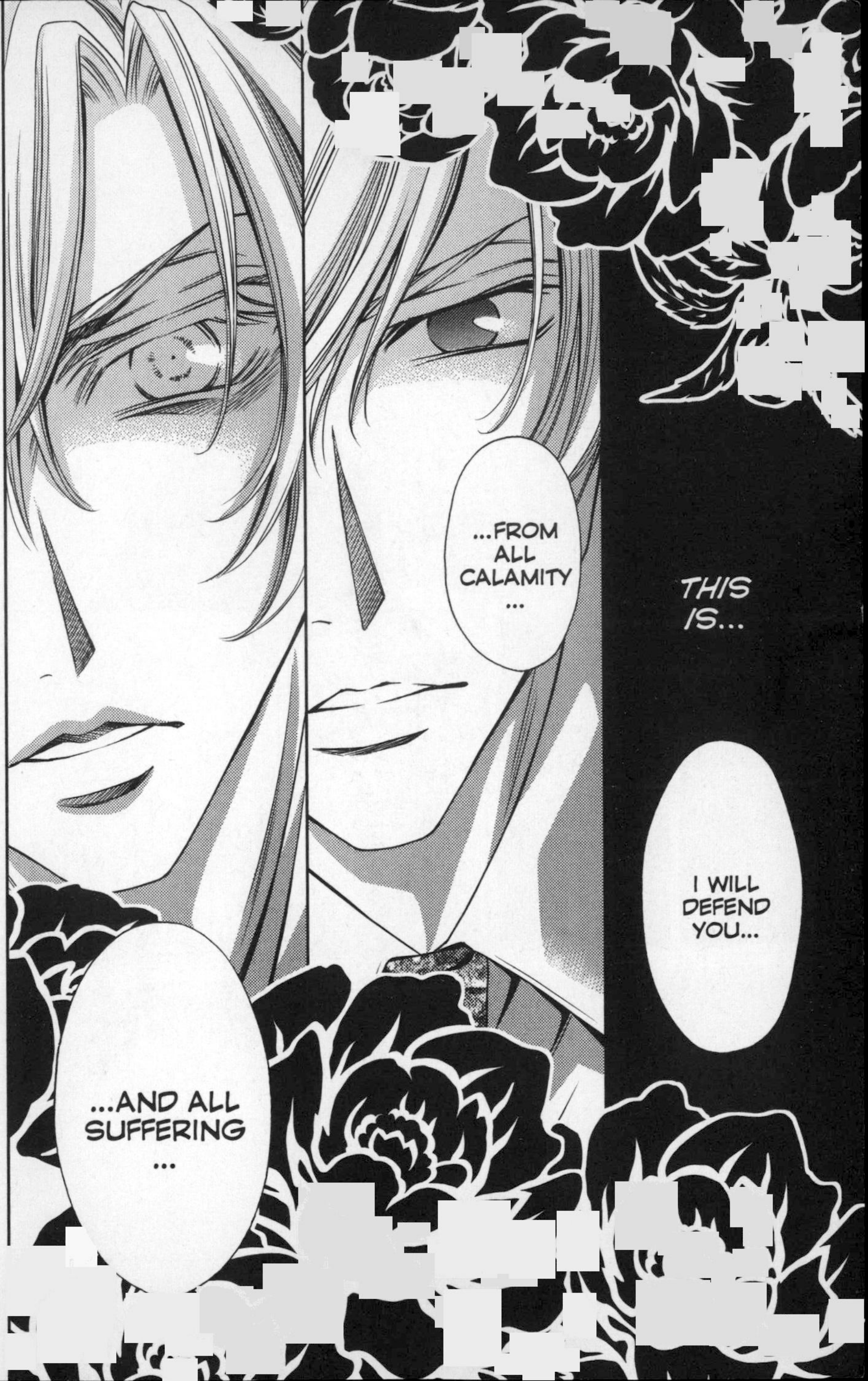
THIS IS...
I WILL DEFEND YOU...
...FROM ALL CALAMITY...
...AND ALL SUFFERING...

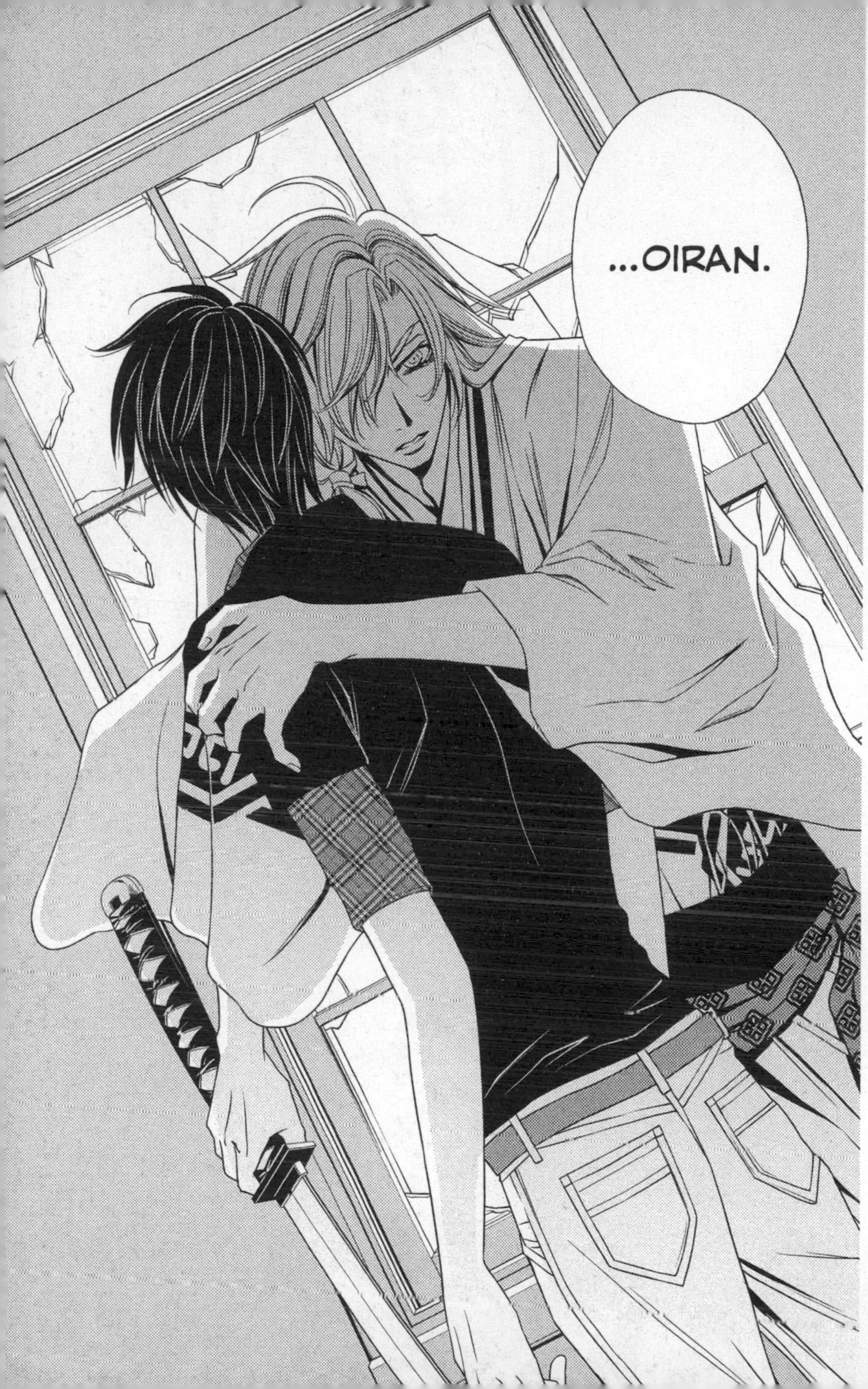
...OIRAN.

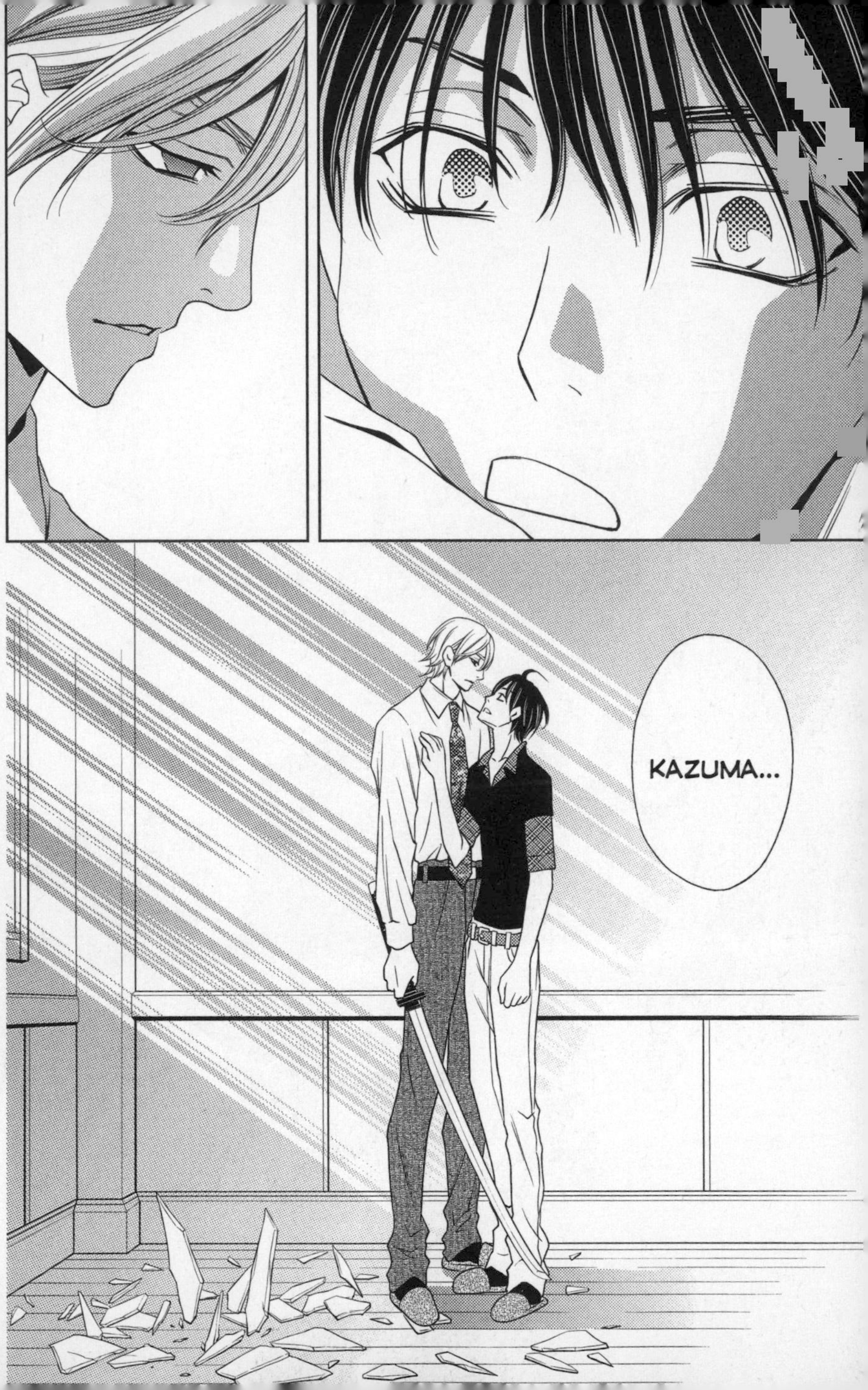
KAZUMA...

Chapter 12

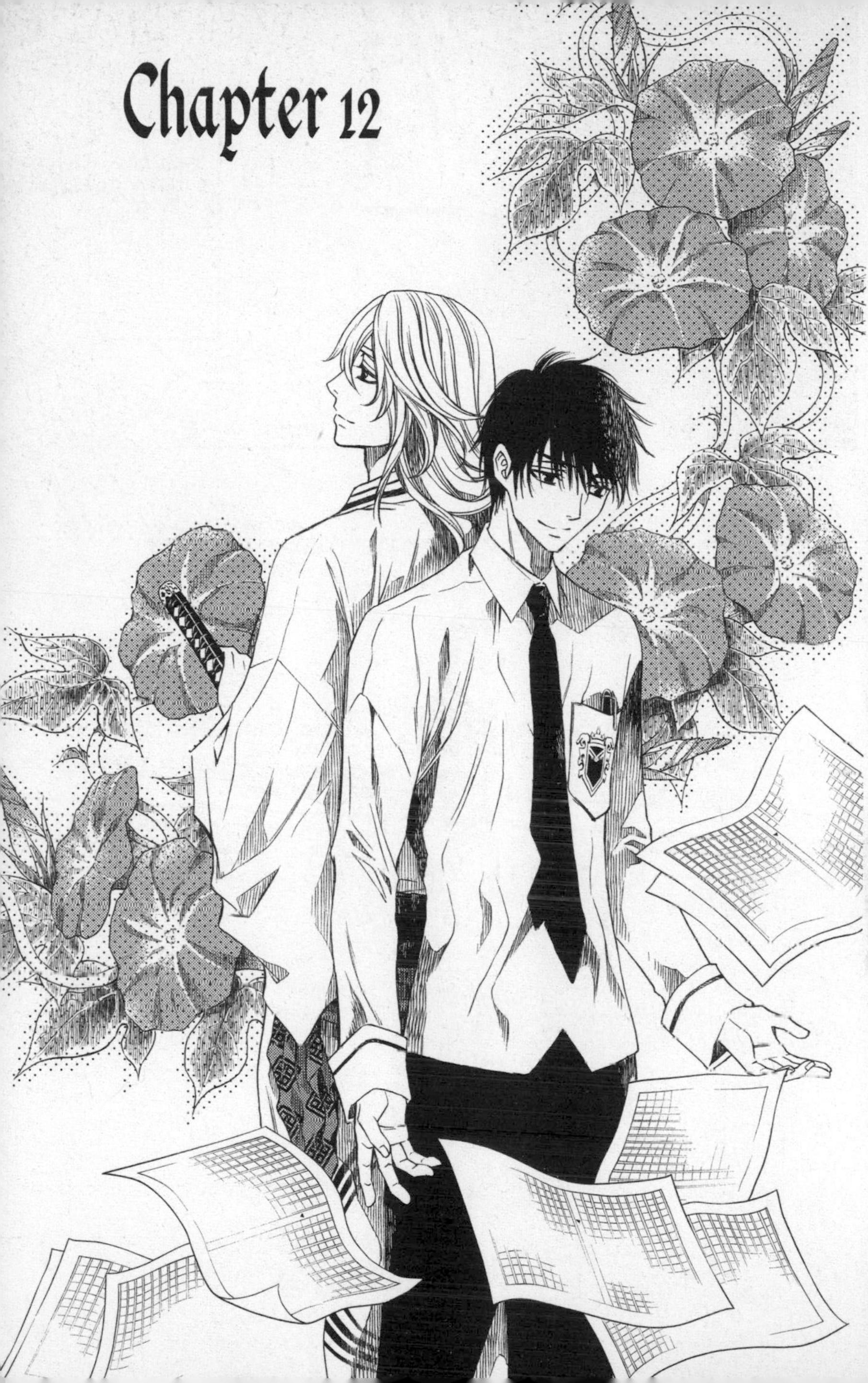

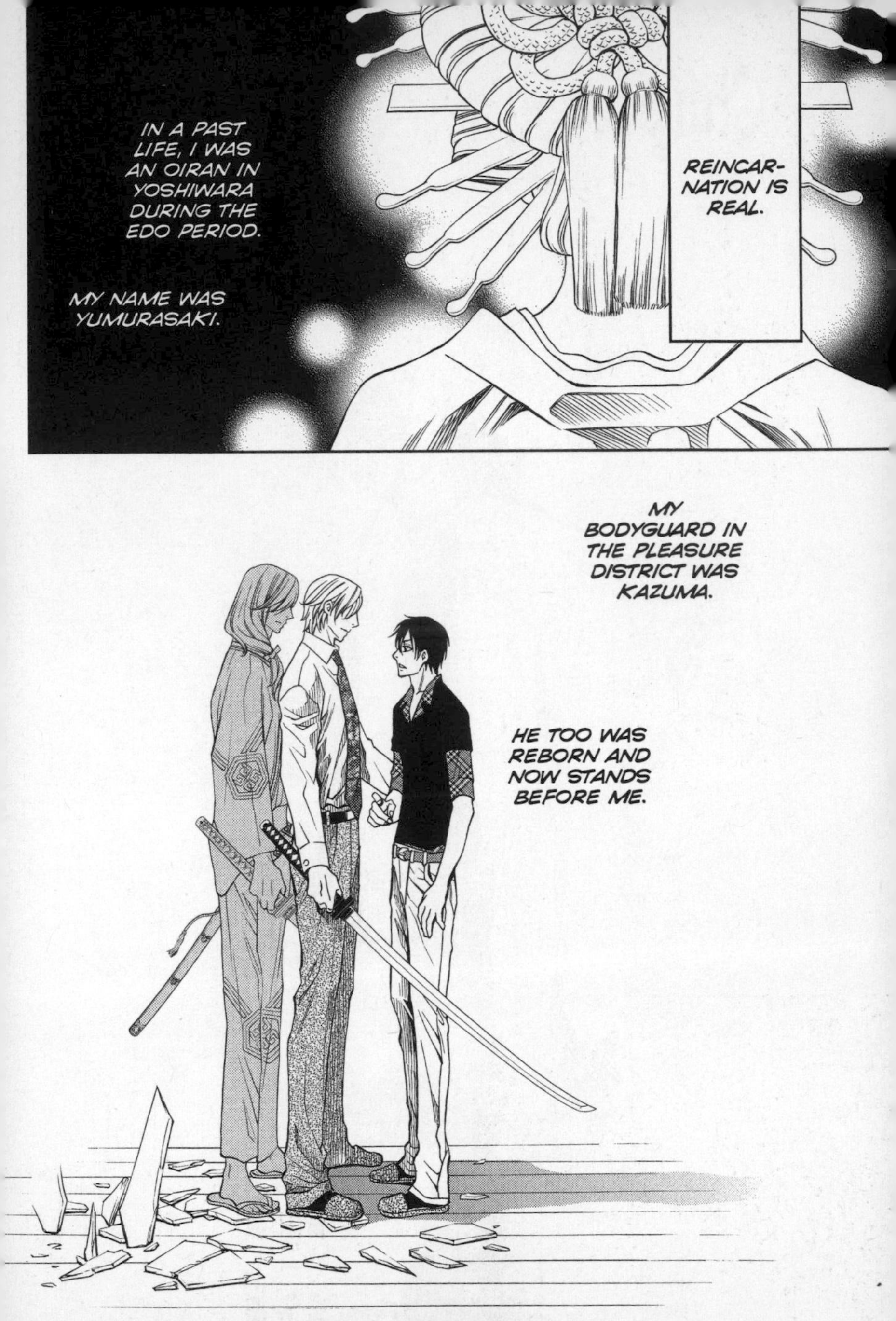
REINCARNATION IS REAL.
IN A PAST LIFE, I WAS AN OIRAN IN YOSHIWARA DURING THE EDO PERIOD.
MY NAME WAS YUMURASAKI.
MY BODYGUARD IN THE PLEASURE DISTRICT WAS KAZUMA.
HE TOO WAS REBORN AND NOW STANDS BEFORE ME.

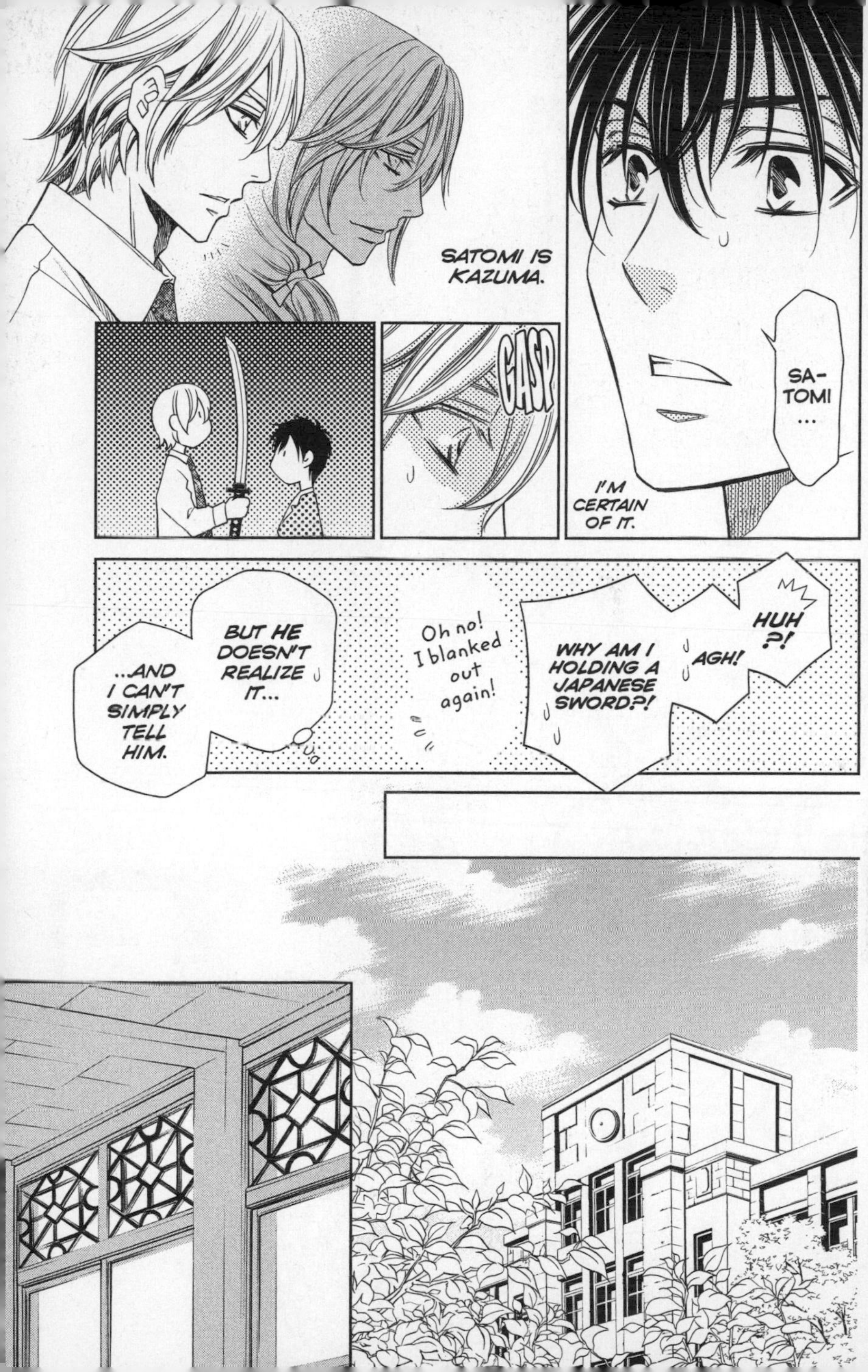
SA-TOMI...
I'M CERTAIN OF IT.
SATOMI IS KAZUMA.
GASP
HUH?!
AGH!
WHY AM I HOLDING A JAPANESE SWORD?!
Oh no! I blanked out again!
BUT HE DOESN'T REALIZE IT...
...AND I CAN'T SIMPLY TELL HIM.

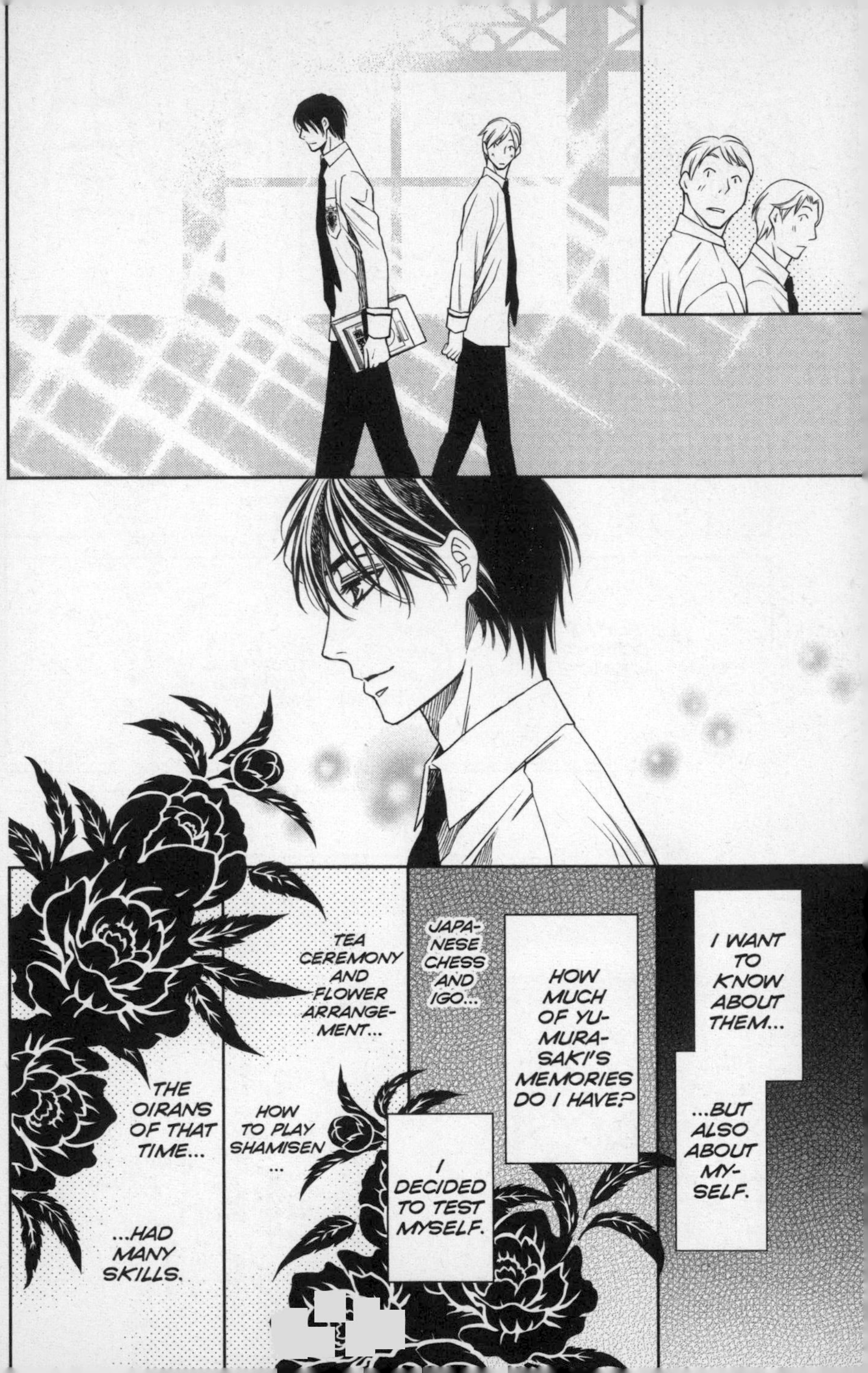
I WANT TO KNOW ABOUT THEM...
...BUT ALSO ABOUT MYSELF.
HOW MUCH OF YUMURASAKI'S MEMORIES DO I HAVE?
JAPANESE CHESS AND IGO...
I DECIDED TO TEST MYSELF.
TEA CEREMONY AND FLOWER ARRANGEMENT...
HOW TO PLAY SHAMISEN...
THE OIRANS OF THAT TIME...
...HAD MANY SKILLS.

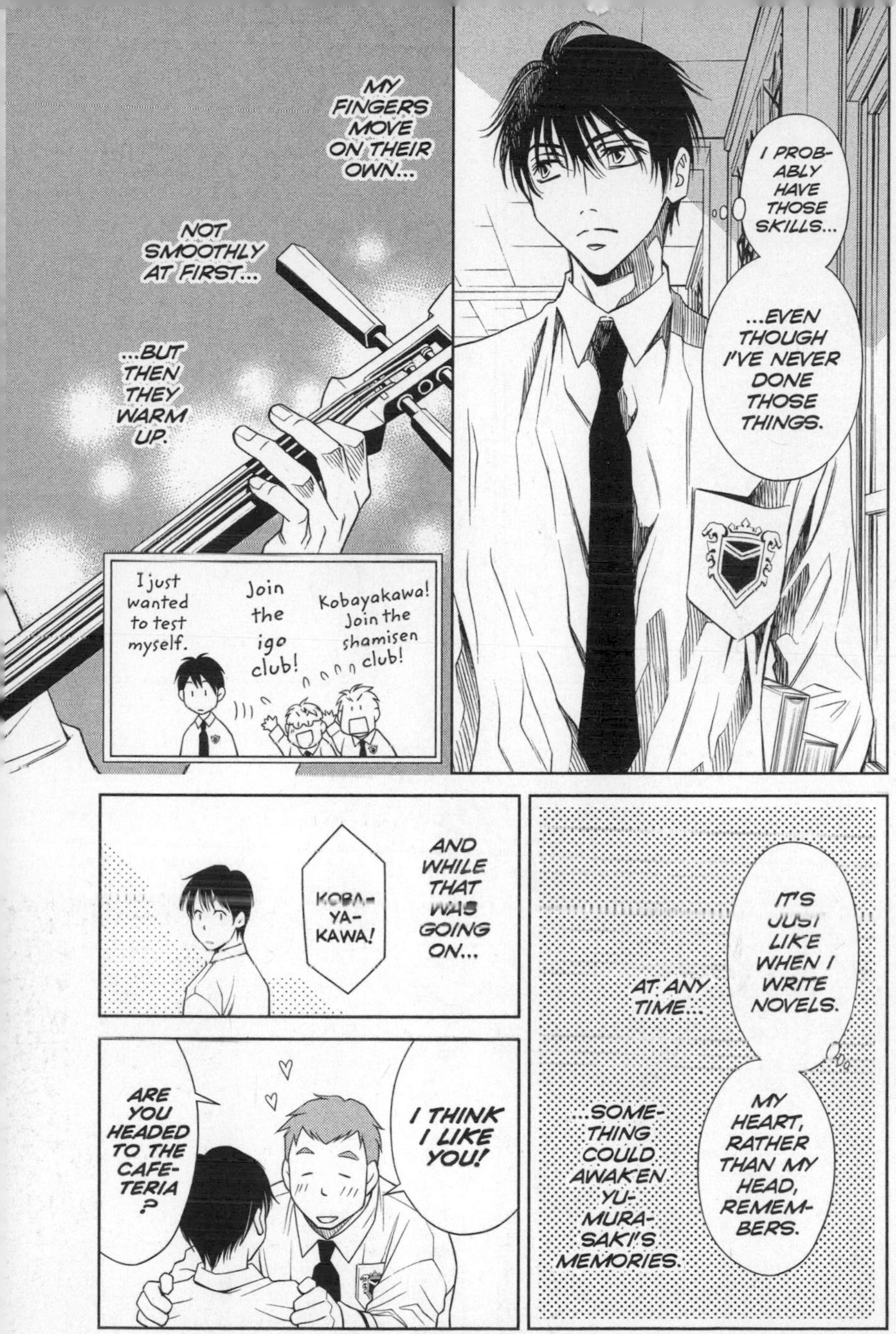
I PROBABLY HAVE THOSE SKILLS...
...EVEN THOUGH I'VE NEVER DONE THOSE THINGS.
MY FINGERS MOVE ON THEIR OWN...
NOT SMOOTHLY AT FIRST...
...BUT THEN THEY WARM UP.
Kobayakawa! Join the shamisen club!
Join the igo club!
I just wanted to test myself.
IT'S JUST LIKE WHEN I WRITE NOVELS.
AT ANY TIME...
MY HEART, RATHER THAN MY HEAD, REMEMBERS.
...SOMETHING COULD AWAKEN YUMURASAKI'S MEMORIES.
AND WHILE THAT WAS GOING ON...
KOBAYAKAWA!
I THINK I LIKE YOU!
ARE YOU HEADED TO THE CAFETERIA?

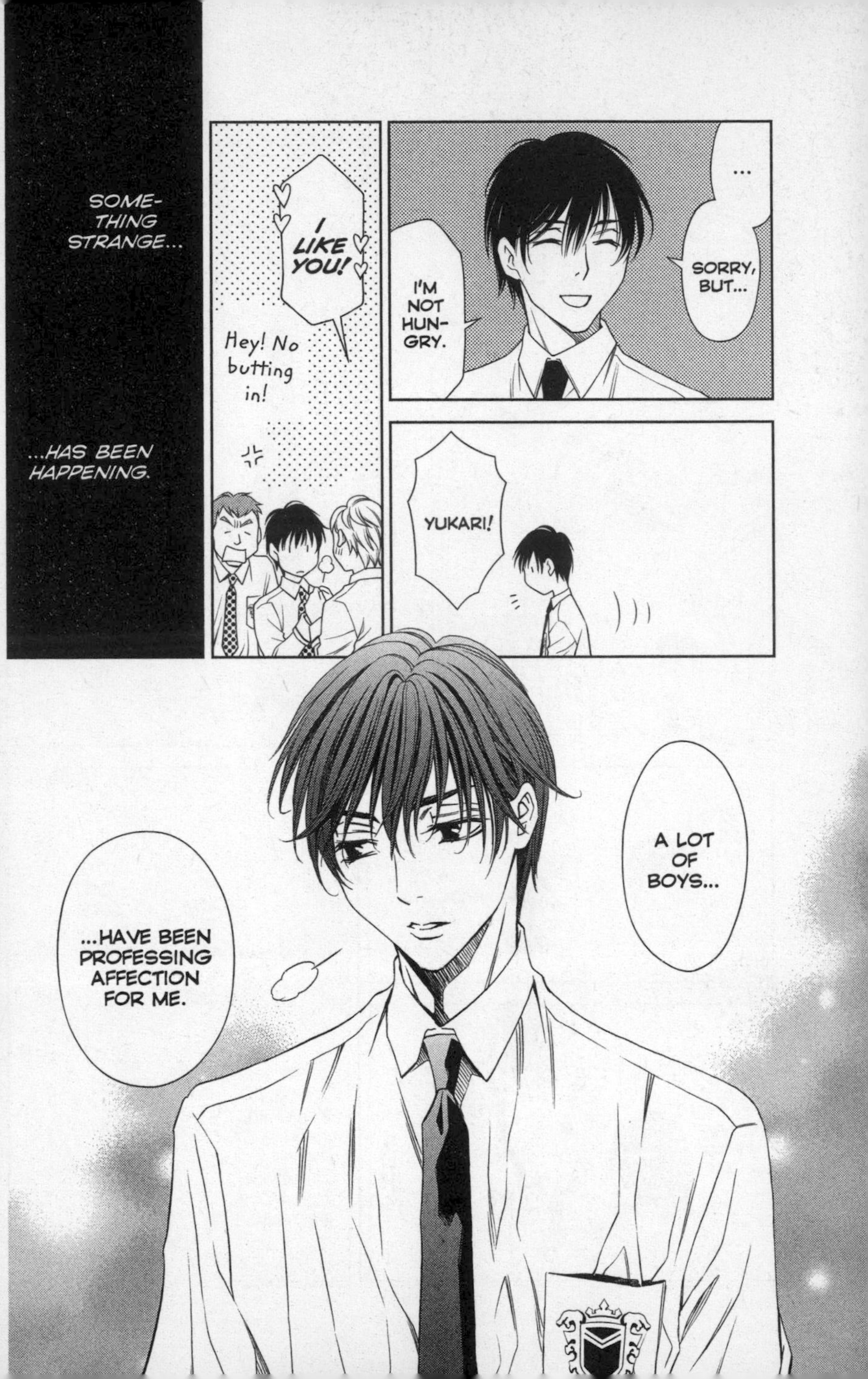
...
SORRY, BUT...
I'M NOT HUNGRY.
YUKARI!
I LIKE YOU!
Hey! No butting in!
SOME-THING STRANGE...
...HAS BEEN HAPPENING.
A LOT OF BOYS...
...HAVE BEEN PROFESSING AFFECTION FOR ME.

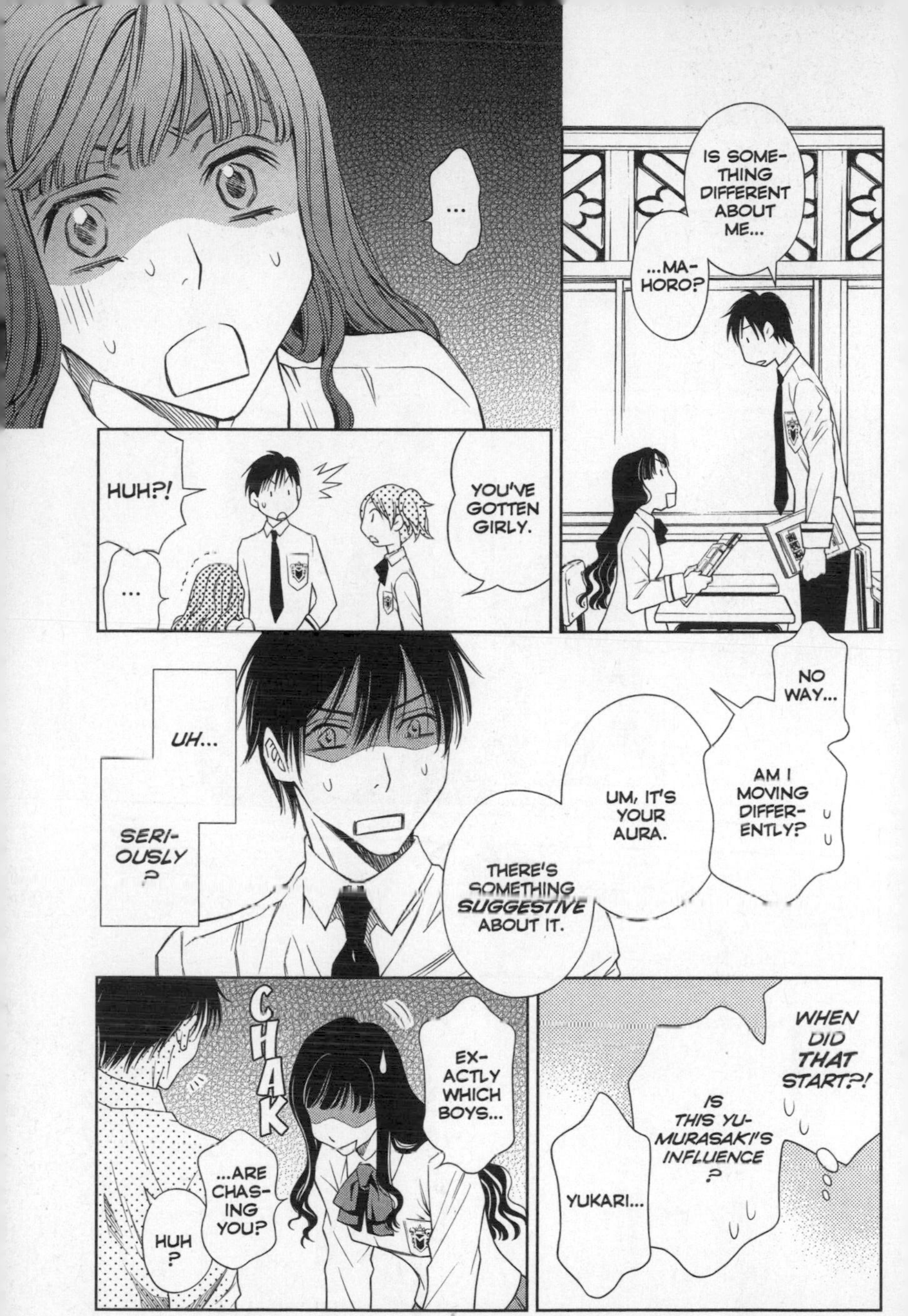
IS SOMETHING DIFFERENT ABOUT ME...
...MAHORO?
...
YOU'VE GOTTEN GIRLY.
HUH?!
...
NO WAY...
AM I MOVING DIFFERENTLY?
UM, IT'S YOUR AURA.
THERE'S SOMETHING *SUGGESTIVE* ABOUT IT.
UH...
SERIOUSLY?
WHEN DID THAT START?!
IS THIS YUMURASAKI'S INFLUENCE?
YUKARI...
CHAK
EXACTLY WHICH BOYS...
...ARE CHASING YOU?
HUH?

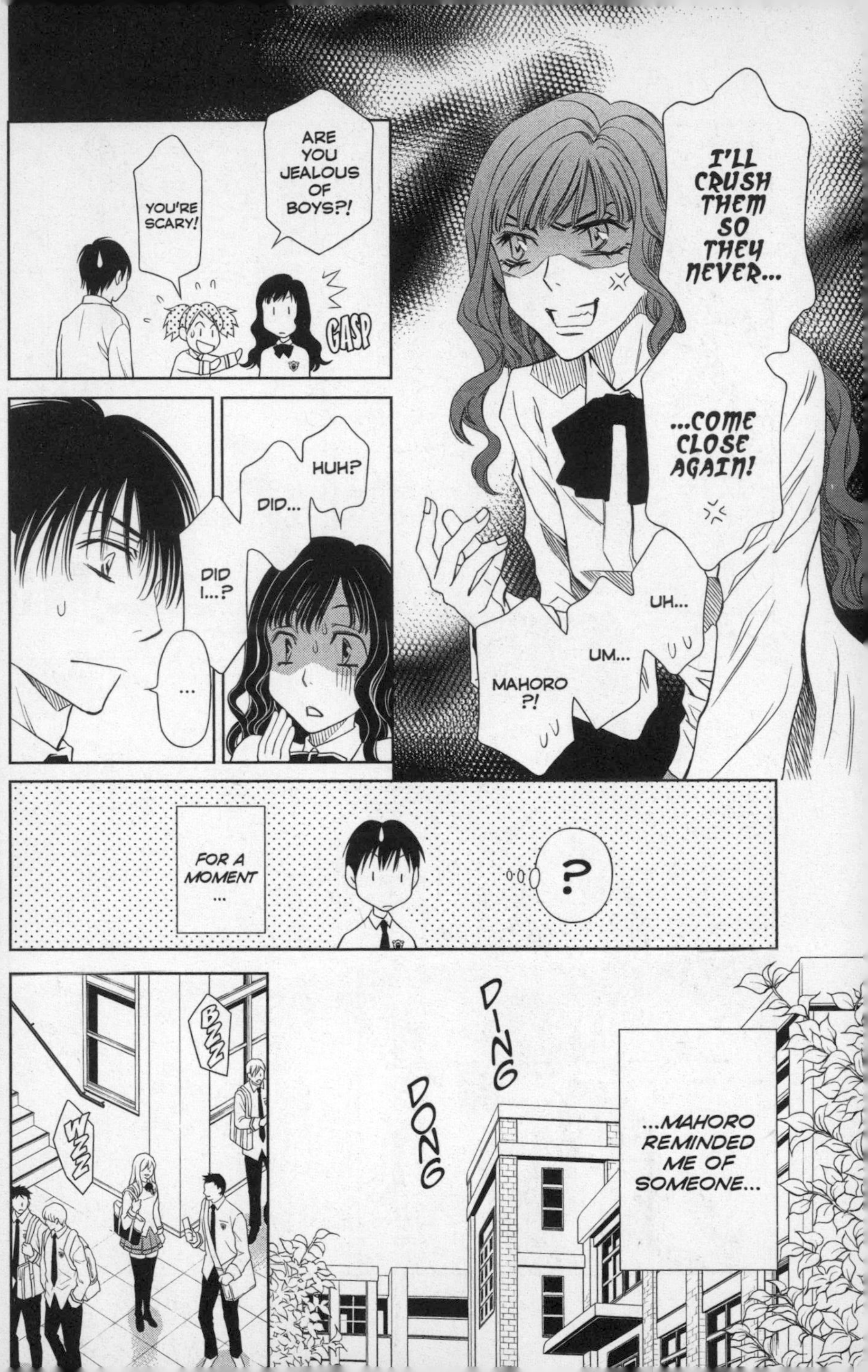
I'LL CRUSH THEM SO THEY NEVER...
...COME CLOSE AGAIN!
UH...
UM...
MAHORO ?!
ARE YOU JEALOUS OF BOYS?!
YOU'RE SCARY!
GASP
HUH?
DID...
DID I...?
...
?
FOR A MOMENT ...
...MAHORO REMINDED ME OF SOMEONE...
DING
DONG
BZZ
WZZ

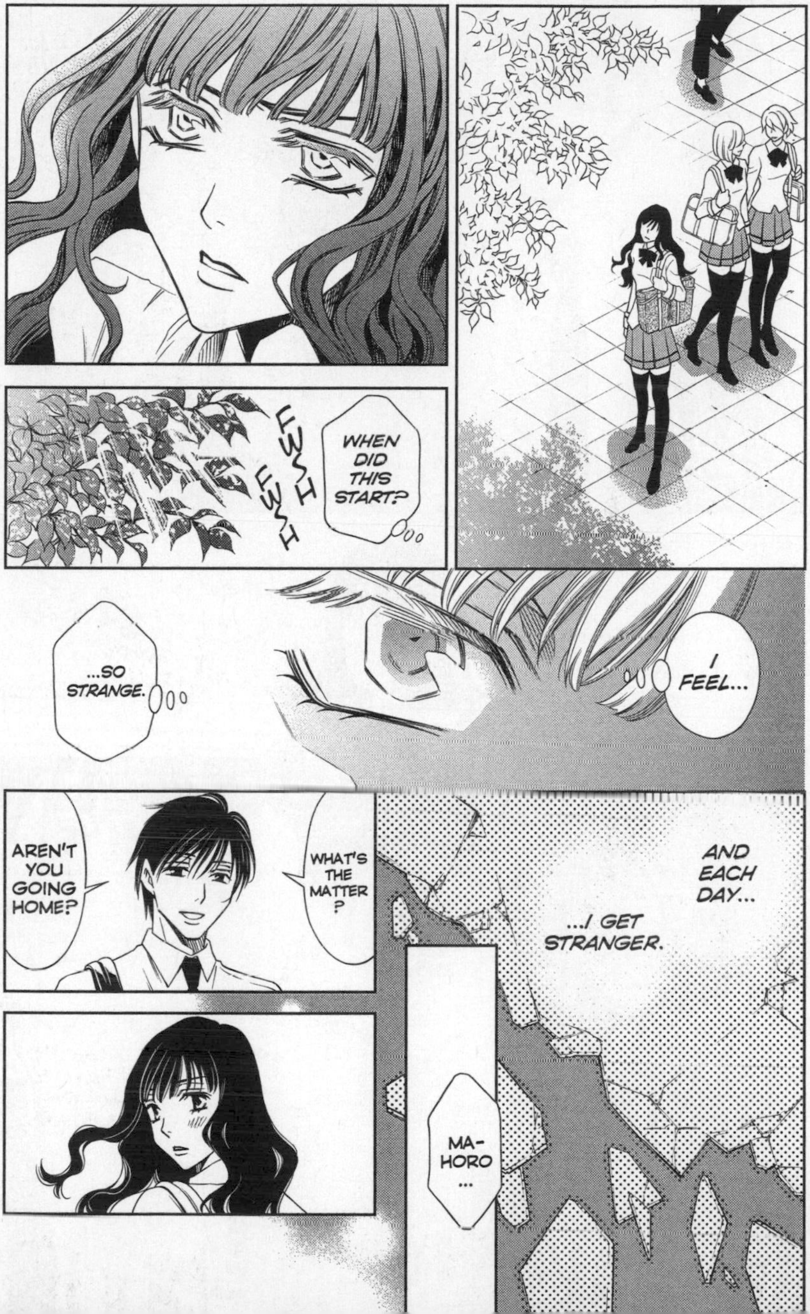

FWSH FWSH
WHEN DID THIS START?
I FEEL...
...SO STRANGE.
AND EACH DAY...
...I GET STRANGER.
MA-HORO...
WHAT'S THE MATTER?
AREN'T YOU GOING HOME?

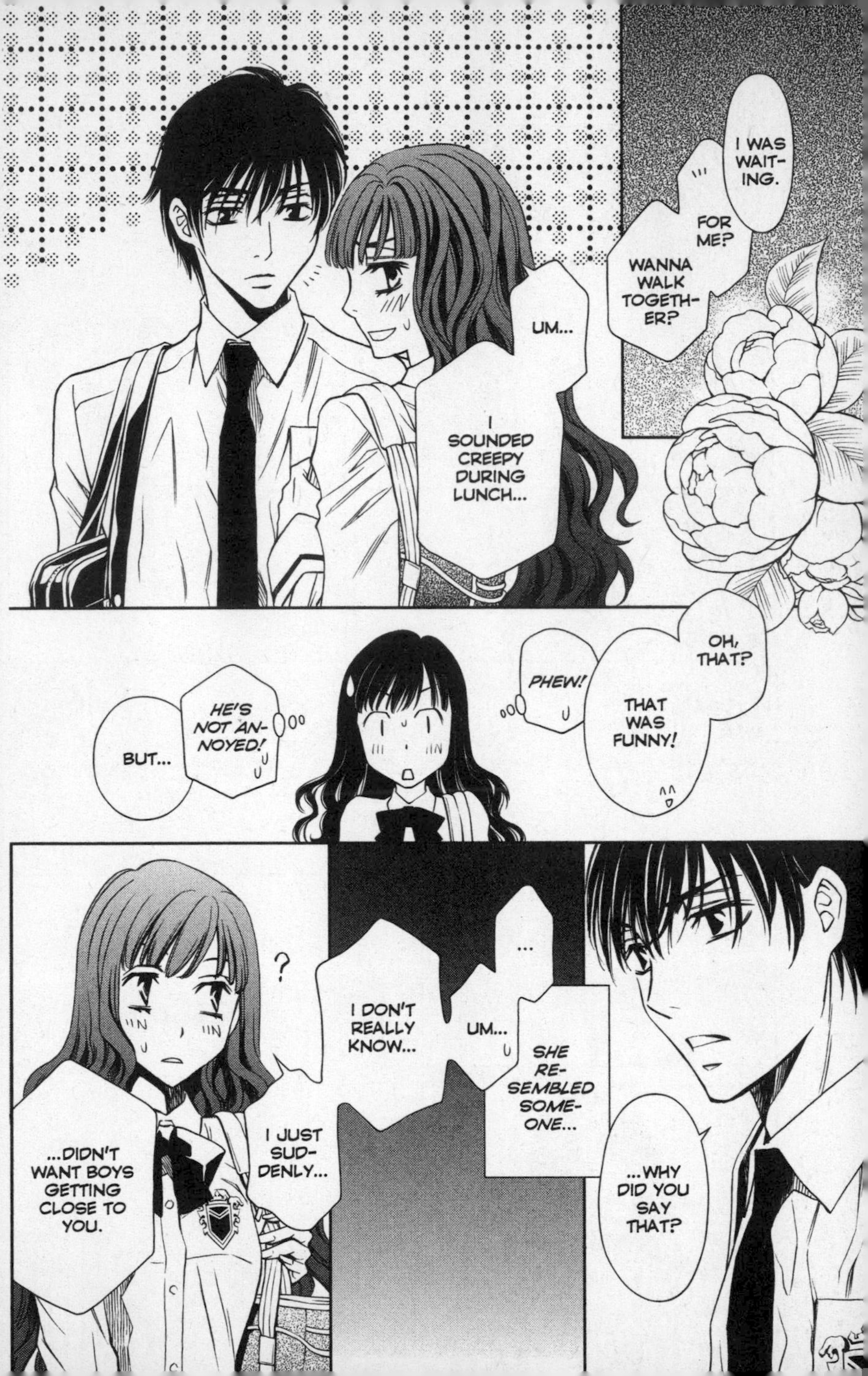
I WAS WAITING.
FOR ME?
WANNA WALK TOGETHER?
UM...
I SOUNDED CREEPY DURING LUNCH...
OH, THAT?
THAT WAS FUNNY!
PHEW!
HE'S NOT ANNOYED!
BUT...
...WHY DID YOU SAY THAT?
...
UM...
SHE RESEMBLED SOMEONE...
I DON'T REALLY KNOW...
I JUST SUDDENLY...
...DIDN'T WANT BOYS GETTING CLOSE TO YOU.

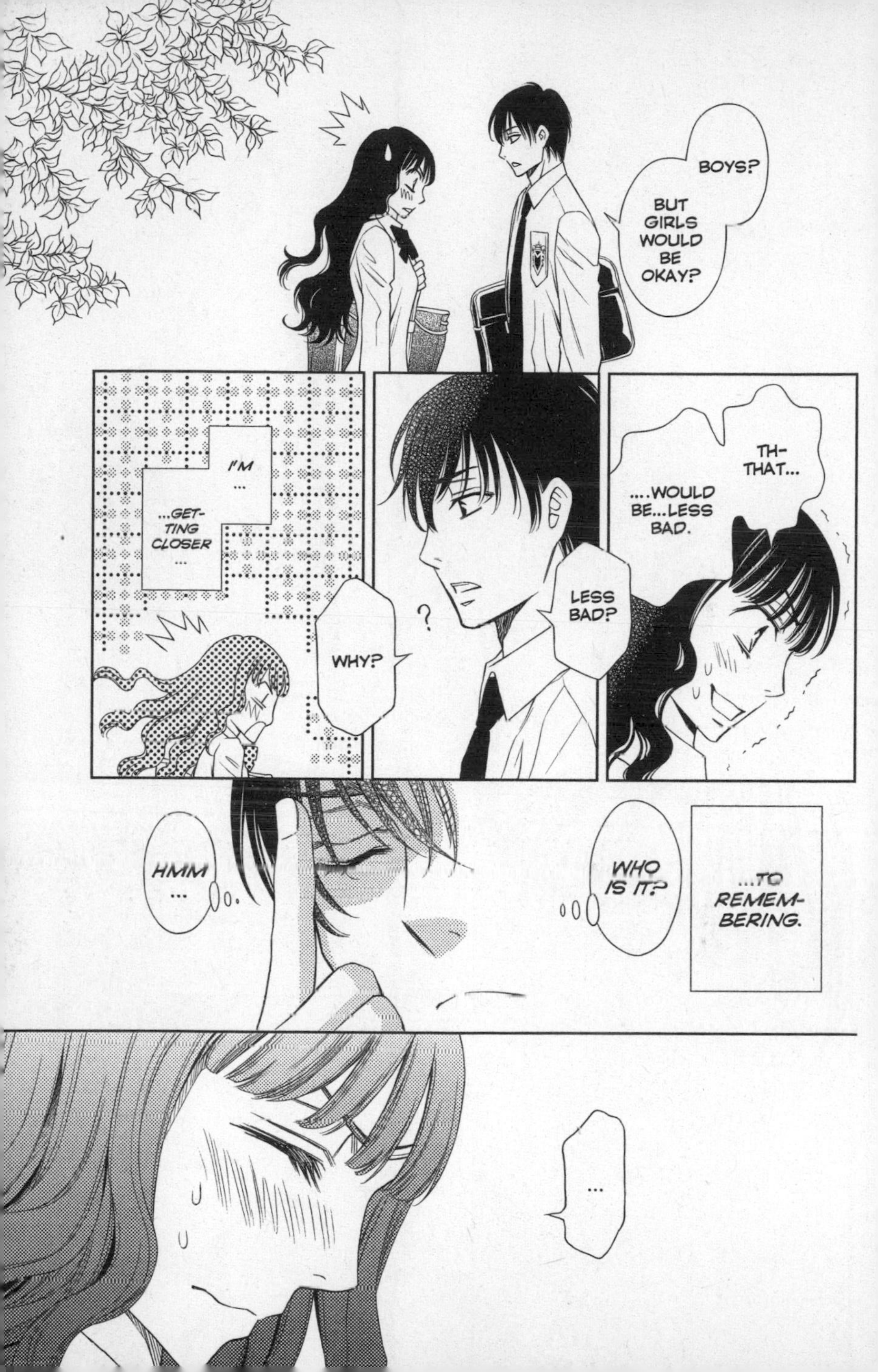
BOYS?
BUT GIRLS WOULD BE OKAY?
TH-THAT...
....WOULD BE...LESS BAD.
LESS BAD?
WHY?
I'M ...
...GET-TING CLOSER ...
...TO REMEM-BERING.
WHO IS IT?
HMM ...
...

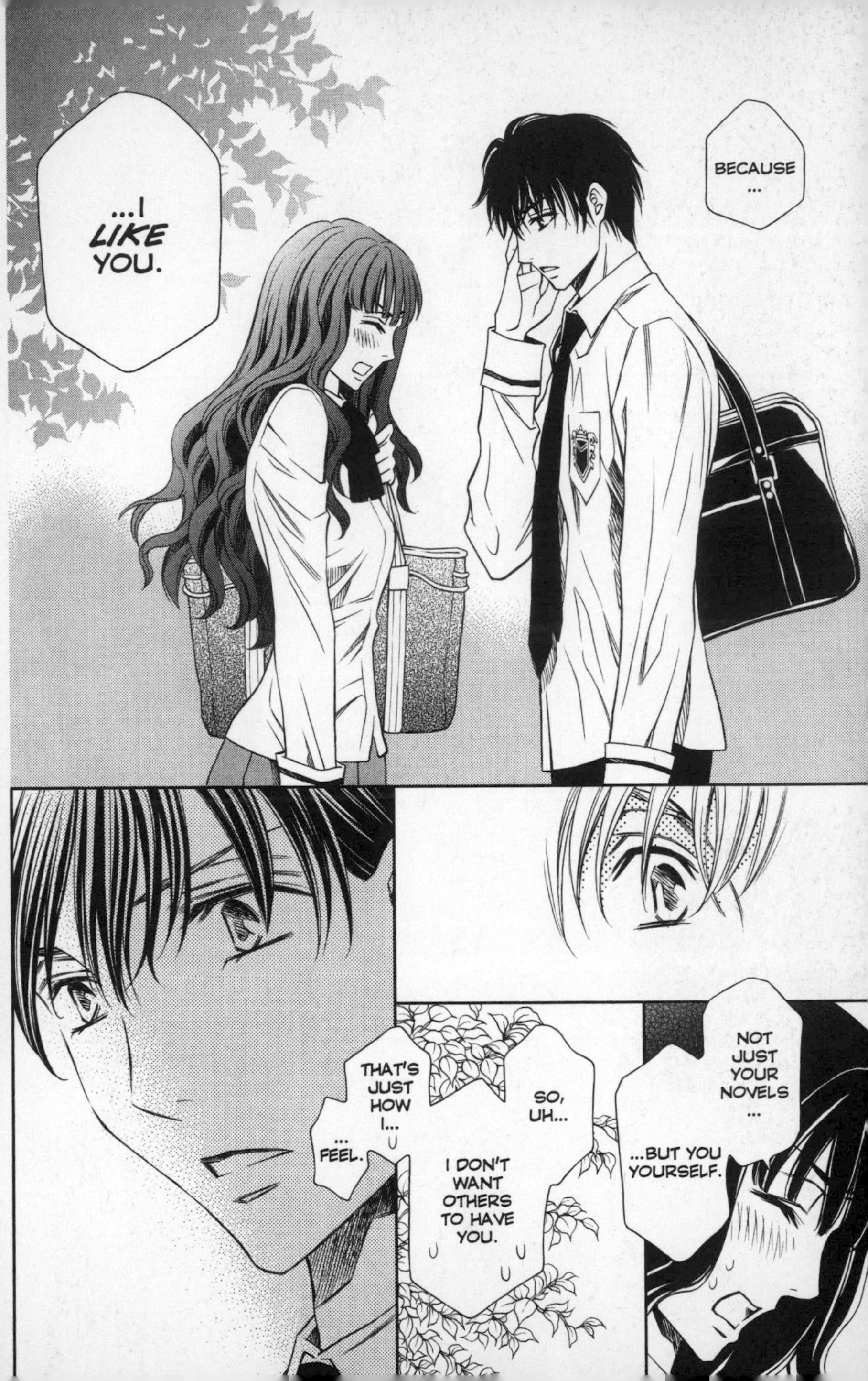
BECAUSE ...
...I *LIKE* YOU.
NOT JUST YOUR NOVELS ...
...BUT YOU YOURSELF.
SO, UH...
I DON'T WANT OTHERS TO HAVE YOU.
THAT'S JUST HOW I...
... FEEL.

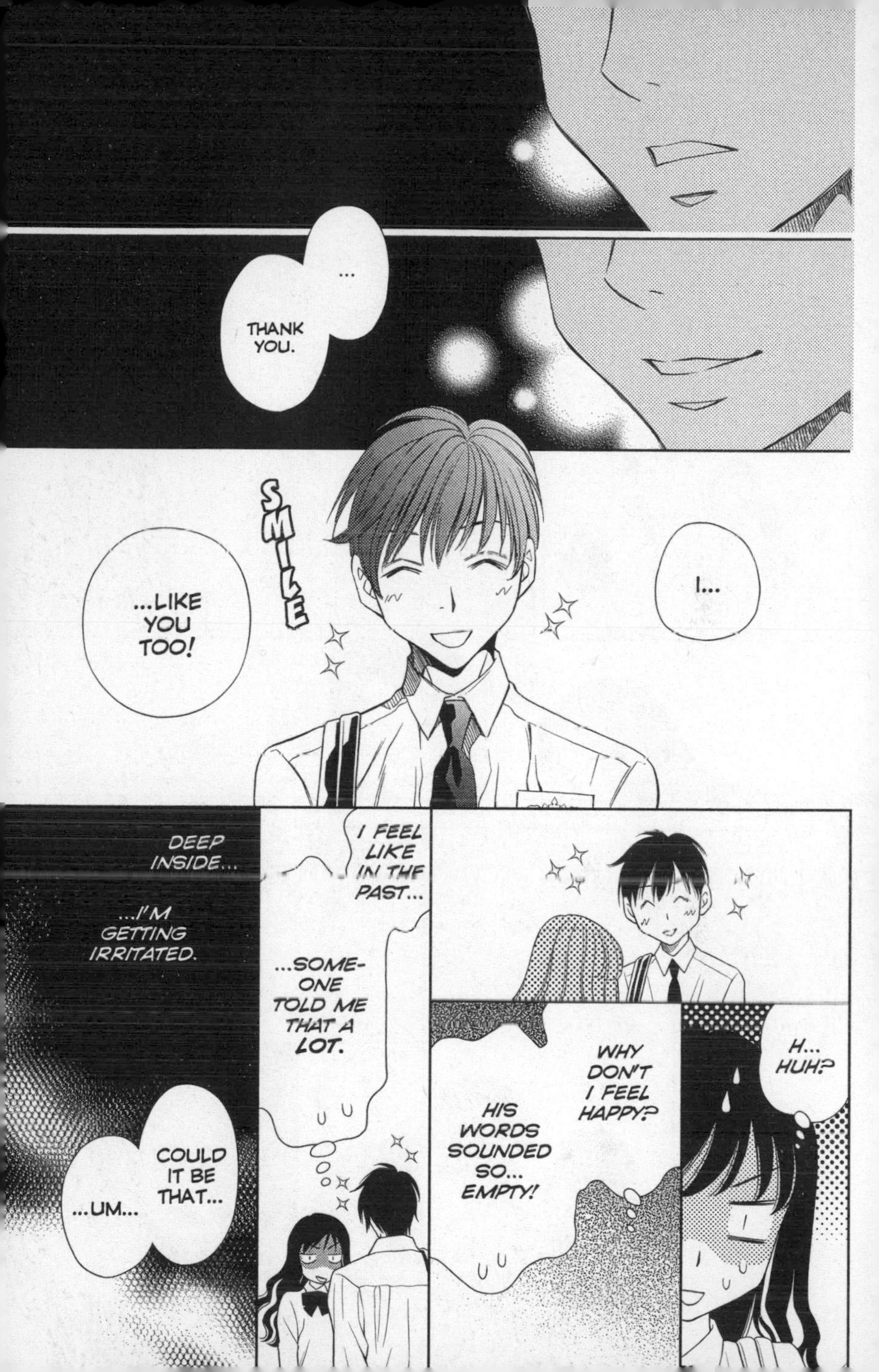
...
THANK YOU.
I...
SMILE
...LIKE YOU TOO!
H... HUH?
WHY DON'T I FEEL HAPPY?
HIS WORDS SOUNDED SO... EMPTY!
I FEEL LIKE IN THE PAST...
...SOMEONE TOLD ME THAT A LOT.
DEEP INSIDE...
...I'M GETTING IRRITATED.
COULD IT BE THAT...
...UM...

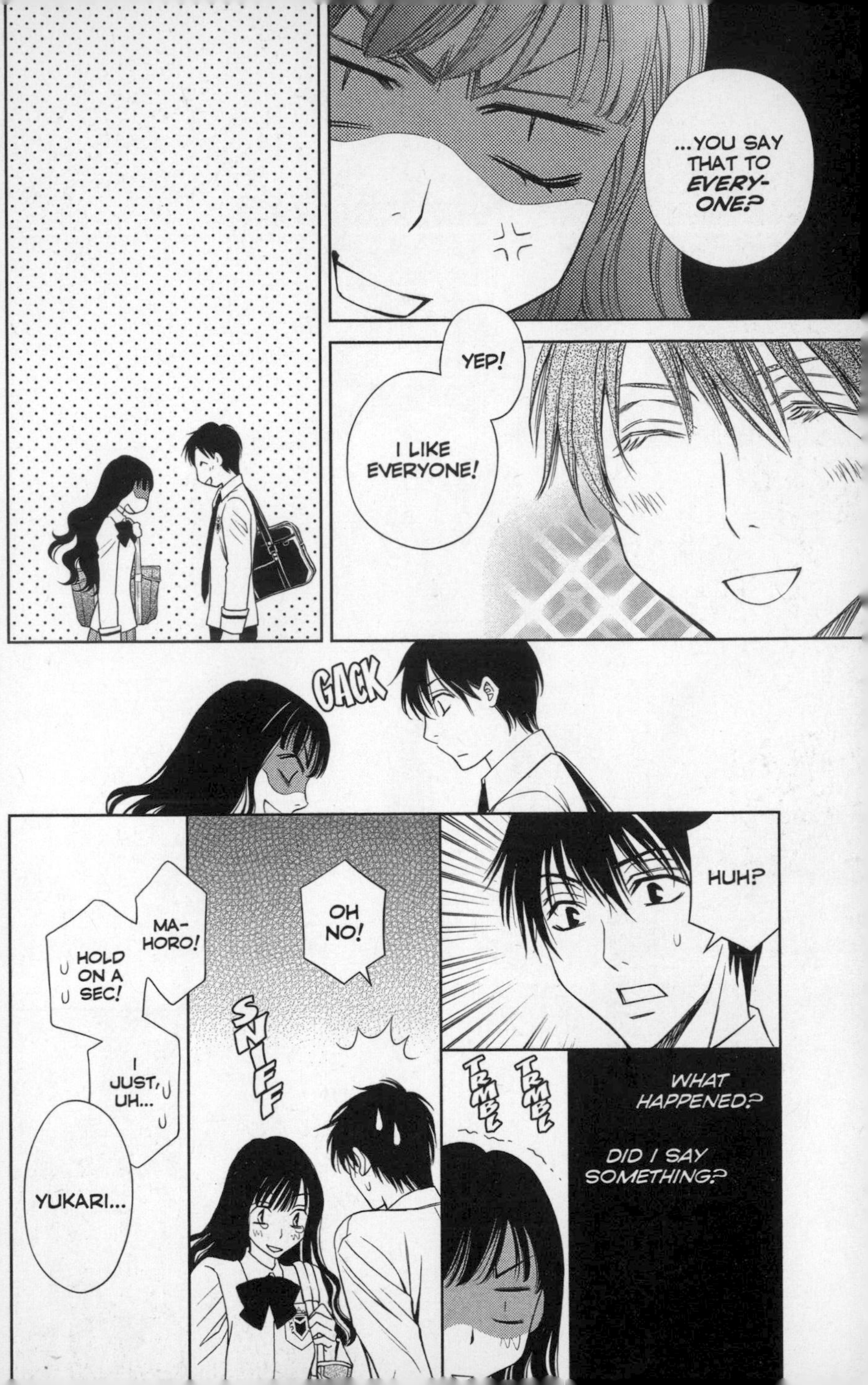
...YOU SAY THAT TO EVERY-ONE?
YEP!
I LIKE EVERYONE!
GACK
HUH?
TRMBL TRMBL
WHAT HAPPENED?
DID I SAY SOMETHING?
OH NO!
SNIFF
MA-HORO!
HOLD ON A SEC!
I JUST, UH...
YUKARI...

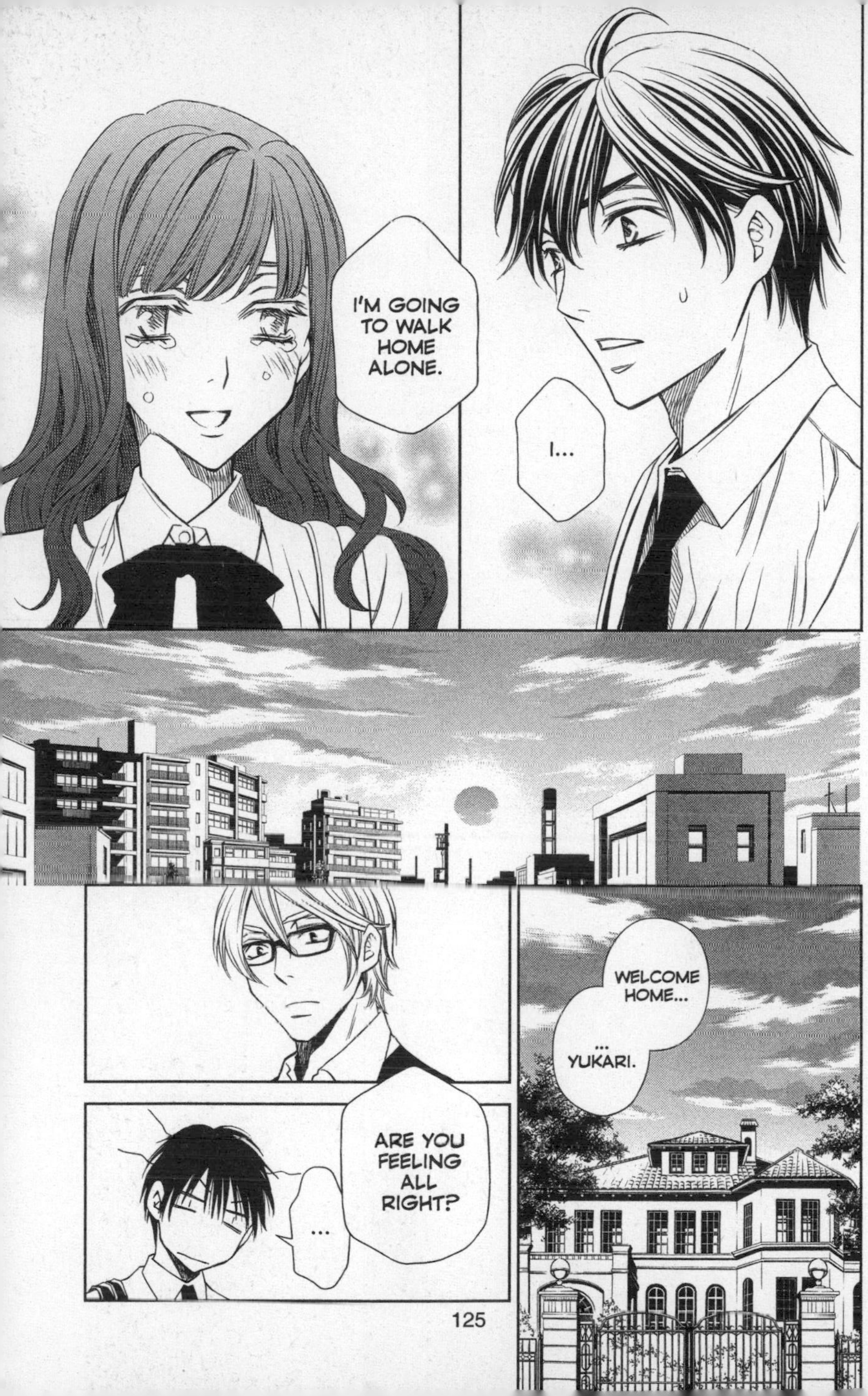
I...
I'M GOING TO WALK HOME ALONE.
WELCOME HOME...
... YUKARI.
ARE YOU FEELING ALL RIGHT?
...

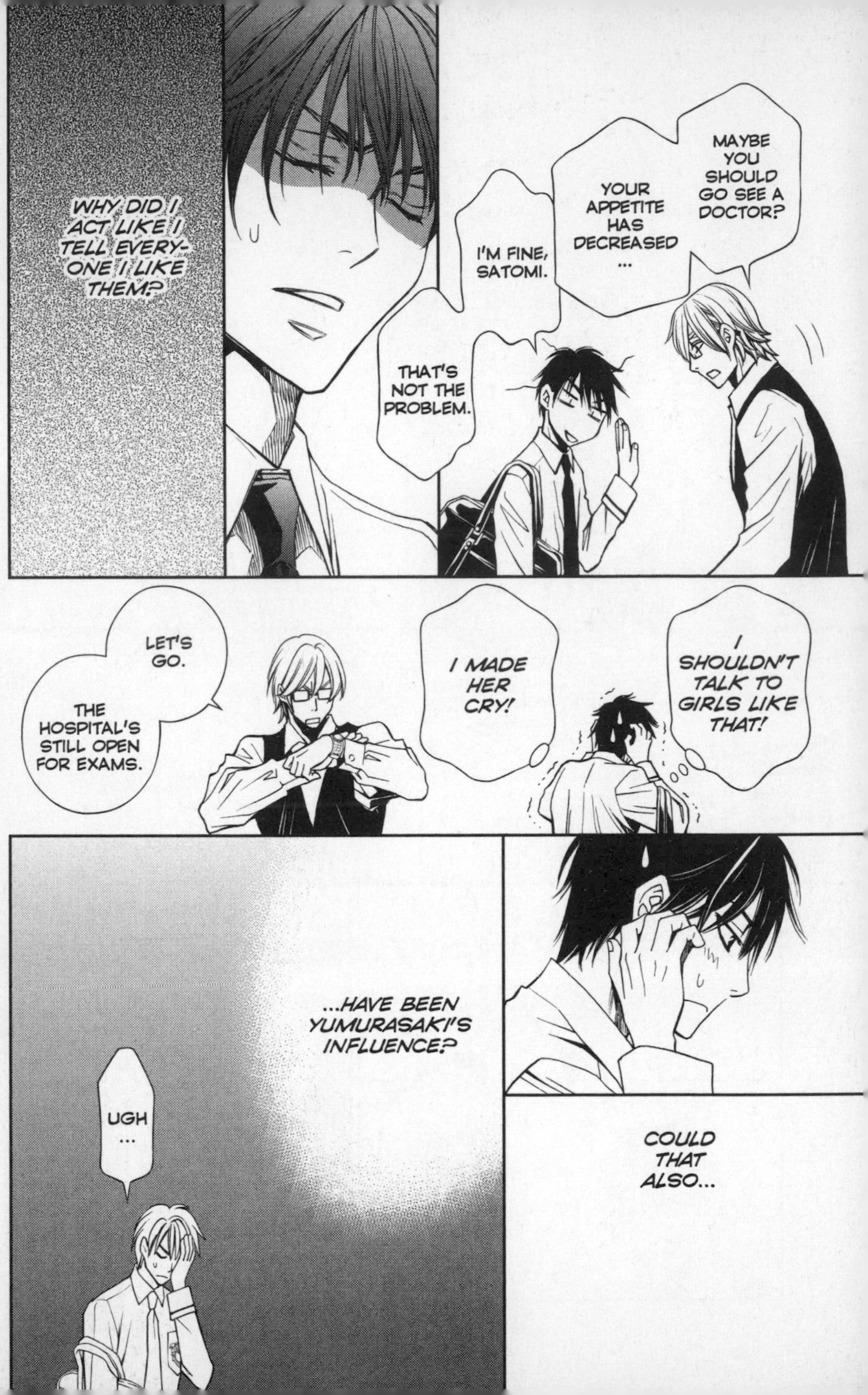
YOUR APPETITE HAS DECREASED ...
MAYBE YOU SHOULD GO SEE A DOCTOR?
I'M FINE, SATOMI.
THAT'S NOT THE PROBLEM.
WHY DID I ACT LIKE I TELL EVERY-ONE I LIKE THEM?
I SHOULDN'T TALK TO GIRLS LIKE THAT!
I MADE HER CRY!
LET'S GO.
THE HOSPITAL'S STILL OPEN FOR EXAMS.
COULD THAT ALSO...
...HAVE BEEN YUMURASAKI'S INFLUENCE?
UGH ...

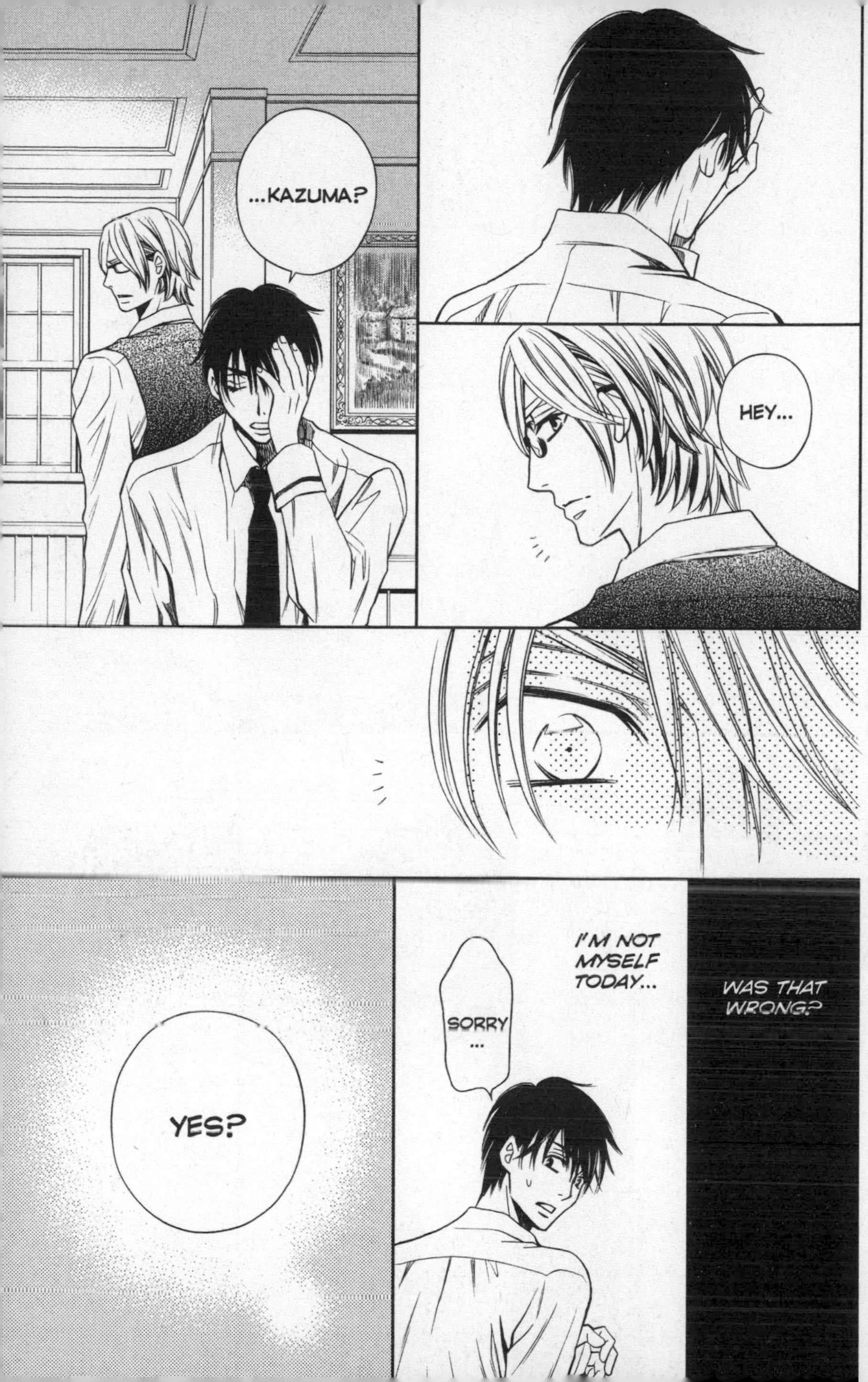
HEY...
...KAZUMA?
WAS THAT WRONG?
I'M NOT MYSELF TODAY...
SORRY ...
YES?

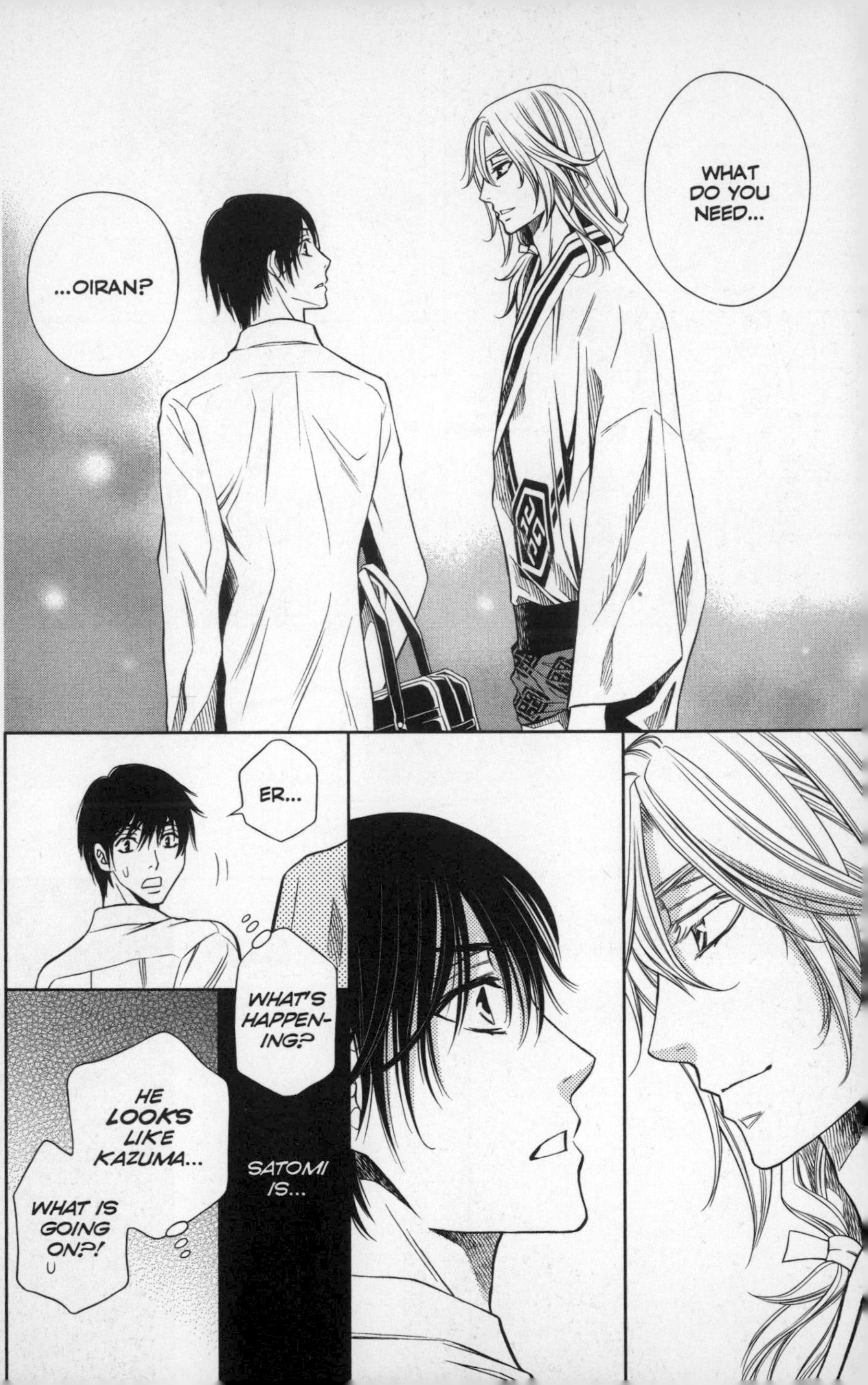
WHAT DO YOU NEED...
...OIRAN?
ER...
WHAT'S HAPPEN-ING?
SATOMI IS...
HE LOOKS LIKE KAZUMA...
WHAT IS GOING ON?!

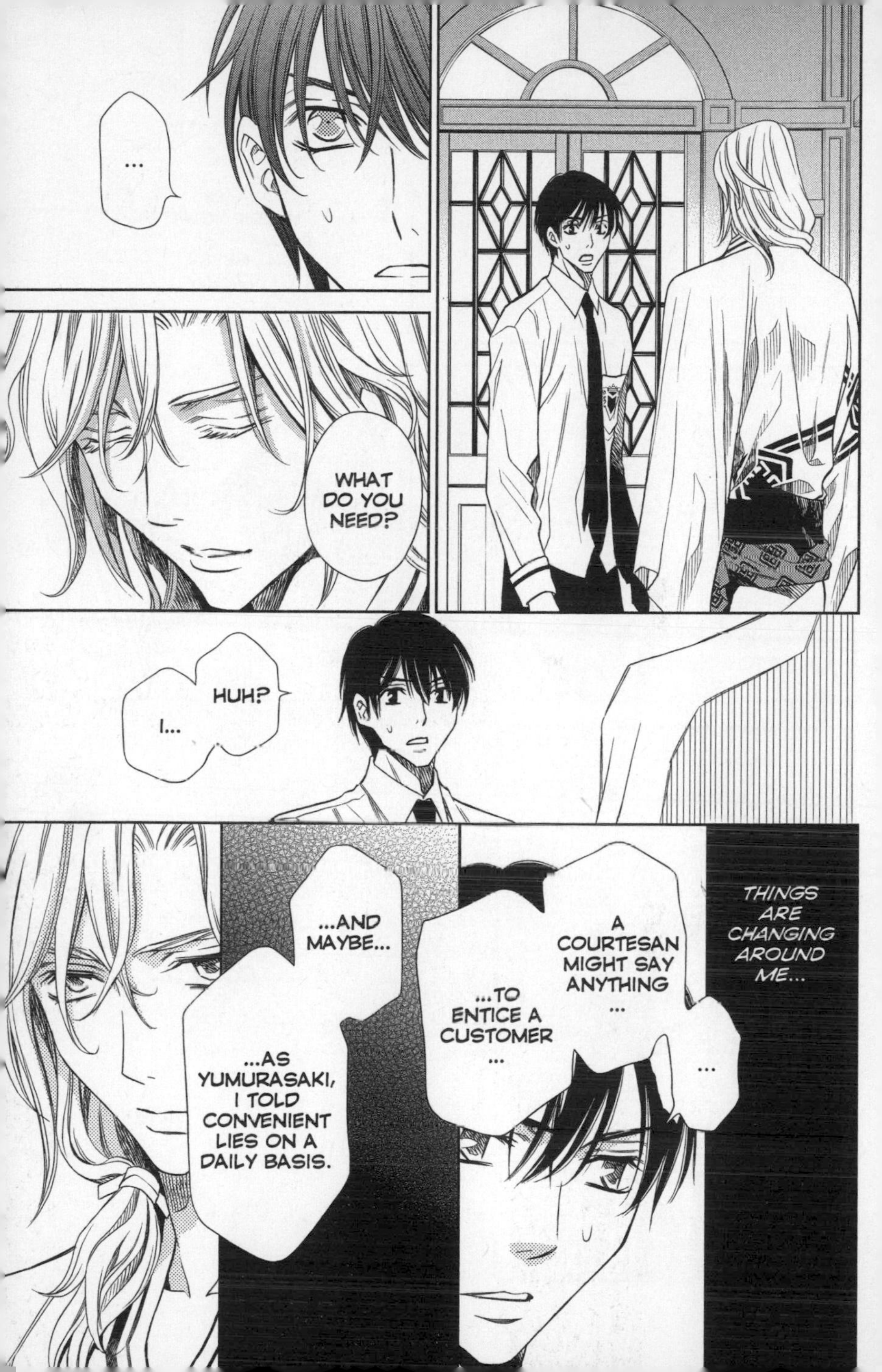
...
WHAT DO YOU NEED?
HUH? I...
THINGS ARE CHANGING AROUND ME...
A COURTESAN MIGHT SAY ANYTHING...
...TO ENTICE A CUSTOMER...
...
...AND MAYBE...
...AS YUMURASAKI, I TOLD CONVENIENT LIES ON A DAILY BASIS.

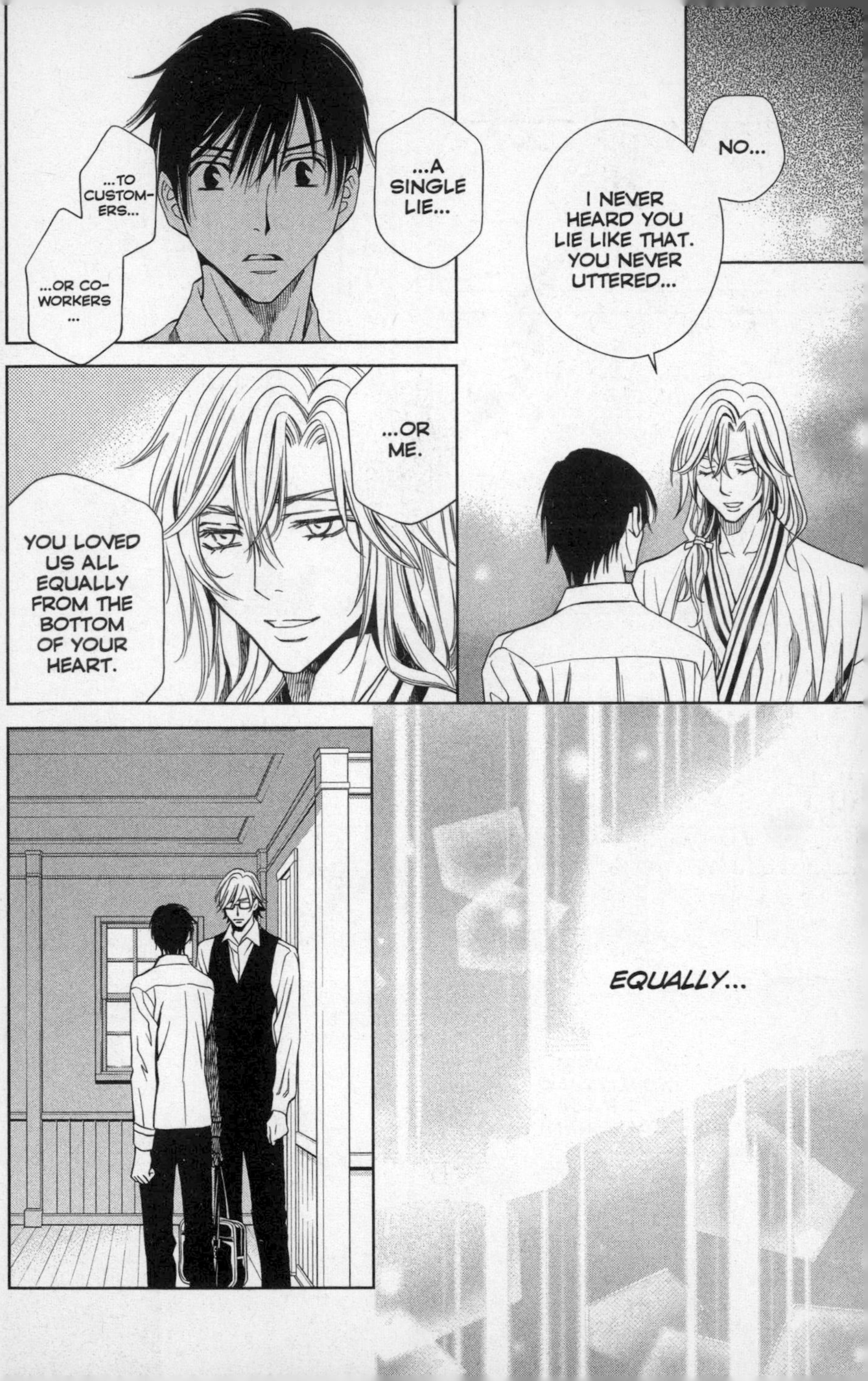
NO...
I NEVER HEARD YOU LIE LIKE THAT. YOU NEVER UTTERED...
...A SINGLE LIE...
...TO CUSTOMERS...
...OR CO-WORKERS...
...OR ME.
YOU LOVED US ALL EQUALLY FROM THE BOTTOM OF YOUR HEART.
EQUALLY...

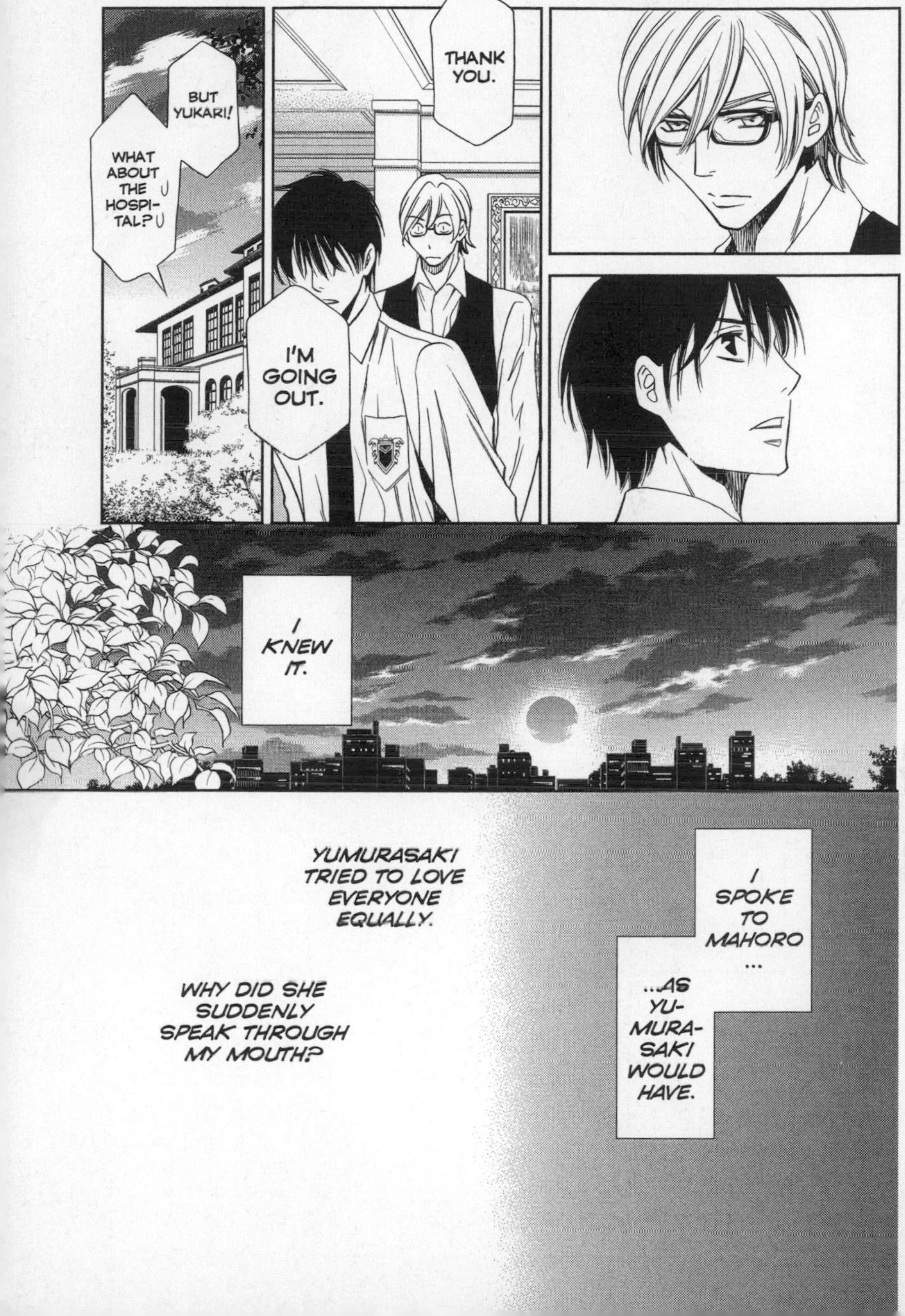
THANK YOU.
I'M GOING OUT.
BUT YUKARI!
WHAT ABOUT THE HOSPITAL?
I KNEW IT.
I SPOKE TO MAHORO...
...AS YUMURASAKI WOULD HAVE.
YUMURASAKI TRIED TO LOVE EVERYONE EQUALLY.
WHY DID SHE SUDDENLY SPEAK THROUGH MY MOUTH?

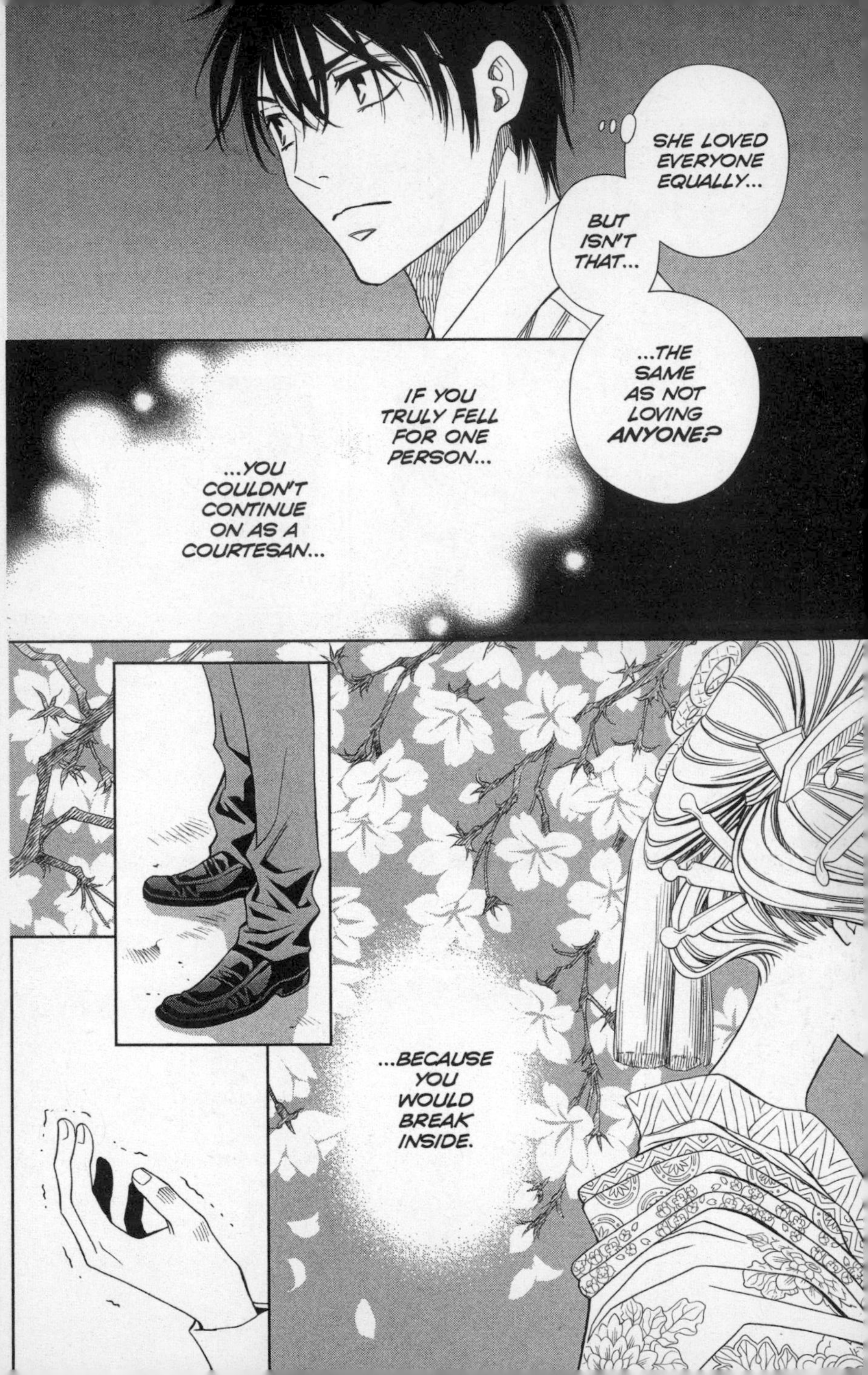
SHE LOVED EVERYONE EQUALLY...
BUT ISN'T THAT...
...THE SAME AS NOT LOVING ANYONE?
IF YOU TRULY FELL FOR ONE PERSON...
...YOU COULDN'T CONTINUE ON AS A COURTESAN...
...BECAUSE YOU WOULD BREAK INSIDE.

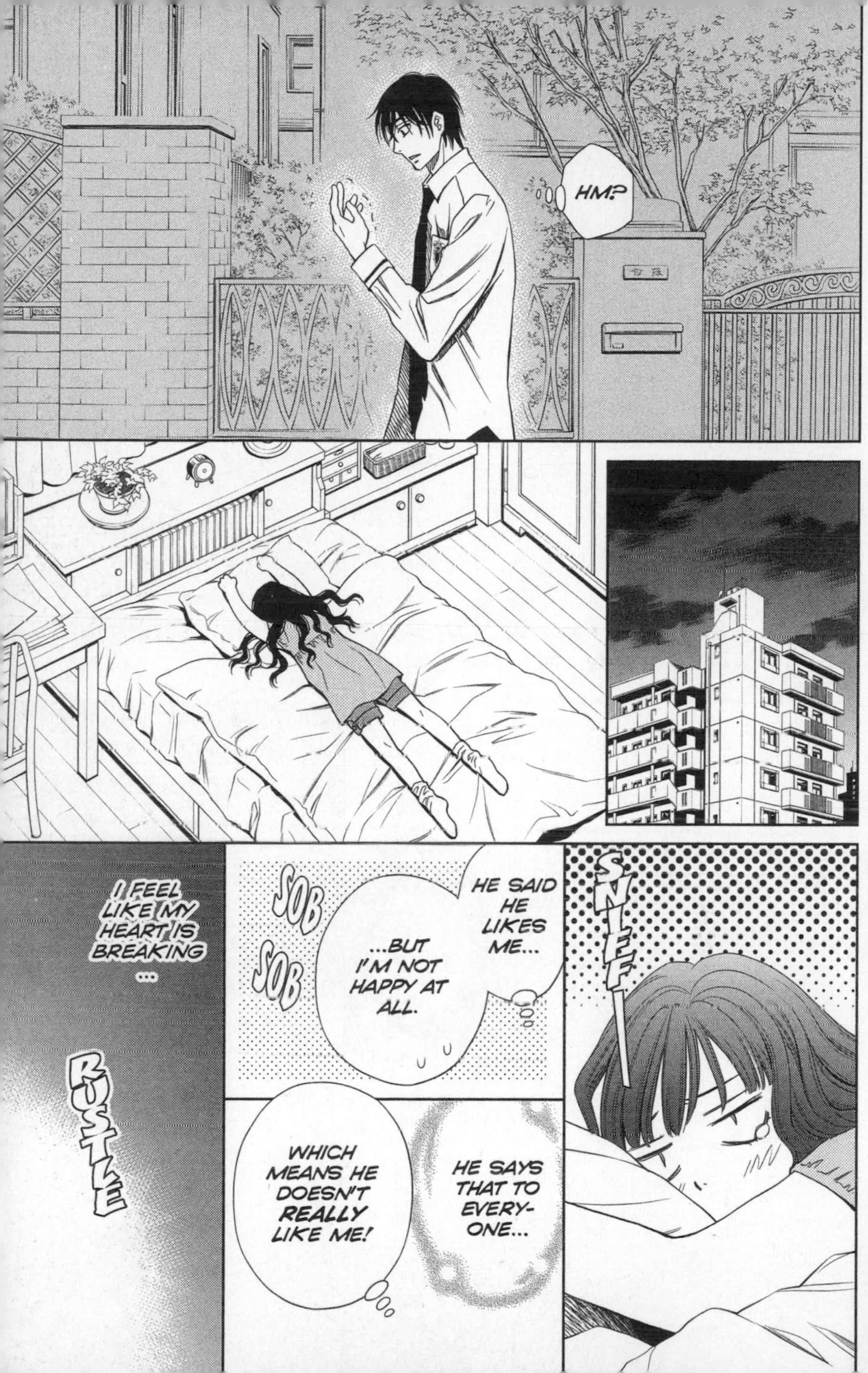
HM?
SNIFF
HE SAID HE LIKES ME...
...BUT I'M NOT HAPPY AT ALL.
SOB
SOB
HE SAYS THAT TO EVERY-ONE...
WHICH MEANS HE DOESN'T REALLY LIKE ME!
I FEEL LIKE MY HEART IS BREAKING...
RUSTLE

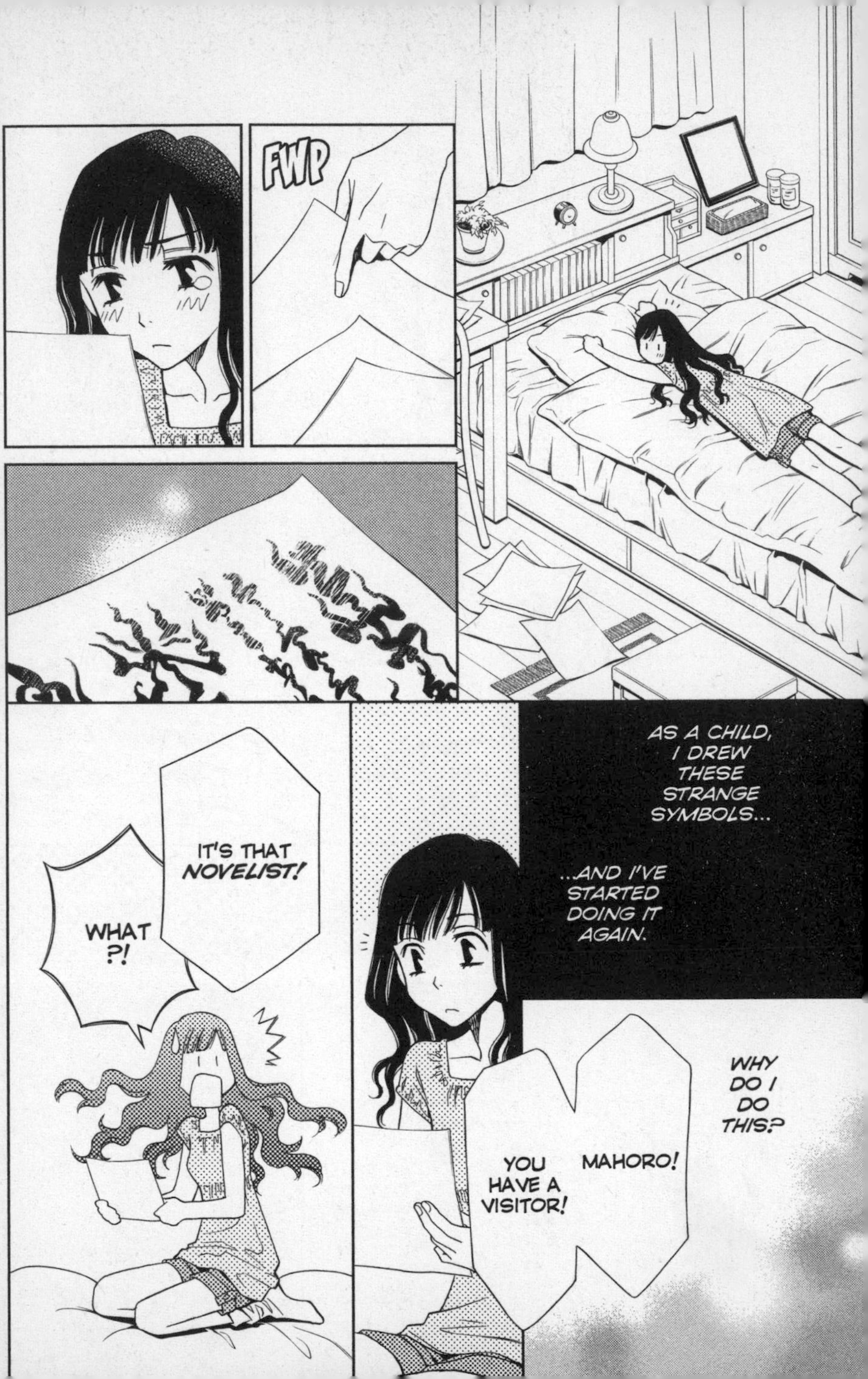
FWP
AS A CHILD, I DREW THESE STRANGE SYMBOLS...
...AND I'VE STARTED DOING IT AGAIN.
WHY DO I DO THIS?
MAHORO! YOU HAVE A VISITOR!
IT'S THAT NOVELIST!
WHAT?!

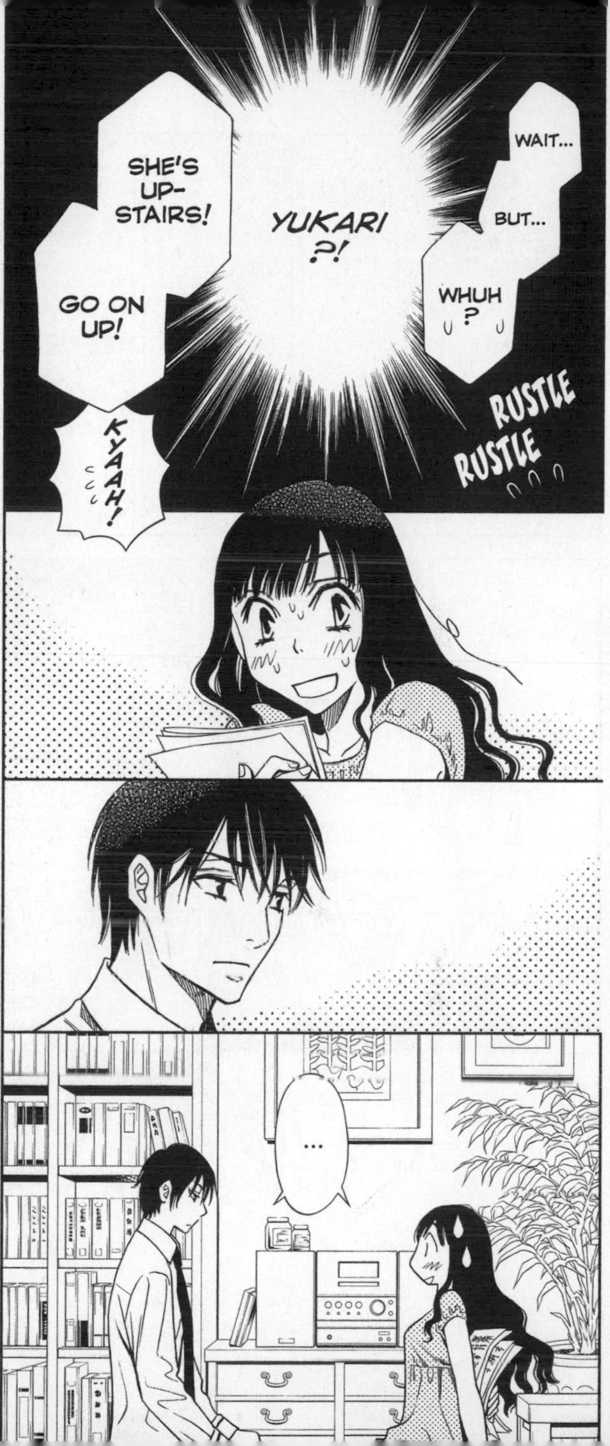
WAIT...
BUT...
WHUH?
YUKARI?!
SHE'S UP-STAIRS!
GO ON UP!
KYAAH!
RUSTLE RUSTLE
...

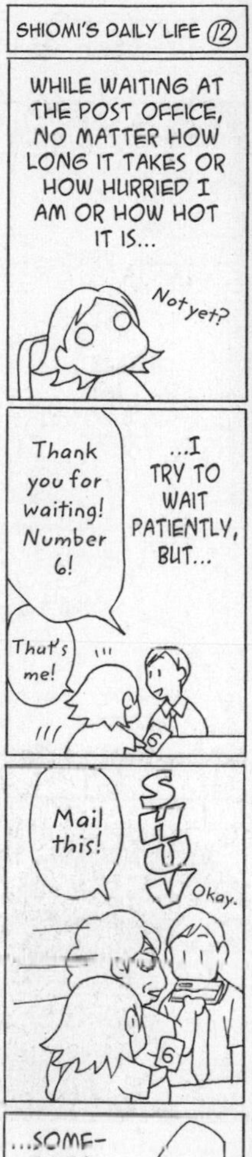
SHIOMI'S DAILY LIFE 12
WHILE WAITING AT THE POST OFFICE, NO MATTER HOW LONG IT TAKES OR HOW HURRIED I AM OR HOW HOT IT IS...
Not yet?
...I TRY TO WAIT PATIENTLY, BUT...
Thank you for waiting! Number 6!
That's me!
SHUV
Mail this!
Okay.
...SOMETIMES I LOSE MY COOL.
Hurry up!
Okay.
TRMBL
TRMBL

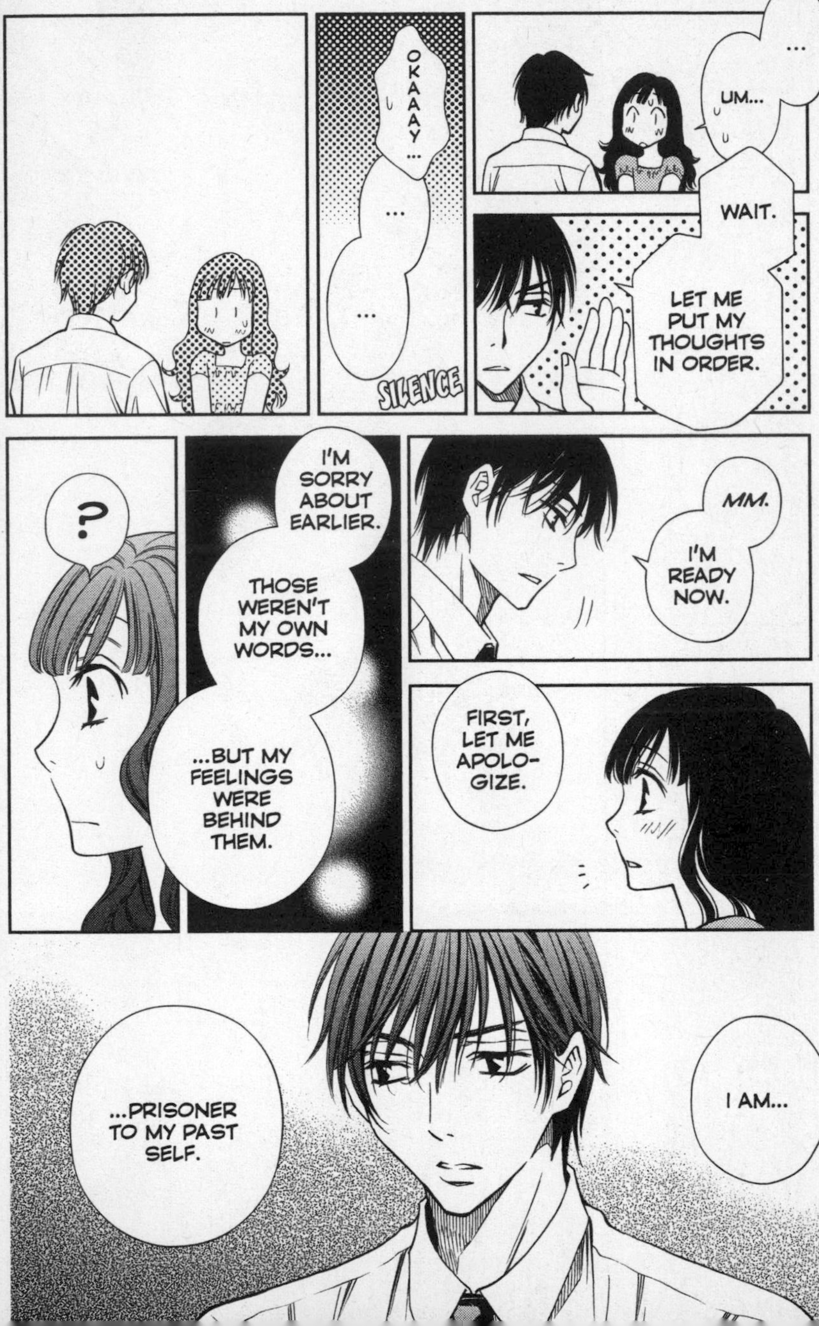
...
UM...
WAIT.
LET ME PUT MY THOUGHTS IN ORDER.
OKAAAY...
...
...
SILENCE
MM.
I'M READY NOW.
FIRST, LET ME APOLOGIZE.
I'M SORRY ABOUT EARLIER.
THOSE WEREN'T MY OWN WORDS...
...BUT MY FEELINGS WERE BEHIND THEM.
?
I AM...
...PRISONER TO MY PAST SELF.

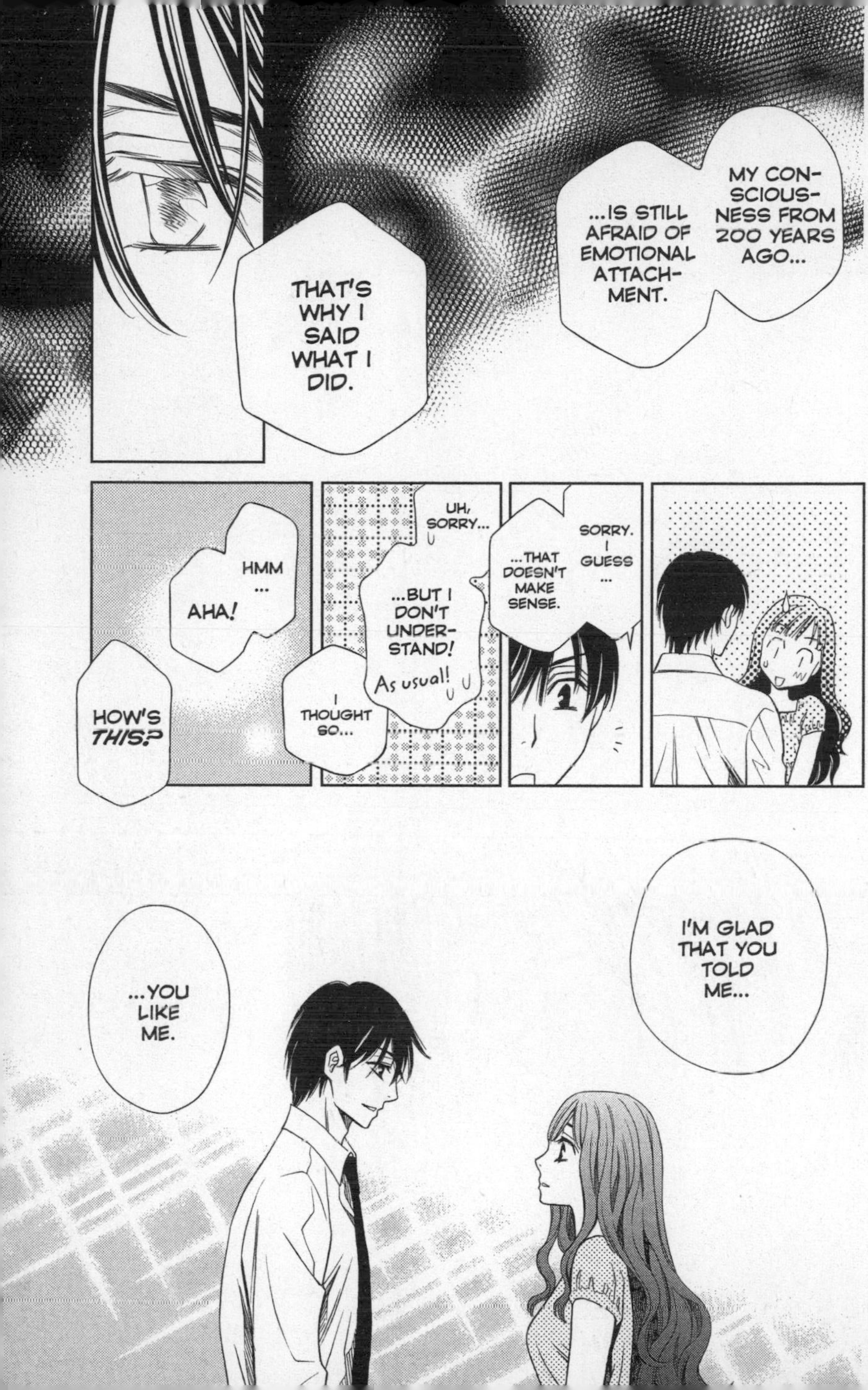
MY CONSCIOUSNESS FROM 200 YEARS AGO...
...IS STILL AFRAID OF EMOTIONAL ATTACHMENT.
THAT'S WHY I SAID WHAT I DID.
SORRY. I GUESS...
...THAT DOESN'T MAKE SENSE.
UH, SORRY...
...BUT I DON'T UNDERSTAND!
As usual!
I THOUGHT SO...
HMM... AHA!
HOW'S *THIS?*
I'M GLAD THAT YOU TOLD ME...
...YOU LIKE ME.

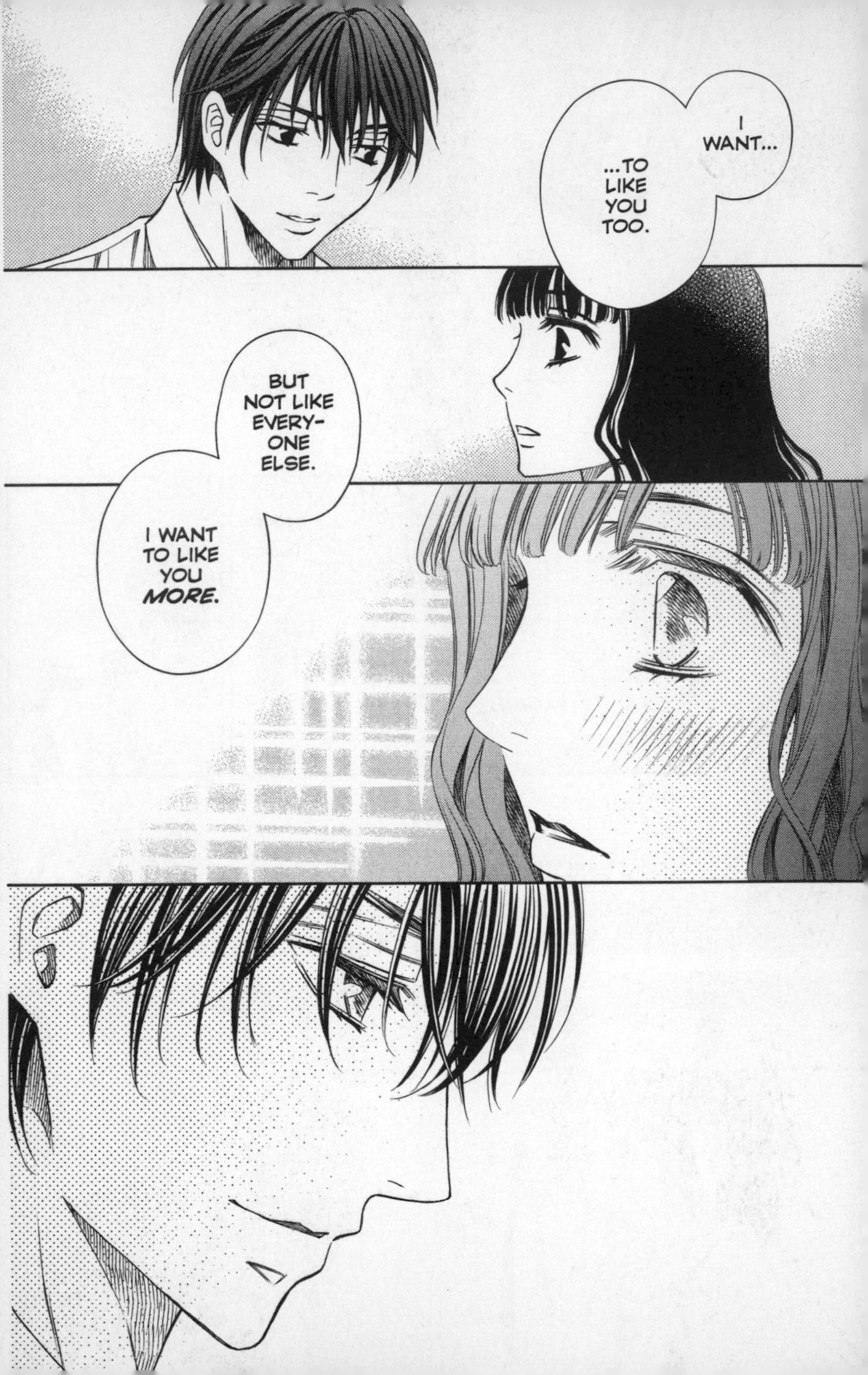
I WANT...
...TO LIKE YOU TOO.
BUT NOT LIKE EVERY-ONE ELSE.
I WANT TO LIKE YOU *MORE*.

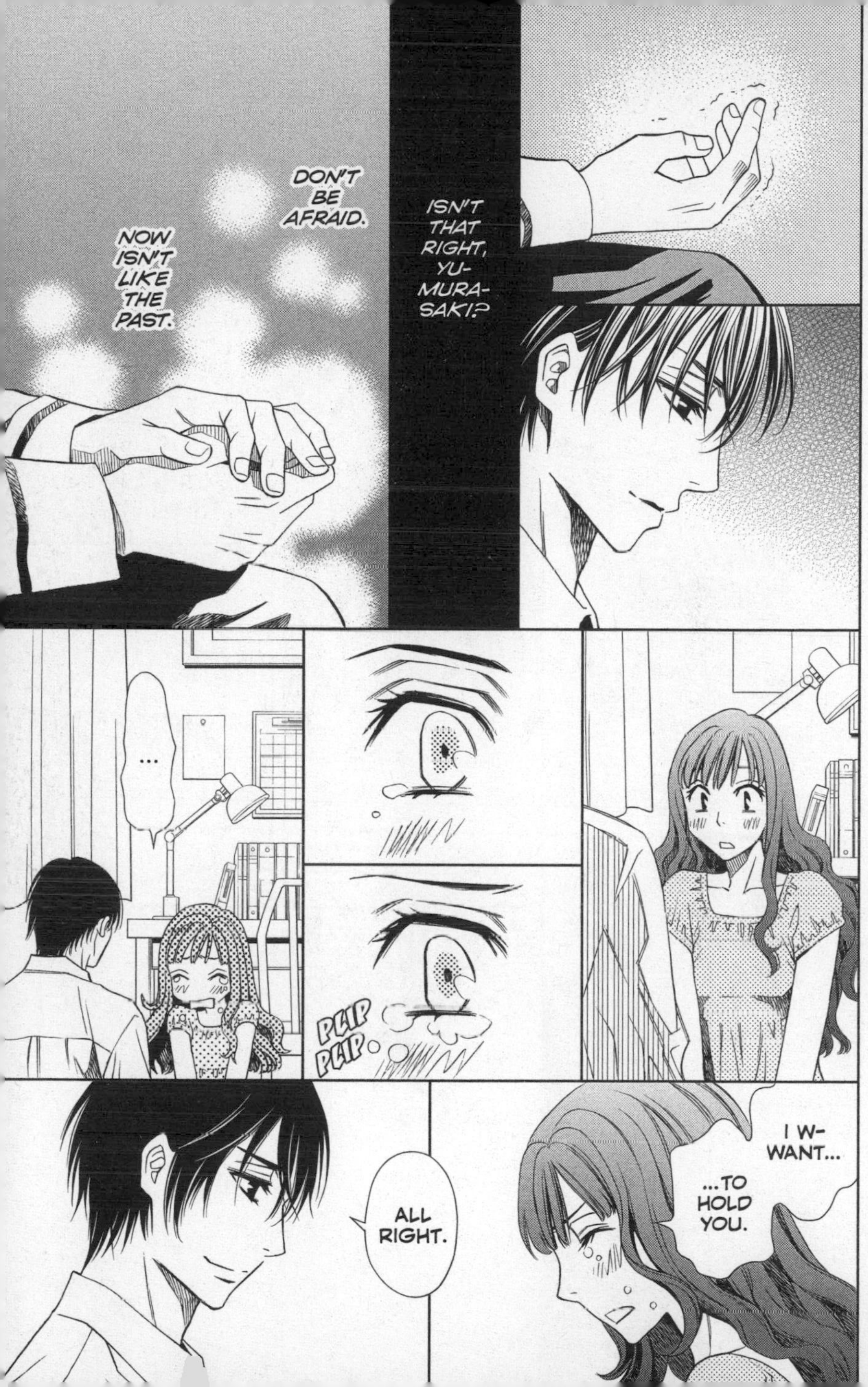
ISN'T THAT RIGHT, YU-MURA-SAKI!?
DON'T BE AFRAID.
NOW ISN'T LIKE THE PAST.
PLIP PLIP
...
I W-WANT...
...TO HOLD YOU.
ALL RIGHT.

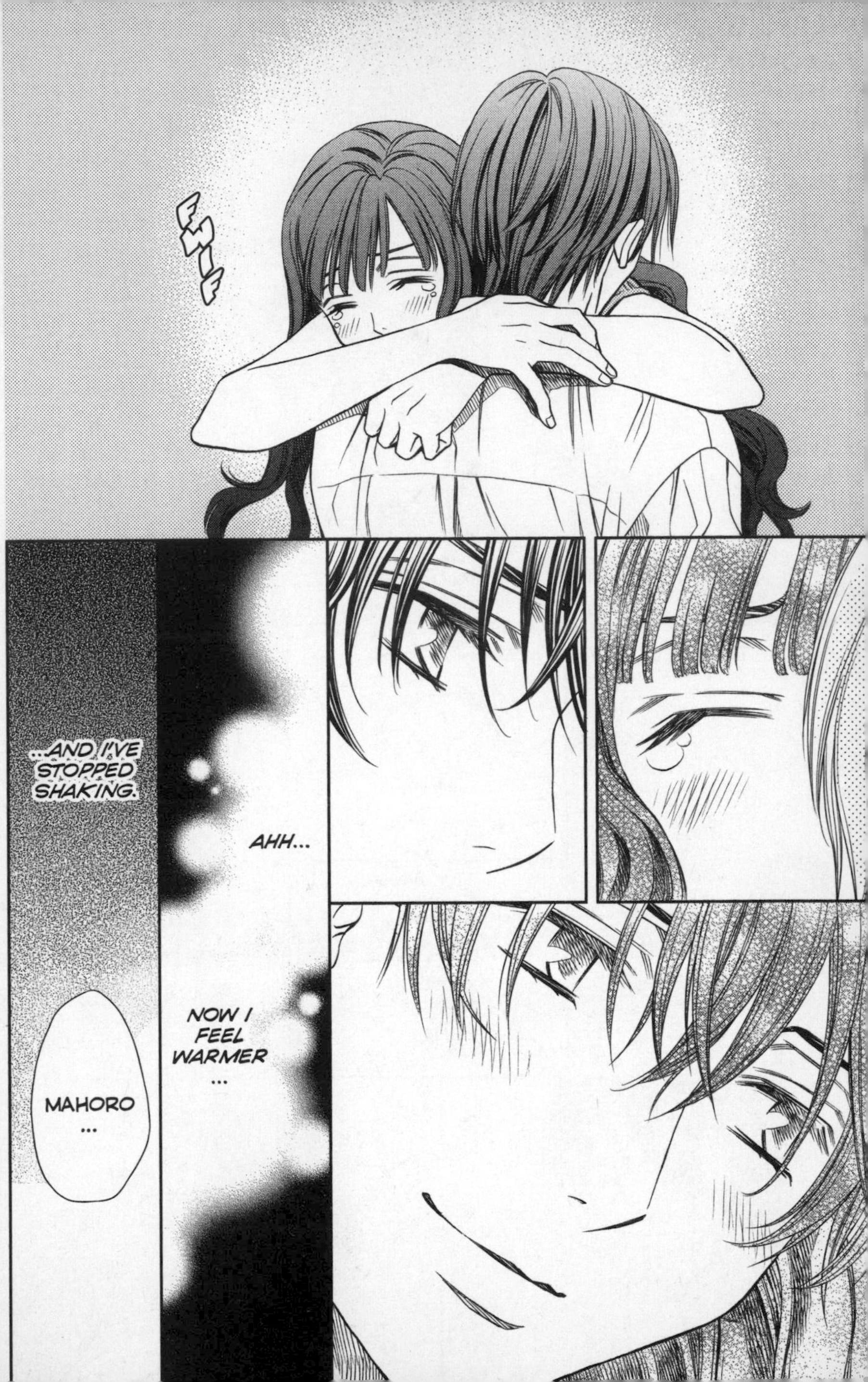
FWIF
AHH...
NOW I FEEL WARMER ...
...AND I'VE STOPPED SHAKING.
MAHORO ...

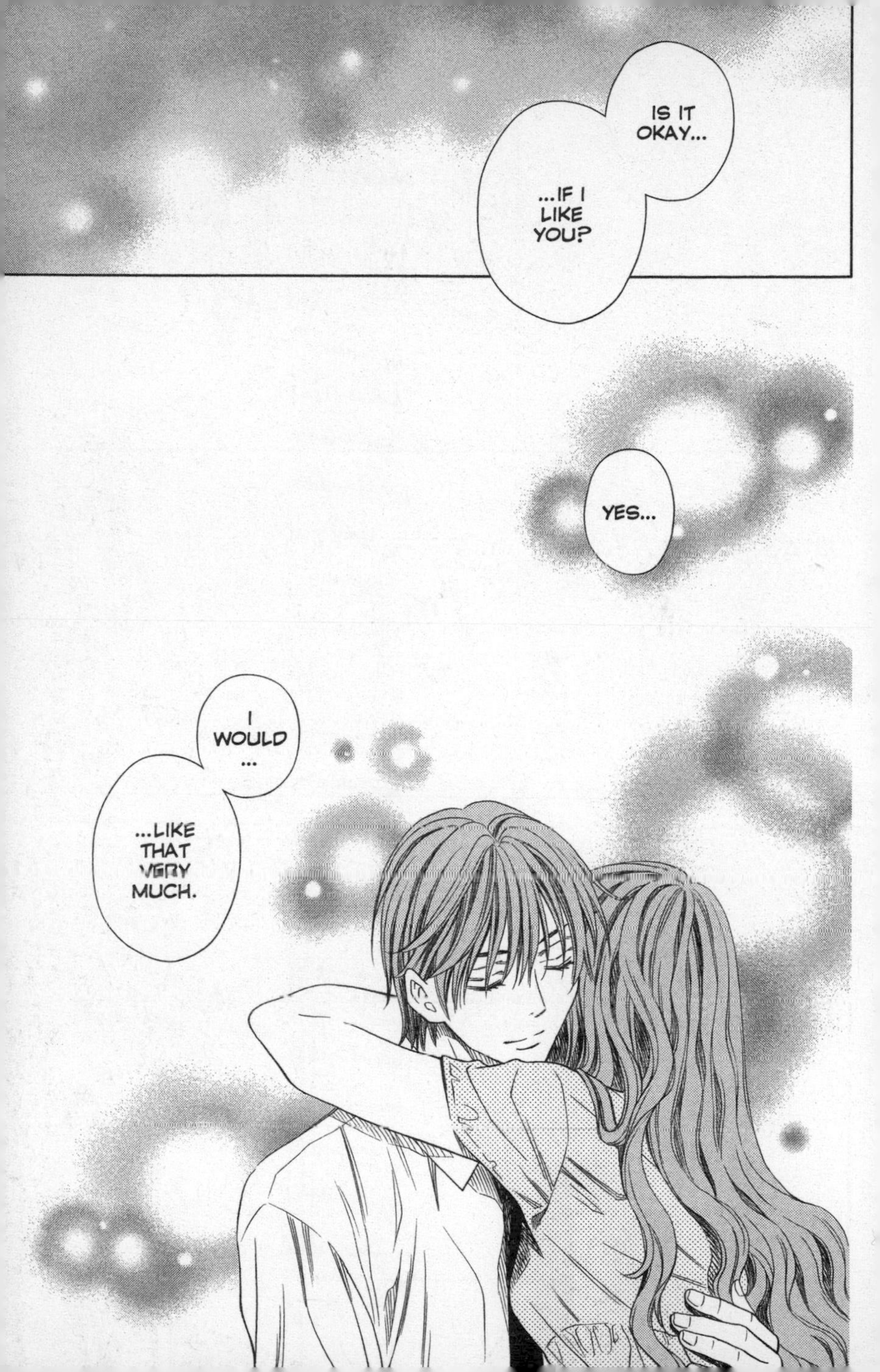
IS IT OKAY...
...IF I LIKE YOU?
YES...
I WOULD ...
...LIKE THAT VERY MUCH.

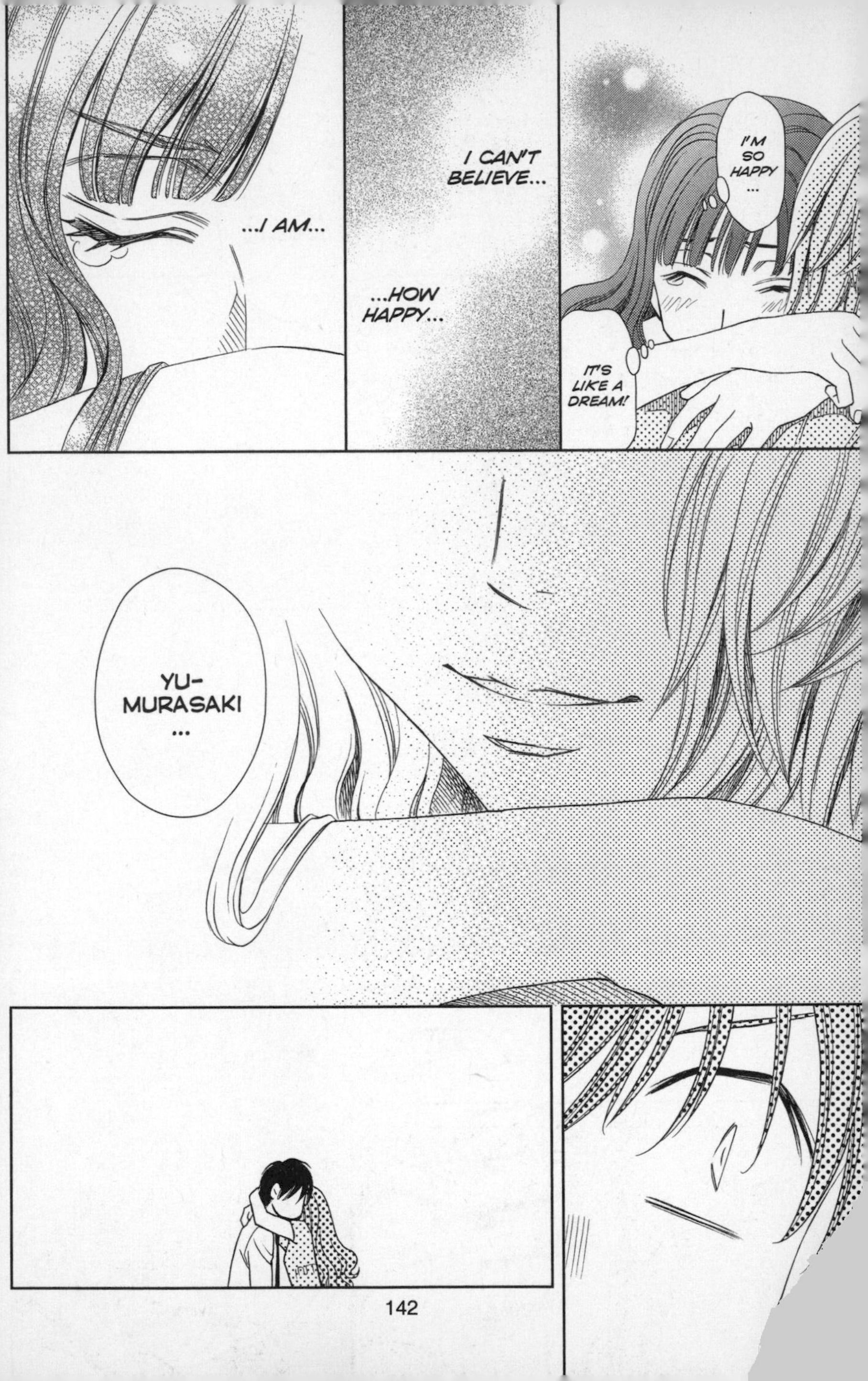
I'M SO HAPPY ...
IT'S LIKE A DREAM!
I CAN'T BELIEVE...
...HOW HAPPY...
...I AM...
YU-MURASAKI ...

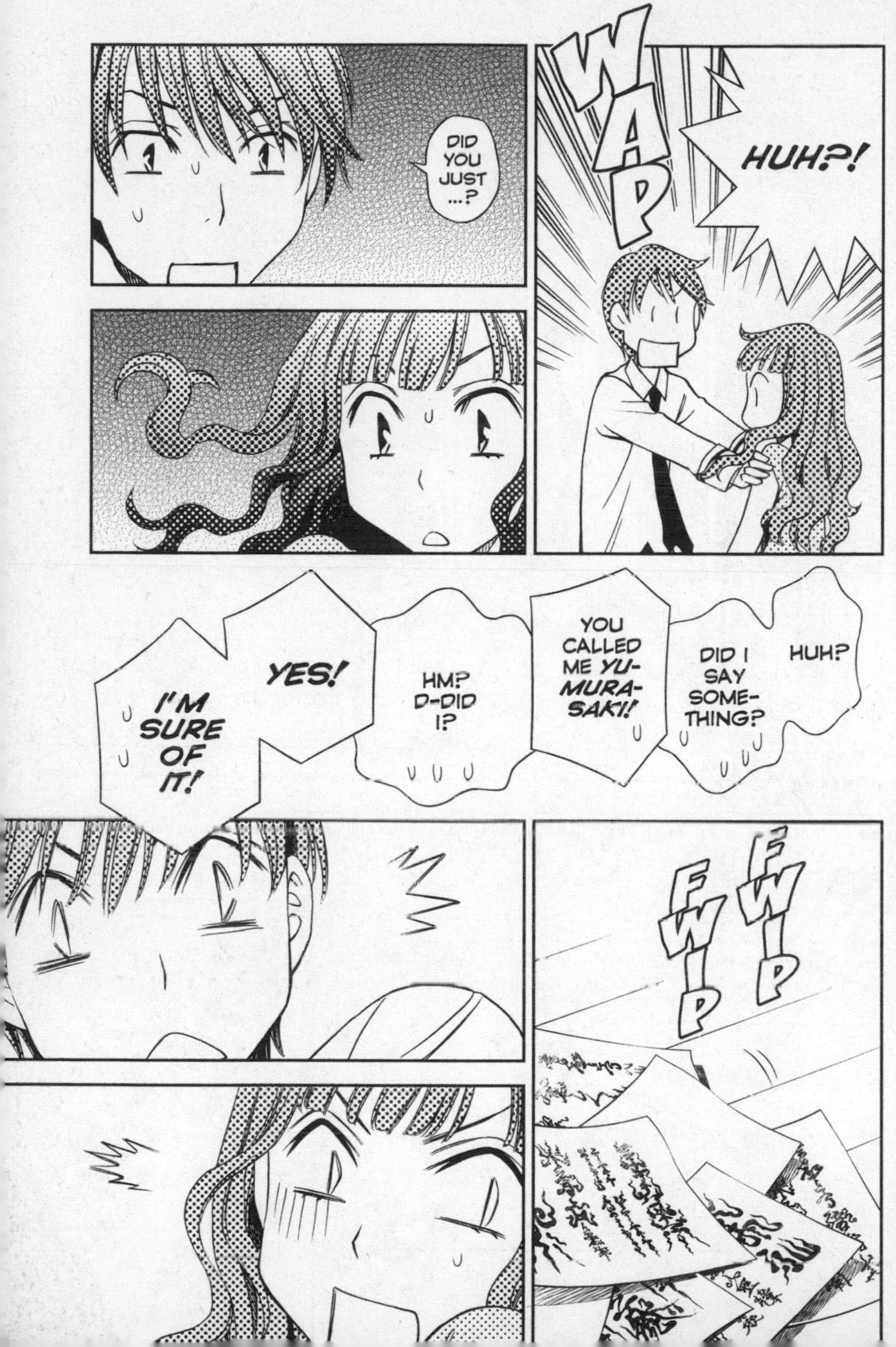
WAP
HUH?!
DID YOU JUST ...?
HUH?
DID I SAY SOME-THING?
YOU CALLED ME YU-MURA-SAKI!!
HM? D-DID I?
YES!
I'M SURE OF IT!
FWIP
FWIP

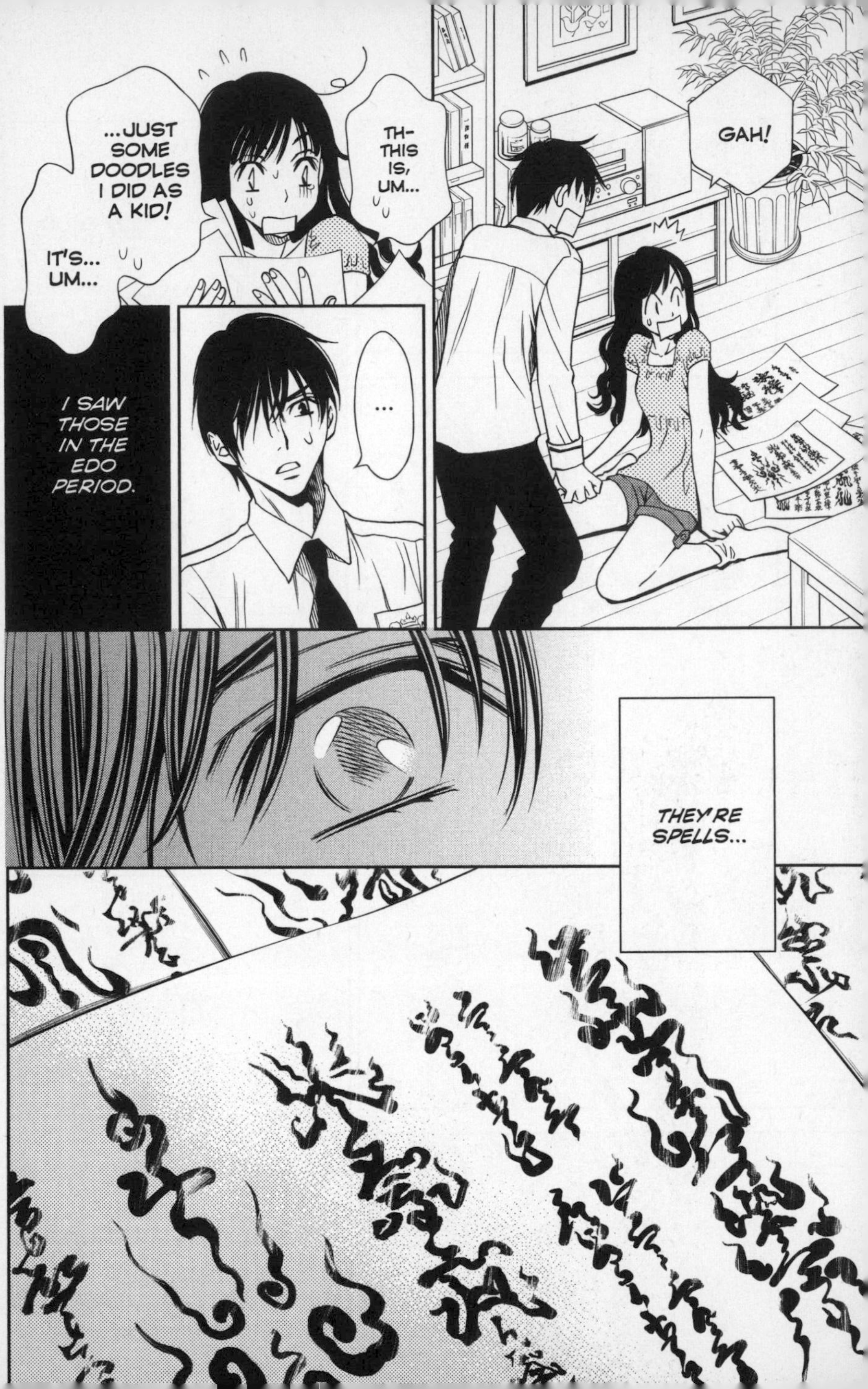
GAH!
TH-THIS IS, UM...
IT'S... UM...
...JUST SOME DOODLES I DID AS A KID!
...
I SAW THOSE IN THE EDO PERIOD.
THEY'RE SPELLS...

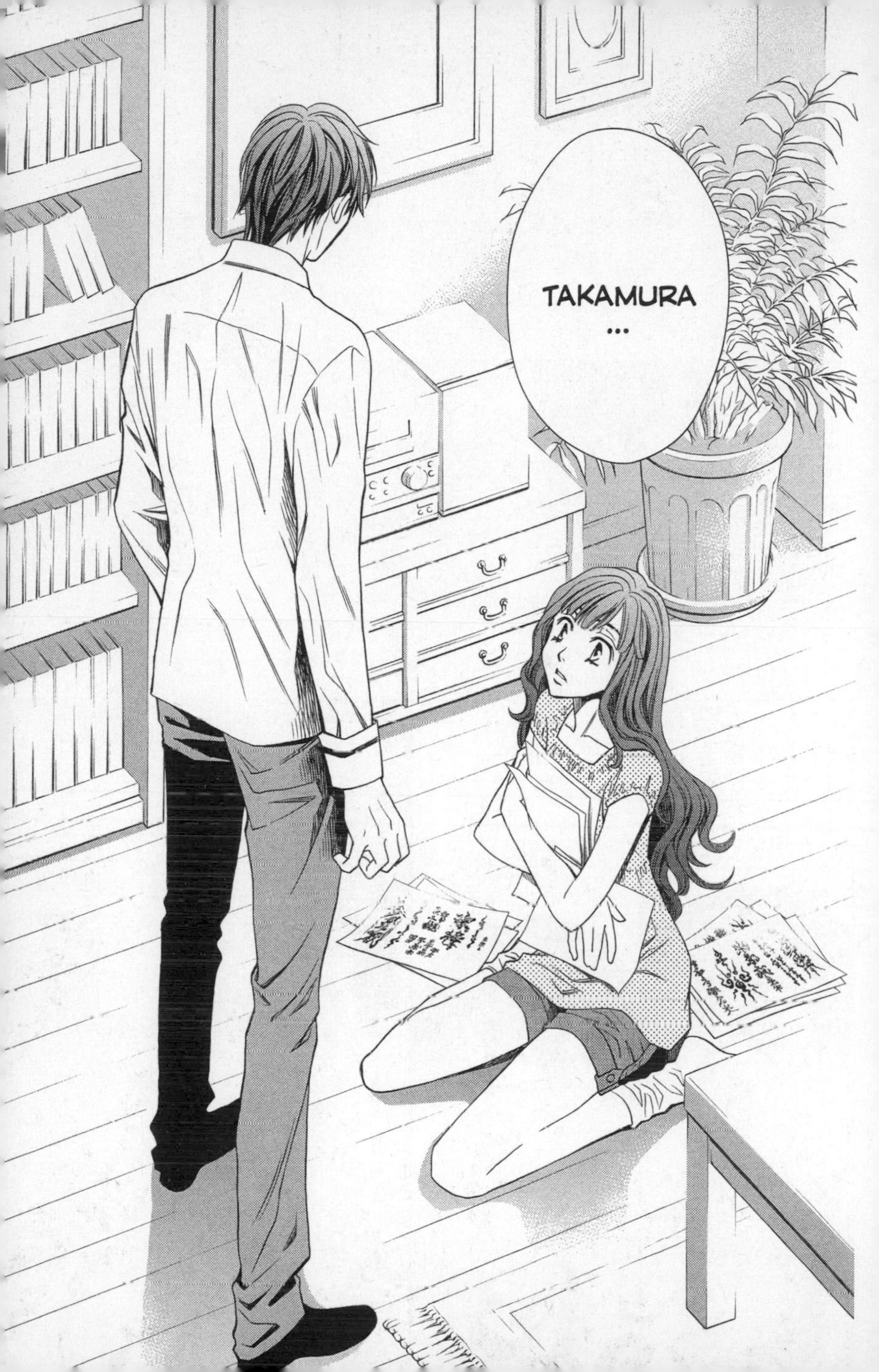
TAKAMURA
...

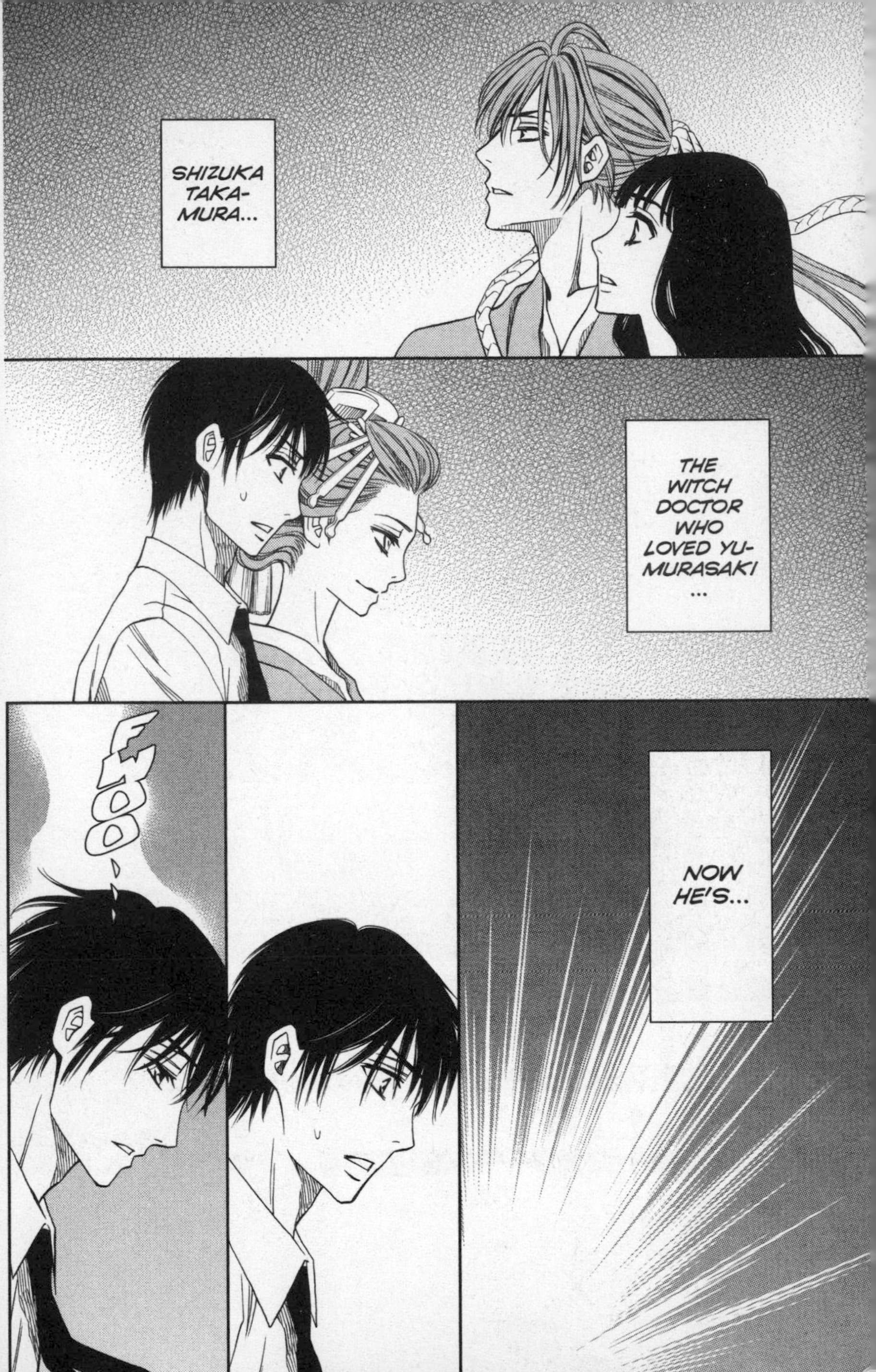
SHIZUKA TAKAMURA...
THE WITCH DOCTOR WHO LOVED YUMURASAKI...
NOW HE'S...
FWOO

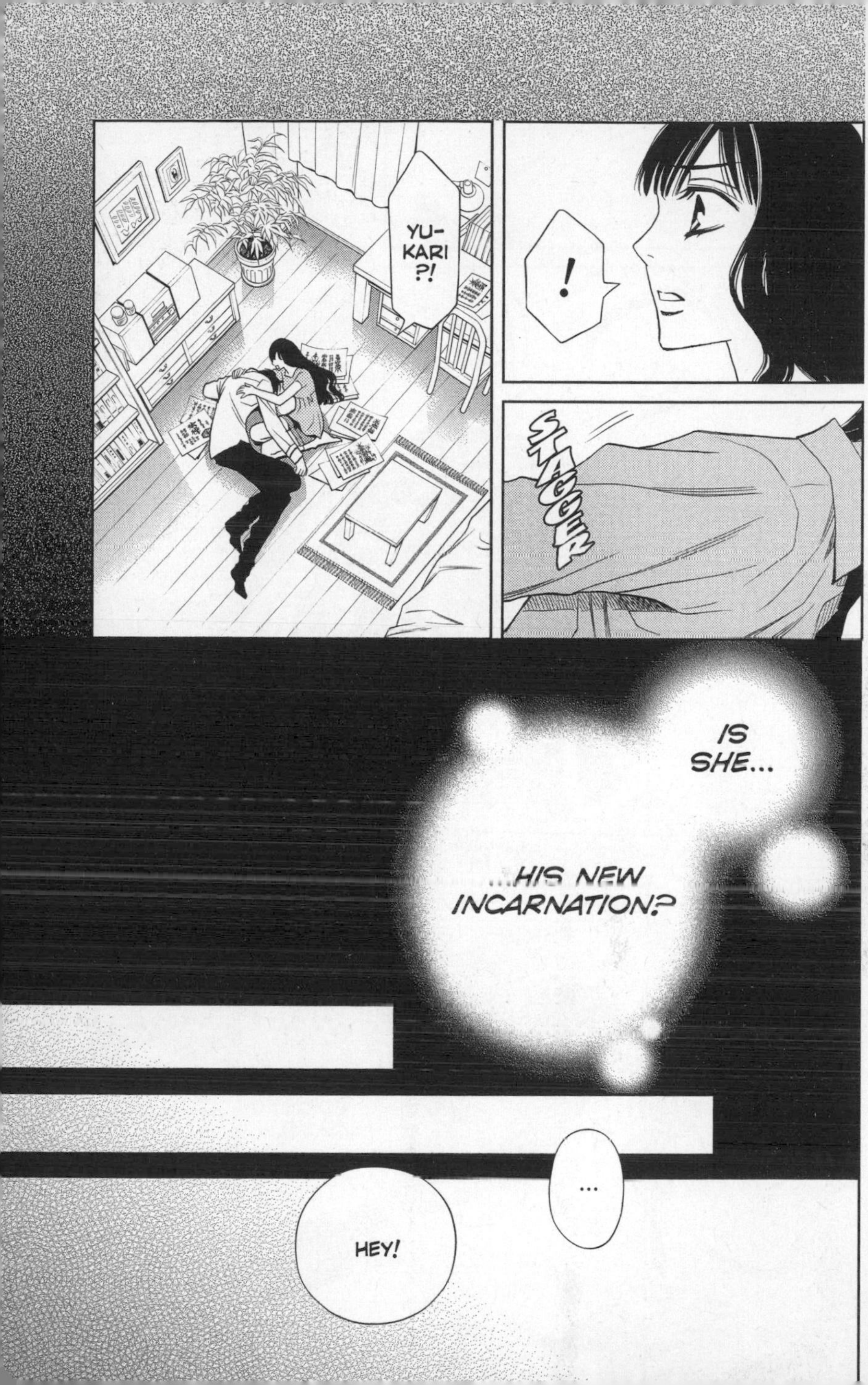
!
STAGGER
YU-KARI?!
IS SHE...
...HIS NEW INCARNATION?
...
HEY!

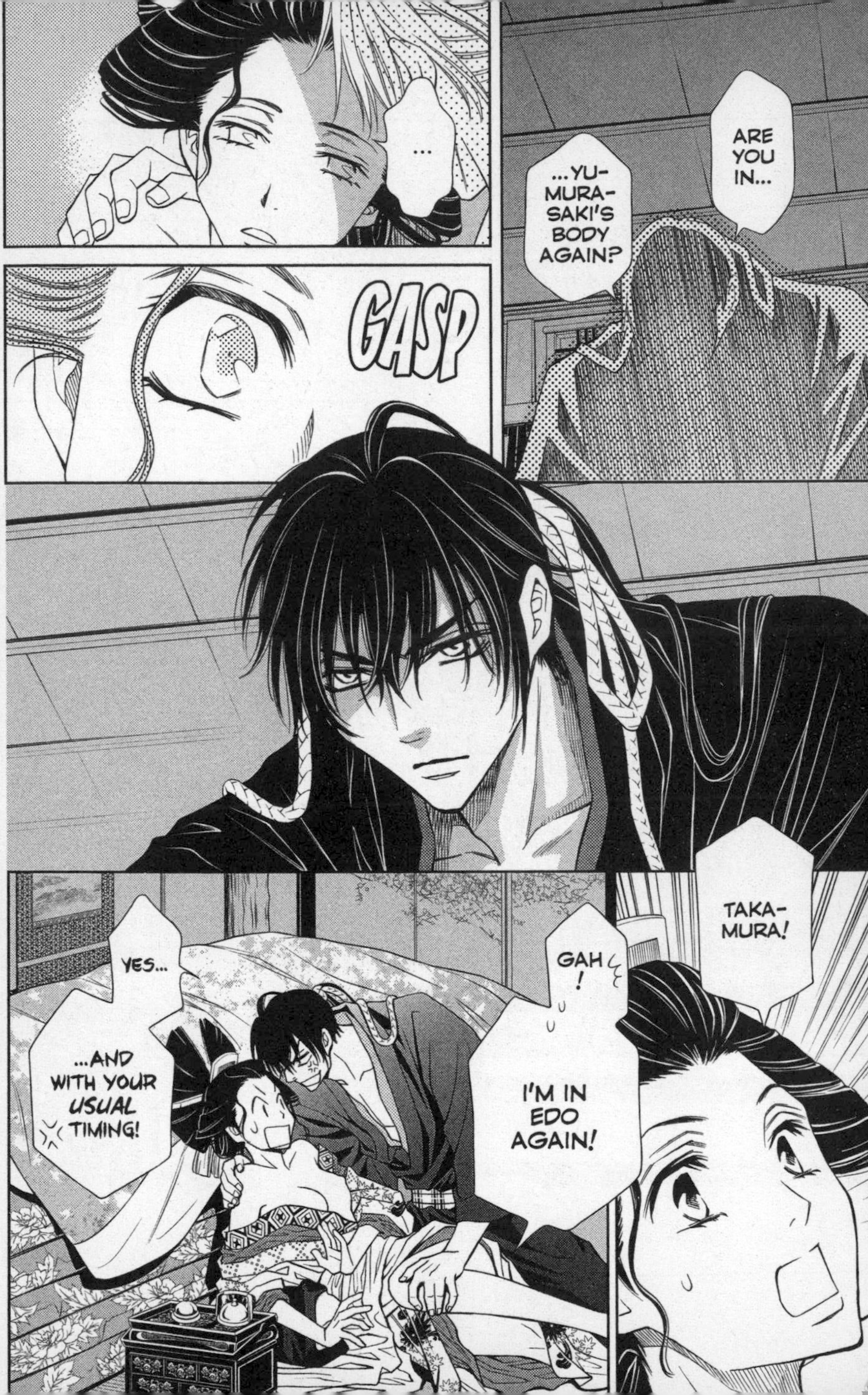
ARE YOU IN...
...YU-MURA-SAKI'S BODY AGAIN?
...
GASP
TAKA-MURA!
GAH!
I'M IN EDO AGAIN!
YES...
...AND WITH YOUR USUAL TIMING!

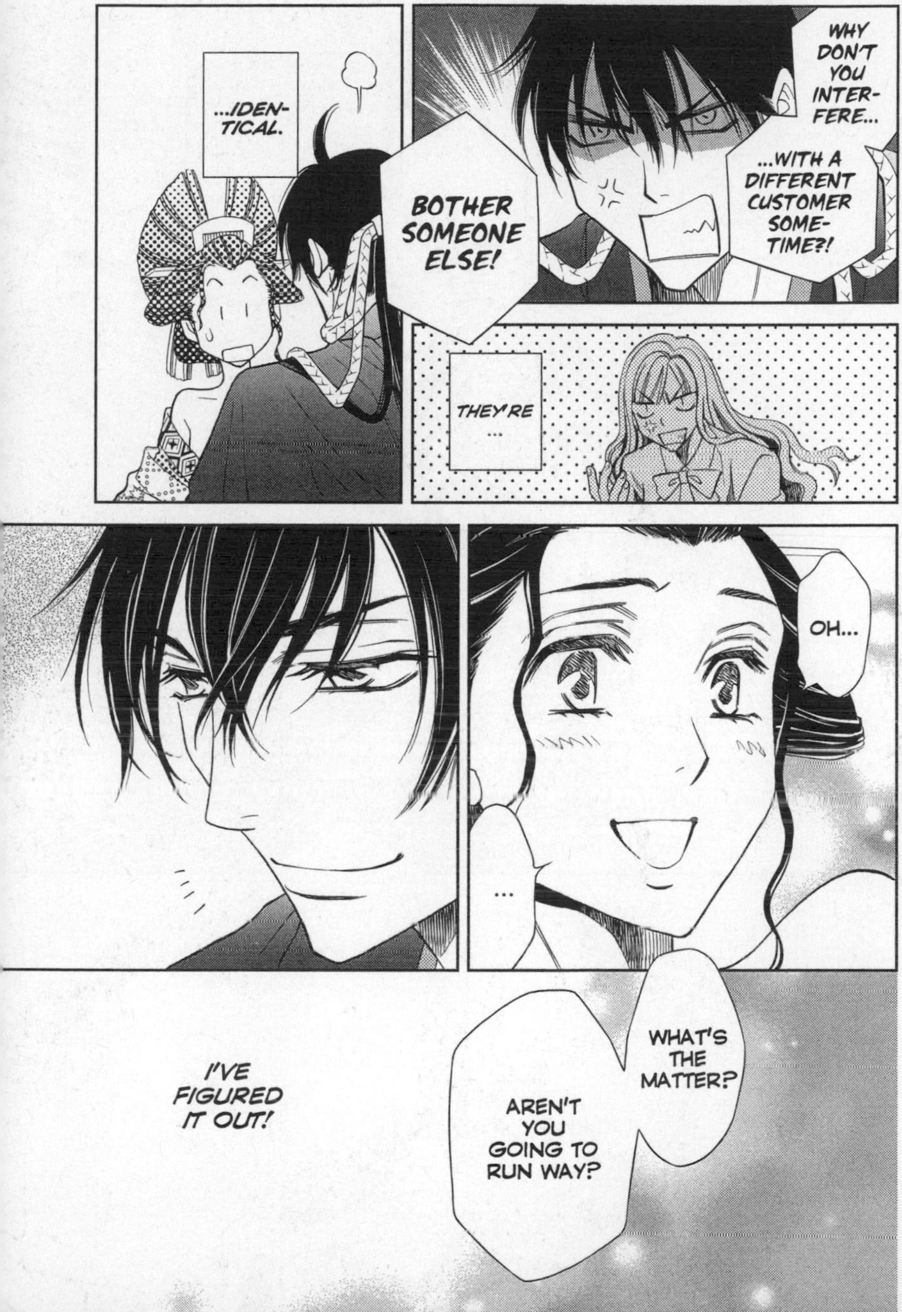
WHY DON'T YOU INTERFERE...
...WITH A DIFFERENT CUSTOMER SOMETIME?!
BOTHER SOMEONE ELSE!
THEY'RE ...
...IDENTICAL.
OH...
...
WHAT'S THE MATTER?
AREN'T YOU GOING TO RUN WAY?
I'VE FIGURED IT OUT!

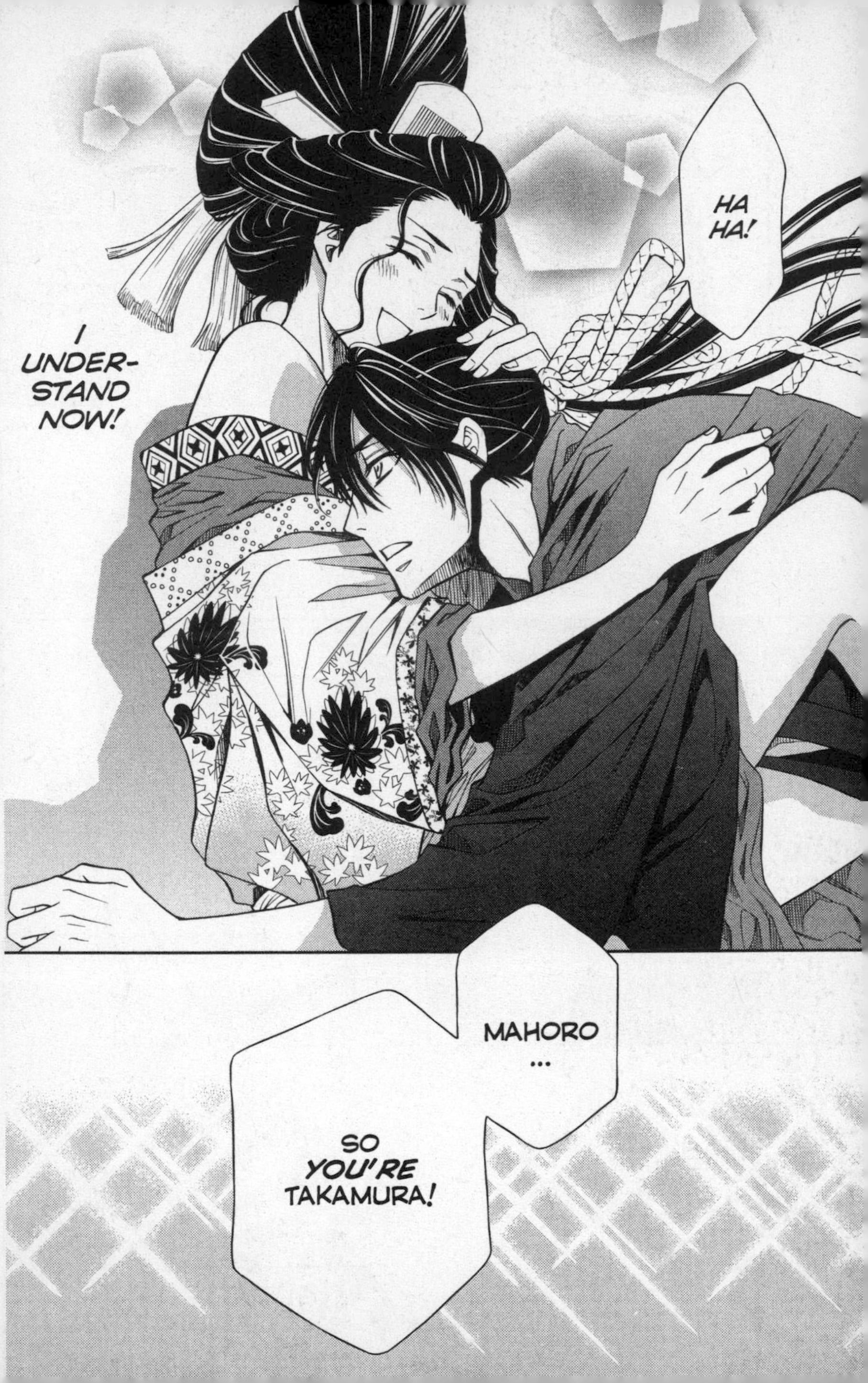
HA HA!
I UNDER-STAND NOW!
MAHORO ...
SO *YOU'RE* TAKAMURA!

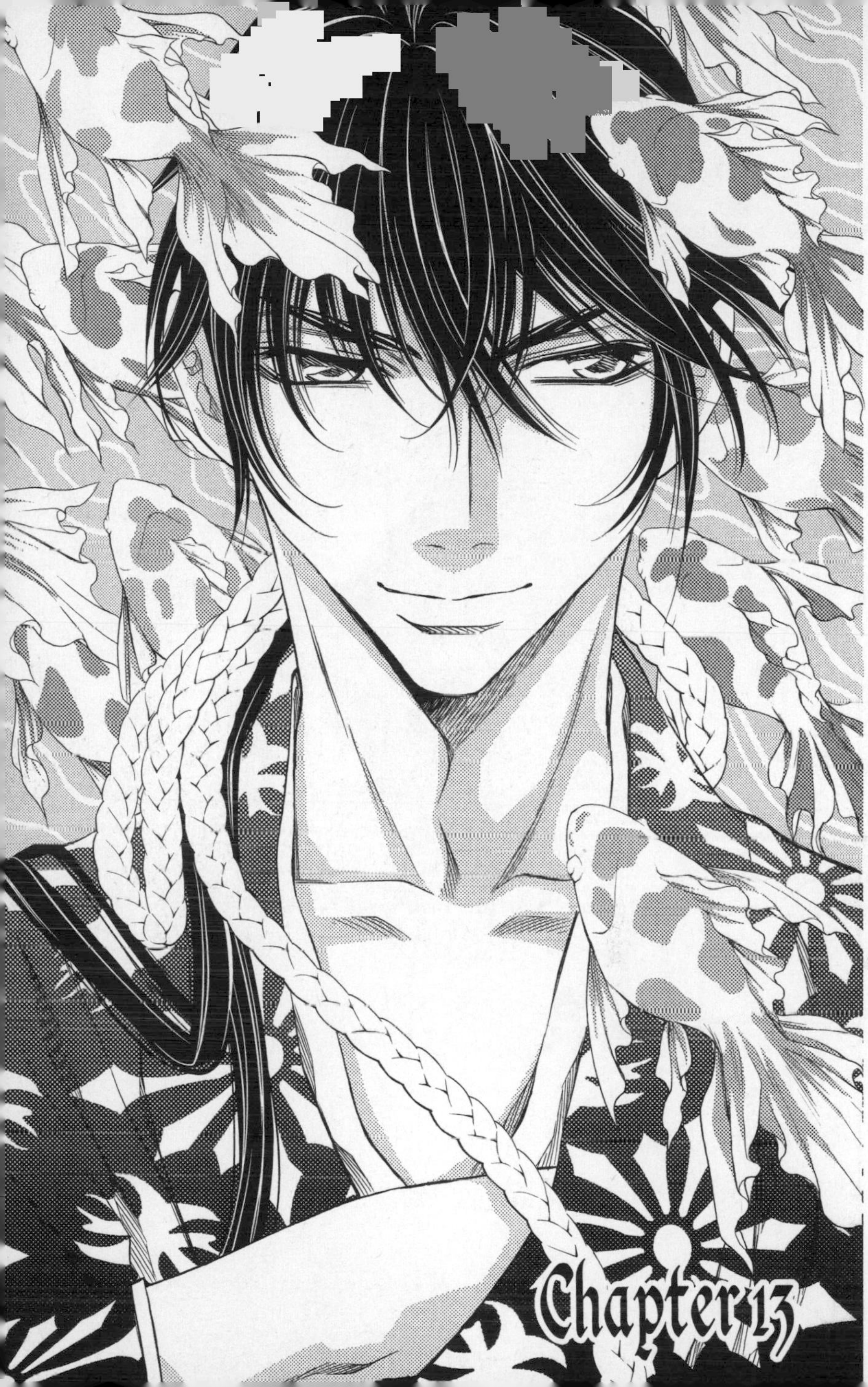
Chapter 13

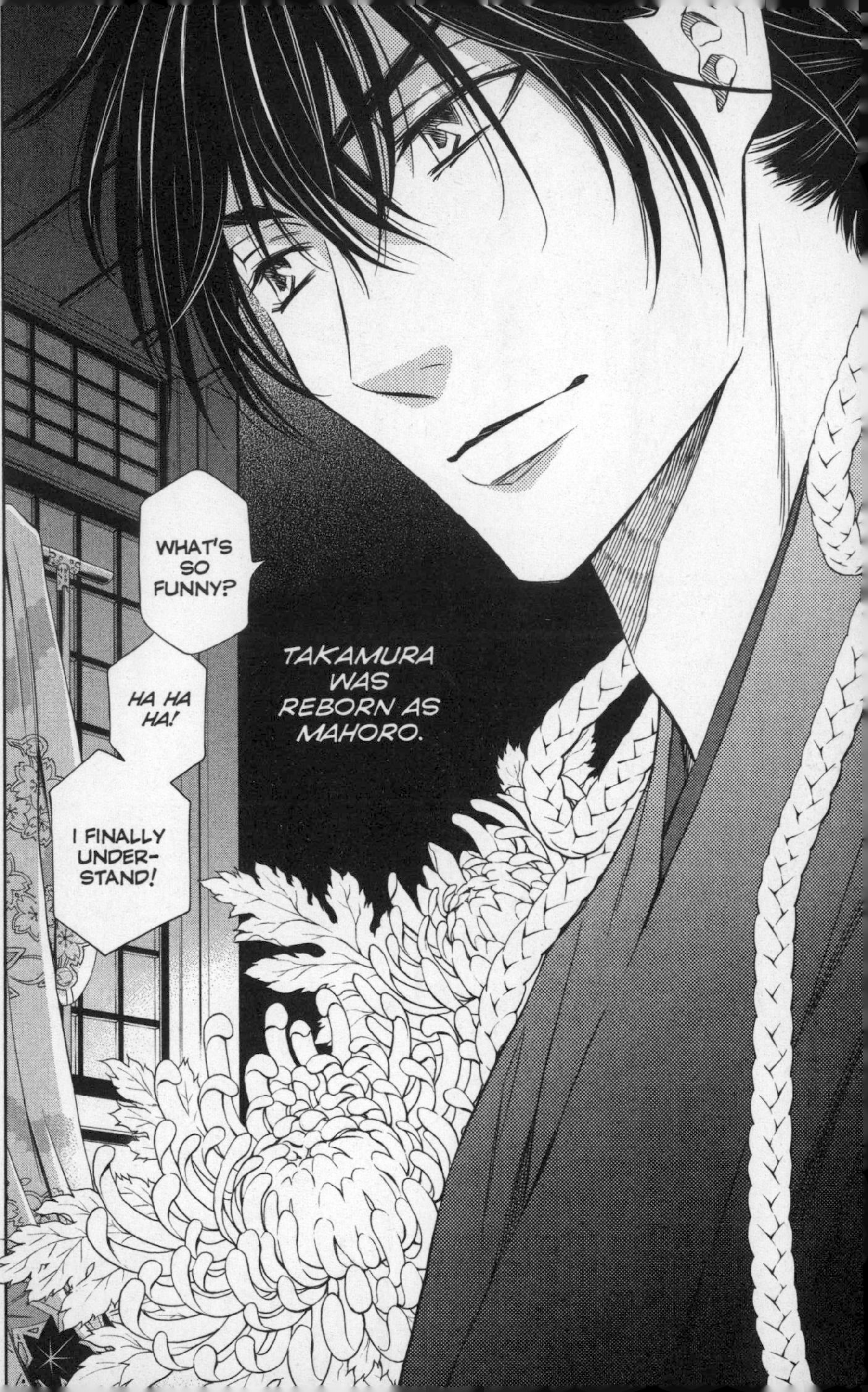
TAKAMURA WAS REBORN AS MAHORO.
WHAT'S SO FUNNY?
HA HA HA!
I FINALLY UNDER-STAND!

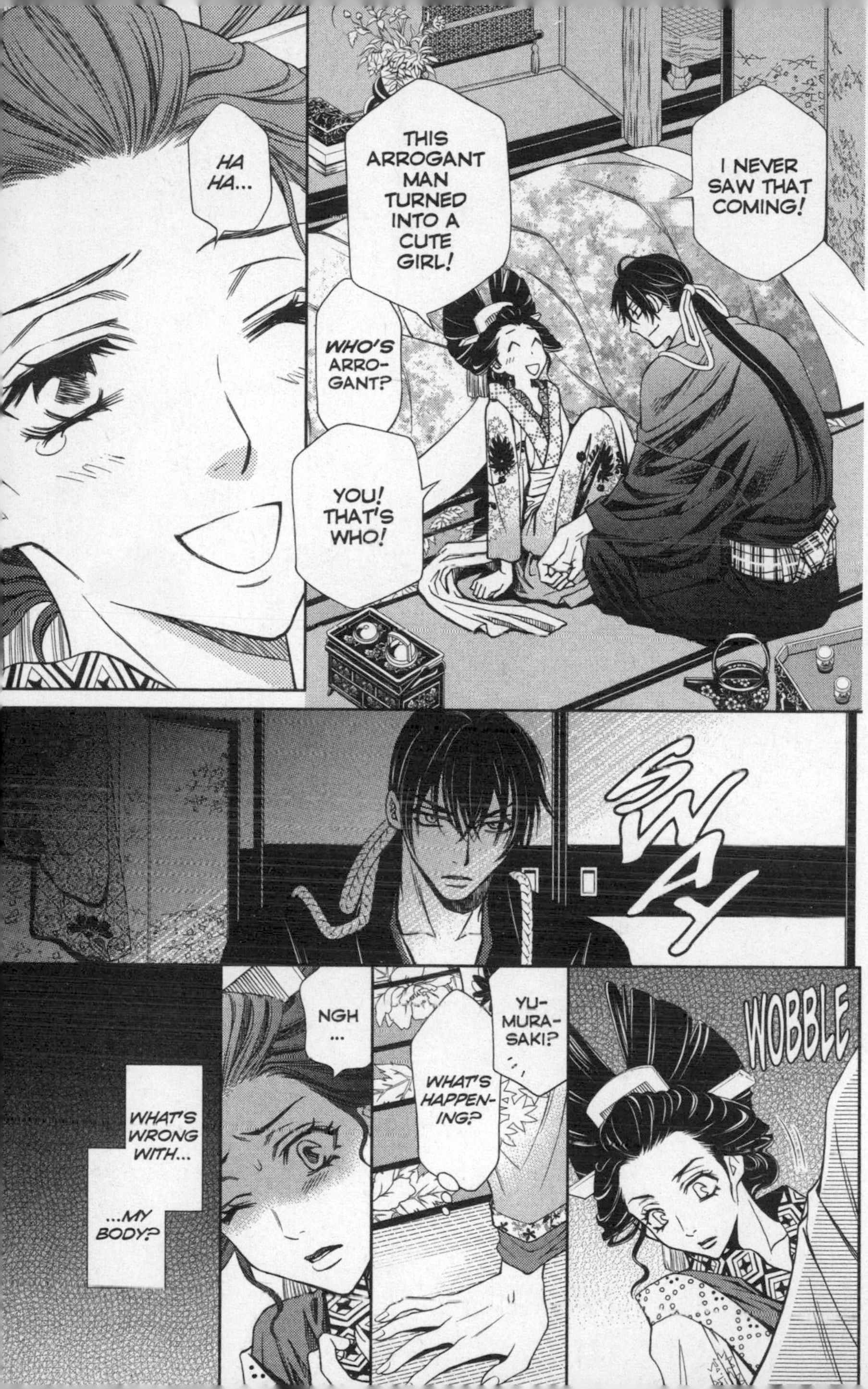
I NEVER SAW THAT COMING!
THIS ARROGANT MAN TURNED INTO A CUTE GIRL!
WHO'S ARROGANT?
YOU! THAT'S WHO!
HA HA...
SWAY
WOBBLE
YU-MURA-SAKI?
WHAT'S HAPPEN-ING?
NGH ...
WHAT'S WRONG WITH...
...MY BODY?

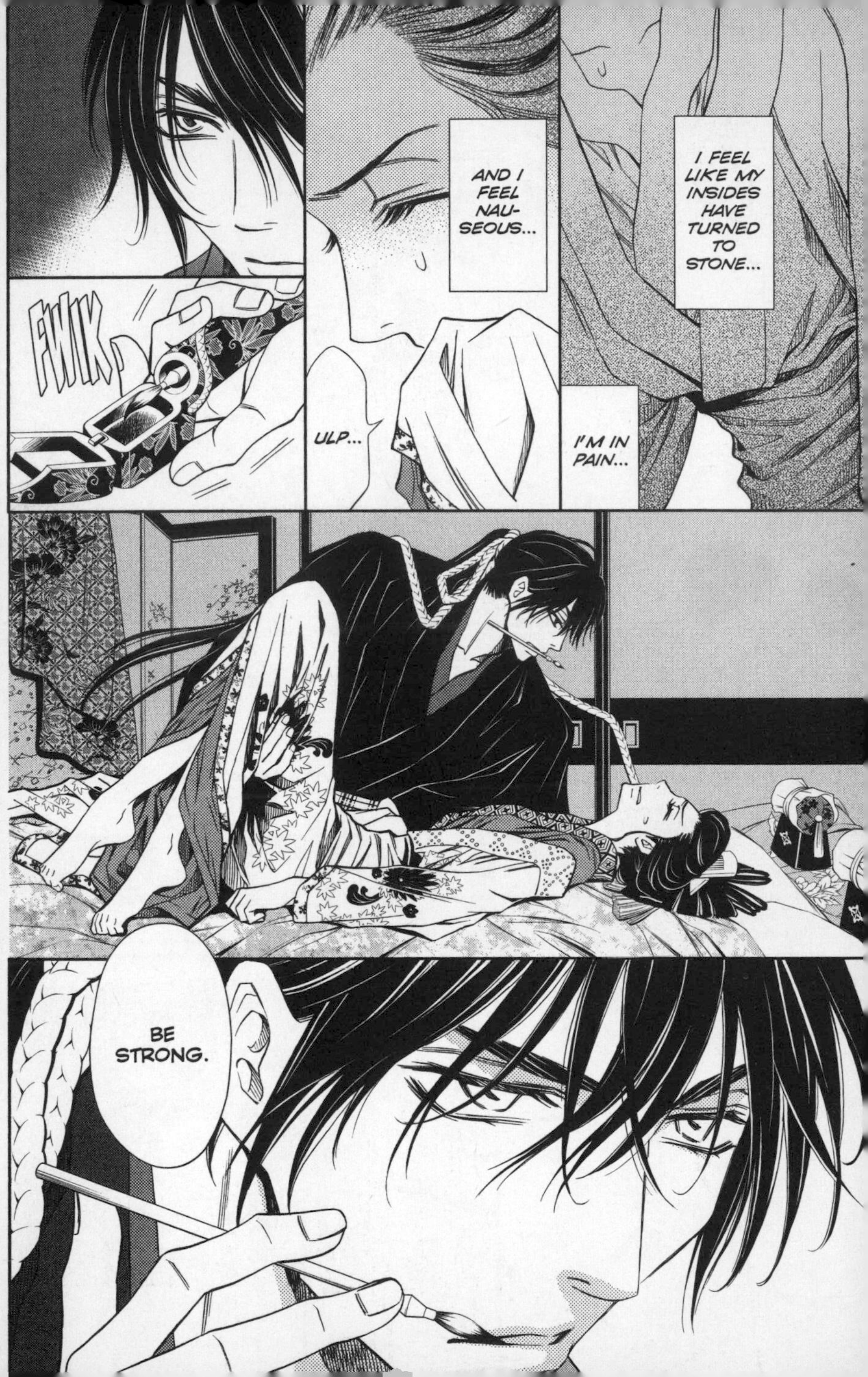
I FEEL LIKE MY INSIDES HAVE TURNED TO STONE...
I'M IN PAIN...
AND I FEEL NAU-SEOUS...
ULP...
FWIK
BE STRONG.

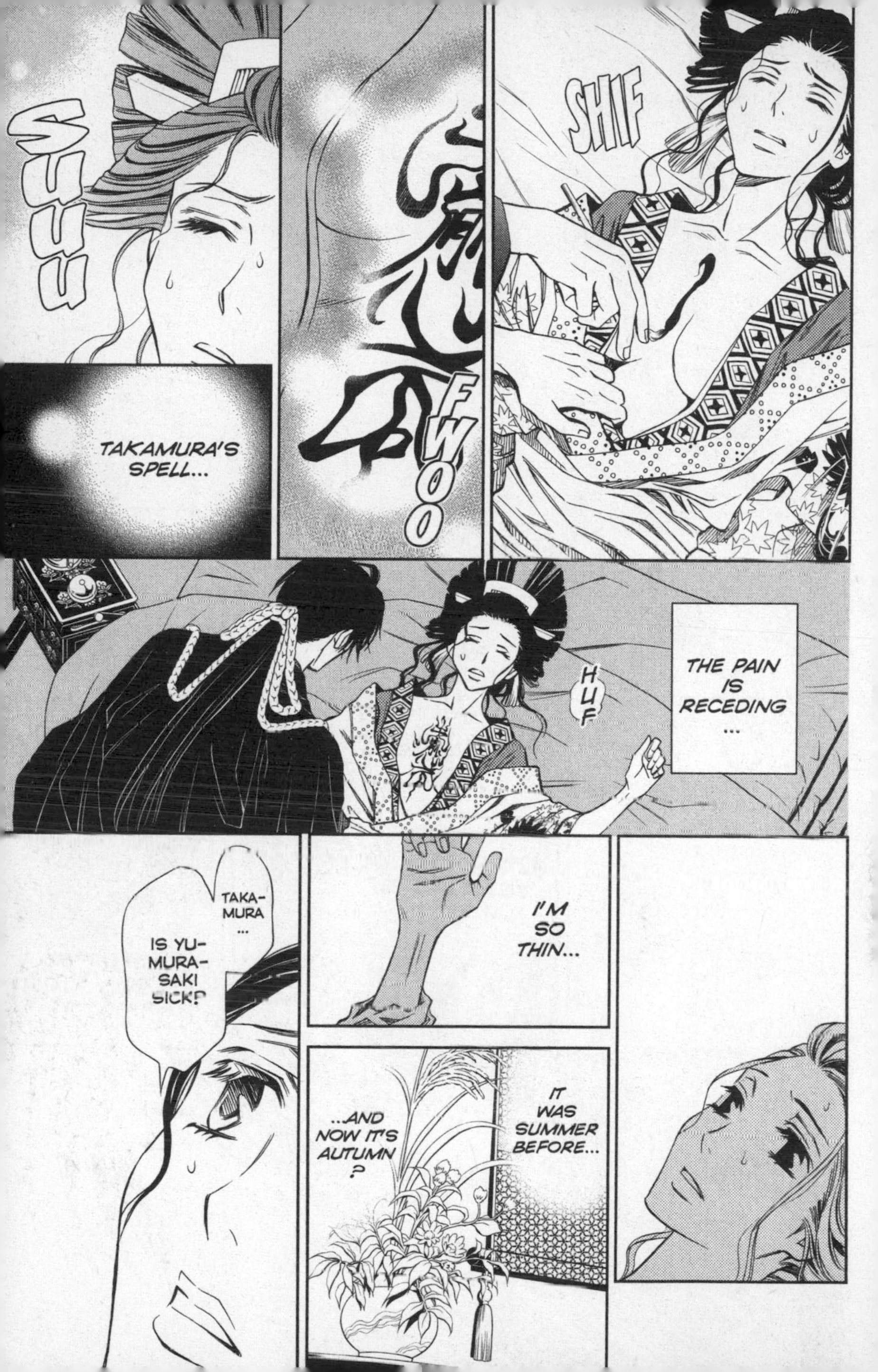
SHIF
FWOO
SUUU
TAKAMURA'S SPELL...
THE PAIN IS RECEDING ...
HUF
I'M SO THIN...
IT WAS SUMMER BEFORE...
...AND NOW IT'S AUTUMN?
TAKAMURA...
IS YUMURASAKI SICK?

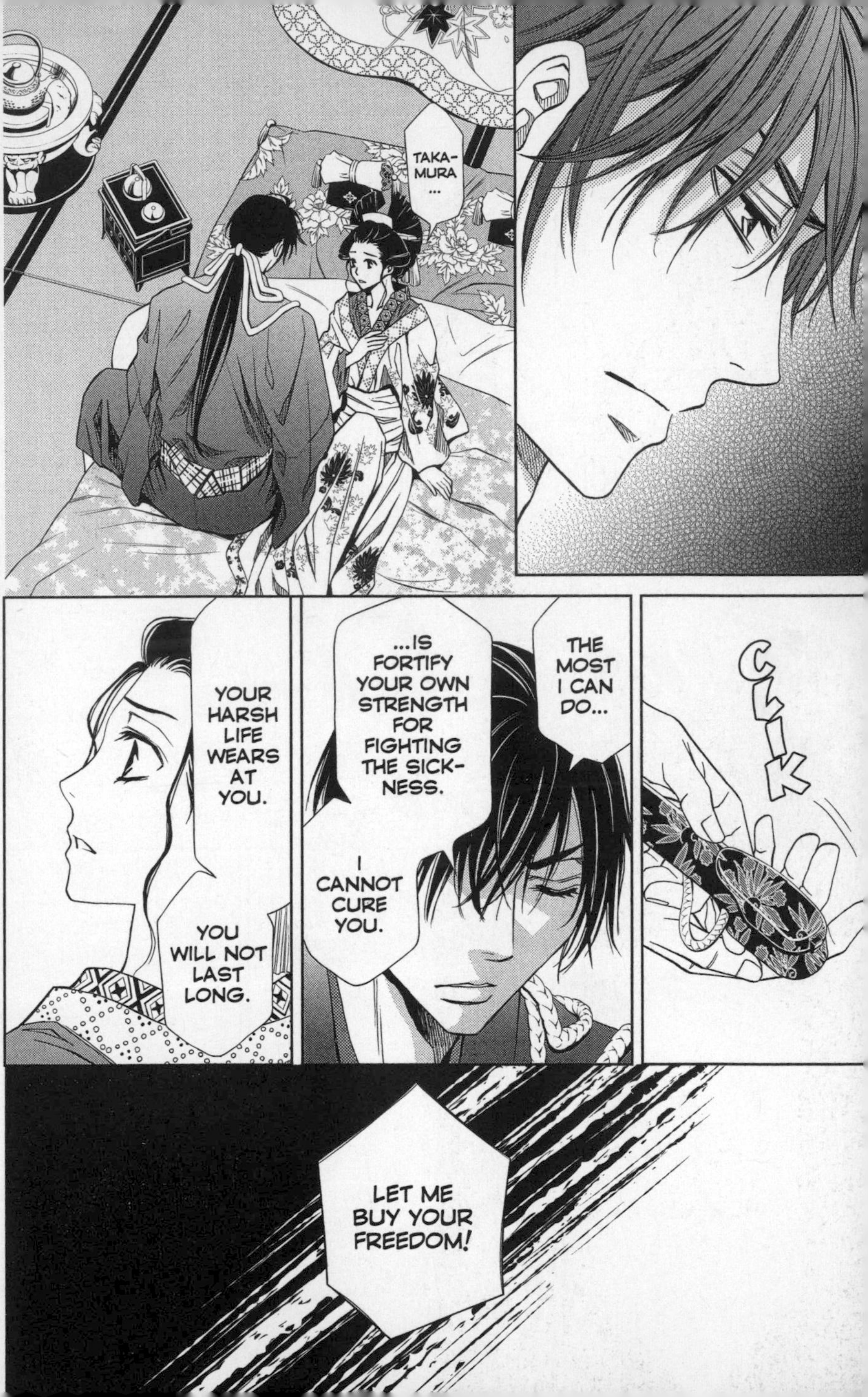
TAKAMURA...
CLIK
THE MOST I CAN DO...
...IS FORTIFY YOUR OWN STRENGTH FOR FIGHTING THE SICKNESS.
I CANNOT CURE YOU.
YOUR HARSH LIFE WEARS AT YOU.
YOU WILL NOT LAST LONG.
LET ME BUY YOUR FREEDOM!

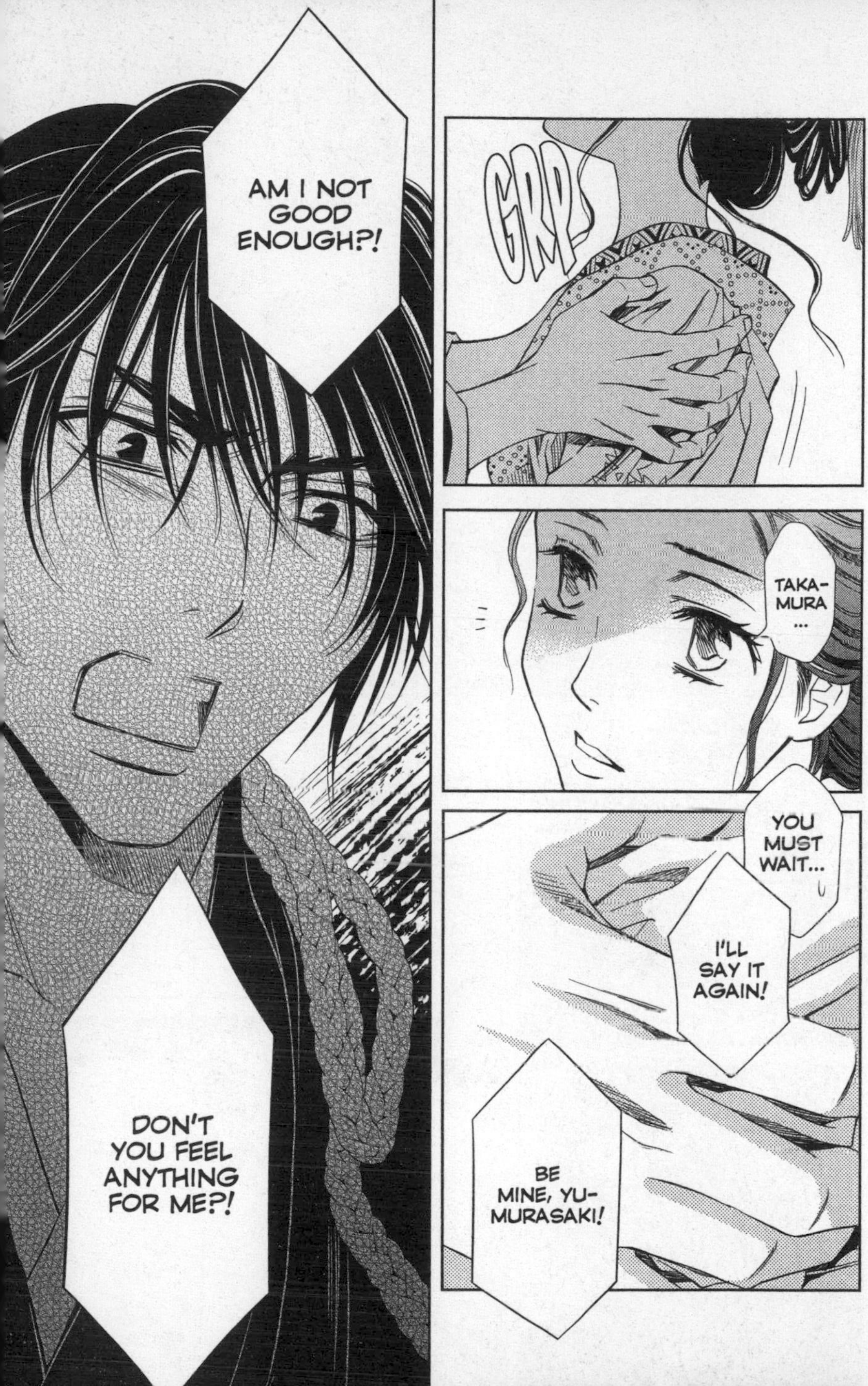
GRP
TAKA-MURA...
YOU MUST WAIT...
I'LL SAY IT AGAIN!
BE MINE, YU-MURASAKI!
AM I NOT GOOD ENOUGH?!
DON'T YOU FEEL ANYTHING FOR ME?!

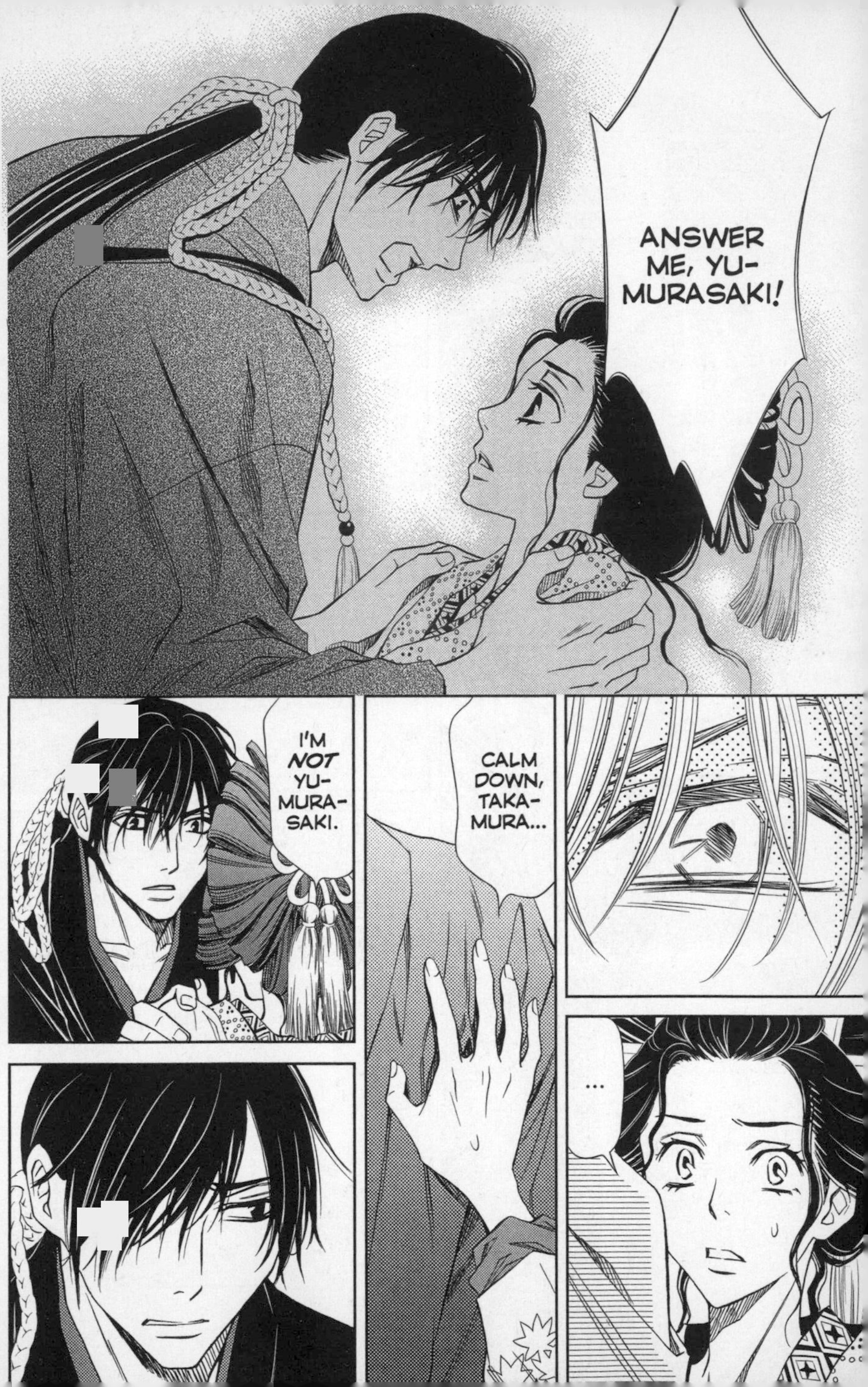
ANSWER ME, YU-MURASAKI!
...
CALM DOWN, TAKAMURA...
I'M *NOT* YU-MURASAKI.

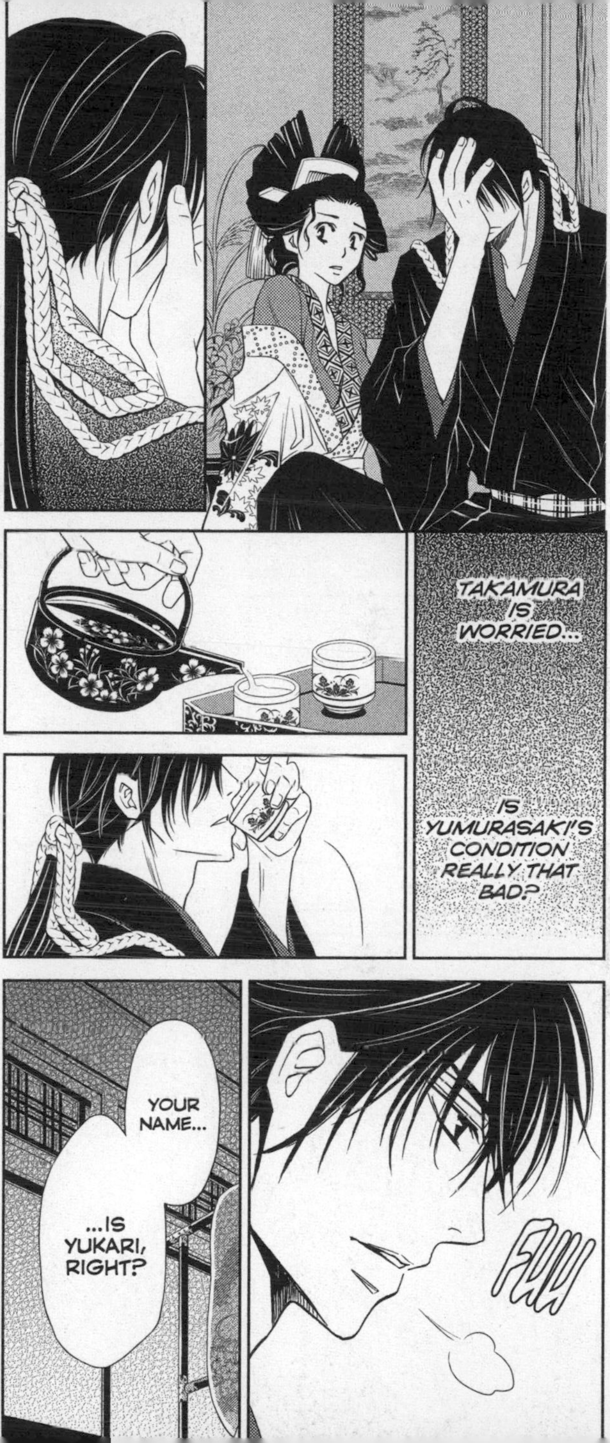
TAKAMURA IS WORRIED...
IS YUMURASAKI'S CONDITION REALLY THAT BAD?
FUU
YOUR NAME...
...IS YUKARI, RIGHT?

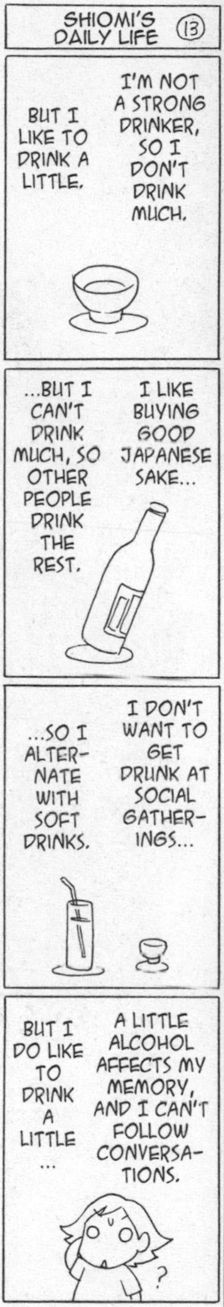
SHIOMI'S DAILY LIFE 13
I'M NOT A STRONG DRINKER, SO I DON'T DRINK MUCH.
BUT I LIKE TO DRINK A LITTLE.
I LIKE BUYING GOOD JAPANESE SAKE...
...BUT I CAN'T DRINK MUCH, SO OTHER PEOPLE DRINK THE REST.
I DON'T WANT TO GET DRUNK AT SOCIAL GATHER-INGS...
...SO I ALTER-NATE WITH SOFT DRINKS.
A LITTLE ALCOHOL AFFECTS MY MEMORY, AND I CAN'T FOLLOW CONVERSA-TIONS.
BUT I DO LIKE TO DRINK A LITTLE ...
?

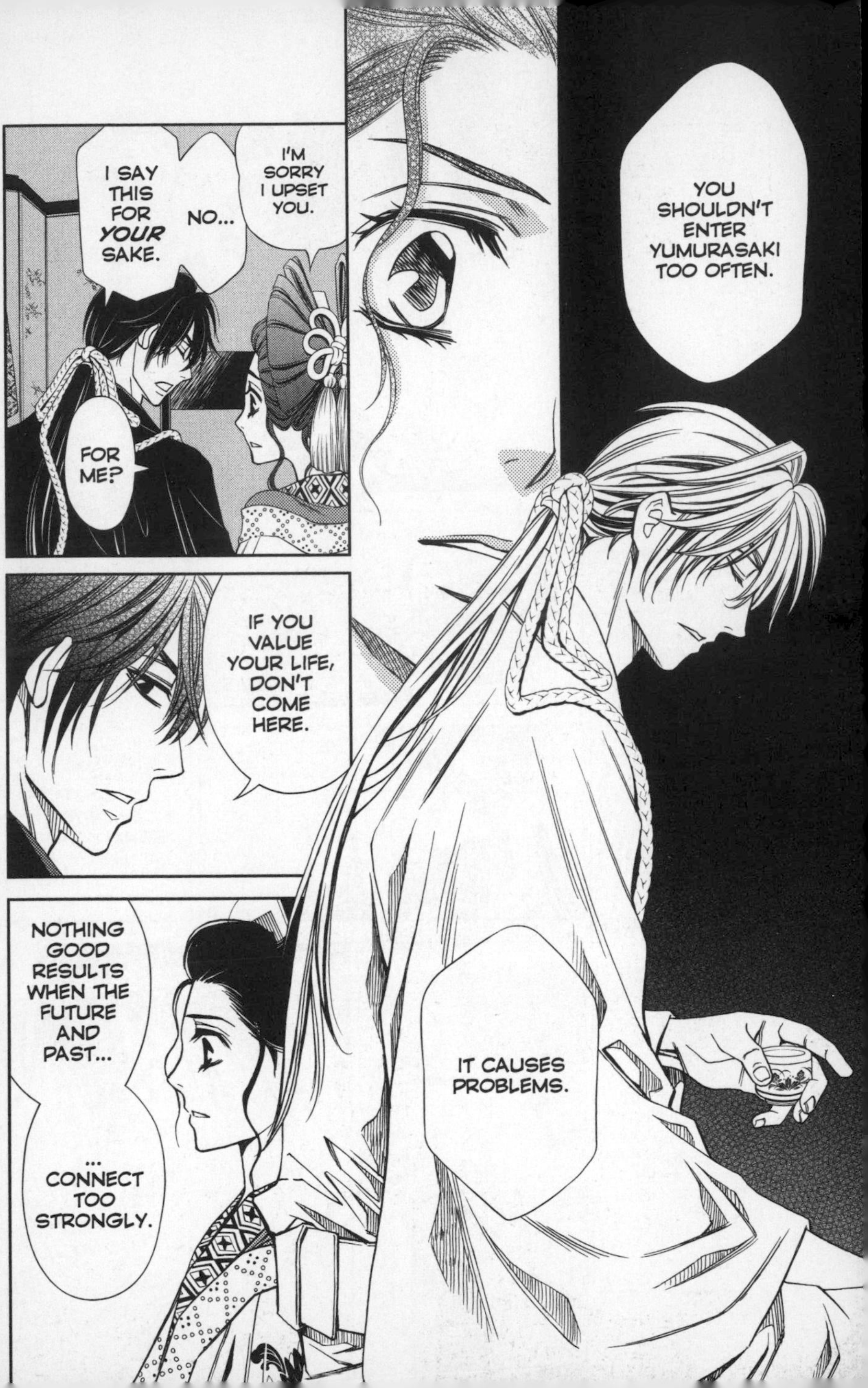
YOU SHOULDN'T ENTER YUMURASAKI TOO OFTEN.
IT CAUSES PROBLEMS.
I'M SORRY I UPSET YOU.
I SAY THIS FOR *YOUR* SAKE.
NO...
FOR ME?
IF YOU VALUE YOUR LIFE, DON'T COME HERE.
NOTHING GOOD RESULTS WHEN THE FUTURE AND PAST...
... CONNECT TOO STRONGLY.

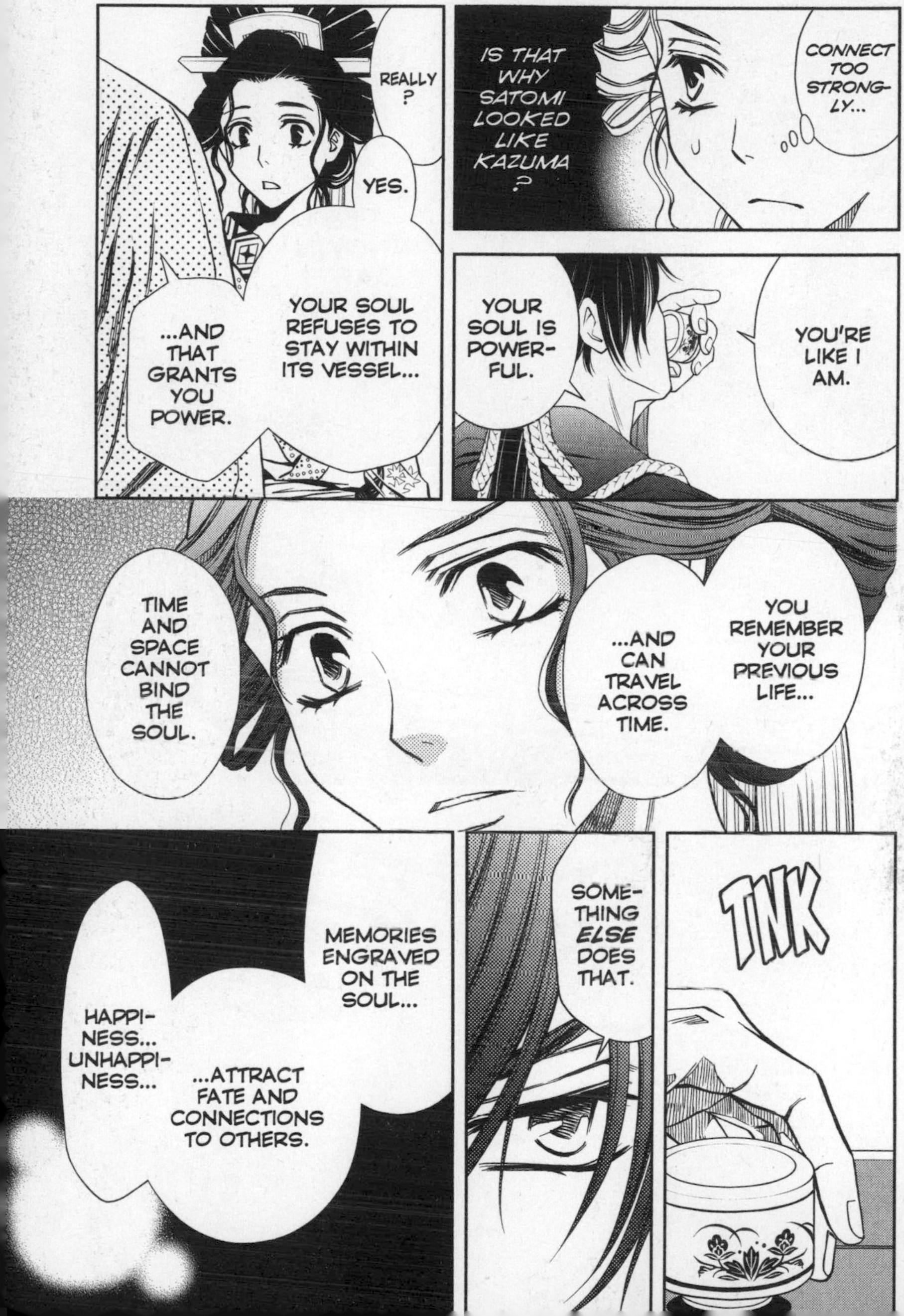
CONNECT TOO STRONGLY...
IS THAT WHY SATOMI LOOKED LIKE KAZUMA?
YOU'RE LIKE I AM.
YOUR SOUL IS POWERFUL.
REALLY?
YES.
YOUR SOUL REFUSES TO STAY WITHIN ITS VESSEL...
...AND THAT GRANTS YOU POWER.
YOU REMEMBER YOUR PREVIOUS LIFE...
...AND CAN TRAVEL ACROSS TIME.
TIME AND SPACE CANNOT BIND THE SOUL.
TNK
SOMETHING *ELSE* DOES THAT.
MEMORIES ENGRAVED ON THE SOUL...
HAPPINESS... UNHAPPINESS...
...ATTRACT FATE AND CONNECTIONS TO OTHERS.

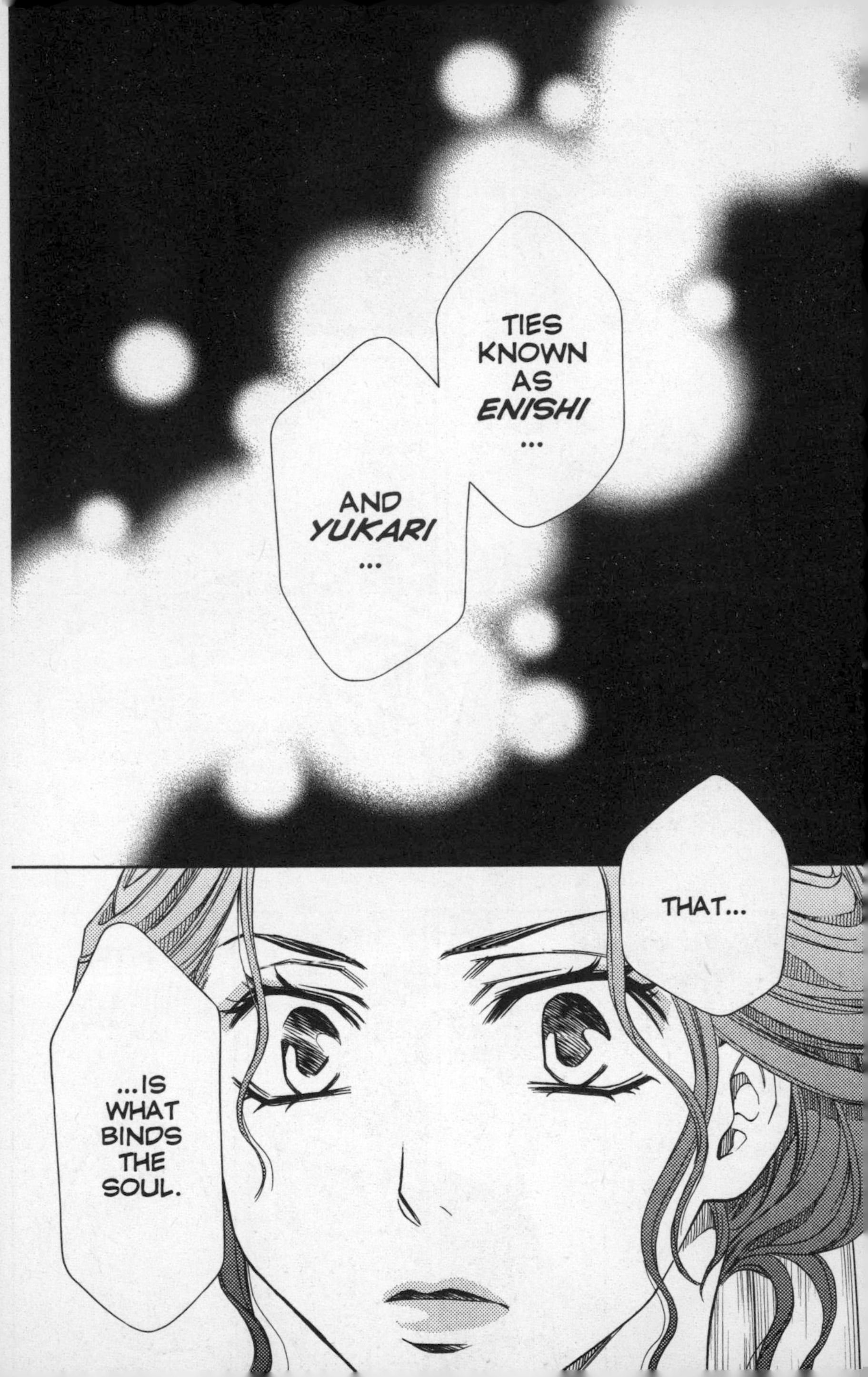
TIES KNOWN AS *ENISHI* ...
AND *YUKARI* ...
THAT...
...IS WHAT BINDS THE SOUL.

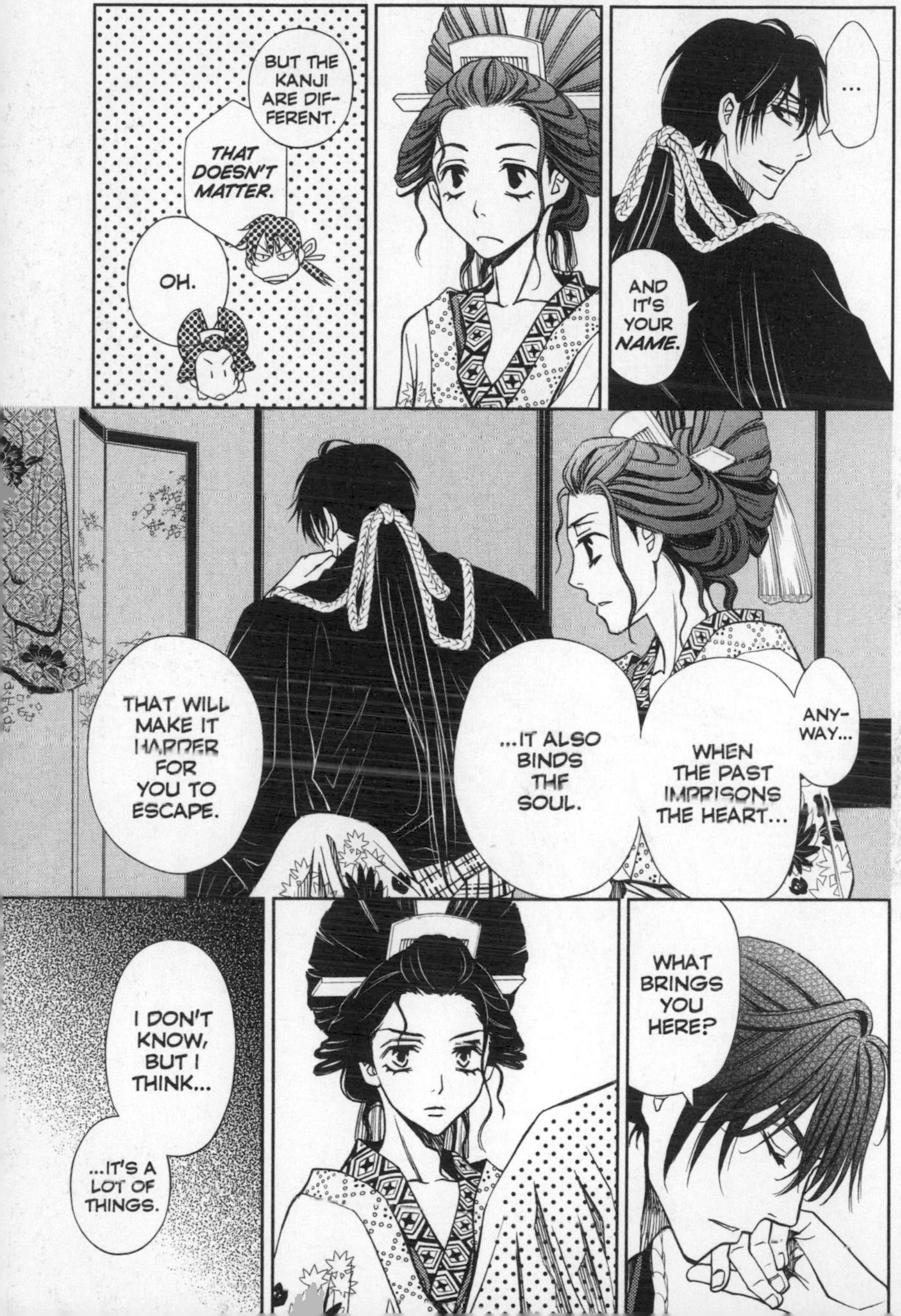
...
AND IT'S YOUR NAME.
BUT THE KANJI ARE DIFFERENT.
THAT DOESN'T MATTER.
OH.
ANYWAY...
WHEN THE PAST IMPRISONS THE HEART...
...IT ALSO BINDS THE SOUL.
THAT WILL MAKE IT HARDER FOR YOU TO ESCAPE.
WHAT BRINGS YOU HERE?
I DON'T KNOW, BUT I THINK...
...IT'S A LOT OF THINGS.

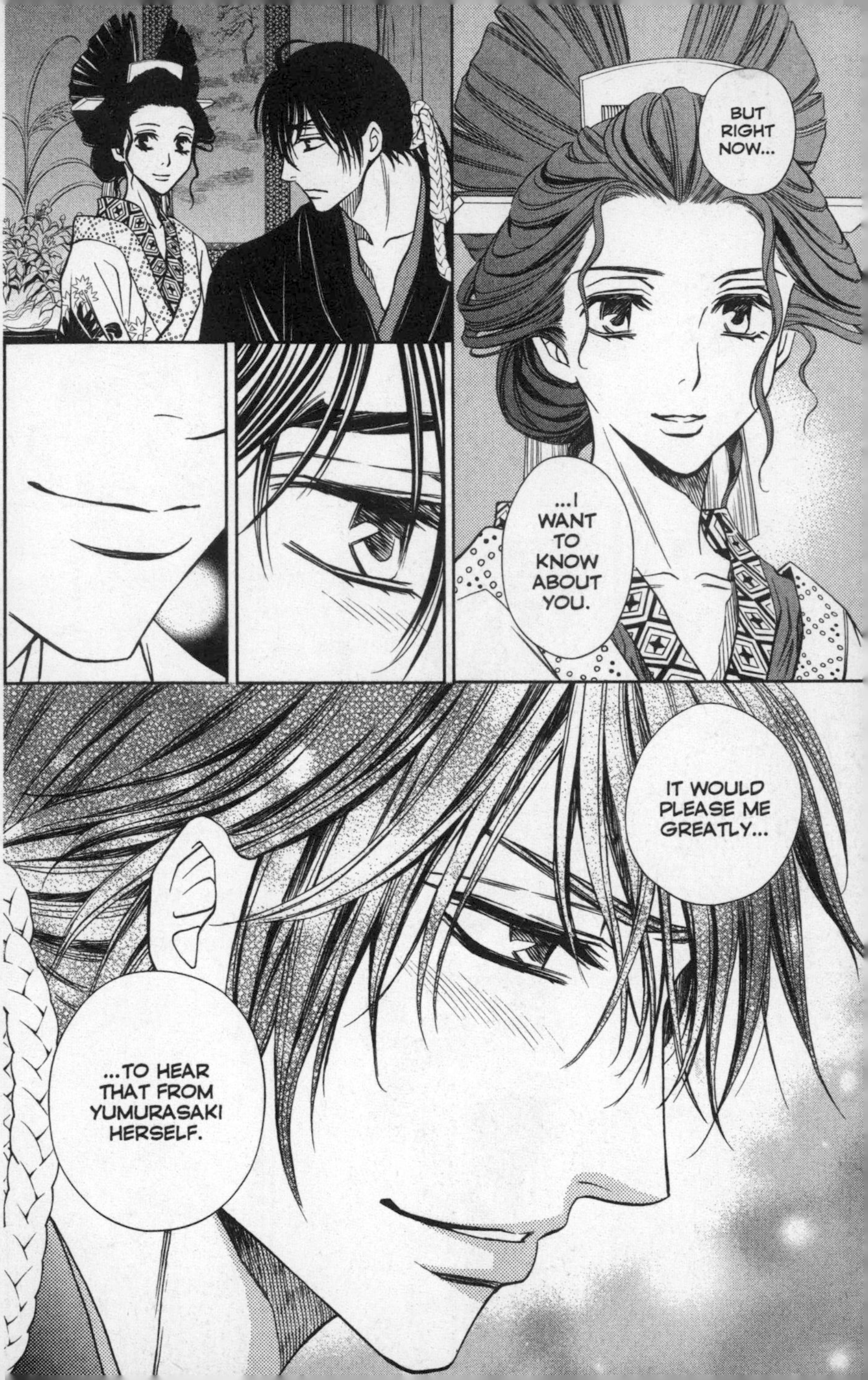
BUT RIGHT NOW...
...I WANT TO KNOW ABOUT YOU.
IT WOULD PLEASE ME GREATLY...
...TO HEAR THAT FROM YUMURASAKI HERSELF.

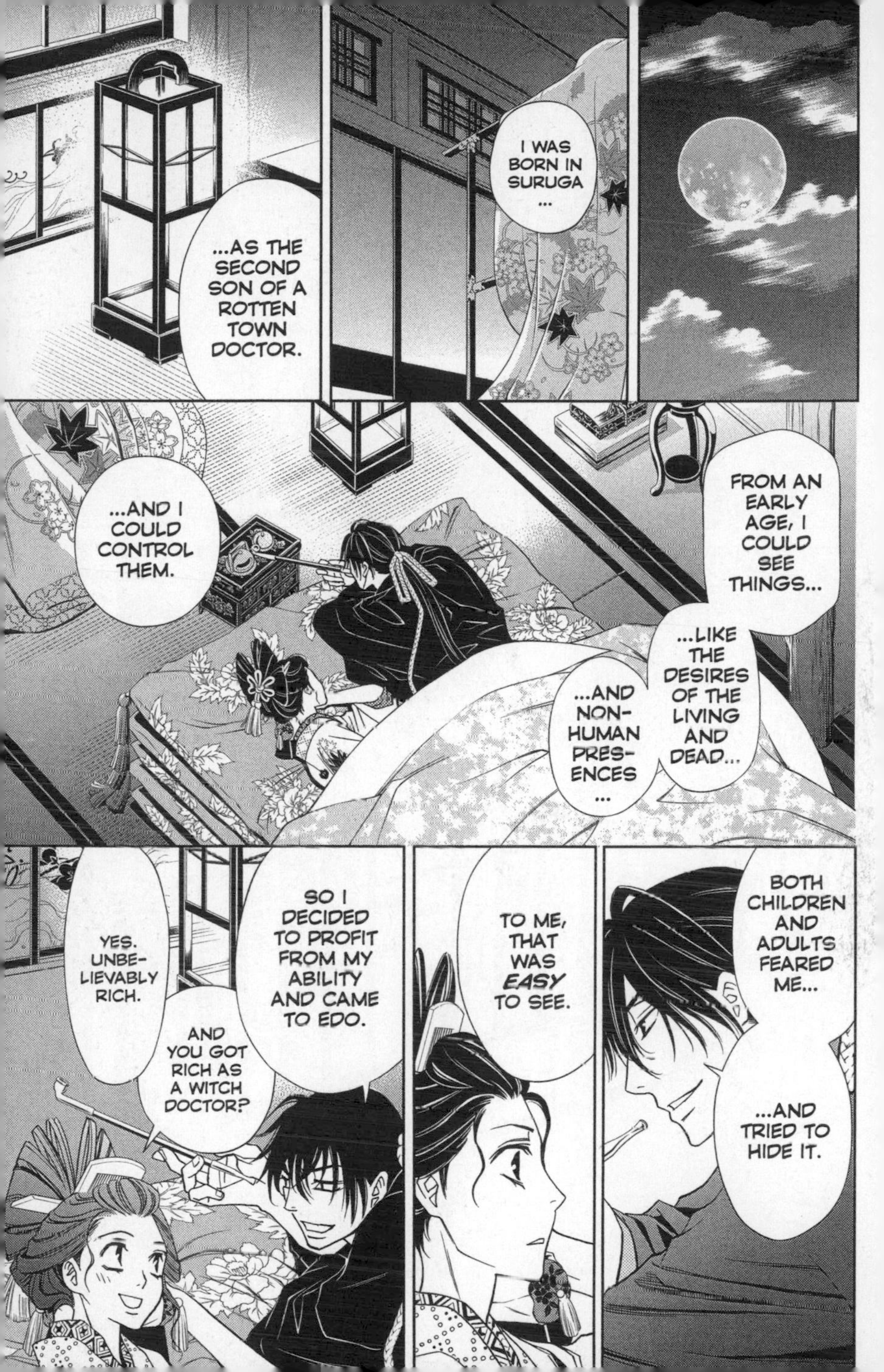
I WAS BORN IN SURUGA ...
...AS THE SECOND SON OF A ROTTEN TOWN DOCTOR.
FROM AN EARLY AGE, I COULD SEE THINGS...
...LIKE THE DESIRES OF THE LIVING AND DEAD...
...AND NON-HUMAN PRESENCES ...
...AND I COULD CONTROL THEM.
BOTH CHILDREN AND ADULTS FEARED ME...
...AND TRIED TO HIDE IT.
TO ME, THAT WAS EASY TO SEE.
SO I DECIDED TO PROFIT FROM MY ABILITY AND CAME TO EDO.
AND YOU GOT RICH AS A WITCH DOCTOR?
YES. UNBELIEVABLY RICH.

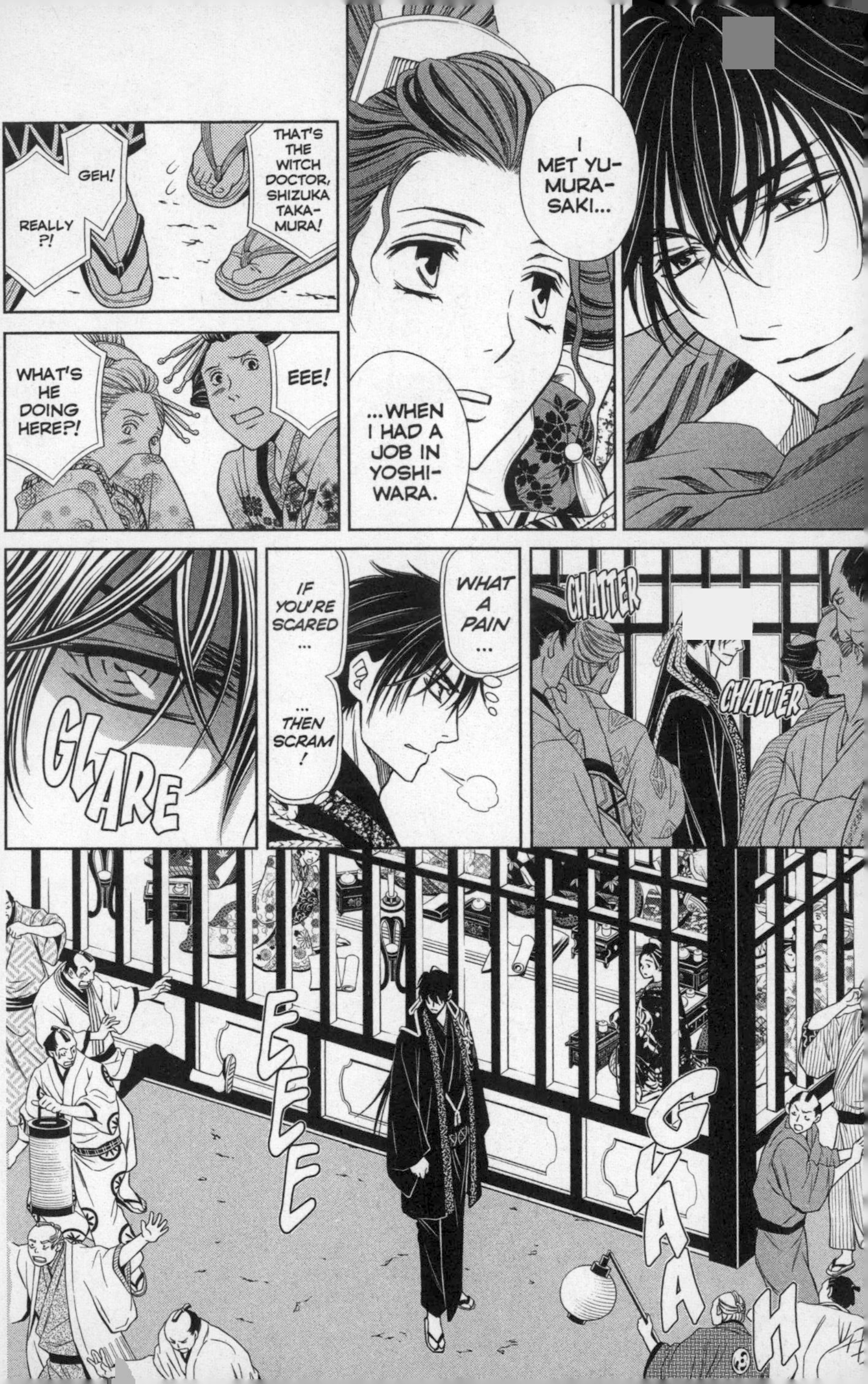
I MET YU-MURA-SAKI...
...WHEN I HAD A JOB IN YOSHI-WARA.
THAT'S THE WITCH DOCTOR, SHIZUKA TAKA-MURA!
GEH!
REALLY ?!
EEE!
WHAT'S HE DOING HERE?!
CHATTER
CHATTER
WHAT A PAIN ...
IF YOU'RE SCARED ...
... THEN SCRAM !
GLARE
GYAAAH
EEEE

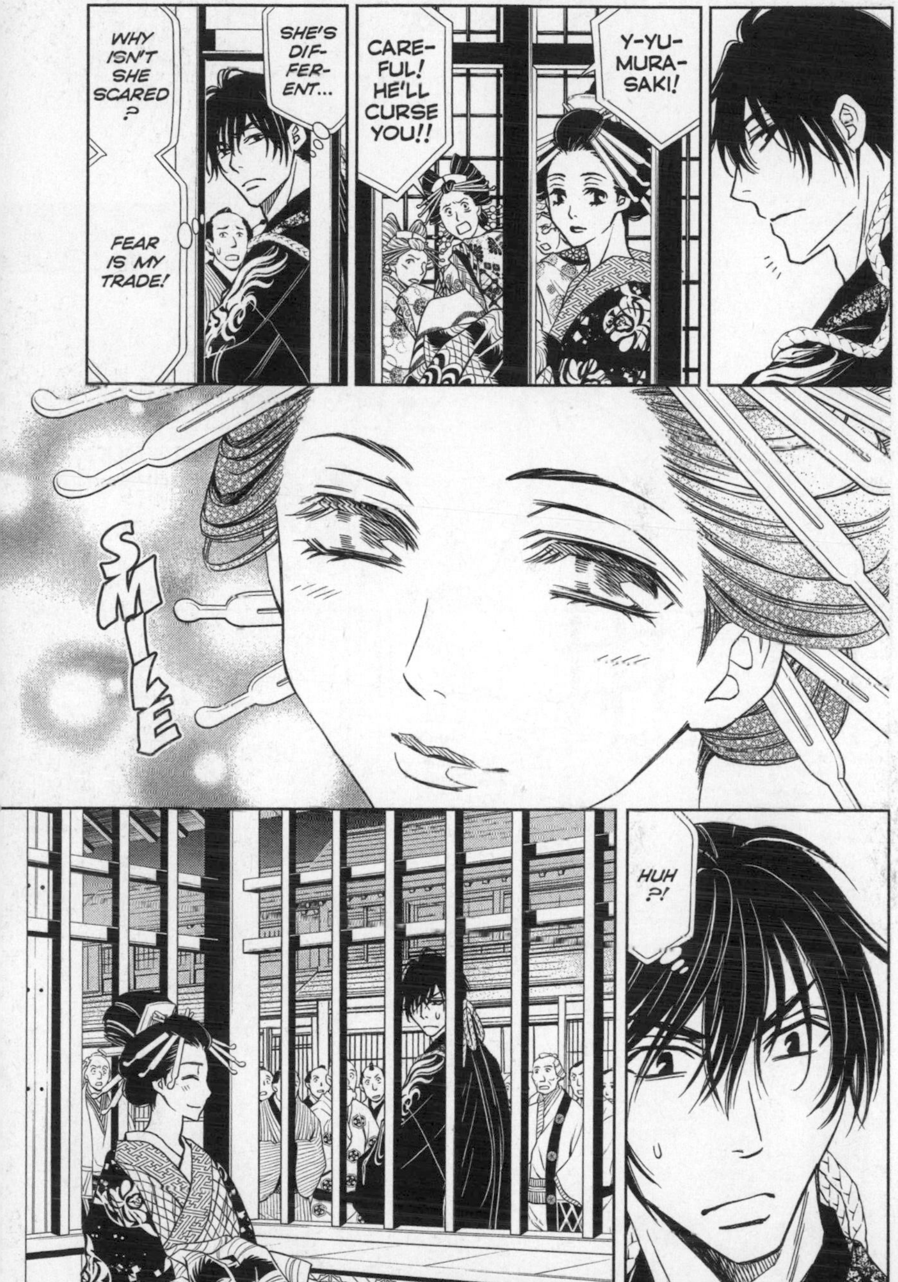
Y-YU-MURA-SAKI!
CARE-FUL! HE'LL CURSE YOU!!
SHE'S DIF-FER-ENT...
WHY ISN'T SHE SCARED?
FEAR IS MY TRADE!
SMILE
HUH?!

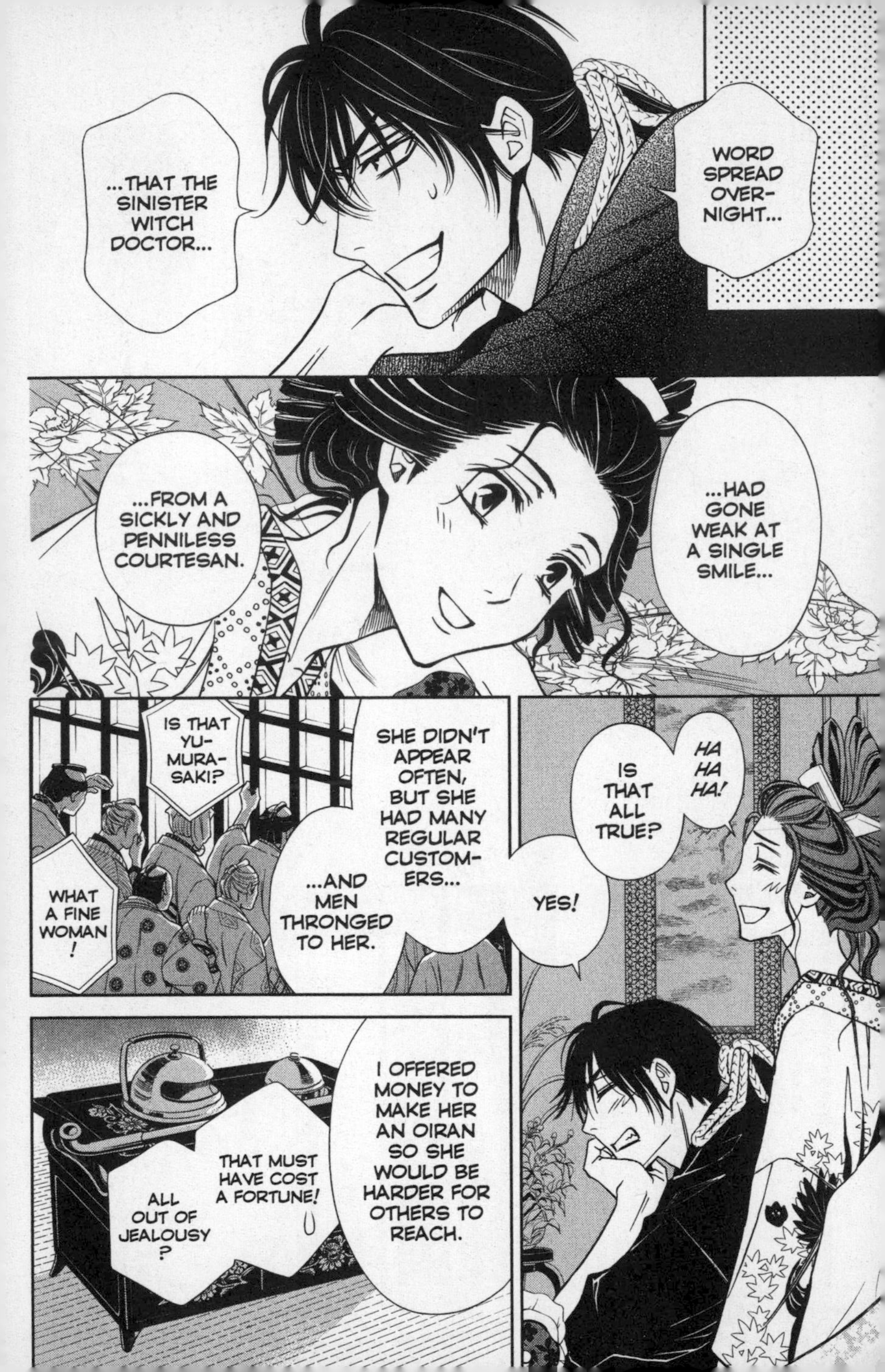
WORD SPREAD OVER-NIGHT...
...THAT THE SINISTER WITCH DOCTOR...
...HAD GONE WEAK AT A SINGLE SMILE...
...FROM A SICKLY AND PENNILESS COURTESAN.
HA HA HA!
IS THAT ALL TRUE?
YES!
SHE DIDN'T APPEAR OFTEN, BUT SHE HAD MANY REGULAR CUSTOM-ERS...
...AND MEN THRONGED TO HER.
IS THAT YU-MURA-SAKI?
WHAT A FINE WOMAN!
I OFFERED MONEY TO MAKE HER AN OIRAN SO SHE WOULD BE HARDER FOR OTHERS TO REACH.
THAT MUST HAVE COST A FORTUNE!
ALL OUT OF JEALOUSY?

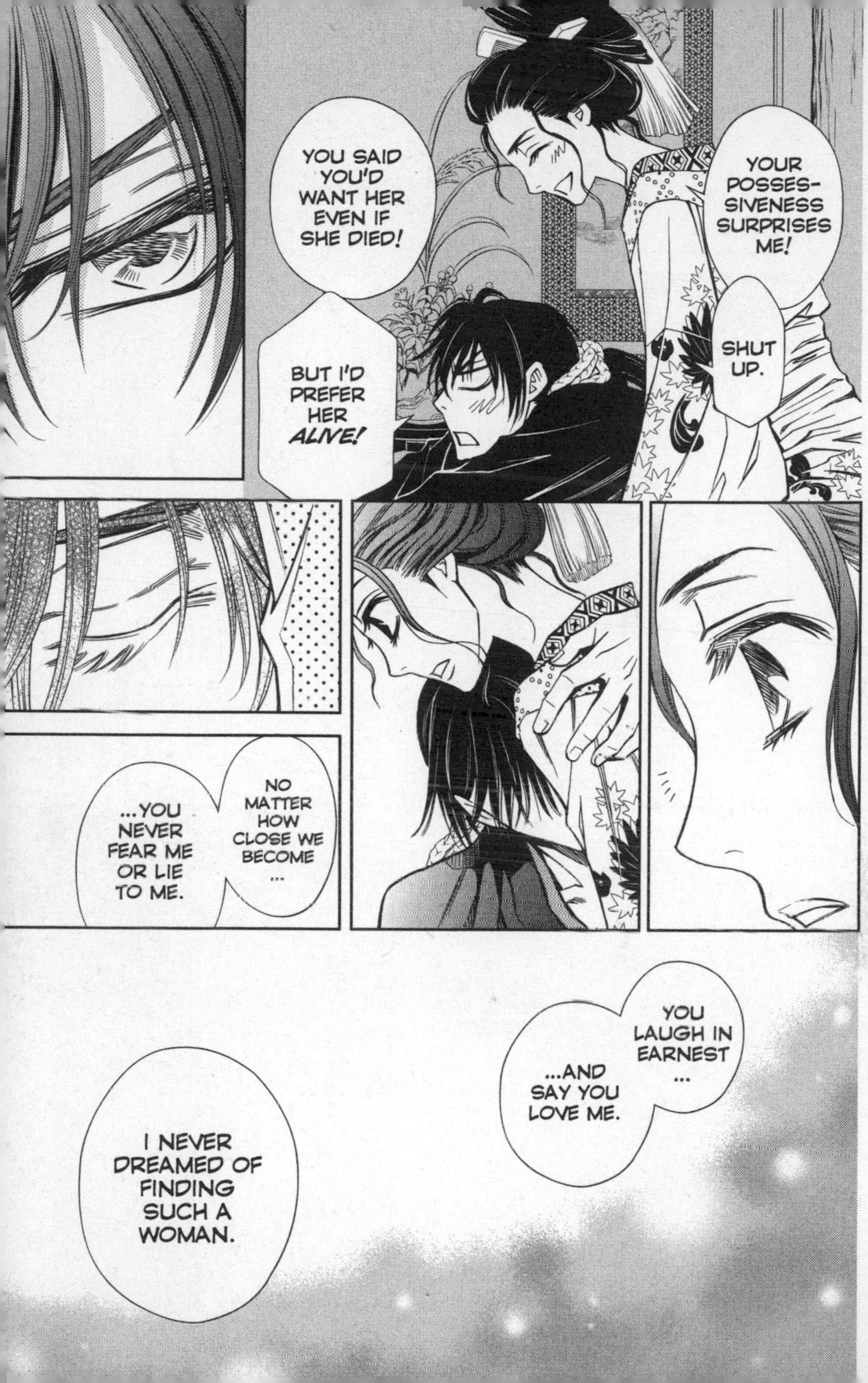
YOUR POSSES-SIVENESS SURPRISES ME!
YOU SAID YOU'D WANT HER EVEN IF SHE DIED!
SHUT UP.
BUT I'D PREFER HER *ALIVE!*
NO MATTER HOW CLOSE WE BECOME ...
...YOU NEVER FEAR ME OR LIE TO ME.
YOU LAUGH IN EARNEST ...
...AND SAY YOU LOVE ME.
I NEVER DREAMED OF FINDING SUCH A WOMAN.

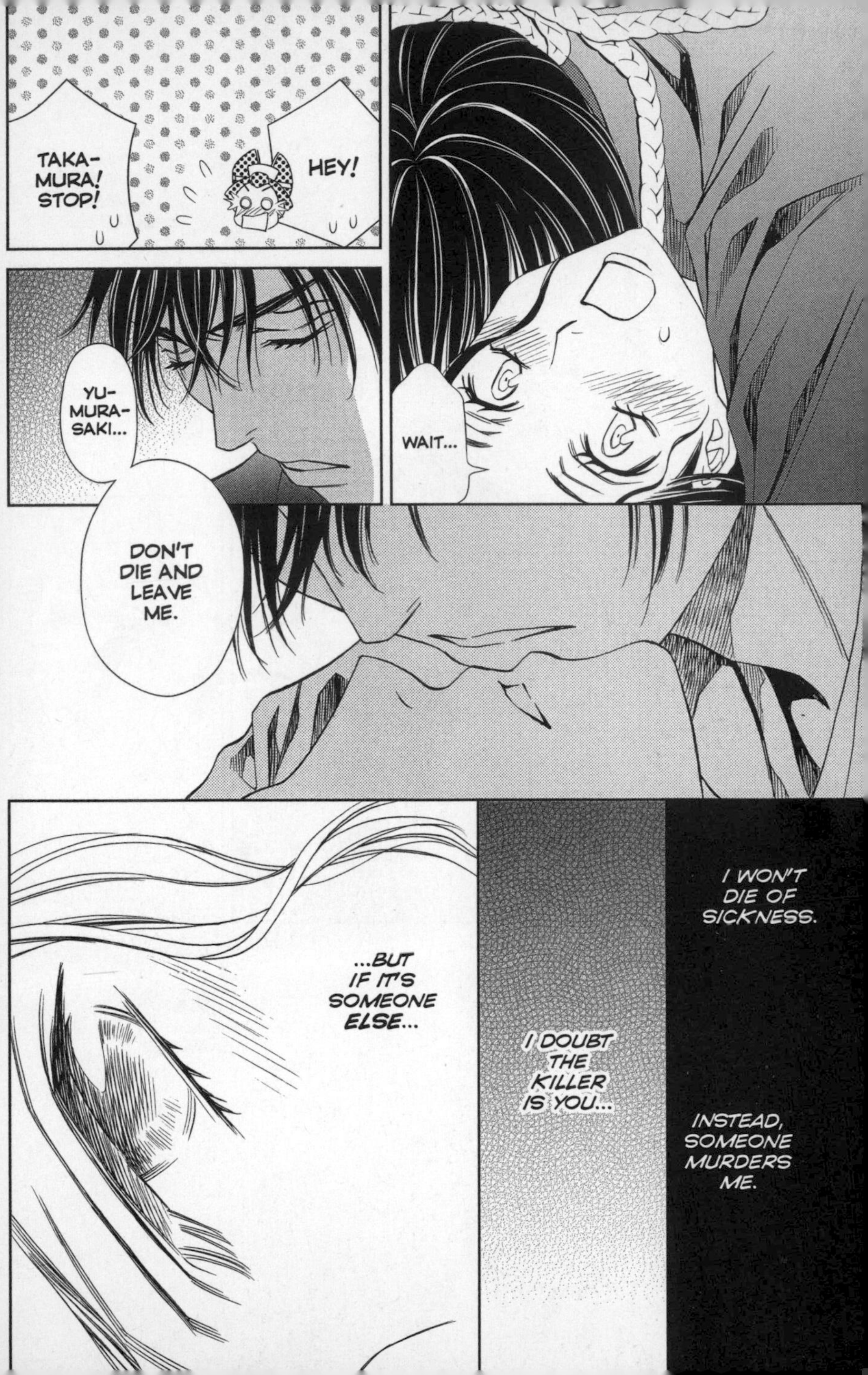
WAIT...
HEY!
TAKA-MURA! STOP!
YU-MURA-SAKI...
DON'T DIE AND LEAVE ME.
I WON'T DIE OF SICKNESS.
INSTEAD, SOMEONE MURDERS ME.
I DOUBT THE KILLER IS YOU...
...BUT IF IT'S SOMEONE ELSE...

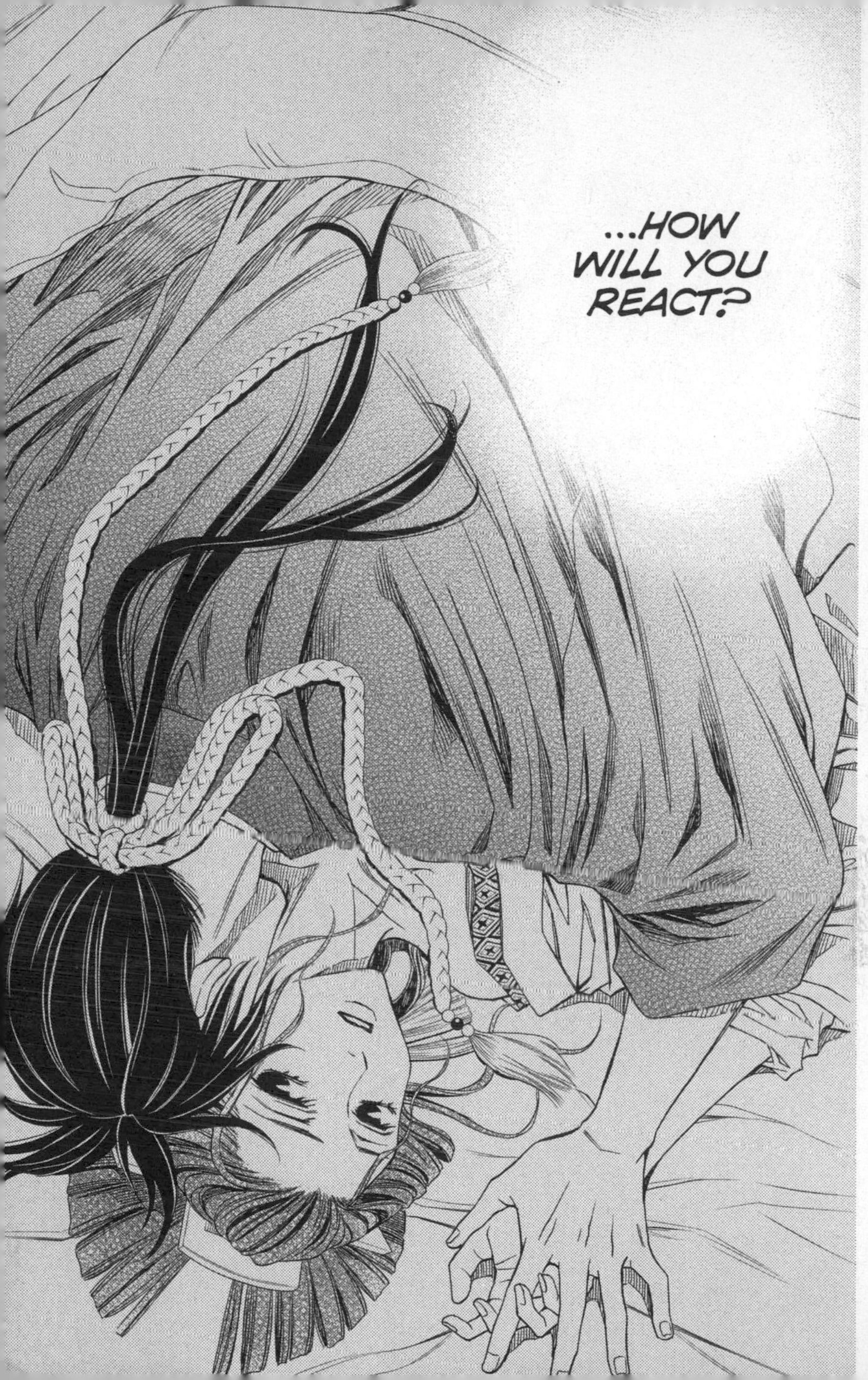
...HOW WILL YOU REACT?

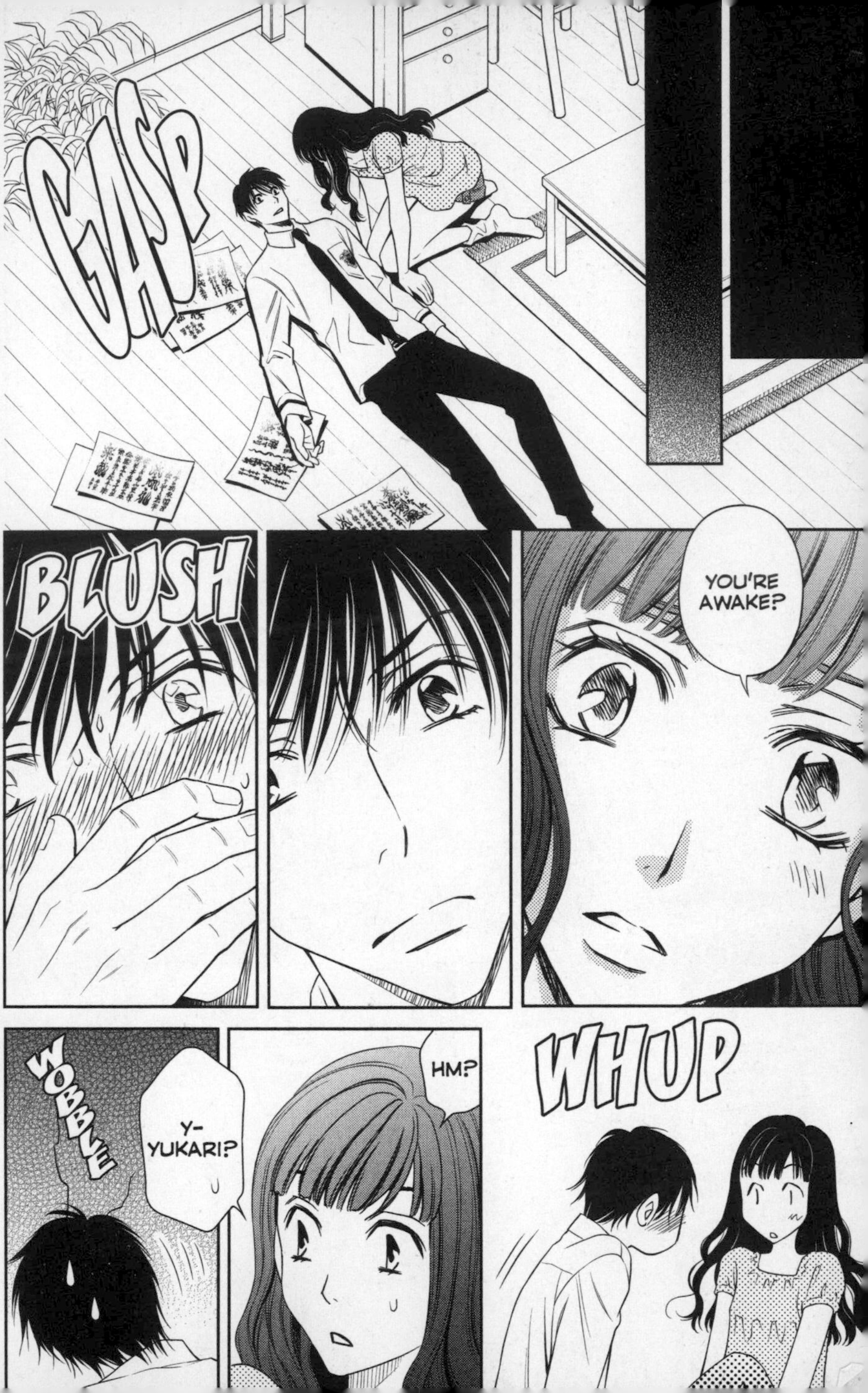
GASP
YOU'RE AWAKE?
BLUSH
WHUP
HM?
Y-YUKARI?
WOBBLE

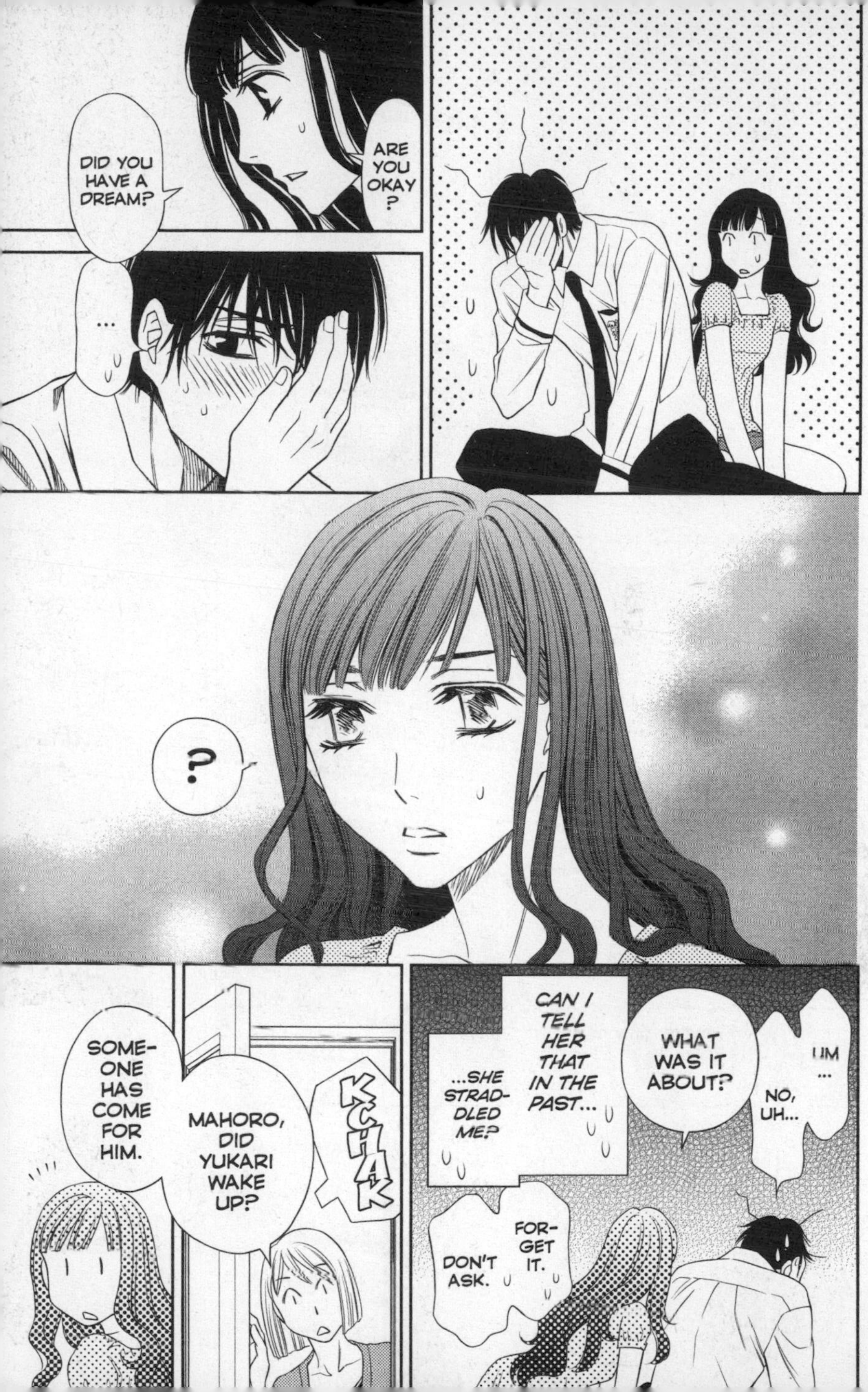
ARE YOU OKAY?
DID YOU HAVE A DREAM?
...
?
UM ...
NO, UH...
WHAT WAS IT ABOUT?
CAN I TELL HER THAT IN THE PAST...
...SHE STRADDLED ME?
FORGET IT.
DON'T ASK.
KCHAK
MAHORO, DID YUKARI WAKE UP?
SOMEONE HAS COME FOR HIM.

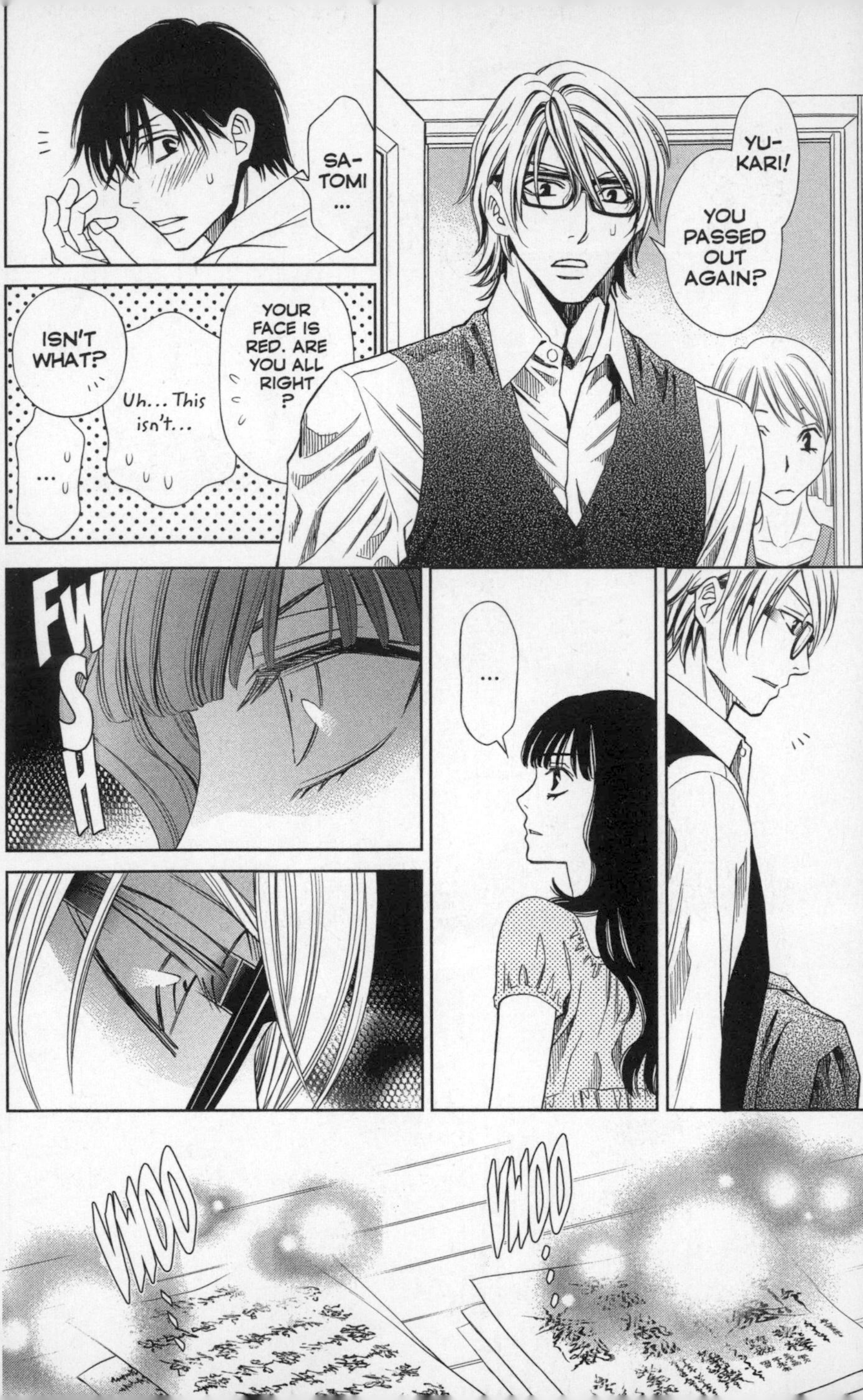
YU-KARI!
YOU PASSED OUT AGAIN?
SA-TOMI ...
YOUR FACE IS RED. ARE YOU ALL RIGHT?
Uh... This isn't...
ISN'T WHAT?
...
...
FWSH
VWOO
VWOO

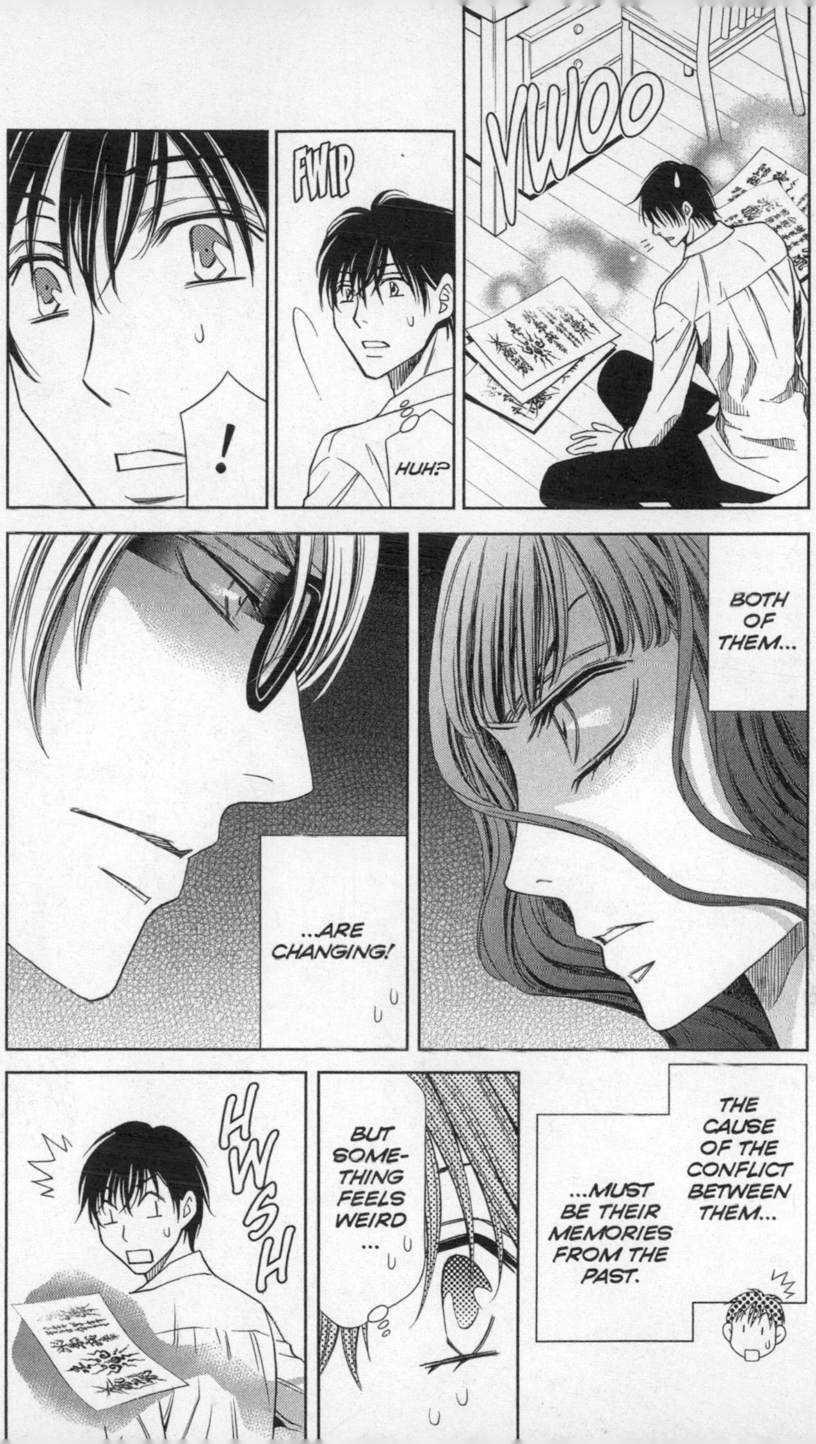
YWOO
FWIP
HUH?
!
BOTH OF THEM...
...ARE CHANGING!
THE CAUSE OF THE CONFLICT BETWEEN THEM...
...MUST BE THEIR MEMORIES FROM THE PAST.
BUT SOME-THING FEELS WEIRD ...
HWSH

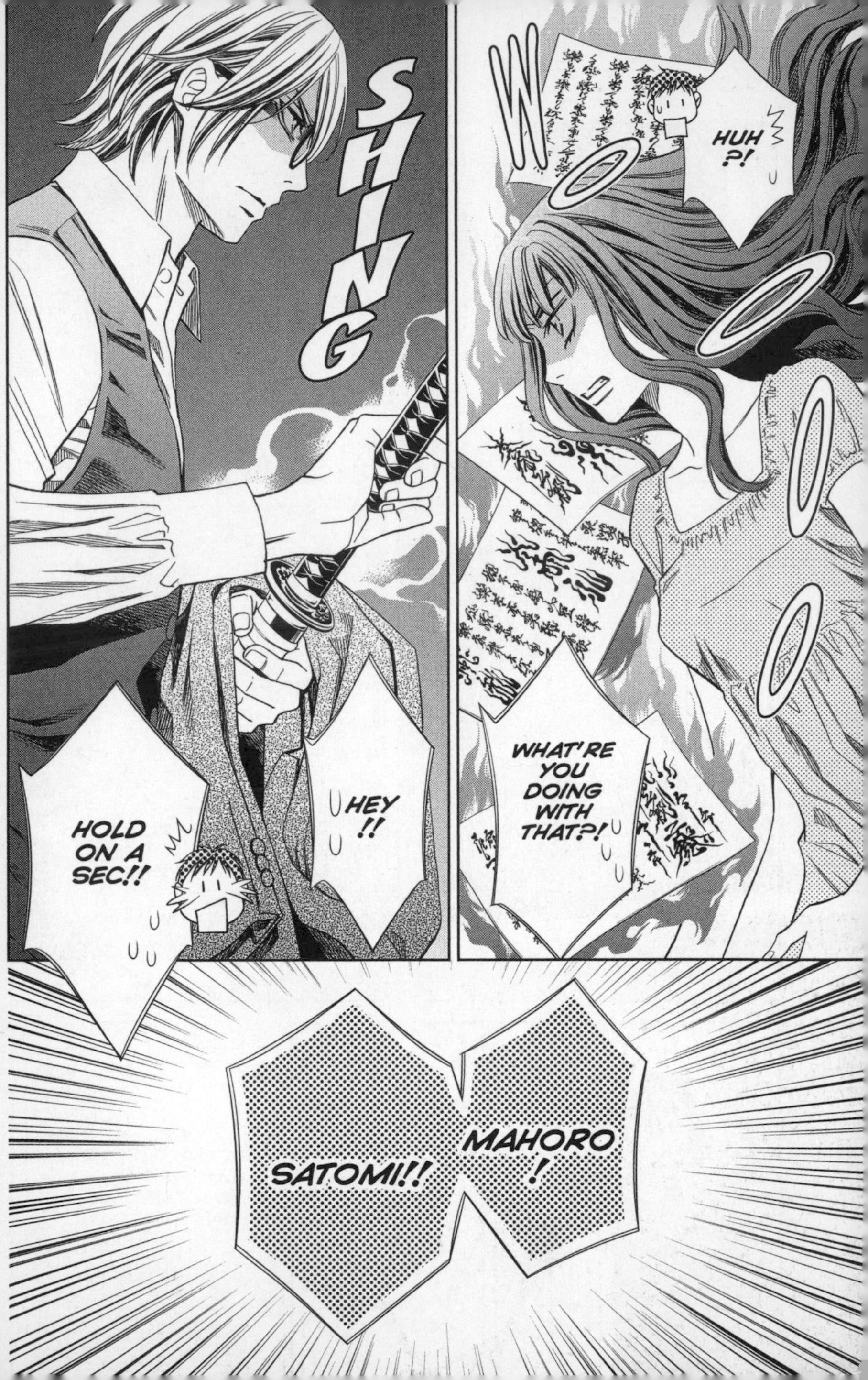
WOOOO
HUH ?!
WHAT'RE YOU DOING WITH THAT?!
SHING
HEY !!
HOLD ON A SEC!!
MAHORO !
SATOMI!!

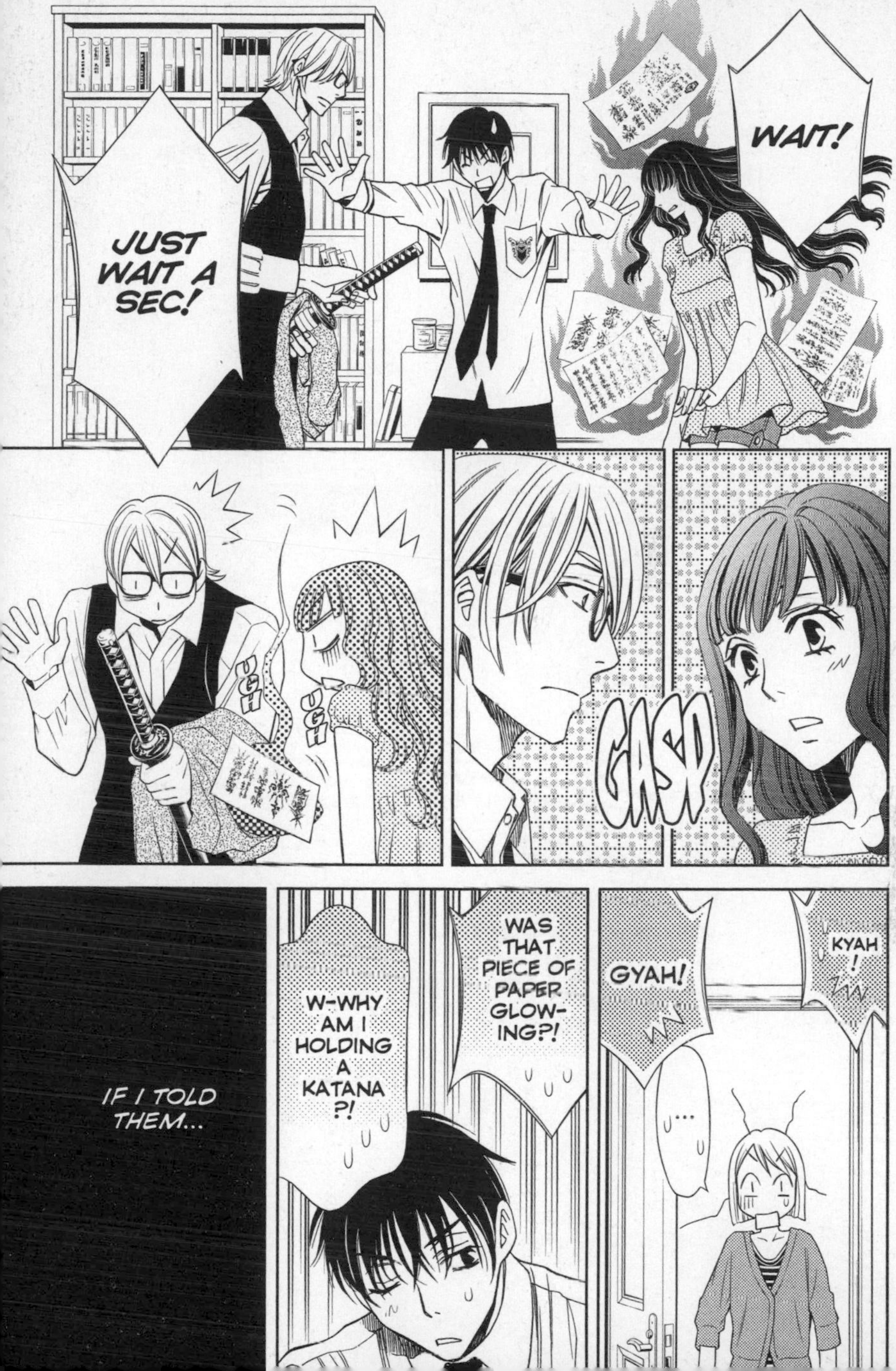
WAIT!
JUST WAIT A SEC!
GASP
UGH
UGH
KYAH!
GYAH!
...
WAS THAT PIECE OF PAPER GLOW-ING?!
W-WHY AM I HOLDING A KATANA?!
IF I TOLD THEM...

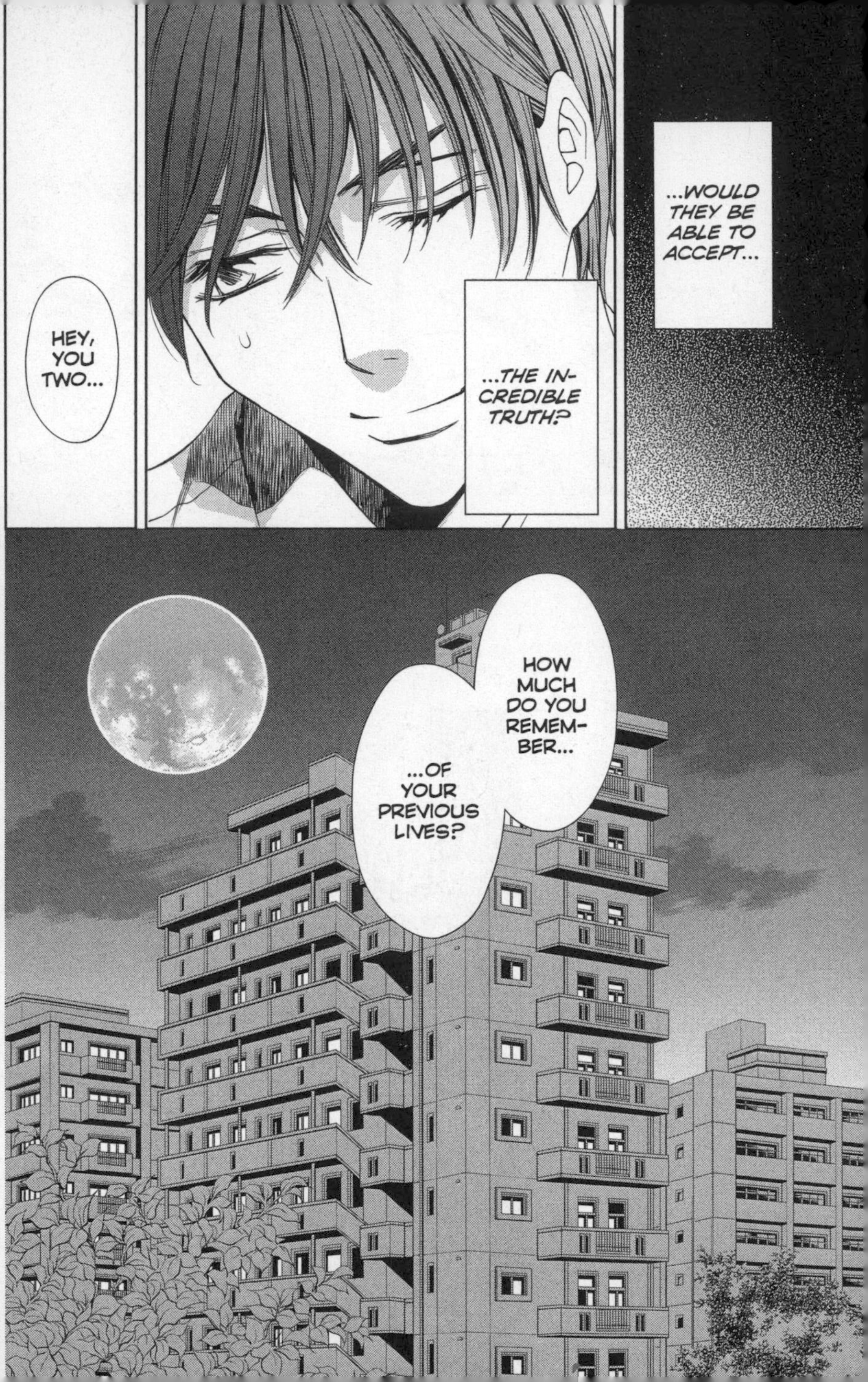
...WOULD THEY BE ABLE TO ACCEPT...
...THE IN-CREDIBLE TRUTH?
HEY, YOU TWO...
HOW MUCH DO YOU REMEMBER...
...OF YOUR PREVIOUS LIVES?

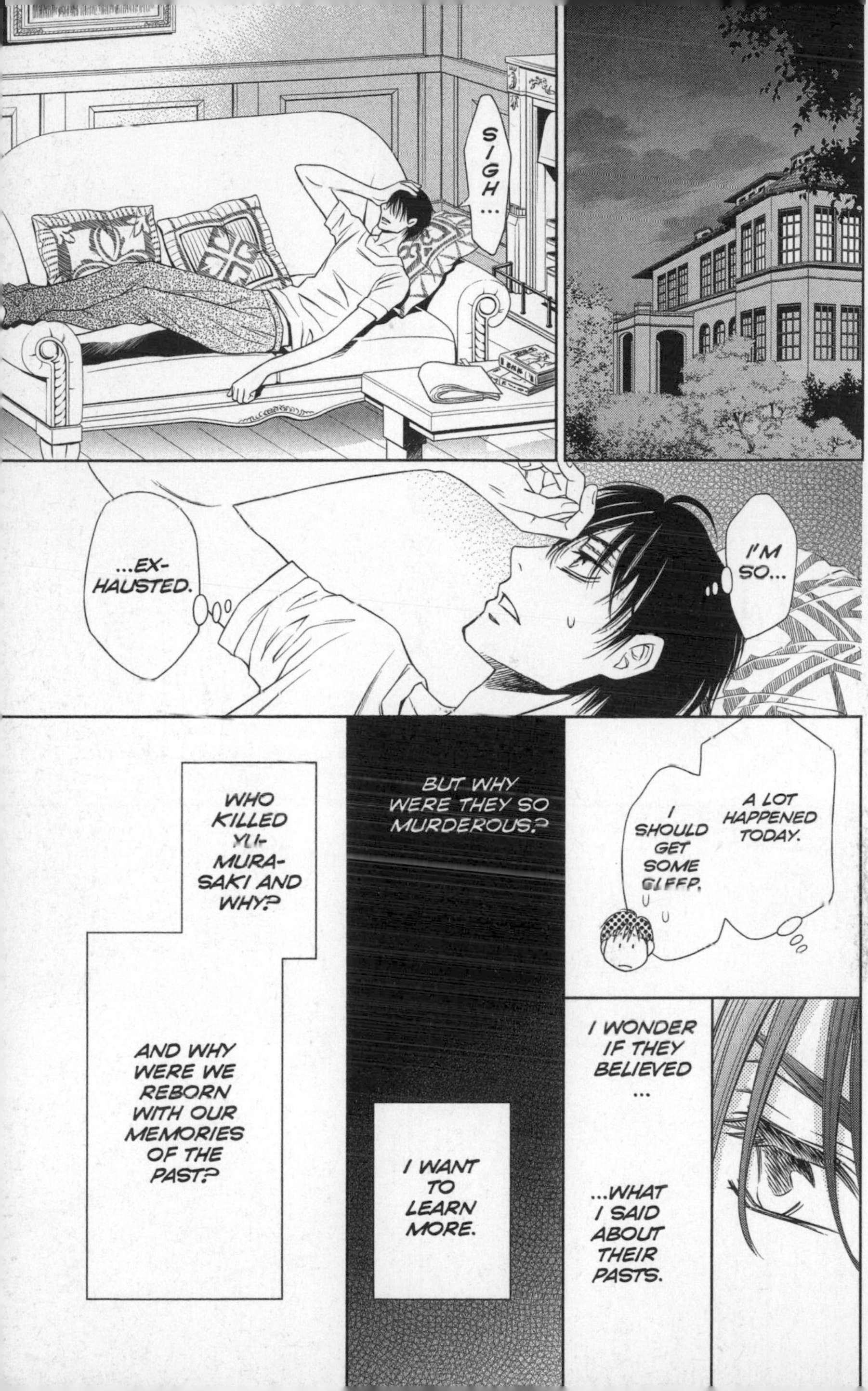
SIGH...
I'M SO...
...EX-HAUSTED.
A LOT HAPPENED TODAY.
I SHOULD GET SOME SLEEP.
I WONDER IF THEY BELIEVED ...
...WHAT I SAID ABOUT THEIR PASTS.
BUT WHY WERE THEY SO MURDEROUS?
I WANT TO LEARN MORE.
WHO KILLED YUI-MURASAKI AND WHY?
AND WHY WERE WE REBORN WITH OUR MEMORIES OF THE PAST?

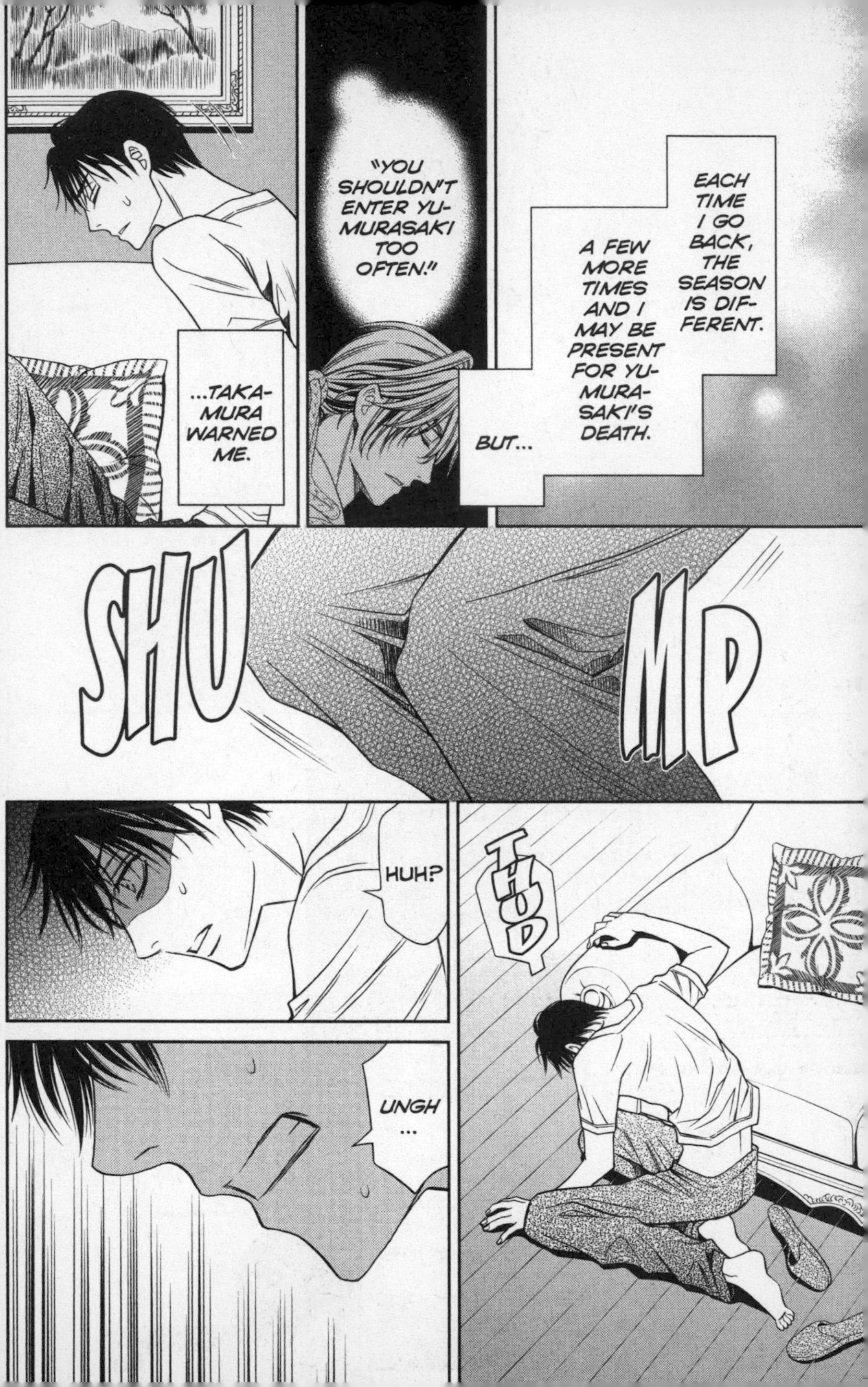
EACH TIME I GO BACK, THE SEASON IS DIFFERENT.
A FEW MORE TIMES AND I MAY BE PRESENT FOR YUMURASAKI'S DEATH.
BUT...
"YOU SHOULDN'T ENTER YUMURASAKI TOO OFTEN."
...TAKAMURA WARNED ME.
SHUMP
THUD
HUH?
UNGH...

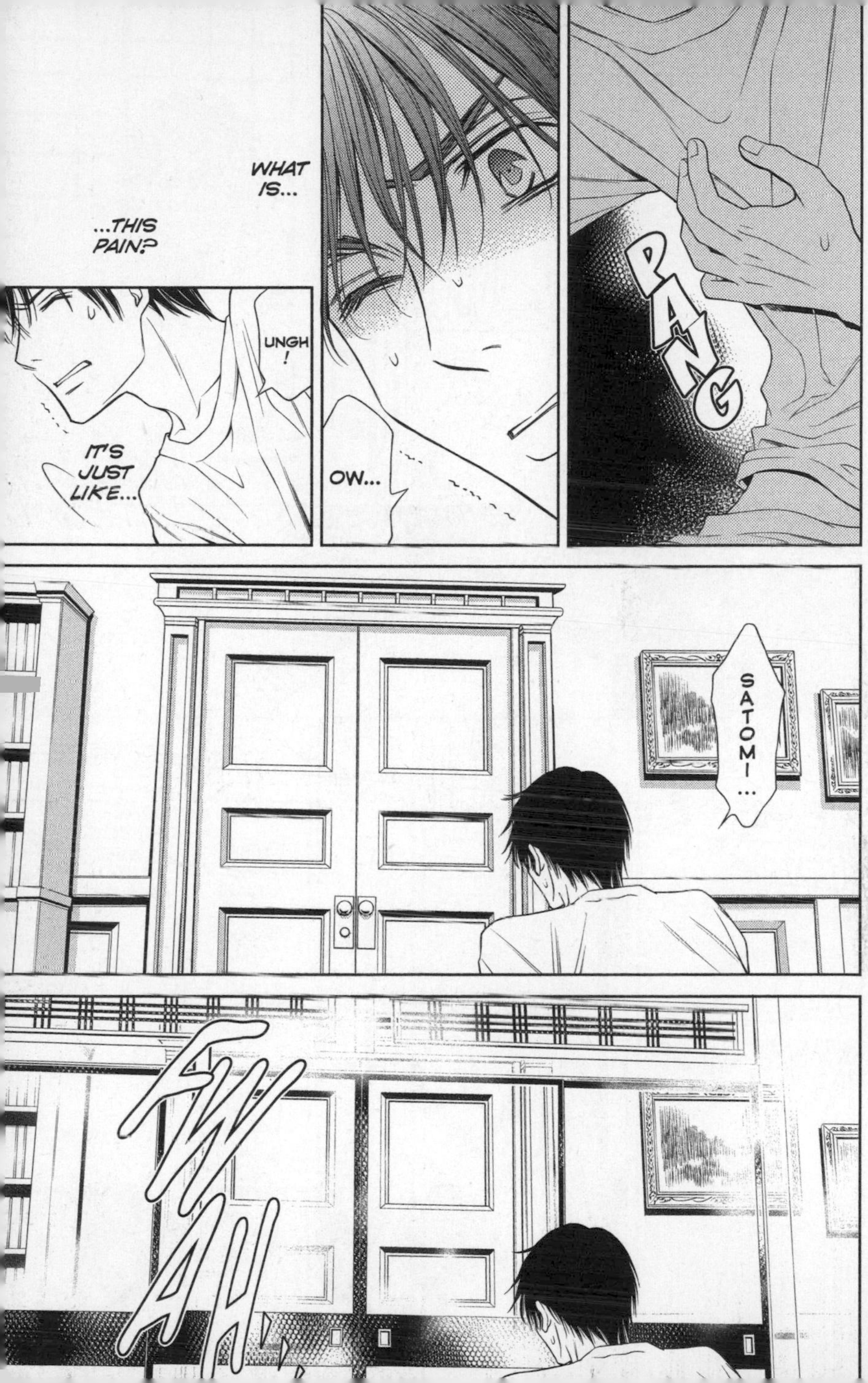
PANG
OW...
WHAT IS...
...THIS PAIN?
UNGH!
IT'S JUST LIKE...
SATOMI...
FWAH!

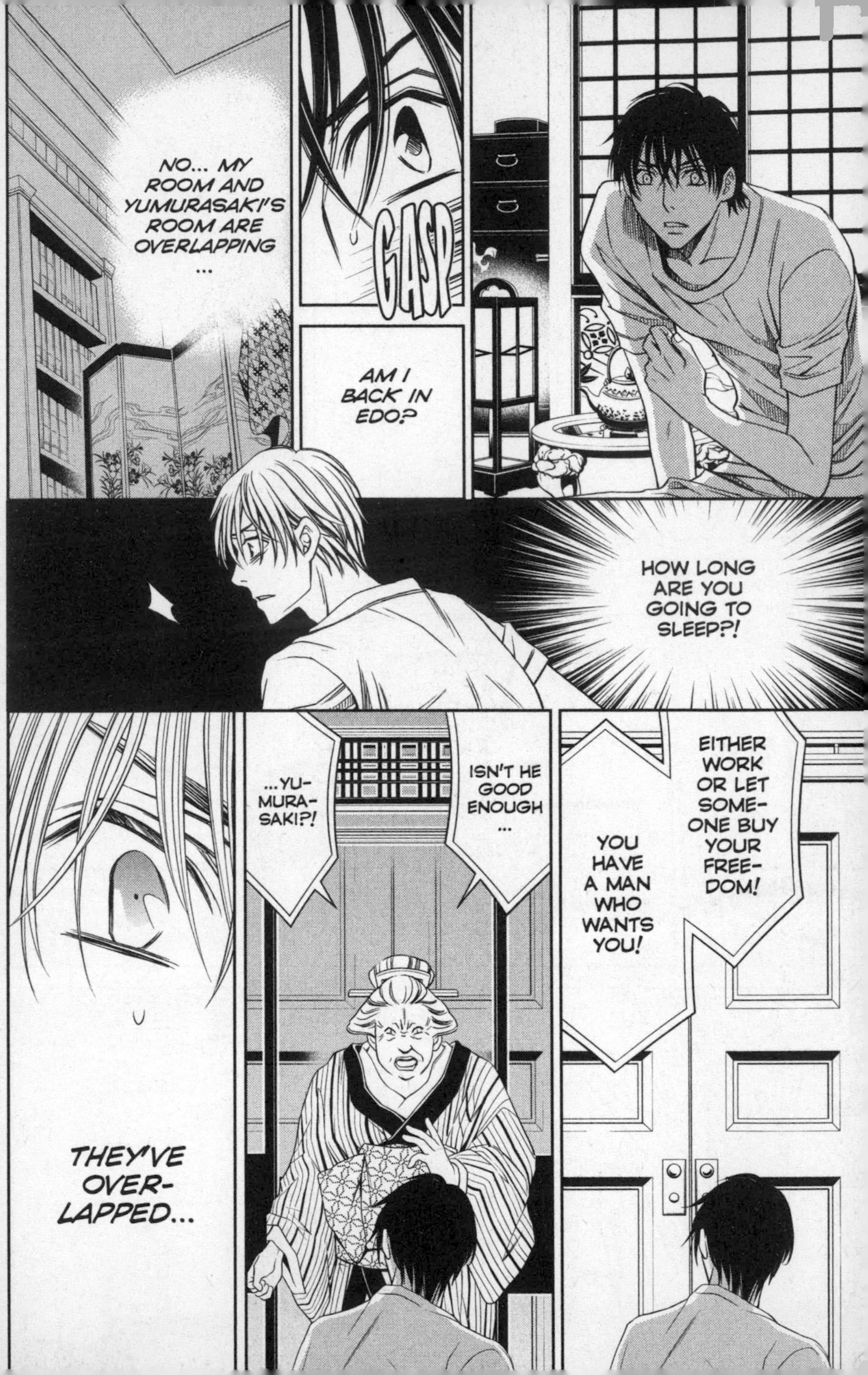
GASP
AM I BACK IN EDO?
NO... MY ROOM AND YUMURASAKI'S ROOM ARE OVERLAPPING ...
HOW LONG ARE YOU GOING TO SLEEP?!
EITHER WORK OR LET SOME-ONE BUY YOUR FREE-DOM!
YOU HAVE A MAN WHO WANTS YOU!
ISN'T HE GOOD ENOUGH ...
...YU-MURA-SAKI!?!
THEY'VE OVER-LAPPED...

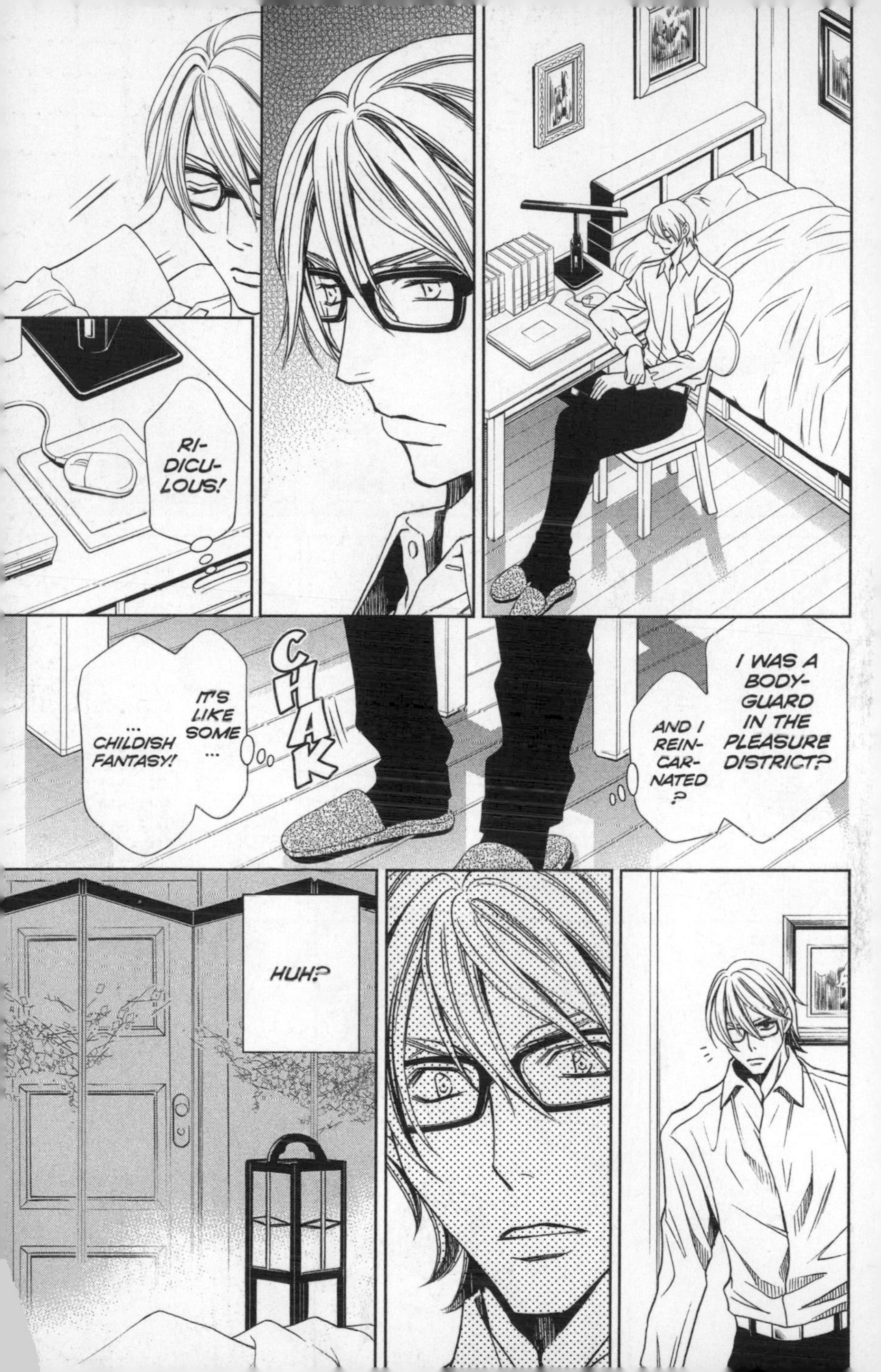
RI-DICU-LOUS!
I WAS A BODY-GUARD IN THE PLEASURE DISTRICT?
AND I REIN-CAR-NATED?
CHAK
IT'S LIKE SOME ...
... CHILDISH FANTASY!
HUH?

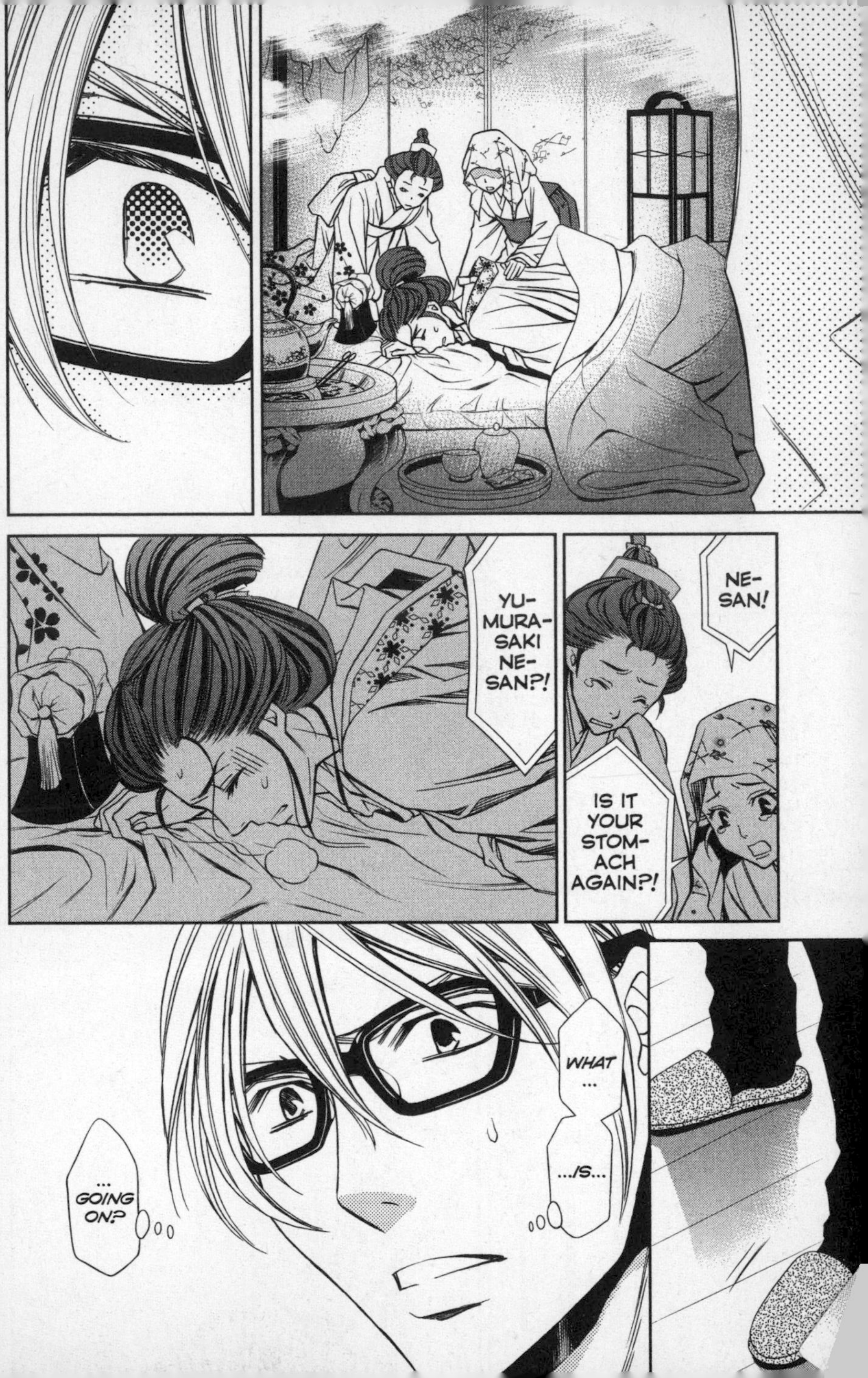
NE-SAN!
IS IT YOUR STOMACH AGAIN?!
YU-MURA-SAKI NE-SAN?!
WHAT ...
...IS...
... GOING ON?

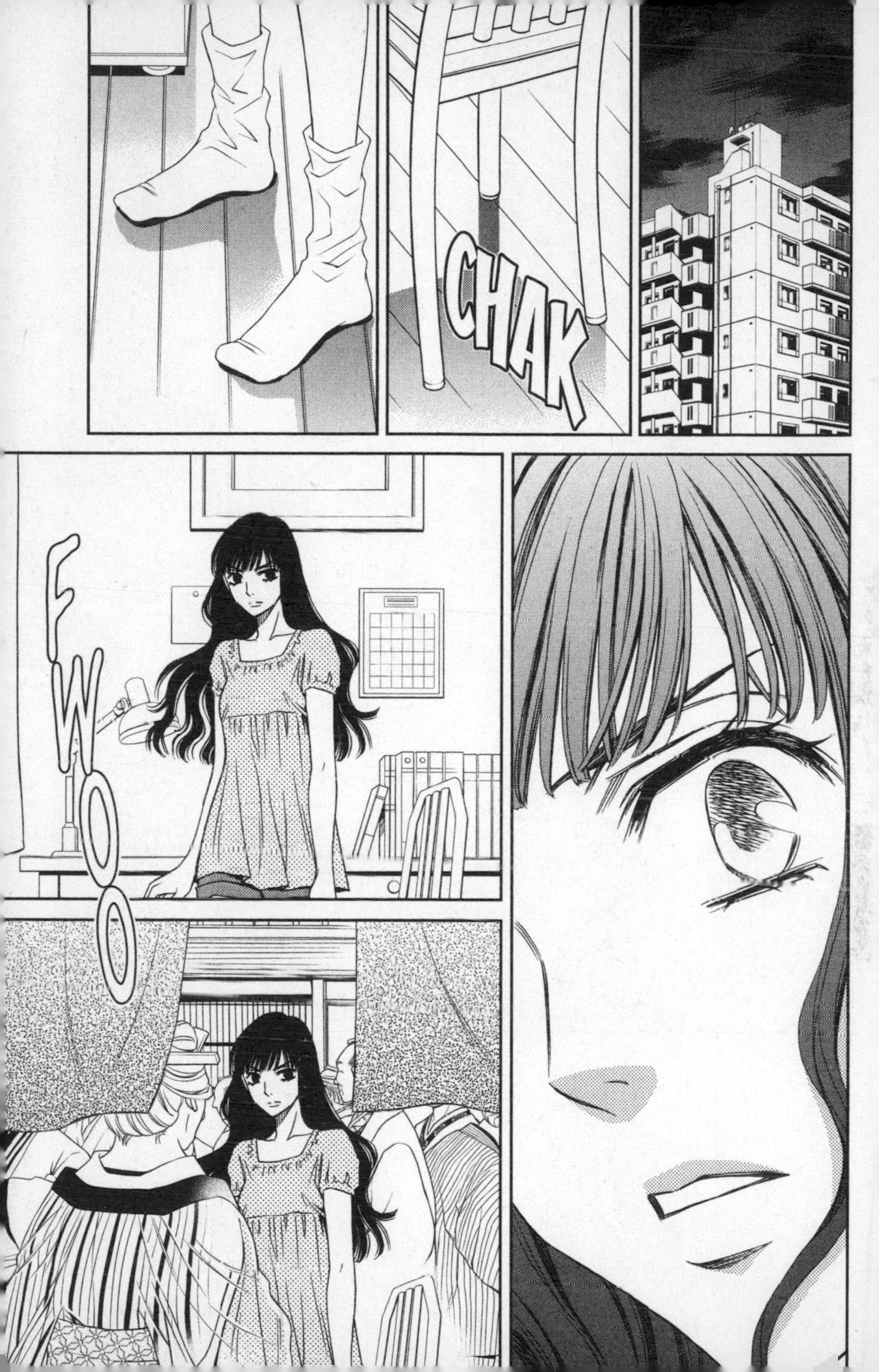
CHAK
FWOOO

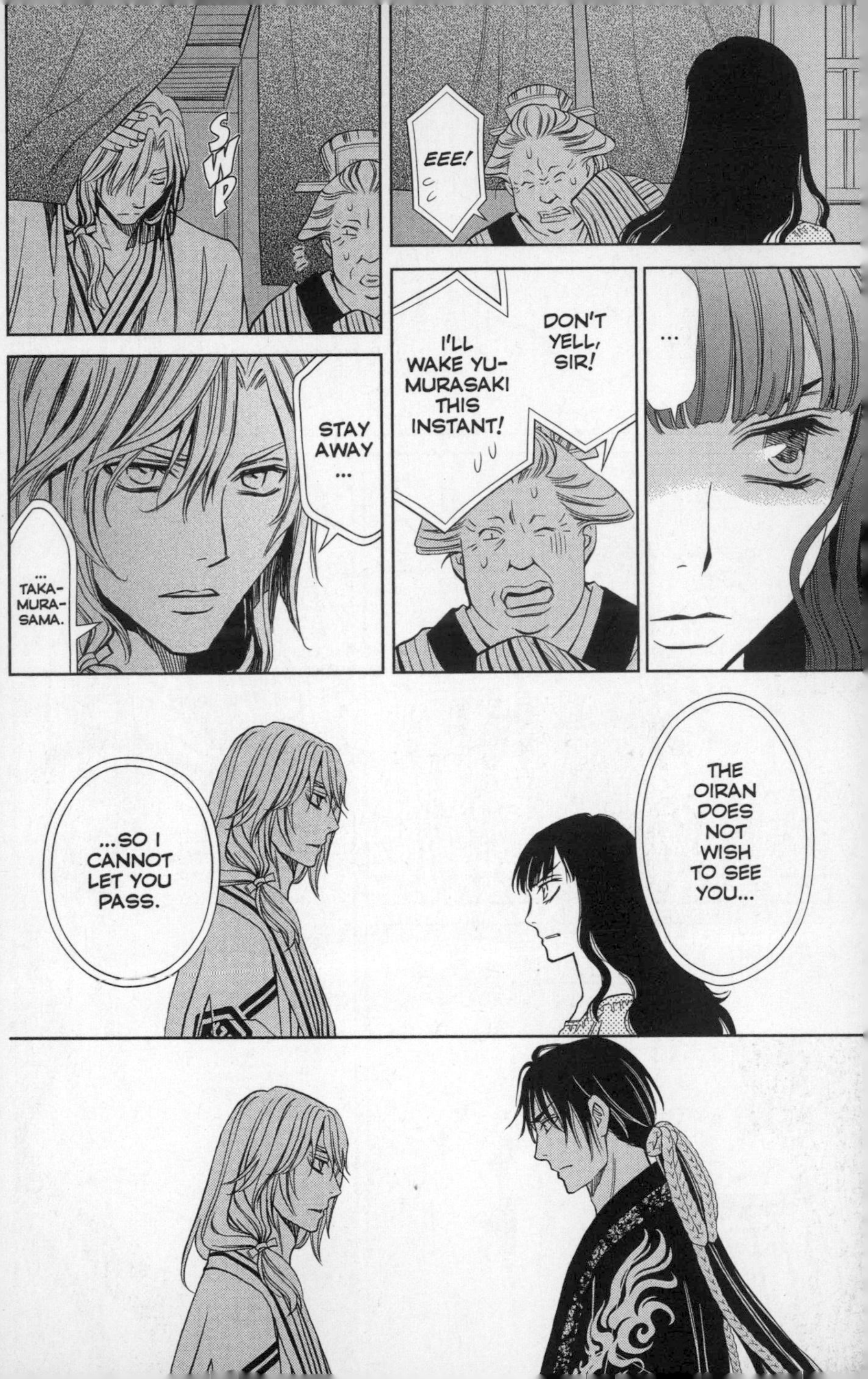
EEE!
SWP
...
DON'T YELL, SIR!
I'LL WAKE YU-MURASAKI THIS INSTANT!
STAY AWAY ...
... TAKA-MURA-SAMA.
THE OIRAN DOES NOT WISH TO SEE YOU...
...SO I CANNOT LET YOU PASS.

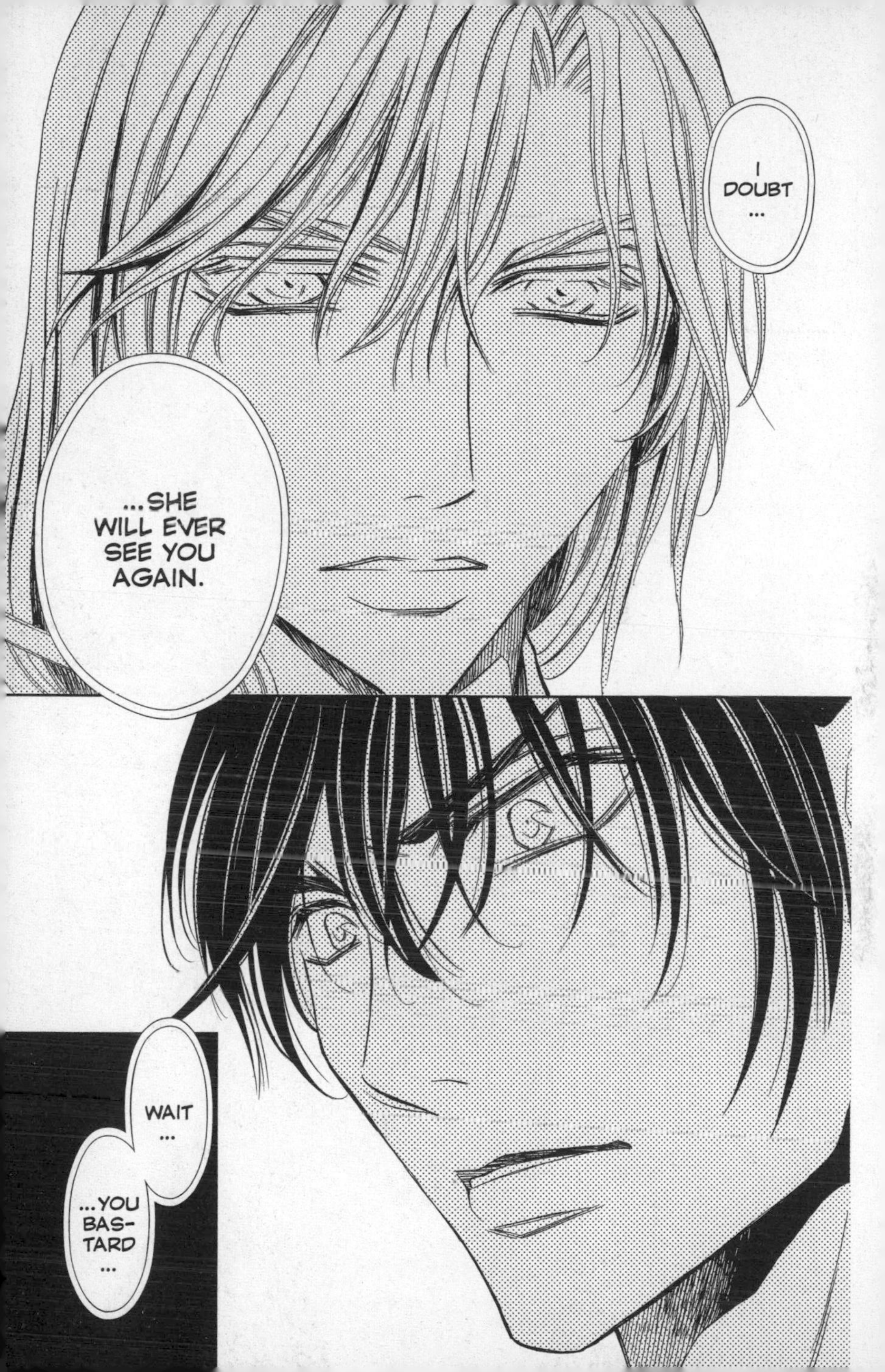
I DOUBT ...
...SHE WILL EVER SEE YOU AGAIN.
WAIT ...
...YOU BASTARD ...

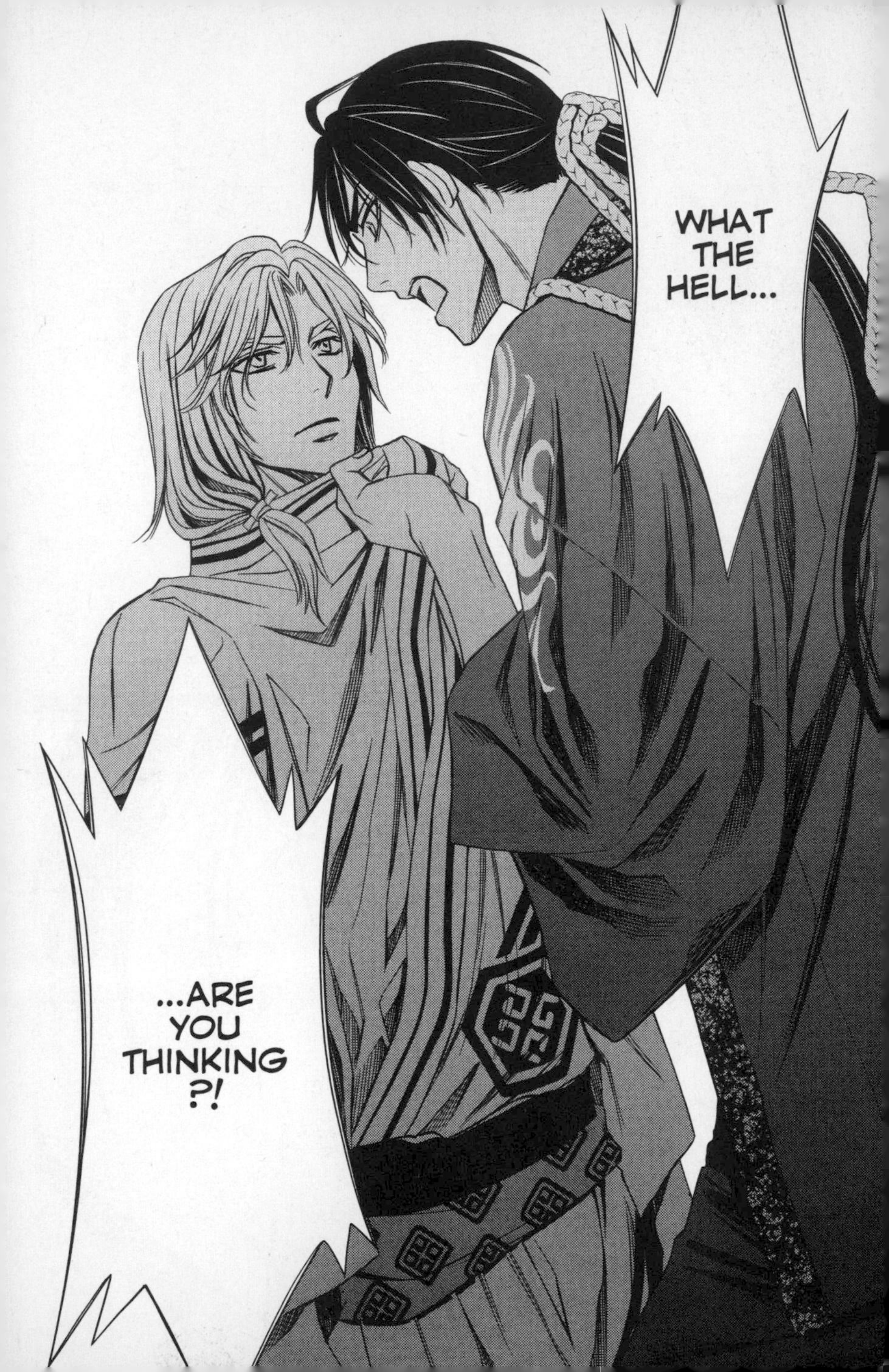
WHAT THE HELL...
...ARE YOU THINKING ?!

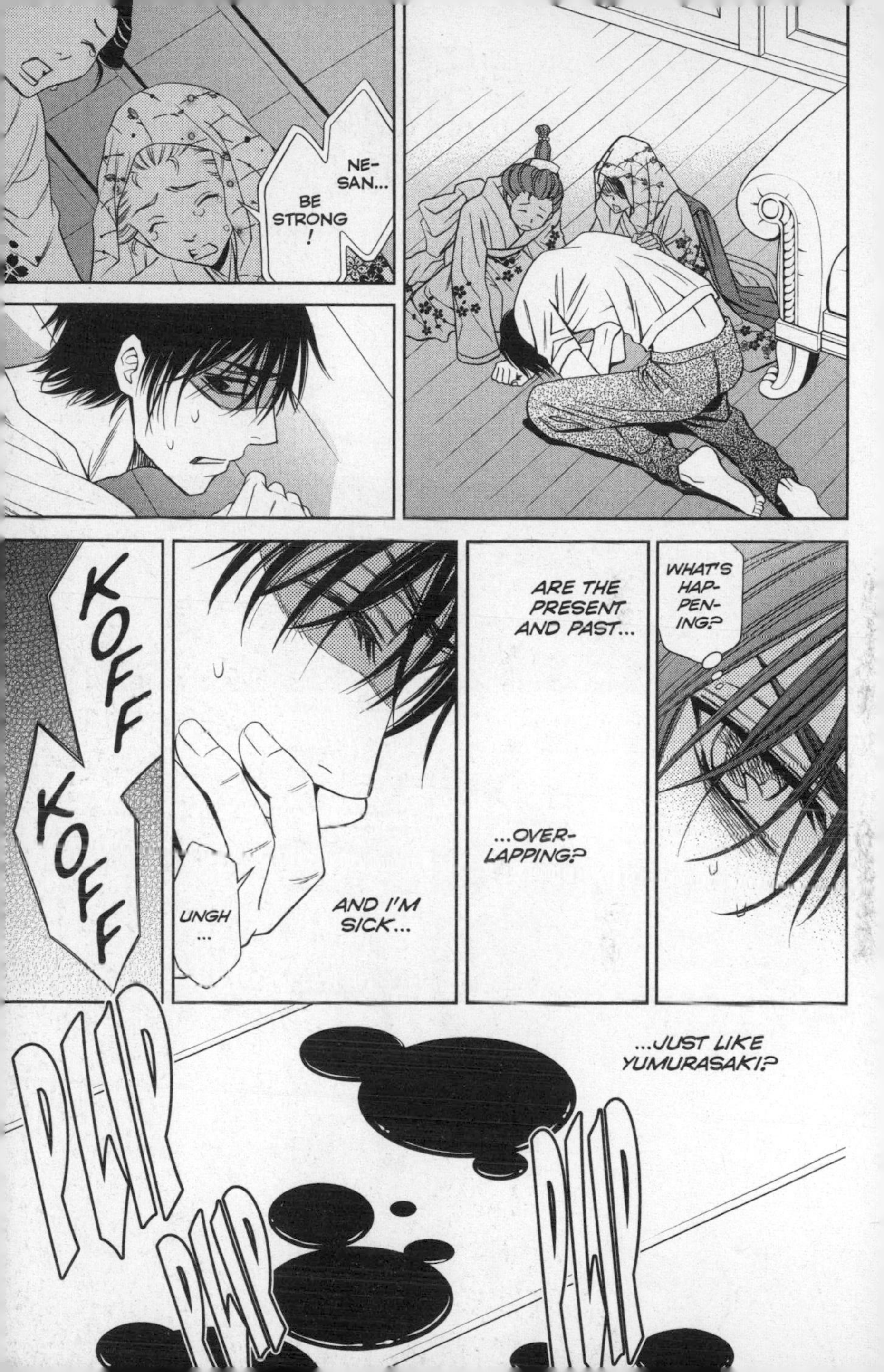
NE-SAN...
BE STRONG!
WHAT'S HAP-PEN-ING?
ARE THE PRESENT AND PAST...
...OVER-LAPPING?
AND I'M SICK...
UNGH...
KOFF
KOFF
...JUST LIKE YUMURASAKI!?

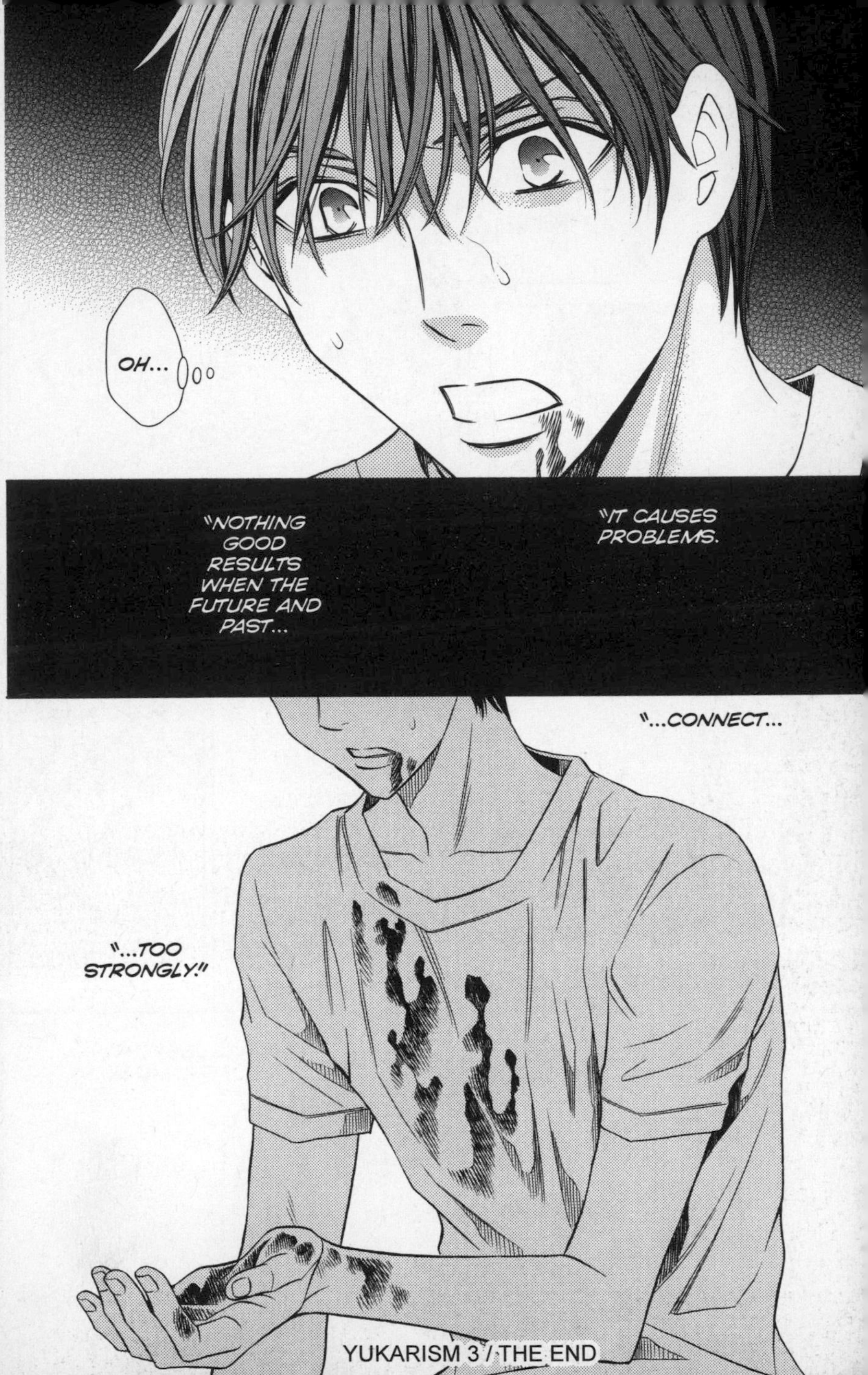
OH...
"IT CAUSES PROBLEMS.
"NOTHING GOOD RESULTS WHEN THE FUTURE AND PAST...
"...CONNECT...
"...TOO STRONGLY!"
YUKARISM 3 / THE END

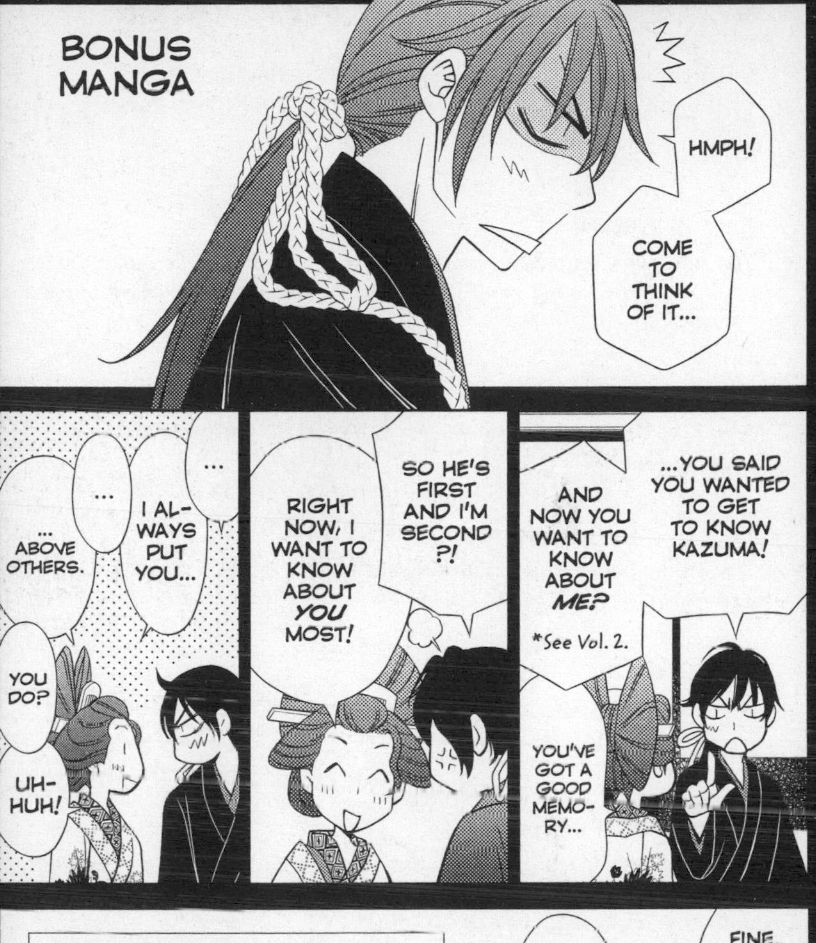
BONUS MANGA
HMPH!
COME TO THINK OF IT...
...YOU SAID YOU WANTED TO GET TO KNOW KAZUMA!
AND NOW YOU WANT TO KNOW ABOUT *ME?*
*See Vol. 2.
YOU'VE GOT A GOOD MEMORY...
SO HE'S FIRST AND I'M SECOND?!
RIGHT NOW, I WANT TO KNOW ABOUT *YOU* MOST!
...
I ALWAYS PUT YOU...
...
... ABOVE OTHERS.
YOU DO?
UH-HUH!

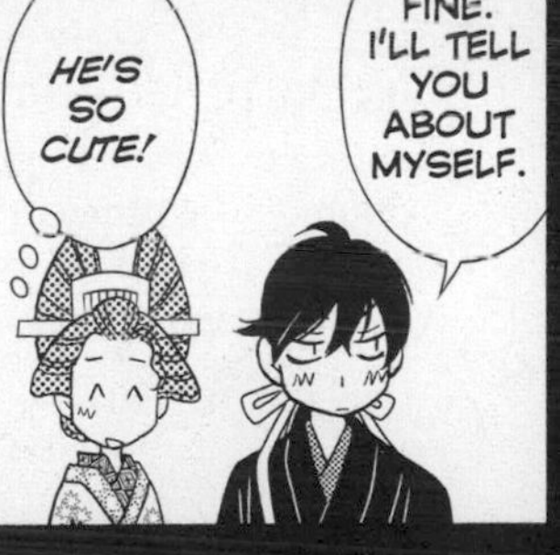
FINE. I'LL TELL YOU ABOUT MYSELF.
HE'S SO CUTE!

PLEASE SEND YOUR LETTERS TO:

CHIKA SHIOMI
C/O YUKARISM EDITOR
VIZ MEDIA
P.O. BOX 77010
SAN FRANCISCO, CA 94107

STAFF:K.YAMADA Y.SHIRAKI
CG WORKS:ERII MISONO
ASUKA SHIZAKI

[Notes]

Yukari's past life occurs during the Edo period of Japan. Check out the notes below to help enrich your understanding of *Yukarism*.

Page 2: Yukari
The kanji character 縁 (pronounced "yukari") means "connection" or "bond." The actual kanji for Yukari's name (紫), however, means "purple."

Page 2: Edo Period
Also known as the Tokugawa period, the Edo period lasted from 1603 to 1868.

Page 3: Yumurasaki
The kanji characters for Yumurasaki's name (夕紫) mean "evening" and "purple."

Page 3: Oiran
A class of courtesan, especially during the Edo period. The kanji characters for *oiran* (花魁) mean "flower" and "harbinger," respectively.

Page 8, panel 4: Ronin
A masterless samurai. Without ties to a feudal lord, ronin wandered the land putting their swords to what use they could, often as mercenaries, bodyguards or bandits.

Page 36, panel 3: Tamagiku Doro
A yearly event held in memory of Tamagiku. Tamagiku (玉菊) was a celebrated courtesan in Yoshiwara who lived from 1702 to 1726. The teahouses of the pleasure district would decorate their eaves with lanterns.

Page 44, panel 1: Hiyamizu

A cool sweet for enjoyment during the hot summer months. In the Edo period, it consisted of rice-flour dumplings in sugar water. In modern Japanese, the word *hiyamizu* simply means "cold water."

Page 48, panel 1: Amazake

A sweet drink, usually slightly alcoholic and made by fermenting rice. In modern-day Japan, hot *amazake* is used to warm up during the winter, especially during a New Year's visit to a shrine. In the Edo period, people drank chilled amazake to stay cool in hot weather.

Page 57, panel 6: Sama

An honorific used to address a person much higher in rank than oneself.

Page 64, panel 2: Ne-san

An honorific that means means "older sister," *ne-san* is used to address an older sister figure (similar to calling someone "Miss").

Page 105, panel 4: Katana

A traditional Japanese sword used during feudal Japan that has a moderately curved, slender, single-edged blade.

Page 114, panel 5: Igo

A strategy game that originated in China. Igo involves two opponents, designated White and Black, who each place stones on a board in an effort to surround and capture as many of their opponent's stones as possible.

Page 114, panel 6: Shamisen

A three-stringed instrument. High-quality *shamisen* often have a body made of cat skin and strings made of silk. Due to the instrument's twangy sound, it is sometimes described as the Japanese banjo.

Author Bio

Chika Shiomi debuted with the manga *Todokeru Toki o Sugitemo* (Even if the Time for Deliverance Passes), and her previous works include *Yurara* and *Rasetsu*. She loves reading manga, traveling and listening to music by Aerosmith and Guns N' Roses. Her favorite artists include Michelangelo, Hokusai, Bernini and Gustav Klimt.

YUKARISM

Volume 3
Shojo Beat Edition

STORY AND ART BY
CHIKA SHIOMI

Translation & Adaptation/John Werry
Touch-up Art & Lettering/Rina Mapa
Design/Izumi Evers
Editor/Amy Yu

Yukarism by Chika Shiomi
© Chika Shiomi 2013
All rights reserved.
First published in Japan in 2013 by
HAKUSENSHA, Inc., Tokyo.
English language translation rights arranged with
HAKUSENSHA, Inc., Tokyo.

Printed in the U.S.A.

Published by VIZ Media, LLC
P.O. Box 77010
San Francisco, CA 94107

10 9 8 7 6 5 4 3 2 1
First printing, July 2015

www.viz.com   www.shojobeat.com

This is the last page.

In keeping with the original Japanese comic format, this book reads from right to left—so action, sound effects, and word balloons are completely reversed. This preserves the orientation of the original artwork—plus, it's fun! Check out the diagram shown here to get the hang of things, and then turn to the other side of the book to get started!

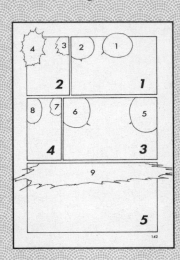